Greek Wisdom Literature and the Middle Ages

Sapheneia
Contributions to Classical Philology

Edited by
Margarethe Billerbeck and Bruce Karl Braswell

Volume 14

PETER LANG
Bern · Berlin · Bruxelles · Frankfurt am Main · New York · Oxford · Wien

Francisco Rodríguez Adrados

Greek Wisdom Literature and the Middle Ages

The Lost Greek Models and Their Arabic and Castilian Translations

PETER LANG
Bern · Berlin · Bruxelles · Frankfurt am Main · New York · Oxford · Wien

Bibliographic information published by Die Deutsche Bibliothek
Die Deutsche Bibliothek lists this publication in the Deutsche Nationalbibliografie; detailed bibliographic data is available on the Internet at ‹http://dnb.ddb.de›.

British Library Cataloguing-in-Publication Data:
A catalogue record for this book is available from *The British Library,* Great Britain

Library of Congress Cataloging-in-Publication Data

Adrados, Francisco Rodríguez, 1922-
[Modelos griegos de la sabiduría castellana y europea. English]
Greek wisdom literature and the Middle Ages : the lost Greek models and their Arabic and Castilian translations / Francisco Rodríguez Adrados.
p. cm. – (Sapheneia contributions to classical philology ; v. 14)
Originally published: Modelos griegos de la sabiduría castellana y europea : literatura sapiencial en Grecia y la edad media. Madrid : Real Academia Española, 2001. Translated into English by Joyce Greer.
Includes bibliographical references and index.
ISBN 978-3-03911-752-9 (alk. paper)
1. Spanish literature–To 1500--History and criticism. 2. Wisdom literature–Criticism, interpretation, etc. 3. Spanish literature–To 1500–Greek influences. I. Greer, Joyce. II. Title.
PQ6060.A3713 2009
880'.9–dc22

2008052927

Francisco Rodríguez Adrados, Modelos griegos de la sabiduría castellana y europea

English Translation by Joyce Greer

This work has been published with a subsidy from the Directorate-General of Books, Archives and Libraries of the Spanish Ministry of Culture.

ISSN 1421-7899
ISBN 978-3-03911-752-9

Hochfeldstrasse 32, Postfach 746, CH-3000 Bern 9, Switzerland
info@peterlang.com, www.peterlang.com, www.peterlang.net

Printed in Germany

Table of Contents

Foreword

In medieval Europe the instruction that was received by the educated and, directly or indirectly, by the common people reached them by two routes which, moreover, sometimes combined with each other.

The first of these routes consists of theological and ascetic writings in Latin, and later in modern languages, as well as preaching in those same languages. The influence of Greco-Latin literature and thought on these genres, both in form and in content, is well known. It comes from the fusion of Hellenism and Christianity in late Antiquity.

The second route is sapiential literature, sometimes in Latin, Arabic or Hebrew, but more frequently, beginning at a certain moment, in Castilian, and then in the other languages of Europe. This literature, of oriental origin (from Mesopotamia, Egypt, Asia Minor) put down deep roots in archaic and classical Greece and has reached us through the Greek literature of the Hellenistic, Roman and Byzantine ages. At times, by way of translations or imitations, it became, secondarily, Latin, Syriac, Arabic or Hebrew literature, to say nothing of literature written in languages like Armenian, Ethiopian, the Slavic languages and others.

So, then, Greek sapiential literature penetrated Europe by various paths: by way of Latin, as I have said, the transmitter of Greek originals and creator of others along the same lines: the *Vita Apollonii*, the *Vita Secundi*, the *Vita Aesopi*, the *Altercatio Hadriani Augusti et Epicteti Philosophi*, Dictys Cretensis, the Pseudo-Callisthenes, the fable, *Barlaam and Josafat*, etc.

But it also came by way of Arabic. This path sometimes derives from Pehlvi and finally from Indian (*Pañcatantra*, *Sendebar*, *The Thousand and One Nights*, etc.). These are works that, on the other hand, came under Greek influence at various times or that have reached us directly through Greek, for example the *Barlaam*. Or they simply derive from Greek, as is the case of the Arabic fables of Lokman, of the Syriac fables and of various *Lives* and gnomologies in these and other languages.

This book is concerned specifically with one sector of the Arabic sapiential literature derived from Greek. It deals with four works translated into Castilian by order of Alfonso X the Wise: the *Libro de los Buenos Proverbios*, *Bocados de Oro*, *Poridad de las Poridades* and *La Historia de la donzella Teodor*.

With Castilian as a starting point, and at times with intermediate Latin translations, this literature spread throughout Europe.

In the histories of Spanish literature, and of European literature in general, these works are treated rather superficially. They speak of "Arabic" or "Oriental" influence, or they attempt to study the themes against the background of medieval Spain. But what there is of Arabic or of Castilian in these works is minimal.

They are actually Greek sapiential works which have a long history within Greek literature and which in the early Byzantine period acquired the form that was later (in the 9th, 10th and 11th centuries especially) translated into Arabic. Sometimes they were preceded by translations into Syriac. I suggest that the final form of the Greek originals, the one that the Arabic translators received, was arrived at in the Syria of the 6th and 7th centuries. That is the thesis of this book.

Enlightened caliphs promoted translations from Greek (at times via Syriac) into Arabic, first in Damascus, later in Bagdad. Then came the translations in the Fatimid court of Cairo. This is a well-known fact. And no less well known is the fact that the main texts translated were scientific and philosophical, texts that were later translated into Latin and Castilian, mostly in the Toledo of the 12th and 13th centuries.

It is also known that the translators from Greek into Arabic were Syrian Christians (especially Nestorians, Melchites and Jacobites) converted to Islam in name only, which was also true of the Persian followers of Zoroaster who translated the Pehlvi literature into Arabic.

But less attention has been given to the fact that the same translators who translated scientific and philosophical works (Hunayn ibn Ishaq, Yahya ibn Batrik and al-Mubassir are the best known) also translated sapiential works from Greek into Arabic, while others were translating them from Pehlvi. Later, many of these works, of one origin or the other, were translated into Castilian in the 13th century through the initiative of Alfonso, the learned king.

Al-Andalus was only a stop on the way, the point of arrival in Spain of the manuscripts from Bagdad and Cairo. Here, and, above all later, in Toledo, lies the key to this fascinating story.

Within the sapiential literature translated from Greek into Arabic and from there into Castilian, the four works we have referred to have never been studied as Greek works. This is the study that we intend to carry out here, or, rather, the study we will begin, as many matters will be left pending.

The four works are the final phase of the evolution of Greek literary genres such as the gnomologies or collections of maxims, sayings and anecdotes, the fictitious letters, the "mirrors for princes" and the novelized *Lives* of sapiential content. Their origins can be studied in remote times in Mesopotamia and Egypt, as I have said. And their successive crystallizations can be studied throughout the history of Greek literature. The last was in Byzantine times. Then came the translations, in which can be found certain slight revisions of a later date, Arabic and Castilian.

And ideology can be studied also, the morality expressed in these works, which added a presentation that at times had a jocular element. This is the old Greek moralism regarding virtue, justice and divinity, a moralism that took an intellectual turn with Socrates, with his insistence on *phronesis* (thought, prudence), knowledge, control of passion, self-sufficiency and care of the soul. This moralism then evolved in Plato, in Aristotle, in the idealized Alexander, in the Stoics and, above all, in the Cynics. They made poverty, effort, asceticism, rejection of the abuse of power and of useless science the center of their philosophy.

Thus arose, in short, a fairly coherent and homogeneous body of doctrine, once certain excesses of the early Cynics had been discarded: their opposition to government, their misogyny, their exhibitionism. Neo-Platonic, Neo-Pythagorean and Hermetic contributions were added. All this can be studied as regards the general orientation and as regards detail as well. In the literature preserved in Greek there are exact coincidences with our treatises.

Now, at a certain moment this whole line merged with the Christian line. The Bible, Basil, Gregory and Johannes Chrysostom entered the gnomologies (and from there entered our treatises). Thus all of Greek sapiential literature acquired a Christian cast. And it crystallized in successive phases, as I have said, in works such as the four that we are studying here. According to them, Socrates and Aristotle are almost Christian saints; Alexander is the good king guided by God (in other works he is the man drunk with power).

In summary, we have before us Greco-Christian works: sometimes they coincide literally with Greek literature that has been preserved, at other times they are, in any case, of similar orientation. Together with other sapiential literature they were translated, in part, into Syriac, then completely into Arabic. With certain exceptions, no Muslim elements were introduced. Neither did they contain Christian dogmatic or hagiographic elements (again with exceptions): they would have been unacceptable, even for the most enlightened of the caliphs.

Ultimately this moral and novelistic Greco-Christian *corpus* became Muslim property, and later, the property of the medieval Christians. It was influential in the creation of a new literature in the Muslim world: a literature dealing with the ancient philosophers, with Alexander and with *The Thousand and One Nights*. And it definitely had an influence on the growth of a Castilian Christian literature; on this I must give more details.

In this Christian Castilian atmosphere sapiential literature, of which we study only four treatises here (though we allude to others), was as important as theology and preaching. Thus, the translated sapiential literature, a good part of it derived, in the end, from Greek via Arabic or Latin, gave an enormous impulse to the development of Castilian prose and to the ideology of Christian virtue and royal government inspired by God. An entire literature arose from this impulse

I feel that, apart from the demonstration of the Greco-Christian origin of the four treatises, there are in the present book matters that can interest a wide public. The Hellenist and the scholar of philosophy can be interested in the creation of a *corpus* of Greek and Greco-Latin sapiential literature which had an influence at the popular level much greater than that of the writings of the most illustrious philosophers. The Hispanist and the medievalist in general might be interested in the proof of the origin of this sapiential literature, which was so decisive for the formation of the Spanish and European man.

A fundamentally uniform line connects this Greek, Latin and Christian sapiential literature with the entire European medieval world. And in close relationship with this literature (in the case of our treatises and various others) Castilian prose arose.

It arose as prose in translation. This fact, which we already knew in some cases, now becomes clearer. Latin, Slavic, Gothic, Armenian and many other literatures also began as literatures in translation. This is only normal.

To settle these two points and to study in detail the roots and phases of the four treatises translated from Greek into Arabic in Bagdad and Cairo and from Arabic into Castilian in Toledo, and then circulated throughout Europe is the objective of this book[1].

Acknowledgements

Juan Rodríguez Somolinos performed the search for the Greek models of specific maxims with the help of the CD-ROM E of the *Thesaurus Linguae Graecae* (Irvine, California, 2000). He also helped me in other aspects of the book and in matters of information technology. And he is the author of the List of works cited and of the final Index. Conchita Gil Gangutia helped me in the research of the Greek authors hidden beneath Arabic transcriptions, at times not at all clear.

In the search for difficult bibliography, often foreign to the classical philologist, I had the help of Carmiña Teijeiro, librarian of the Madrid Institute of Philology.

My most sincere thanks to all of them.

1 As an advance of the book, I published a first version of Chapter I ("Nuevos textos sapienciales griegos en obras árabe-castellanas", *Emerita* 67, 1999, pp. 195–217) and of Chapter IV ("Tradición sapiencial antigua y obras árabe-castellanas", in *Studia Graeca in memoriam Jesús Lens Tuero*, Granada, Athos-Pérgamos, 2000, pp. 1–17).

Chapter 1

Four Castilian Works That Come from Arabic and in the Final Analysis from Lost Greek Originals

I. The problem

We are dealing with four Castilian sapiential texts translated from Arabic by order of Alfonso X the Learned toward the middle of the thirteenth century: the *Libro de los Buenos Proverbios*, *Poridad de Poridades*, *Bocados de Oro* and *La Historia de la Donzella Teodor*. They in turn are translations from Greek, as the Arabic translators of two of them tell us and as can easily be inferred in the other two.

In contrast, for the *Calila*, another sapiential work translated from Arabic, there is no earlier Pehlvi version, but we do have approximate models in Sanskrit. And for the *Libro de los engaños e los asayamientos de las mujeres* or *Sendebar*, also translated from Arabic in this same period, we can construct a fairly close image of the Pehlvi model, possibly derived from an earlier Sanskrit model, although there are clear additions which come from the Greco-Roman tradition[1].

In all these cases we are dealing with works belonging to the sapiential literature that reached the Arab world from various sources; *The Thousand and One Nights* is another example. In the case of the four works mentioned above, the origin, I insist, is Greek translated into Arabic (in a few cases, it seems, with an intermediate Syriac version). The thesis of this book is that with the Castilian texts (and, naturally, the Arabic ones) as a starting point, the lost Greek models can be reconstructed to a certain extent.

For this reason, the repeated affirmations in books and articles on Castilian literature regarding an "Arabic" or "oriental influence" are completely

1 On *Calila* and *Sendebar* see my *Historia de la fábula greco-latina*, vol. II, Madrid, Universidad Complutense, 1985, pp. 560 ff. (= pp. 615 ff. of the English edition, Leiden, Brill, 2000).

incorrect: it is a Greek influence, by way of intermediate Arabic sources to be sure (and sometimes Latin ones). A different matter is the date of the Greek originals, early Byzantine in my opinion, from the 6th or 7th century, but representing the culmination of an ancient tradition, although a certain amount of Arabic reworking (with Syriac as an intermediate language at times) cannot be dismissed *a priori*. Because this is clearly a matter of Greek texts found by the Arabs in the libraries of Damascus, Antioch and Alexandria. It was only later that there was direct contact with Byzantium.

The existence of Arabic translations of Greek texts, especially scientific and philosophic works, is well known, as is the fact that in certain cases only the Arabic text has been preserved. This has given rise to an extensive bibliography, to which I will allude later. The same is true of the translation of scientific-philosophical texts at the school of translators in Toledo, but there has been much less scholarly attention given to the sapiential texts. What the scholars of Castilian literature tell us about these origins is extremely vague (this will be discussed later); apparently this is a subject that is unrelated and unfamiliar to them. The subject has generated more interest among a few Arabic scholars, although in general they have been more concerned with translations of scientific-philosophical texts, as I have already remarked[2].

2 For example, on Aristotle's *Lives* in Arabic and on his doctrine, see authors like A. Baumstark, *Aristoteles bei den Syrern vom 5. bis 8. Jahrhundert*, Leipzig, Teubner, 1900 [= Aalen, Scientia-Verlag, 1976 (reprint)], pp. 4 ff., and S. Pohl, "Die Aristotelische Ethik im *Kitab al-Sa'ada wa-l-is'ad*", in G. Endress/R. Kruk (eds.) *The Ancient Tradition in Christian and Islamic Hellenism. Studies on the transmission of Greek philosophy and sciences dedicated to H. J. Drossaart Lulofs on his ninetieth birthday*, Leiden, 1997, pp. 206 ff. For the subject of sapiential literature, including the gnomologies, the epistolary novels and, to a lesser extent, some of our treatises, an appropriate bibliography will be given later (also see below, notes 12 and 13): works by Gutas, Strohmeier, Grignashchi, Rosenthal, Manzalaoui and others. The scant attention given to these Arabic-Castilian texts is remarkable in works of a general type such as those by F. Rosenthal (mentioned above) and J. Vernet, which will be discussed later.
The whole movement of translation from Greek into Arabic in Abbassid Bagdad was the theme of a comprehensive study by D. Gutas in his *Greek Thought, Arabic Culture*, London-New York, Routledge, 1998; but as I pointed out in my review in *Saber Leer*, 129, 1999, pp. 6–7, the attention given to sapiential literature is minimal. More information can be obtained from another book by D. Gutas, *Greek wisdom literature in Arabic translation. A study of the Graeco-Arabic gnomologia*, New Haven, Conn., American Oriental Society, 1975, especially from the bibliography and from allusions to his commentary on the *Philosophical Quartet*. Further information can also be obtained

The following are the arguments in favor of a strictly Greek origin of the Arabic texts translated into Castilian (i.e. not various texts converted into a new work by the Arabs):

1. The Arabic authors themselves say so. Hunayn, for example, the translator of *Buenos Proverbios* (among many other translations from Greek), mentions using "ancient books", evidently Greek ones, and he goes on to say that *los romanos* (that is, the Greeks) *"fata oy en dia fazien sus libros e sus psalmos escriptos con oro y con plata en pargaminos tintos de la color que dixiemos"* (the Romans even today write their books and psalms in gold and silver on parchment dyed the color we said), and he continues, *"falle escrito en unos libros de los griegos que un rrey fue en Grecia [...]"* (I found written in certain books of the Greeks that there was a king in Greece [...])[3]. The translator of *Poridad*, Yahya ibn al-Batrik (John, son of Patrick), parallels this, saying that, having been charged by the ruling *Miramamolin* (the Caliph al-Ma'mon) with searching for this supposedly Aristotelian text, he found it (among others with letters of gold) in a temple of Homer the Greater (Hermes Trismegistus), that is, in a temple of late Antiquity, and he translated it from the language of the "gentiles" (from Greek) into Latin (i.e. to Syriac, see below) and from that into Arabic[4].

   Nothing is said about the originals either by al-Mubassir, author of *Bocados*, or by the unknown translator of *La donzella Teodor*. Nor does either of the two speak of himself, as the translators of the first two works do. So it seems insufficient to say, for example, that *Bocados* uses "Diogenes Laertius and other late sources"[5], or that *La donzella Teodor* comes "from the Orient"[6], given the connection of both with strictly Greek genres.

---

from individual articles such as the one dedicated to Mubassir by K. Merkle, Leipzig, 1921. The subject of previous translations, sometimes from Greek to Syriac, will be discussed in Chapter III.

3 *Buenos Proverbios*, ed. by H. Sturm, *The Libro de los buenos proverbios. A critical edition.* Lexington, University Press of Kentucky, 1971, pp. 43 and 46. L. Kasten. "Poridat de las Poridades. A Spanish Form of the Western Text of the Secretum Secretorum," *Romance Philology* 5, 1951–52, pp. 180–190, studies the relation with the *Secretum Secretorum* and considers that the coincidences of *Buenos Proverbios* with *Poridad* do not come from this work but from Hunayn.

4 See *Poridat*, ed. L. A. Kasten, p. 31.

5 Ed. M. Crombach, p. XIII.

6 Ed. W. Mettmann, p. 77.

2. In the controversy over to what extent Arabic texts like these, including pseudo-epigraphs as in *Poridad*, are translations or recreated original texts, the opinion of the scholars tends to favor the first hypothesis. Note that there is nothing Muslim in the texts and that they come from a non-Muslim circle in Bagdad[7].
3. Above all, due importance must be given to the constant presence in our texts of the themes and literary genres associated with the cultural and literary universe of Greece.

In effect, we encounter:

a) Texts derived more or less indirectly from the legend of Alexander, sometimes at a considerable distance from the Pseudo-Callisthenes original, preserved in recension *a*, and others closer to it.
b) The combination of *Lives* of Greek wise men and philosophers, normally combined with a physiognomic description and with series of maxims and of questions and replies between a disciple and a philosopher, all of this closely related to the ancient *Lives* and gnomologies that have come down to us. And with different variants: the *Life* can be missing, there may be anonymous maxims, etc. We find this freedom to combine elements already present in the Greek tradition of the imperial period.
c) The variant consisting of the episode in which someone escapes from a dangerous situation by giving intelligent answers to a series of questions of the type "What is...? What is the most...?", which also include enigmas; at other times it is only a contest of knowledge. The *Life of Aesop*, the *Life of Secundus* and Plutarch's *Banquet of the Seven Wise Men* are the best-known examples but not, by any means, the only ones.

All of this is clearly Greek and, with exceptions in the case of Homer (in the *Life*) or Solon (in Herodotus), centers, within the philosophy that extends from Socrates to Diogenes, on the body of sapiential literature that involves Alexander and Aristotle (adherents, according to this tradition, of

7 See G. Ziakas, "On the problem of the Origin of the pseudo-Aristotelian Arabic Works," *Graeco Arabica* 2, 1983, pp. 39–50, especially pp. 45 ff. It is not only a question of the pseudo-Aristotle; since ancient times the gnomologies have been full of false attributions of maxims, and the same thing happens with the attributions of letters. All of this comes from a late Greek tradition. I provide below more details on the Greek origin of our treatises and on the Bagdad circle of translators later.

the same philosophy) and in some others on texts derived from the theme of the debate on knowledge.

But the theme of Aristotle and Alexander is expanded in the sapiential literature through later strata, Christian (quotations from 4th and 5th century Fathers of the Church, references to Our Lord and to Christian morality) and Byzantine (themes regarding royalty and the ambience of the court). Actually, between the Socratic ethic with its multifarious branches and the Christian one, there are many coincidences, so that the syncretism that arose between them should cause no surprise. This occurs in all four of our works.

The syncretism among the doctrines of the various representatives of the Socratic schools was promoted fundamentally by the Cynics in the pre-Christian period[8]. And this line of thought merged with the Christian current: the Church Fathers of the 4th century (Basil, Gregory of Nazianzus, John Chrysostom) were admitted to the Byzantine gnomologies along with Socrates, Plato, Aristotle, Diogenes, Aesop, Plutarch, Galen and all the others). There are beginnings of this fusion in writings dating from the 3rd century A.D.

Of course it will be necessary to study the different strata in more detail, but typically Greek thematic elements, maxims, anecdotes, and *khreîai*, for example, are frequently preserved exactly in the Castilian texts. And in other cases we must conclude that other elements parallel to these in form and content are also Greek, although they are not preserved literally in Greek. There are scarcely any Arabic elements (see below), or Castilian ones either, except in the vocabulary referring to institutions, as when in *Poridad* Alexander makes Aristotle his *alguazil* or the philosophers meet *"en una eglesia"*, or where *Poridad* speaks of *"el rey mayor, el hondrado Dulcarnayn* (the Arabic name of Alexander, which had already appeared in the Koran)".

The different chronological and ideological sectors of the Greeks combine variously, at times somewhat arbitrarily, as when the legend of Alexan-

8 Thus D. Gutas, *Greek wisdom literature in Arabic translation. A study of the Graeco-Arabic gnomologia*, already mentioned, pp. 453 ff. In this work and in bibliography that he quotes on the Arabic gnomologies, the fact that they are translations from Greek, more or less retouched or modified, is not questioned; furthermore, he studies the subject in depth for the Arabic gnomology that he published, the *Siwan alhikmah* or "The wisdom salon" by al-Sijistani, which coincides in may instances with the others, including ours. Apparently this bibliography has gone unnoticed by scholars of Castilian literature.

der becomes mixed with the Socratic and later gnomologies. And, as has already been said, there are clear indications of an internal evolution. The great problem is whether all these accretions and combinations were already present in the Greek models of the Arabic translations done in the 9th to the 11th centuries (and even earlier, it is thought), or whether part of them can be ascribed to the translators themselves who made use of Greek material found in the library of the caliphs of Bagdad. This question will be studied. In any case, all, or almost all of the materials translated are of Greek origin.

There can, however, be intermediate solutions. And whatever the reply may be, the matter, already mentioned, of the development of this literature from classical to Byzantine Greece is pending, and deserves study. This topic will be discussed, but we can say in advance that the Aristotle/Alexander theme in one or more novels, in letters and in narratives about meetings of philosophers has been supplemented with gnomologies that have been added over time.

For, as I have already explained, we are dealing with the concept of sapiential literature, which is a literature written in multiple languages and with an open structure. It comprises fables, maxims, dialogues and debates, Lives, anecdotes, various erotic and philosophical themes (including novelistic ones), parodies and letters, all this combined in various ways. There are changing attributions to the authors of the maxims and the protagonists of the anecdotes and false attributions of letters or works: pseudo-epigraphic literature, as we say.

We encounter this sapiential literature in Mesopotamia (from the time of the Sumerians) and Egypt, then in the Bible, in the Greek of all periods, and also in India and in Persia. From Greece and India (via Persia) a double tradition reached the Arab world of Bagdad (and later of Egypt, etc.) and from there we now know that it reached Castile and then all of Europe. It also reached Syria (either from Greek or from Arabic), Armenia and Ethiopia, and the Slavic lands. And there is the tradition going from Greece to the West via Latin. No one has ever described this sapiential literature as a whole – it is too extensive, it has become a part of too many languages and cultures – but we do know its essential features.

The matter of transmission is complicated. In some cases the Indo-Persian tradition reached Greece (as occurs with the *Barlaam*); in others the Greek tradition has passed into Latin (the various collections of fables, Julius Valerius's *Life of Alexander,* the *Life of Secundus*), or we assume that this is the case, but the Greek originals are missing (as is the case for the works of Dictys Cretensis and Dares the Phrygian, the *Historia Apollonii regis Tyri*, etc.); and there are Latin works along the same lines as well (collections of fables, the *Altercatio Hadriani et Epicteti*, etc.). All this literature passed from the Latin of the Empire to the European Middle Ages.

But it is also true, and I have put this idea forth in earlier texts of mine, that certain Byzantine sapiential literature (of oriental origin or otherwise) reached Spain by way of Roman Europe. This is the case, to give one example, of various fables that appear in the works of the Archpriest of Hita[9].

Here I simply make brief reference to matters that are well known (although not all of them are, for instance the route Byzantium-Roman Europe-Spain), in order to situate our texts in the literary environment to which they belong. The fact is that the descendants of Greek literature reached Spain by two routes: the route of the Arabs (who also brought with them literature of Persian origin that in turn was, at times, Indian in origin), and that of Roman Europe. Thus there is a convergence of the various sapiential literatures: in our manuscripts works of all these traditions appear side by side in perfect harmony. The concept of sapiential literature as a composite whole maintains its vigor, and Spain was the launching site that sent this amalgam of literatures into Roman and Germanic Europe. But it is important to note that the oldest wave of Greek literature is the one that reached Spain by way of our treatises in Arabic.

Needless to say, I became interested in this topic through my studies of sapiential literature, studies that began with the fable and whose principal representative is my aforementioned *Historia de la fábula greco-latina* (1979–1987). In this work and various later ones, some of them mentioned above (collected in a book, *De Esopo al Lazarillo*, University of Huelva, 2003), I traced the history of these multiple routes for the fable and related genres, with Spain as the point of convergence, and gradually I extended the panorama, dealing, apart from the fable, with the Lives and with debates, the anecdote and the story, the maxim, erotic literature and the novel.

9 See, for example, my articles "The earliest influences of Greek Fable on Medieval Latin writing", *Classica et Mediaevalia* 35, 1984, pp. 243–263; and "Aportaciones al estudio de las fábulas del Arcipreste", in *Philologica Hispaniensia in honorem Manuel Alvar. III. Literatura*, Madrid, Gredos, 1986, pp. 459–473. Also *Historia de la fábula greco-latina* (cited in note 1) II, pp. 511 ff. (p. 559 ff. in the English edition).

In continuation of these studies, this book simply attempts to reconstruct a missing link: the Greek origins of the Arabic translations subsequently rendered into Castilian in the four works dealt with here.

II. Sapiential literature and the concept of an open tradition

The concept of an open tradition refers to the stories, anecdotes, romances, maxims, etc. for which it is not possible to establish an archetype that all later tradition derives from. The discrepancies between the various versions are not "errors" but rather innovations of the scribes, writers or oral transmitters who considered themselves authorized to introduce a bit of creativity. Or they unwittingly confused or contaminated the texts.

I have personally treated this theme in detail with regard to the transmission of the fable and also of the erotic tale and the novel[10]. I have pointed out themes such as the Greek elements that entered the *Calila* and the *Sendebar* in Bagdad (in this case following Perry's precedent), the presence of others in the *Haggadah*, *The Thousand and One Nights* and Petrus Alphonsus, the inclusion of oriental elements in the Syriac fables of Greek provenance, the combination of oriental-Byzantine and Greco-Byzantine traditions in the medieval Latin fable, etc.

I believe that this must be borne in mind in our context, because it is a fact that the school of translators in Bagdad, when it was translating phi-

10 See, for example, "Desiderata en la investigación de la fábula antigua", in *Actas del V Congreso Español de Estudios Clásicos*, Madrid, 1978, pp. 215–235; "Problemas de crítica textual en la transmisión de la fábula greco-latina", in *La Crítica textual y los textos clásicos*, Murcia, 1986, pp. 131–148; "Documentación suplementaria de la fábula greco-latina", *Euphrosyne* 18, 1990, pp. 213–226; "La fecha de la Augustana y la tradición fabulística griega y bizantina", *Prometheus* 18, 1992, pp. 139–149; "El cuento erótico, de los cínicos al final de la Edad Media", *Argos* 12, 1990–91 [1992], pp. 185–194; "Literatura sapiencial antigua en la *Haggadah* y en Pedro Alfonso", *Illinois Classical Studies* 18, 1993, pp. 229–236 (studies collected in the above-mentioned book *De Esopo al Lazarillo*); "La fábula en Bizancio, entre Grecia, Oriente y Occidente", *Studi Italiani di Filologia Classica* 11, 1993, pp. 195–204; *El cuento erótico griego, latino e indio*, Madrid, Ediciones Clásicas, 1994. See especially my *Historia de la fábula greco-latina II*, 1985, pp. 511 ff. (pp. 559 ff. in the English edition) ("La fábula medieval griega y latina de tradición oriental e influjo de la fábula griega en Oriente").

losophical-scientific texts (philosophers, physicians, astrologers, mathematicians, geographers, etc.), was doing precisely that: producing translations that were more or less exact. We know the method of translation as described by the key man of the Bagdad school of translators, Hunayn ben Ishaq, which is comparable to the method of any modern translating team and which we could call scientific.

Naturally, the task was different for various reasons (defective manuscripts, want of precise knowledge about certain points) and errors are not lacking[11]. But the translator considered himself just that: a translator. Any commentary or interpretation was left to later scholars, numerous commentators and original thinkers like Averroes and the others.

But in the case of sapiential literature we do not know to what extent it was simply "translated" and to what extent it was amplified or reworked. Since these procedures already existed in Byzantium and existed later in Castile, as we shall see, when there is no precise data, it is difficult to establish the Arabs' part (and at times, earlier, that of the Syriacs) in those recreations. It was an important part, for example, in *The Thousand and One Nights*[12] and in the legend of Alexander, but it is more doubtful in our four texts. We will return to this topic.

On the other hand, our knowledge of the oldest Arabic manuscripts of our four works is, at the present time, far from complete, and even the oldest Castilian versions must be reconstructed to a certain extent[13]. The

11 On all this see J. Vernet, *La cultura hispanoárabe en Oriente y Occidente*, Barcelona, Ariel, 1978, pp. 85 ff. And, in the substantial bibliography among other works, various studies in G. Endress/R. Kruk (eds.) *The Ancient Tradition in Christian and Islamic Hellenism. Studies on the transmission of Greek philosophy and sciences dedicated to H. J. Drossaart Lulofs on his ninetieth birthday*, Leiden, 1997. But especially the book by D. Gutas, *Greek thought, Arabic culture. The Graeco-Arabic translation movement and early 'Abbāsid society (2nd–4th / 8th–10th centuries)*, London-New York, Routledge, 1998 (and my review in *Saber Leer*, 129, 1999, pp. 66–7). More about this below.

12 For *The Thousand and One Nights* see my study "Documentación suplementaria de la fábula greco-latina", *Euphrosyne* 18, 1990, pp. 213–226, as well as G. E. von Grunebaum, "Greek Form Elements in the Arabian Nights", *JAOS* 62, 1942, pp. 277–292 and T. Hägg, "The oriental reception of Greek Novels", *Symbolae Osloenses* 61, 1986, pp. 99–131. The Alexander legend is dealt with in Chapter III.

13 Thus the *Libro de los Buenos Proverbios*, cf. J. K. Walsh, "Versiones peninsulares del *Kitāb ādāb al-falāsifa* de Hunayn ibn Ishaq. Hacia una reconstrucción del `Libro de los buenos proverbios'", *Al-Andalus* 41, 1976, pp. 355–384. For the Arabic text of *Poridad* there is a good study by M. Manzalaoui, "The pseudo-Aristotelian Kitāb Sirr al-āsrār",

fact is that the first three works to be dealt with suggest considerable contamination and amplification, while the story of *La donzella Teodor* (in which, paradoxically, there is no mention of the author or his sources) has a much more closed structure.

In any case, something can be said about this, though I will leave the matter of sources for later. To begin with, the whole atmosphere of these works points to the Greek world in its most recent, Byzantine, phase, the obsessive themes being, as I have already said, the king and his court, his palaces, war and splendor, instruction in the ten arts; and also Christian themes in the maxims (sometimes attributed to the Church Fathers of the 4th and 5th centuries).

Strictly speaking, there is no Muslim phase, only rare allusions, especially to the Caliph in the prologues of the works: he is referred to by name, but he is called "king". The only precise references are that of the *Buenos Proverbios*, p. 55 of H. Sturm's edition, when it says that *"los moros pintan en sus mezquitas"* (the Moors paint in their mosques), which suggests the Ommiad period, and when he quotes Locanen, or Loginem (Lokman) in *Buenos Proverbios*, p. 50, and in *Poridad*, where the translators themselves speak, acting as narrators.

In any case, an attempt will be made to show a difference between the method of Hunayn, in the 9th century, and that of the 11th century writers ibn Sindi and al-Mubassir. The former is a translator, although it is possible that he managed to join fragments of an epistolary novel about Alexander (thought to have been translated into Syriac and Arabic in the first half of the 8th century) with various gnomologies; the latter two worked on Arabic texts, surely translated from Greek, although perhaps through Syriac[14].

There are already certain traces of modifications or variants in the 9th century texts, but they do not seem to have reached the extent of the Arabic and Jewish variants in the legend of Alexander or of the multiple addi-

---

Oriens, 23–24, 1974, pp. 147–247. In the following chapter I provide more bibliography on this subject.

14 Thus D. Gutas, *Greek wisdom literature*, pp 444 ff. For the earliest origins of the translations of the Alexander novel, see M. Grignaschi, "Le roman épistolaire classique conservé dans la version arabe de Sālim Abū-l-'Alā", *Le Muséon* 80, 1967, pp. 211–264; "Les *Rasā'il Aristātālisa ilā-l-Iskandar* de Sālim Abū-l-'Alā et l'activité culturelle à l'époque Omayyade", *Bulletin d'Études Orientales de Damas* 19, 1965–66, pp. 7–83. The translations into Syriac of Greek sapiential literature in general will be dealt with in Chapter IV.

tions to *The Thousand and One Nights*. After Syriac precedents that introduced variants, in the 9th century court of Bagdad we come upon a circle of Christians (and followers of Zoroastrianism) who are only formally Muslim. And al-Ma'mon, the creator of this school, was a fanatic regarding Aristotle, who appeared to him in his dreams. All of this went on outside the limits of the official religion. Still, some contamination or alterations could have been introduced here, and errors as well, although I believe that the greater part comes from the Greek texts of that first Byzantine era of which I have spoken. We will return to this topic.

Later I will discuss what the scholars of Castilian literature say. As for Arabic literature, it is important, as I have said, to note the scant attention given to these Arabic-Castilian texts in works such as J. Vernet, *La cultura hispano-árabe en Oriente y Occidente*, Barcelona, 1978, F. Rosenthal, *Das Fortleben der Antike im Islam*, Stuttgart, 1965 and M. Cruz Hernández, *Historia del pensamiento en el mundo islámico*, two vols., Madrid 2000, especially vol. 1, pp. 53 ff. and 159 ff., which deal only, and rather superficially, with the *Calila*, the *Sendebar*, *The Thousand and One Nights*, certain stories and the sources, real or supposed, of Dante and the Archpriest. But there is some valuable Arabic bibliography[15].

Very little is said, either, in the most widely disseminated works on the tradition of the life of Alexander that reached the Arabic models for our Castilian translations[16]. And the Hellenists (the scholars of ancient and

15 Nevertheless, see, for example, J. Lippert, *Studien auf dem Gebiete der griechisch-arabischen Übersetzungsliteratur. I. Quellenforschung zu den arabischen Aristotelesbiographien*, Braunschweig, Richard Sattler, 1894; A. Baumstark, *Syrisch-Arabische Biographien des Aristoteles*, Leipzig, Teubner, 1900; K. Merkle, *Die Sittensprüche der Philosophen, Kitāb ādāb al falāsifa*, Leipzig, O. Harrassowitz, 1921; M. Brocker, *Aristoteles als Alexanders Lehrer in der Legende*, Bonn, 1966; F. E. Peters, *Aristotle and the Arabs*, New York, University Press, 1968; G. Strohmaier, "Ethical sentences and Anecdotes of Greek Philosophers in Arabic Tradition", in *Actes du Ve Congrès d'Arabisants et d'Islamisants, Correspondance d'Orient*, 11, Bruxelles, 1971, pp. 436–471 and "Die arabische Sokrateslegende und ihre Ursprünge", in P. Nagel (ed.), *Studia Coptica*, Berlin, Akademie Verlag, 1974, pp. 121–136; D. Gutas, *Greek Wisdom Literature* and *Greek Thought, Arab Culture*, cited above; G. Endress/R. Kruk (eds.) *The Ancient Tradition in Christian and Islamic Hellenism. Studies on the transmission of Greek philosophy and sciences dedicated to H. J. Drossaart Lulofs on his ninetieth birthday*, Leiden, 1997. And what E. García Gómez says in his extensive introduction to *Un texto árabe occidental de la Leyenda de Alejandro*, Madrid, 1929.

16 Cf. G. Cary, *The Medieval Alexander*, Cambridge, University Press, 1956, but see pp. 21 ff., 105, 146, 151; R. Merkelbach, *Die Quellen des griechischen Alexanderromans*, Munich, Beck, 1954; E. García Gómez. *Un texto árabe occidental de la leyenda de Alejandro*, cited

Byzantine Greek) evidently have never seen the texts, yet not only do the authors of the Arabic texts themselves speak of Greek sources, but the very content of these texts demonstrates this origin clearly. Any Hellenist can see this[17]. There is, then, a need for an independent study based, to be sure, on the bibliography of Aristotelic studies.

The same is true of another sapiential text, earlier than the four mentioned and written in Latin – the *Disciplina Clericalis* by Petrus Alphonsus (c. 1115 A.D.), where the author himself speaks of Arabic sources, and it is also true of various sapiential texts of the Jewish *Haggadah*, as I have already mentioned. I have discussed the Greek sources of these texts in an article mentioned in note 10; here I will do the same for Castilian literature. I will also add some details about Petrus Alphonsus. Not everything that is Arabic (and before was Greek) in his text comes from the tradition that we are considering: not, for example, the anecdote about Diogenes in the barrel, attributed to Socrates because of the assimilation of both philosophers into the Cynic tradition and the later confusion in the Arabic tradition[18].

Furthermore, it must be understood that our four Arabic-Castilian treatises are merely a part of the sapiential works translated from Greek into Arabic, that most of them were never transferred to Western works and that many were not even published. This is the context in which our works must be placed. In this book we will refer repeatedly to Gutas's abovementioned 1975 book, which deals with four gnomologies by Pythagoras, Socrates, Plato and Aristotle, related to *Buenos Proverbios* and *Bocados de Oro*. We will consider as well the likewise related gnomology of Ibn Durayd, edited by F. Rosenthal[19]. And there are several others that we know of mainly through references, which we will discuss below.

Here I will present the principal points of the problem: the characteristics of our four texts, the Greek sapiential literature in which they are in-

above. They are important books but they contribute little to the variants of our works. Nevertheless, I will provide information about this. Here I mention again the two works by M. Grignaschi cited above.

17 Note the scant attention paid to the translations of sapiential literature in the most important work on the 9th century Bagdad school of translators: Dimitri Gutas's book *Greek Thought, Arabic Culture*, cited above. On the Syriac translations prior to the Arabic ones, see pp. 20 ff.; on Hunayn see pp. 138 ff.

18 See G. Strohmaier, "Die arabische Sokrateslegende und ihre Ursprünge", in P. Nagel (ed.), *Studia Coptica*, Berlin, Akademie Verlag, 1974.

19 F. Rosenthal, "Sayings of the Ancients from Ibn 's *Kitab al-Mujtanā*", *Orientalia* 27, 1958, pp. 29–54.

cluded and that render them comprehensible, and the date of arrival of the Arabic originals in the Iberian Peninsula. In later chapters I will study certain specific aspects of the Greek sapiential texts that reached us through Arabic: variants of the legend of Aristotle and Alexander, together with the maxims of both, which are not preserved in the Byzantine versions of the Pseudo-Callisthenes that have come down to us; the composite formed by certain Lives of ancient philosophers and writers and certain series of maxims and replies referring to them, especially in the cases of Socrates, Plato and Diogenes; and the precedents of *La donzella Teodor.* Needless to say, there remains a multitude of matters for others to investigate.

There are two things that I would like to recall first of all: one, that the translations or recreations of the Greek texts under consideration must be situated in Bagdad toward the middle of the 9th century A.D. As I have said, we are dealing with the school of translators, both from Greek and from Pehlvi, founded in the 9th century by the Caliph al-Ma'mon, on Syriac precedents and later the precedents of Al-Mansur and Harun al-Rashid toward the end of the 8th century. (Hunayn was the main translator.) It continued in the 10th century and especially in the 11th (al-Mubassir, a Syrian who worked with the Fatimids of Cairo, was the principal translator). I have already mentioned the Syriac and Ommiad precedents.

Naturally, the translation of scientific and philosophical works was the most important activity, but there was no lack of sapiential works, coming both from Greek and from Pehlvi, at times via Syriac translations. Something must be said here about the characteristics of these successive oriental schools of translators, because otherwise their treatment of the Greek texts that interest us here could not be understood.

Another matter is the arrival in Al-Andalus, far to the west, of the Arabic texts in question, the models for the Castilian texts. In general, nothing is said about this, only that the Arabic originals, both scientific-philosophical and sapiential, were translated into Latin and Castilian in the school of translators at Toledo, which was already in existence in the 12th century and reached its peak in the central years of the 13th with Alfonso X[20]; and that the texts were imitated in later Castilian literature. This is correct but insufficient.

20 On the Toledo school of translators, its history and working methods, see G. Menéndez Pidal, "Cómo trabajaron las escuelas alfonsíes", *Nueva Revista de Filología Hispánica*

For it is clear that these Arabic originals were known in Al-Andalus from the time of their origin in the 9th or the 11th century, as the case may be. It is true that there was no school of translators in Al-Andalus; they had only the books that came from the Orient, the translations done in Abbassid Bagdad. Later western Arabic science (the Platonizing Ibn Hazam, the Aristotelian Averroes, Avempace, etc.) depended on these translations no less than did oriental Arabic science (Avicenna, etc.). It should not be necessary to say this, as it is quite evident, but there are too many commonplaces regarding the culture of Al-Andalus; without denying its fruits, it is evident that it stems from the Arabic translations of Bagdad.

For, I repeat, in Al-Andalus there was never a school of translators nor was Greek known. We need only recall what we know about the story of the text of Dioscorides, translated into Arabic in the Abbassid period (by Stephen, son of Basil, later revised by Hunayn) and used in Spain according to Ibn Yulyul of Cordoba: Romanos, emperor of Byzantium, sent a Greek Dioscorides to Abderraman III as a gift, in the year 948. But as no one in Cordoba knew Greek, Abderraman had to ask Romanos for a translator. Romanos sent a monk named Nicholas, who became an important figure among the physicians of Cordoba[21].

There is, then, a great "window" between the 9th and the 13th centuries during which the Arabic texts translated from Greek circulated throughout Al-Andalus and, doubtless, among certain learned men of Christian Spain as well, Petrus Alphonsus being one of them. I have shown that he was at least partially acquainted with the Greco-Arabic tradition a century and a half before the Alphonsine translations. I will return to this topic. Also, see below the comments on translations of *Poridad* into Latin and Hebrew earlier than the Castilian translation of Alfonso X.

In short, the school of Bagdad and later that of Toledo, both understood in a broad sense, are one of the routes by which oriental and Greek learning penetrated the West. The other is the Latin translations from late Antiquity and their medieval continuations. Here we simply amplify this panorama as regards the sapiential literature that arrived in Spain by way of Arabic and that in many cases later passed on to Europe via translations into Latin and other languages.

5, 1951, pp. 363–380. A useful article which, however, does not deal with our four works.

21 See J. Vernet, op. cit., pp. 69 ff.

III. Preliminary remarks on the *Libro de los Buenos Proverbios*

Like the other three, this is a little-known text to which literary histories devote only a few lines. Before continuing, it would be useful to give some essential information about the four works, and then, as I have already said, center on how they fit into the frame of sapiential literature. *Buenos Proverbios* is the work that is least reflected in the medieval literatures.

The *Libro de los Buenos Proverbios*[22] is known through two manuscripts in the Escorial (L–III–2 and h–III–1, here called L and H). It was translated by Hunayn ibn Ishaq (b.803–d.873), the most important figure in the al-Ma'mon circle of translators. He was a Nestorian Christian who learned Greek and Syriac in Syria and was taken to Bagdad by the caliph. There, surrounded by an authentic team, he translated innumerable philosophico-scientific works (Hippocrates, Plato, Ptolemy, Galen, etc.). We have information about his working method, as I have said: comparing manuscripts, giving certain translations to other members of the team, reviewing. The problem is that for sapiential literature the methods could be different, as will be seen below.

He translated, as I say, this work of sapiential literature. He describes the original manuscript as a sumptuous volume in parchment with letters of gold and silver and, on the opening page, a picture of the philosopher sitting in a chair and surrounded by disciples who are receiving instruction. It was a Greek manuscript, as I have said: the Castilian translation speaks of *"los romanos"* (that is, *rumís*, Greeks), and the prologue states that Hunayn (whom it calls Joaniçio, son of Ysaac) translated the book from Greek into Arabic and *"nos agora del aravigo al latín"* (and we now from Arabic into Latin) that is, into Castilian.

Note that in both manuscripts the work follows the model of *Poridad* and is found among other sapiential works, some derived from Arabic and

22 See H. Knust, in *Mitteilungen aus dem Eskurial*, Tübingen, 1879, pp. 1–61; H. Sturm, *The Libro de los buenos proverbios. A critical edition.* Lexington, University Press of Kentucky, 1971; J. K. Walsh, "Versiones peninsulares del *Kitāb ādāb al-falāsifa* de Hunayn ibn Ishaq", *Al-Andalus* 1941, 1976, pp. 355–384. For the collections studied here and Castilian sapiential prose in general see Mª J. Lacarra and F. López Estrada, *Orígenes de la prosa*, Madrid, Júcar, 1993, pp. 31–43, and F. Gómez Redondo, *Historia de la prosa medieval castellana*, I, Madrid, Cátedra, 1998 (*Poridad*, pp. 273–286; *Buenos proverbios*, 440–455; *Bocados*, 455–463; *Donzella Teodor*, 282–502).

some from Latin: for the Alphonsine scriptorium they constituted a single corpus. The text had varying repercussions in Europe through translations into Latin and from there into other languages, but not in the case of *Buenos Proverbios*, which was forgotten and was never translated.

It seems that modern scholars do not pay sufficient attention to such explicit affirmations about the Greek origin of *Buenos Proverbios*, in which, furthermore, we constantly find the action taking place in Greece among the Greeks, with Greek characters named. H. Sturm considers this to be, rather, a literary device to lend authority to the proverbs, distancing them from the translator (but the translator is mentioned quite explicitly).

As for sources, the coincidences with *Bocados* and *Poridad* are pointed out (which is not saying much) and reference is made, or course, to the Pseudo-Callisthenes. There is no doubt about this, but it is too general: many of the things that are in the *Buenos Proverbios* cannot be found in any of the known works. And apart from that there is the central part of the work: meetings of philosophers with maxims of each of them, maxims of Socrates and Plato. All of this seems to come from a different source.

The general conclusion is, therefore, clear. But before studying the topic in detail, an analysis of the work will be useful. This will be done giving the chapters and pages of H. Sturm's edition cited above.

Pp. 41–42. External prologue, I. Joaniçio describes the manuscripts he is translating.

I, pp. 42–45. Internal prologue. The history of Anchos, murdered by thieves and avenged by the cranes that witnessed the deed and revealed it. It is suggested that this comes from the legend of the poet Ibycus, whose death was revealed by the cranes[23].

II, pp. 46–47. External prologue, II. Joaniçio: it was God who caused the cranes to pass by. He says who the philosophers are and presents their seals.

III, pp. 48–50. Proverbs written on the seals (and on the "sashes" and on the houses) of the philosophers: these are Greek philosophers that go from Socrates to Alexander and Galen, plus one Christian (Garagorios, Gregory), one Arab Locanem (Lokman) and others difficult to decipher.

IV, pp. 50–51. Assembly of four philosophers who give maxims of wisdom. Joaniçio closes this part.

V, pp. 53–54. Assembly of five philosophers who speak of wisdom.

23 See another Arabic version of the same legend in F. Rosenthal, op. cit., p. 258.

VI, pp. 55–61. Councils of philosophers. Joaniçio narrates the episode of when at the meeting near the royal palace, after the failure of Nitaforius, son of the king, Aristotle is chosen by Plato to be his disciple. His maxims.

VII, p. 62. A philosopher teaches his disciples the Greek sciences. Plato teaches Aristotle the ten arts.

VIII, pp. 63–64. Meeting of seven philosophers in the palace of gold, each one gives a maxim.

IX, pp. 65–66. Assembly of ten philosophers. Their maxims.

X, pp. 67–68. Assembly of thirteen philosophers in a royal cloister. Their maxims.

XI, p. 69. Assembly of four philosophers. At the king's request each one gives his maxim.

XII, pp. 70–82. Teachings of Socrates the philosopher: maxims not preceded by a *Life*.

XIII, pp. 83–92. Plato's advice or teachings for his disciples, not preceded by a *Life*.

XIV–XVI, pp. 93–99. Letters from Aristotle to Alexander, urging him to treat the conquered peoples well, not to be arrogant. Alexander, "lord of the two horns".

XVII, p. 100. Alexander proves that sadness destroys the heart, as Aristotle said. Words by Alexander.

XVIII, pp. 101–105. Advice that Alexander requested of Aristotle, dialogue with his counselors, questions put to Plato regarding how to govern the kingdom, dialogue with the man who lived in the cemetery.

XIX, pp. 106–108. Alexander's words when he learned that he was going to die of poisoning, letter of consolation to his mother. Banquet and words by his mother after his death.

XX, pp. 109–111. Letter of Alexander to his mother: he consoles her and begs her not to weep for him.

XXI, pp. 112–113. Letter from his mother: I will soon be with you.

XXII, pp. 114–115. Alexander is placed in the golden casket, laments of the court ladies.

XXIII, pp. 116–127. Words of each of the philosophers around the casket in Babylonia. Arrival in Alexandria: words of the mother and the court officials, closing by the mother.

XXIV, pp. 128–131. Words of the philosophers around the casket with comments and closing by the mother.

XXV, pp. 132–135. Letter of consolation from Aristotle to Alexander's mother, words of the mother, who retires to her chamber; arrival of two philosophers, each of whom gives a maxim.
XXVI, pp. 136–137. Reply of Alexander's mother to Aristotle.
XXVII, pp. 138–141. Teachings of Diogenes the Wise.
XXVIII, pp. 142–145. Teachings of Fayagoras (Pythagoras) to his disciples.

Narrated by Joaniçio (although at one point the narrator disappears), there is the rather artificial juxtaposition of the anecdote about Anchos y its moral development (I–II); various proverbs of anonymous philosophers (III–XI)); teachings of Socrates, Plato and Aristotle (XII–XIII); the letters, stories and mourning relating to the life and death of Alexander, which is the center of the work (XIV–XXVI); and an appendix with the teachings of Diogenes, Pythagoras and Hippocrates (XXVII–XXIX).

Altogether, we are presented not with a *Life* of Alexander, but with a moral treatise dealing with his schooling in government and with his death, with commentaries by the philosophers, his mother and the court. It is a treatise on government and an ascetic treatise. All of this has doubtless attracted moral elements of other origins. This topic will be studied in Chapter III. I believe that it was Joaniçio who added a series of Greek gnomologies to the central topic.

In the Pseudo-Callisthenes, apart from the great humanity of Alexander, there are few precedents, as we shall see: the death by poisoning, the golden coffin (III 31) and others. It is by no means the only source. Neither the teachings nor the moral letters and letters of consolation nor the assemblies of philosophers, nor the gnomologies appear in it. It is, in short, a completely different work, although it is concerned with the life and death of Alexander. Searching for these new elements, we find only the themes of the golden casket and of the maxims of the philosophers grouped around it in Petrus Alphonsus XXXIII, but this is derived from the Arabic original of our work, as is also, without doubt, the citing of some of these maxims in the Arabic historian 'Izz ad-Din ibn al-Athir[24]. And from Petrus Alphonsus or *Buenos Proverbios* or *Bocados* come the European references to this topic[25].

24 Cf. M. M. Mazzaoui, "Alexander the Great and Arab Historians", *Graeco-Arabica* 4, 1991, p. 39.

25 Cf. C. Cary, *The Medieval Alexander*, Cambridge, University Press, 1956, p. 151. For late Arabic references, F. D. Gutas, op. cit., p. 43; and S. P. Brock, "The laments of the philosophers over Alexander in Syriac", *Journal of Semitic Studies* 15, 1970, pp. 205–218.

It seems, a priori, that the initial novel about Plato, Aristotle and Alexander, followed by a series of Aristotle's maxims, is a Greek element, as is the novel about the death of Alexander, a combination of letters and the philosophers' lamentations on Alexander's death. The other gnomologies, at the beginning and at the end, are also of Greek origin. Naturally a detailed study must be made of these elements, as they present problems of chronology and possible additions. The piecing together of the two novels with each other and with the other gnomologies is a different matter: it could be Greek or later; I believe it is later. And, of course, the external prologue is Arabic.

IV. Preliminary remarks on *Poridad de las Poridades*

Once again we are dealing with a translation into Arabic in the Bagdad of the 9th century, this time by the Syrian Christian Yahya ibn al-Batrik, John son of Patrick, translated, as we have said, from Greek into Syriac and from Syriac into Arabic[26]. This is the only text that has reached us, in two versions: one more extensive, or the oriental one (probably amplified secondarily). Of this oriental version there was a Latin translation by Philip of Tripoli (Secretum secretorum) in the 15th century, from which, in turn, come the European versions, among them a Castilian one from the 15th century. Of the shorter version, there was, prior to the Castilian Alphonsine version, a partial translation into Latin by Johannes Hispalensis, as well as a Hebrew version by al-Harizi, both from the 12th century.

And again we have before us a kind of *Fürstenspiegl* ("mirror for princes"), or rules of government, organized around the figure of Alexander. But little remains of that figure: after ibn al-Batrik's prologue, narrating the king's order for a search and an introduction about Alexander, there comes the discovery of the book, supposedly written by Aristotle, in the

26 We follow the edition of L. A. Kasten, *Poridat de las poridades*, Madrid, 1957. See also by the same author "Poridat de las poridades. A Spanish Form of the Western Text of the Secretum secretorum", *Romance Philology* 5, 1951–52, pp. 180–190 (which suggests that there are Syriac accretions); F. Gómez Redondo, op. cit., pp. 273 ff. and G. Cary, op. cit., pp. 21 f. Consider also the article by M. Manzalaoui, cited above. There is an edition of the Arabic of the oriental recension text in A. Badawi, Cairo, 1954.

temple of Hermes Trismegistus, and then eight treatises on government, or rather, seven; the eighth is a recent *Lapidarium.*

In other words, we have an external prologue with the search for and discovery of the book, something that was habitual in this Arabic sapiential literature: the same thing appears in the *Calila.* But the prologue permits the insertion of a narrative about Alexander, his great deeds and his humane behavior after receiving a letter from Aristotle. This procedure is not very different from that used by Hunayn. Now, the fiction consists in the fact that the seven treatises are part of the letter: from time to time a paragraph begins with a vocative *"Alexandre".* We have, then, a letter that is really a "mirror for princes", continuing the tradition of Isocrates and also a much earlier tradition from the ancient Orient, the education of the prince by the philosopher, except that here there is a variant: the disciple, Alexander, becomes a real philosopher. There are no maxims, strictly speaking.

To summarize, with the page numbers according to Kasten:

- P. 29. External prologue. The Miramamolin, or Caliph, charges ibn al-Batrik with finding the work.
- Pp. 29–31. Internal prologue. Eulogy of Aristotle, now an old man, having been made an *alguacil* or governor by Alexander (God told him that *"mas çerca eres de auer nonbre de angel que de omne"* (you are closer to being called an angel than a man) and spoke of *"los grandes fechos que fizo"* (the great deeds that he did), referring to Alexander. Alexander's letter to Aristotle consulting him on the treatment to be given to his subjects; Aristotle's reply recommending moderation, which brought good government to Persia.
- Pp. 31–32. The external prologue continues. Ibn al-Batrik finds the book in the temple of Hermes Trismegistus and in it a letter in which Aristotle replies to another from Alexander expressing his regret that the philosopher could no longer advise him and asking him for a book on government. Aristotle sends this in the letter, but recommends great secrecy (hence the title). He gives the index of the book.

The seven treatises follow: definition of the king; the king's state; the value of justice; governors; the king's agents; the king's nobles; battles and armies. After the device of the search for the book and the letter, everything centers on the king and the court with its staff, using a medieval terminology,

The initial prologue deserves attention. It coincides, as I have said, with the *Calila* in the journey to find the book. Evidently a prologue with a mythical or exotic background was de rigueur: it is also found in *Buenos Proverbios* and in *La donzella Teodor*, as well as in oriental and Greek precedents (Ahikar, Pañcatantra, *Life of Aesop*, *Banquet of the Seven Wise Men*, etc.). What is of interest here is the Hermetic component, Egyptian in origin as the book states, present not only in the discovery but also in the request for secrecy. Whether this component was introduced at an early date, in Egypt, where it is thought that the Pseudo-Callisthenes was also written, or in the Arabic period, in which there remained Hermetic elements[27], could be a matter of discussion. We consider the first hypothesis as valid and will return to this question. We will also see old models of the Alexander/Aristotle relation, of the device of the letter, of the use of false attribution to Aristotle and of other points.

V. Preliminary remarks on *Bocados de Oro*

This work[28], another translation from Arabic, is known through nine 15th century Castilian manuscripts, to which can be added three printed editions from the 15th and 16th centuries.

In seven of the manuscripts it appears with no title, while in the other two and in the printed editions it is preceded by a late prologue that speaks of the discovery of the book in India by a Persian king, Bonium, who gives it its name. This is a late addition, not present in the Arabic original. It reveals the wide diffusion of this literature with a prologue of this type, traditionally ascribed to India. Indeed, the work was used in the *Segunda Partida*, in the works of D. Juan Manuel, in *La Gran Conquista de Ultramar*, etc.

27 There are maxims of Hermes from Arabic gnomologies, cf. D. Gutas, *Greek Wisdom Literature*, cited above, pp. 45, 246, 309.

28 We follow M. Crombach's edition, Bonn, 1971 (after that of J. Knust, cited above, pp. 558 ff.). Cf also Mª J. Lacarra and F. López Estrada, *Orígenes de la prosa*, Madrid, Júcar, 1993, p. 33, and R. Gómez Redondo, cited above, pp. 455 ff., where there is mention of the 13th century Latin version by Giovanni Procida (there is a fragmentary version, Ptolemy's maxims, earlier than the Castilian one) of the amplified Castilian versions of the 15th century etc. Crombach, p. XIX mentions the European translations based on the Latin one.

The translation, which can be dated around 1048–49, is the work of the Syrian physician and philosopher al-Mubassir, who worked in the Fatimid court of Cairo under the Caliph az-Zahir[29]. Unlike the two previous works, the text begins abruptly with no prologue, that is, without any indication about its origin or the translator. This is the reason, I think, why certain scribes believed they were called upon to add the prologue, according to which the book had been brought from India. It seems, then, that it is nothing more than a gnomology.

All modern authors consider that in it can be found Greek sources: We read of "writings of late Antiquity now filtered through Diogenes Laertius" (Gómez Redondo, p. 455); Crombach, p. XIII speaks of "sources" that have been partially researched for the maxims attributed to Zeno, Aristotle and Alexander. See the works of Endress, Lippert and Strohmaier cited in note 15, and of Rosenthal (note 19). But this is not a matter of systematic studies either of the details or of the gnomological collections that refer to the various authors of Antiquity, but only of certain general ideas. More concrete are the coincidences that D. Gutas finds with various gnomologies, especially with the one he edited (the above-mentioned Philosophical Quartet), a recension of the gnomology of al-Sijistani. We will look into this theme in more detail below.

On the other hand, there are coincidences with *Buenos Proverbios* and *Poridad*, undoubtedly loans, as we are dealing with a more recent work, of the Fatimid environment of Egypt, and not of Bagdad. We have already said that in this environment works that were already in Arabic were contaminated, but it could have happened that sometimes it was a matter of using the same source.

The work is organized in a series of chapters that speak of the sayings, sometimes preceded by the acts, of a number of different personages, most of them Greek sages, but at times hard to recognize. I list them using Crombach's page numbers.

1. Sayings of Sed (Seth).
5. Acts of Hermes the Wise.
6. His sayings.
18. Counsels of Tad (Tat, Thot).
20. Counsels of Çagalquius (Asclepius), disciple of Hermes.

29 The Arabic text was edited by A. Badawi, Madrid, 1958, as I have said. For this text see M. Crombach, op. cit., pp. XII ff.

21. Words of Homer.
24. Acts of Solon. His words.
26. Acts of Rabion (Zeno). His words.
28. Acts of Ypocras (Hippocrates).
30. His words.
32. Acts of Pythagoras. His advice and his teachings.
39. Counsels of Diogenis (Diogenes, with Greek iotacism) the Dog.
45. Acts of Socrates. His counsels.
71. Plato's acts.
72. His sayings and teachings.
79. Plato's counsels to Aristotle.
98. Aristotle's acts.
101. His counsels.
117. Deeds of Alexander.
133. Alexander's counsels.
139. Ptolemy's acts. His counsels.
143. Counsels of Assaron (?).
146. Counsels of Loginem (Lokman or Aesop).
157. Counsels of Enesio (Eusebios? Eunapios?)
158. Counsels of Medargis (?).
160. Counsels of Thesileus (Basil?).
162. Counsels of Gregory.
163. Chapter on Galieno (Galen).
165. His counsels.
168. Sayings of many sages.
182. Sayings *que no sopieron quien los dixo* (that no one knew who said them).

The organization is not so chaotic as it might seem. Two groups must be differentiated:

1. Hermes and three other personages included in the Hermetic legend. There is a notable coincidence with *Poridad*. The earlier gnomologies were evidently adopted by the Hermetic circles.
2. Chapters referring to Greek sages who go from Homer to Galen in approximately chronological order. There are various enigmatic figures plus a Christian (Gregory) and a teller of fables in whom the Greek tradition of Aesop is reflected in an old Arabic character (Lokman). In the case of the more important characters, we have the combination *Life* (with physiognomy) + maxims; in the others there is only the second

part (in Medargis, physiognomy and maxims). This combination *Life* + maxims is present for Homer, Solon, Zeno, Hippocrates, Pythagoras, Socrates, Plato, Aristotle, Alexander, Ptolemy and Galen, and is especially extensive for the Socratic line from Socrates to Alexander, who is included here as a sage. This coincides with *Buenos Proverbios*, as does the great number of the maxims of Diogenes (but with no *Life*). There are also maxims of Assaron (?), Loginem (Lokman), Enesius (?), Medargis, Thesileus (Basil), Gregory and Galen.

In short, we have an orientation in common with that of *Buenos Proverbios*, but without the axis of Alexander's biography (which, to be sure, is incomplete there, as we have seen)[30].

3. Two final chapters, evidently taken from the gnomologies: some maxims by authors found infrequently in these texts and others anonymous.

The Socratic tradition with its Cynic and Christian descendents, including Alexander, dominates; the themes are the same: justice, self-control, friends, knowing when to keep silent, etc. All of this coincides with the other works we are studying and with the main line of the Greek gnomologies that we know in their ancient and Byzantine phases.

Of course, the great problem is whether all this comes from the ancient gnomologies and from what dates, or if there are recreations, and also there is the problem of the relation with the other sapiential works we are dealing with. Does the combination *Life* + maxims of Socrates, for example, origi-

30 To these Greek sages are added, here and there, various others, some not identified. The citation follows Crombach's page numbers. 168. Proteus (Plutarch), Plinit (Apollonius of Tyana), Dimicratis (Democritus, Democrates, or Demosthenes), Aseus (Aesop), Asigranis (Archigenes), Escalibus = Çagalquius (Asclepius); 169. Aracanus (?), Calides (Euclid), Aplinus (Apollonius of Tyana), Aseres (Hesiod); 170: Silus (Basil?, Zosimus?), Tenparastis (Theophrastus), Abrachis (Hipparchus), Dimigratis (Democritus), Nichomatus (Nicomachus), Grenes (?); 171: Asajagonis (Archigenes), Polutucus (Plutarch), Quedaras (Pindar?), Domiciatis (Democritus), Plimes (Philemon); 172: Dicomes (?), Anicos (Anytus?), Polos (Polus?), Ocason (?), Critus (Crito); 173: Amaron (?), Tisemus (?), Armesis (?), Milisius (Melissus), Pirgonos (Phaedrus); 174: Quedaris (Pindar), Eugenius (Xenophon), Ocriton (Crito), Eclimon (Philemon); 175: Aderando (?), Aclines (?), Crianus (?), Quenis (?); 177: Vastacos (Pittacos), Bracalitos (Heraclitus); 178: Ascidus (Hesiod), Senus (Simonides), Acasagoras (Anaxagoras), Malisius (Melissus), Arsides (Euripides). As can be seen, alongside the Greek sages there are characters from the Hermetic legend, others from Plato's *Dialogues*, Alexander and Ptolemy, Church Fathers and perhaps some Persians. I return to the topic in Chapter VII. I was assisted in the interpretation of these names by Dr. Conchita Gil.

nate in some ancient source or have the maxims been taken from various gnomologies organized by topics? The fact that we have a compilation of early Byzantine gnomologies, with a fusion of Christian and Hermetic doctrine, is evident. Were they joined together in late Antiquity or at a later time, or is the reply a combination of the two?

An important problem, as Strohmaier has seen, is whether there are additions that could be Syriac or Arabic; he suggests this for a Socratic maxim that is in *Bocados* and in the mausoleum of Tamerlane's sister in Samarkand. And there is also the problem of whether the ancient collection could have been enlarged, since the scheme *Life* + work in the Socratic line is, without any doubt, ancient.

It is difficult, however, to give a definitive reply to all this until there is a computerized list of each and every one of the maxims with their Greek or later sources, but strong probabilities can be proposed.

VI. Preliminary remarks on *La donzella Teodor*

This work[31] closes the cycle of the four translations from Arabic, derived from Greek, that were translated into Castilian in our 13th century. It is preserved in five 15th century manuscripts (in some as an appendix to *Bocados*) and three printed editions from the 15th and 16th centuries. In these versions there are important variants that are included in Mettmann's edition. The tale was very popular in Spain; there were many editions and it was the basis for a play by Lope de Vega, *Historia de la donzella Teodor.* On the other hand, in this case not one, but various Arabic sources are known, which, too, are notably discrepant from each other, especially the version of *The Thousand and One Nights* and that of a manuscript belonging to the Madrid Academy of History, closer to our Castilian texts. See below.

31 W. Mettman's edition, *La historia de la donzella Teodor. Ein spanisches Volksbuch arabischen Ursprung*, Mainz, Akademie der Wissenschaften und der Literatur, 1962. See also Mª J. Lacarra and F. López Estrada, op. cit., pp. 51 ff., and G. Gómez redondo, op. cit., pp. 483 ff. Also A. Wesselski, "Die gelehrten Sklavinnen des Islams und ihre Byzantinischen Vorbilder", *Archiv Orientálni* 9, 1937, pp. 353–378.

This is the tale of a maiden, a slave, who defeats the wise men in an examination. I will narrate first, and summarily, the theme of the Castilian work (which at times differs from the Arabic versions; for this see Chapter VIII of this book):

A bankrupt merchant is advised by his slave Teodor to sell her to the king for ten thousand *"doblas"* (doubloons) of gold. She assures him that she possesses such wisdom in all kinds of science and art that she is well worth that price. The scene takes place, depending on the version, in Babylonia (referring to Babylonia of Egypt, the place where Cairo was founded, according to Castilian manuscripts) or in Tunis (in the printed Castilian version B). And the king is called "Abomelique Almançor" or "Miramamolín". Then comes the scene of the examination before an *alfaquí "sabedor de justiçias e de leyes"* (learned in justice and law), a physician or doctor and a poet *"sabedor de la gramática e de la lógica e de la buena fabla"* (learned in grammar and logic and in rhetoric). The examination consists of a series of questions and a series of riddles (What is ...?, What is the most ... thing ?).

The wise men are defeated and the last of them must pay the maiden ten thousand *"doblas"* in order not to be obliged to remove all his clothing, as he had promised. And the king tells the maiden to request a favor; in reply she asks to be returned to her master. The king complies, giving her ten thousand ducats and returning her to her master in rich garments.

The tale has a certain Christian atmosphere: there is frequent mention of "Nuestro señor Jesu Cristo," of the "Virgen Santa María", etc., and in some versions Teodor is a Christian slave from Spain. There is no doubt about the parentage being Arabic versions, which I will mention briefly:

1. The version of *The Thousand and One Nights*, where the story of the slave Twadduh is narrated by Scheherazade between nights 436 and 462. The setting is Bagdad, in the court of Harun al-Rashid, and in this version it is the bankrupt son of the slave's master who is going to sell her to the caliph, on her advice, for ten thousand dinars. But the caliph, in view of the slave's demonstration of her wisdom, submits her to an examination, this time before seven wise men (the last of them the philosopher an-Nazzam, whose death in 885 gives the *terminus ante quem* of the work). The themes are the same (medicine, astronomy, philosophy, rhetoric) besides other Koranic themes that do not appear in the Castilian text and that must be considered Arabic additions to the Byzantine model. The maiden, in turn, poses questions to the judges, who must remove their clothing and turbans if they are defeated.

2. A version in Arabic in a manuscript belonging to the Madrid Academy of History. The action continues to be in the Bagdad of Harun al-Rashid, but now it is the master of the slave, not his son, who takes her to be sold. A number of the questions are missing, and the slave does not pose questions or require changes of clothing in the case of the first two examiners, religious men. There is another Arabic manuscript with variants in the School of Arabic Studies in Granada. Neither of the two corresponds exactly to the Castilian versions, although they are closer than that of *The Thousand and One Nights.*
3. A. Wesselski[32] has pointed out the existence of a Persian version, translated from Arabic and situated once again in the court of Harun al-Rashid. There are a number of variants, among them that the slave is now called Hasaniya. She is threatened with death because she is a Shiite, and the examination before the mullahs is on the theological differences between Shiites and Sunnis. The maiden wins once again and receives 100,000 gold coins plus the sultan's promise that he will not persecute the Shiites. An-Nazzam appears again, but the date is not made clear. Naturally this is a much modified version at the service of Muslim themes.
4. Finally, Wesselski and Mettmann speak of an Arabic work whose title is given in the *Fihrist* as the "Book of the philosopher who was examined by the slave Qitar and the tale of the philosopher about this topic": it says that it is a translation from Greek. Teodor is clearly a predecessor of the other slaves and this time is included in a story, lost for the most part, that comes from Greek, we are told. This is the only explicit mention of a Greek source, which there is no reason to doubt.

I consider that we are indeed once again confronted with a Hellenic tradition that this time appears in Arabic and then Castilian versions that have undergone recreative processes and the addition of variants. But the bibliography gives little precise information, except to speak of "wise maidens" in the case of Tarsiana of the *Life of Apollonius* and in the case of Saint Catherine, submitted to an examination before the doctors. It also mentions the parallel of the literature of disputes, for example that of Hadrian and Epictetus and that of certain stories of wise monks in the Indian Jataka[33].

32 Article cited above, pp. 358 ff. (and for the old version of the slave Qitar, pp. 368 ff.).

33 See Gómez Redondo, op. cit., p. 483; Mettmann, op. cit., p.76; Wesselski, op. cit., pp. 370 f.

All this is true, but it can be made much more precise by situating the story within the Mesopotamian (and then Indian, Hebrew and Greek) genre of disputes in which a philosopher (or a slave or a maiden or a child) challenges a powerful person (king, master, false sage, etc.). There are questions and riddles in which the supposedly inferior character triumphs, saving himself from the grave danger he was in. This genre found its maximum popularity in late Antiquity. I have dealt with it in general terms elsewhere[34].

In short, we have one more version of the very frequent novel about the inferior person who is at risk but who saves himself or herself by triumphing over his high-ranking opponents by using his wisdom. But while in other versions, such as the *Life of Aesop*, the novelesque element dominates, here, as in the *Life of Secundus* and the *Altercatio* of Hadrian and Epictetus, it is only a setting or pretext for the exposition of ingenious replies, which for the most part are Teodor's definitions and solutions of enigmas (She is called Teodora in some of the printed versions). Something similar occurs in a complex text like Plutarch's *Banquet of the Seven Wise Men.* The following is a succinct resume of the work, following the page numbering of Mettmann's edition:

103. First Title. The good merchant educates his slave and, bankrupt, he finds he must sell her, but first he asks her advice. She gives the answer that we already know. Her master takes her to the market, where he buys her clothing and jewelry, and then to the Miramamolín Almançor.

107. Second Title. Dialogue of the merchant and the king, who is astounded at the high price being asked and wants to know the nature of the maiden's learning. She shows herself, is introduced and speaks of her knowledge: the Law of God and his commandments, foods, the stars, the animals, necromancy, the seventy-two languages of the world, medicine and surgery, geometry, grammar and logic, poetry and music, the dance, singing and playing instruments, making clothing and embroidering, illuminating books, precious stones, etc.

34 See my "Elementos cínicos en las *Vidas* de Esopo y Secundo y en el *Diálogo de Alejandro y los gimnosofistas*", *Homenaje a Eleuterio Elorduy*, Bilbao, Universidad de Deusto, 1978, pp. 323 ff.; "The Life of Aesop and the Origins of the Novel in Antiquity", *Quaderni Urbinati di Cultura Classica* N.S. 1, 1979, pp. 93–112; "Géneros helenísticos en el Banquete de los Siete Sabios de Plutarco", in *Estudios sobre Plutarco: Aspectos Formales*, Salamanca, Ediciones Clásicas - Universidad, 1996, pp. 125–142.

110. Third Title. The king is astonished and orders his wise men, the three mentioned above, to come to examine her. Dialogue between the first of them and the maiden.
111. Fourth title. The first wise man questions her on the creation; she answers with the planets and the stars. The questions continue: what is the best way to attain paradise; the properties of the months (a calendar for agriculture and regimen for living). Triumph of the maiden.
112. Fifth Title. She is questioned by the second wise man, a master of the seven liberal arts, about the human body and the regimen for living and nourishment. Then comes an erotic interrogation, which discomfits the maiden, but she shows her wisdom in this topic too. And another question on women, the characteristics of each age, their "signs." Triumph of the maiden.
120. Sixth Title. Dispute with the third wise man, "Abraam the troubadour and master of music," a Jew. His boastful words. The maiden's proposal that the one who is defeated give all his clothing to the winner, which the king approves.
123. Seventh Title. Questioning by the third wise man: enigmas of the type "What thing is?" (heaviest, sharpest, fastest, most enjoyable for an hour or for various periods of time, etc.) And others of the type "What thing is?" a man, a woman, the thing *"de la que hombre no se puede ver farto"* (which man cannot get enough of), etc. The two types alternate, together with others: "Who holds up the world?", "Who was the first king?", etc. All this reveals knowledge of the Bible, myths, Christianity and ancient science. This part closes with an encomium of man, superior to all creatures.
124. Eighth Title. Abraam admits his defeat. Then comes the dispute about the clothing, which the wise man does not want to take off because he wants to pray to Our Lord. The maiden, out of piety, agrees and receives ten thousand *"doblas"*. Final scene with the king.

Thus, between two novelesque episodes that open and close the work there is an interrogation that is the real climax. The work is well composed; it is, without doubt, the result of a recreation that reduces the number of wise men to three and introduces certain medieval themes, some Byzantine, some Castilian. But the themes are not new: especially for the interrogation in which definitions and the resolving of enigmas are demanded, there are clear parallels in works of Antiquity. Also for the themes of the calendar and doctors and the erotic themes. Nevertheless, the difference with the Arabic versions does not reside entirely in modifications introduced by the Castilian version; it is evident that the Arabic ones also modified the Greek original, introducing specifically Muslim themes, as I have already pointed out.

The parallels with the frame novel and with the oldest sapiential elements must still be determined exactly. Note that this work stands somewhat apart from the others because it contains no maxims of the Socratic-Cynic tradition attributed to specific authors, nor does it contain the theme of Alexander, which had been assimilated into that tradition.

VII. The acceptance of Greco-Arabic literature

The first thing that must be remembered is that the Greco-Arabic works were known in Spain prior to the time of their translation into Castilian in the middle of the 13th century through the initiative of Alfonso X. To what has been said above regarding Petrus Alphonsus and the translations of *Poridad* before the Alphonsine translation, we must add the *Libro de los Siete Sabios*, composed by order of Fernando III, c. 1237, which clearly imitates the theme of the assembly of the sages who give advice to the prince.

Before returning to the topic of the Greek origins of our treatises, considering them as accepted in the light of what has been said, it seems appropriate to offer a rapid review of the reception of this tradition in medieval Castilian literature and in all European literature. Because the reconstruction of the evolutional line of sapiential literature, which is what we are attempting, encompasses both its origins, be they Indo-Persian or Greek, and its decisive influence in the creation of new literatures. In their origins these were, at least in the case of prose, literatures in translation, just like the case of early Latin literature, which was translated from Greek. History repeats itself.

But the picture we are offered in the treatises and studies on medieval literature is greatly distorted, as I have already suggested. For example, in a publication by a specialist as important as Maxime Chevalier[35], it is stated as an incontrovertible fact that in the double culture of medieval Spain, there was a confluence of "the apologues of the oriental collections" and the "*exempla* that Christian Europe had collected". Not so: the traditions that came together (either by way of Spain-Europe or by Europe-Spain) are on the one hand the Greco-Arabic tradition (which we are studying here) and the Persian-Arabic one; and on the other hand the Greco-Latin tradition.

There are two Greek traditions and a Persian one, moreover with various examples of contamination, all three heirs of older, Mesopotamian traditions. As regards the fable, I have studied its development in my book *Historia de la fábula greco-latina* and in other bibliography that I will not repeat here. There is the Indo-Persian-Arabic tradition, contaminated with the Greek tradition in cases like the *Calila*, the *Sendebar* and *The Thousand and One Nights*, a tradition which, on the other hand, sometimes comes by way of Byzantine Greek and Latin Europe; the case of the *Barlaam* can be included here. In cases like the Archpriest of Hita, as I have pointed out (see note 8), there is a confluence of the fables of the Persian line with those of the Greek line which arrived via imperial or medieval Latin, which is the case of *El Conde Lucanor* and other works.

But then there is this other line that we are studying in our four Castilian treatises and that can also be seen, for example in the Arabic fables of Lokman, which are basically Greek.

Leaving aside, now, the collections of fables, and giving, here also, only a few general lines, we must point out that there is a confluence of our four works with the sapiential literature which arrived via the other routes: with the Persian-Arabic literature which we have mentioned and about which we have the clearest ideas. The *Calila* and the *Sendebar* are considered as forming part of the same literary genre; they are used together in the new productions. Likewise the *Barlaam*, a special case, in which a Persian original and a Greek one must be accepted, with perhaps an intermediate Georgian one. The same is true of the Greco-Latin literature (or simply Latin based on Greek models) that is frequently found in the same manuscripts and is used in reconstructions; for example, in some manuscripts of *La donzella Teodor* passages from the *Disputa de Hadriano y Epicteto* (or *Epito*) have been

35 "Prólogo" to *Cuento y Novela corta en España. I. Edad Media*, Mª J. Lacarra, Barcelona, Crítica, 1999.

added. And there is contamination among the works that we are studying: in *Bocados* and *Poridad* there are passages from *Buenos Proverbios*[36].

We have given some examples of this type of literature above: literature which has Greek origins although it has reached the West by way of Latin (*The Life of Secundus*, *The Life of Alexander* by Julius Valerius), and the literature whose origins are Latin only, the Greek origins having been lost or never existed (*The Life of Apollonius king of Tyre*, the *Trojan Histories* of Dares and Dictys, Valerius Maximus, the above-mentioned *Altercatio*, the *Ioca Monachorum* and other literature of disputes, etc.).

In short, there was created by the confluence of various sources (contaminated, moreover, since early times and, in the final analysis, of common origin) a sapiential literature that extended throughout Europe. Frequently the point of departure was Castilian, from which *Bocados* was translated into Latin and then passed into various other languages, but not always: the European translations of *Secretum Secretorum* come from a Latin translation of a different branch from the one that reached Castilian, as we have said. And conversely, the Castilian *Libro de Alexandre* comes basically from the French of Walter of Châtillon, the *Historia Troyana* and its version in verse from the *Roman de Troie*. In these cases the route that comes from Antiquity passes, conversely, through France.

What is of interest is that by diverse paths a sapiential literature was created whose fundamental end was the education of the prince and the doctrine of government by the kings. It is not surprising, then, that in the royal milieu of Castile works should be recovered which, disregarding their ancient strata, refer to political and moral teachings in Byzantium, under the guise of Alexander and the ancient sages. This was the recognized intention of the *Pañcatantra* in India and afterwards.

All of this, as I have said, comes from the sapiential literature of Mesopotamia, whose best-known text (not the only one or the oldest) is the *Book of Ahikar*, which was translated into Greek, as is known. The moralistic tradition of the Socratic school was inserted into this old tradition and adapted to the monarchical period, which saw its model in Alexander. Our medieval literatures did nothing but follow this model in an equally monarchical milieu. It must be added that this entire tradition acquired, at various times and places, a Christian content that fit into the Socratic tradition with

36 For *Poridad* see L. Kasten, cited above; in general, Mª J. Lacarra and F. López Estrada, op. cit., pp. 32 ff. See also note 3.

no difficulty. The ancient formula of combining a novelistic presentation with maxims of good conduct and good governance was always maintained.

We should add here that all this literature continued the system of an open tradition that was characteristic of it, as we have said. But sometimes it is difficult to see whether the recreations and contamination are from the Arabic or from the Christian period, or even older (we will leave this last topic for the moment).

For example, the two versions of *Poridad*, the western or short one and the oriental or extensive one, are without doubt Arabic; we have already seen that they are earlier than the arrival of the former in Spain. We have already mentioned the Muslim additions to *La donzella Teodor*. But this work also has many important variants in different Castilian manuscripts, even taken from the *Altercatio*. We saw that in manuscripts of *Bocados* there is an introduction about a king Bonium who journeys to India in search of the book, a theme copied from the same theme in the *Calila*, in *Buenos Proverbios* and in *Poridad*. In this last work we have already seen that there was a *Lapidarium* that had been added. Furthermore, we are not well enough acquainted with either the Arabic or the Castilian tradition of these works and we might encounter surprises.

The tradition of additions and summaries was perpetuated in the Castilian imitations of this literature, as I will explain below, and it was old, too, in the tradition of works like the *Life of Secundus* or the *Altercatio* or the *Life of Aesop*[37]. And, of course, in the gnomologies, which I will discuss in a later chapter. *The Life of Apollonius*, from the 5th or 6th century, appears in two versions that adapt a Greek original of the 2nd or 3rd century[38].

Now, on occasion the possibility that at some moment there have been modifications or syntheses or additions of this type derives from a simple internal analysis, and the problems of if and when remain, as I have mentioned.

37 On the first two works (and many more) see L. W. Daly and W. Suchier, *The Altercatio Hadriani Augusti et Epicteti philosophi and the question-and-answer dialogue*, Urbana, Illinois, University of Illinois Press, 1939. In this work the multiple secondary recensions of the text are pointed out. On the *Life of Aesop* see my works cited: in recensions G and W and in papyri there are traces of diversification from the original text going back to ancient times.

38 Cf. the edition of Mª C. Puche López, *Historia de Apolonio rey de Tiro*, Madrid, 1997, pp. 13 ff, 29.

The point that is still unresolved, also mentioned previously, is the growth of this literature, its role as a model for all Castilian sapiential literature. On the one hand, there is the replica of our works in later Castilian literature. J. K. Walsh has made a good study of this topic[39] in relation to *Buenos Proverbios*; and we have already mentioned *La Donzella Teodor*. The *Bocados* was used in the works of D. Juan Manuel, in the *Gran Conquista de Ultramar*; there are echoes of these works in the historical works of Alfonso X the Wise. It is necessary to make detailed studies of sapiential literature in general. In the *exempla* of the homilies, in maxims, stories and anecdotes we encounter all kinds of transpositions of ancient sapiential literature[40]. On the more specific topic of Alexander, I refer the reader to the study by Mª Rosa Lida in a review of Cary's book, quite deficient on this subject[41].

But of more interest is the fact that through the influence of our works there was created a whole literature of education of princes, aided by moral maxims, sermons and fables, always with a short prologue in which the commissioning of the book or some other incident concerning its origin is related. Of special interest in the 13th century is the *Flores de Filosofía*, which opens with a dialogue between a king and a preacher: the latter propounds his doctrine by chapters and subjects. It contains things from *Buenos Proverbios* and *Bocados*[42]. The *Libro de los Cien Capítulos* seems to be an amplification. And especially important is the *Libro de los doce sabios*[43], by Ferdinand III, called the Saint, assembled to advise his son: a classic theme. It is dated c. 1237, but there is an addition from 1255, by then in the reign of his son Alfonso the Wise, who called twelve philosophers together to give maxims worthy of being recorded in the sepulcher of his father, a clear echo of our familiar theme

Of a later period is the *Castigos de Sancho IV*, addressed by the king to his son. And later, in the 14th century, we have the works of D. Juan Manuel: the *Libro de los estados*, the *Libro del Cavallero y el Escudero*, *El Conde Lucanor*

39 In "Versiones peninsulares...", cited.

40 See *Cuento y novela...*, cited, pp. 29 ff (themes of the son of the prostitute who may, unwittingly, stone his father; and of Demades and the swallow, transposed to a Christian background).

41 See Mª R. Lida, "La Leyenda de Alejandro en la literatura medieval", in *La tradición clásica en España*, Barcelona, Ariel, 1975, pp. 175–197.

42 See the edition of H. Knust, Madrid, 1878, prologue.

43 See, apart from the general bibliography, H. Bizarri, "Consideraciones en torno a la elaboración de *El libro de los doze sabios*", *La Coronica* 18, 1989, pp. 85–89.

and the *Libro del Consejo*, all of the same type. In the first of these works the prologue is of note, with echoes of the *Barlaam*, in which the pagan king Moravan is looking for a preceptor for his son Joas, who, after seeing visions of Buddha, asks to be taught about the human soul. The work is developed through a series of dialogues in which the preceptor Julius takes part. The influence of Christianized sapiential literature is perfectly clear. Furthermore, having various strata, it is a good example of Byzantinization starting from an original that is probably Pehlvi: a true pastiche or cento[44]. As for the *Conde Lucanor*, the prologue is between the count and his adviser Patronio; here there is a very elaborate composition[45], but the starting point is the same.

Then we could go on to speak of the *Libro del Cavallero Zifar* and of various other works, also of collections of examples (the *Libro de los Enxemplos* by D. Juan Manuel) and proverbs (the *Libro de los proverbios*, by the same author, the *Proverbios Morales* of Sem Tob, etc.), in which the old gnomologies are continued, with no framework. They are collections of varied material, similar to the last chapter of *Bocados*, but with the possibility of innovation and originality.

The fact is that this Castilian literature of the 13th to the 15th century, sometimes in other peninsular languages also (e.g. the *Libro de la Saviessa* in Catalan, attributed to James the Conqueror), revives the ancient Greek sapiential literature that comes from various sources and whose unity is recognized now. There is, of course, the confluence of the Indo-Arabic literature of which we have spoken. Perhaps it is useful to have given a brief idea of the prolongation of this tradition in order to mention as well several aspects of the Greek sources of the Arabic originals that were translated and that constitute one of its essential roots.

44 See P. Bádenas, *Barlaam y Josafat: redacción bizantina anónima*, Madrid, Siruela, 1993, pp. XXV ff.

45 Cf. J. Gimeno Casalduero, "El *Conde Lucanor*: composicion y significado", *Nueva Revista de Filología Hispánica* 24, 1975, pp. 101–112.

VIII. A panoramic view of the Greek sources of this literature

I have already taken a stand in favor of the Greek origin of the model or models of our works. I will go into this more specifically later, but some points must be added here.

I repeat that the topic of the Greek sources has hardly been treated in the bibliography of Castilian literature, somewhat more (but very little regarding our works) in the bibliography of Arabic literature; I have given the pertinent bibliography. The book by Mª J. Lacarra, cited in note 35, is paradigmatic: of *Buenos Proverbios* it says (p. 49) that "the critics seem to have in mind a version direct from the Arabic, without paying much attention to the words of the prologue" (in which Joaniçio speaks of the Greek original). Now of course, there is an Arabic version, but this is, in turn, a version of one or various Greek originals.

Without going into this difficult question of the singularity or plurality of the models for the moment, I want to emphasize here certain things already said. For example, the life of Alexander serves as a pretext to write moral treatises, as do the old gnomologies. This is all the result of successive treatments in the imperial and Byzantine eras, with little traces of Muslim influence. There is, to be sure, a process of Byzantinization and of Christianization, whose fundamental features I have already presented.

Let me insist that this process is far from being unique. We see it, for example, in the *Barlaam*, and also in the tradition of the Pseudo-Callisthenes: only the Byzantine recensions derived from B (Œ, l, ms. L, g, e) present a series of new themes such as the visit of Alexander to Jerusalem or the blocking of the mountains to impede the passage of the peoples of Gog and Magog. These recensions continued to grow, as also occurred with the collections of fables, until the 7th century. I will discuss this topic in more detail below.

And the same thing happens in the case of the gnomologies in our works, which are based on others with citations that go back to the 5th century B.C.[46], and which were later remodeled in various ways. Here is where the stratification can be seen best: there are gnomologies of Socrates (and of Diogenes) from the end of the 4th century B.C. containing maxims,

46 See I. Gallo, *Frammenti biografici da papiri.* II. *La biografia dei filosofi*, Rome, Edizioni dell'Ateneo, 1980, pp. 176 ff.

or *khreîai*, that sometimes come from Xenophon or Plato while others were incorporated more recently; and many of them reached the gnomologies of Maximus the Confessor and Antonius Melissa, in the Byzantine period, via other intermediate ones. New maxims and also attributions to Socrates of Cynic material appeared. The gnomologies of *Bocados* and the others have this origin, but sometimes they offer new material, whose date of incorporation is uncertain. This is a topic that must be researched. In other words, the theme of the Greco-Arabic gnomological tradition should be studied apart from the Alexander novel or novels and the novel of the maiden Teodor.

Note that the regal background, the palaces and the jewels and, of course, the Christian atmosphere must be attributed to the Byzantine world. And gross errors like attributing maxims to the wrong authors or attributing to Homer Aesop's fable of the two knapsacks (as in *Bocados*) are typical of this tradition. And thus in the gnomologies preserved in Greek (often in Byzantine collections of the 9th century or later), one already finds errors such as saying that Socrates died in a fall from a cliff (thus in the *Gnomologium Vaticanum* 478). From the 4th century B.C. to the 8th century A.D. the gnomologies (and the collections of *Lives* + maxims) increased, almost always under Cynic and then Christian influence. The Byzantines enlarged them enormously, with increasingly less rigor. It is quite probable that the greater part of the gnomologies in our works is theirs, although some Arabic contributions cannot be excluded.

And we must always take into account unschooled writers, more interested in moral subjects than in historical accuracy, this going back to the Hellenistic period (embryos of the Pseudo-Callisthenes, of the *Life of Aesop*, of the gnomologies) and increasingly more thereafter.

In short, summarizing these things and adding others, and putting aside for the moment the assembly of the various elements, there is a long series of these elements that must be attributed to the first Byzantine period and that crowns a sequence of strata that come from the classical period. Without considering the combination *Life* + maxims of which I have spoken, I can cite, for example:

1. Alexander as a philosopher, who is actually the equal of his master Aristotle and who pronounces a series of maxims that reach the gnomologies, sometimes coming from the Pseudo-Callisthenes. In that work we

already encounter his humanity again and again, and it is an image that some of the biographies of Alexander maintained[47].

2. The theme of the master's "secret", taught only to his disciples (acroamatic works), already existed in Antiquity; it is discussed, for example, in the (apocryphal) letters from Alexander to Aristotle and from the latter to the former in *Simplicius in Physicorum* I 1. This theme, which is important in *Poridad* and which explains the union of the tradition we are studying with the Hermetic tradition (in *Poridad* and also in *Bocados*), comes, then, from Antiquity.

   Therefore, the Hermetic doctrine that enters sapiential literature in the places mentioned comes, naturally, from Antiquity. It is not, therefore, an Arabic element, although they continued this tradition. It appears in Egypt beginning in the 2nd century A.D.[48].

3. Epistolary novels, like the ones we find in the Pseudo-Callisthenes and much more extensively in *Buenos Proverbios* and *Poridad*, are a specialty of the Hellenistic and Roman ages, which Merkelbach studied[49]. He comments on the epistolary novels about Themistocles, Chion of Heraclea, the Seven Wise Men, the letters of the *hetairai* in Alciphron. On the other hand, the pseudo-epigraphists in general and the false attribution of works (for example the *Poridad* attributed to Aristotle) are frequent in the imperial period. I have already referred to this subject in relation to an article by G. Ziakas.

4. The theme of the debate on wisdom between the king (or master, etc.) and the philosopher (or slave, etc.), in which the apparently inferior person triumphs, is definitely Greek although its roots be oriental, as I have explained in various publications of mine cited herein. The best-known examples, but by no means the only ones, are those of Aesop and his master *(Life of Aesop)*, Secundus and Hadrian *(Life of Secundus)* and Alex-

47 See P. Hadot, "Fürstenspiegel", *Reallexikon für Antike und Christentum*, VIII, Stuttgart, 1972, col. 582 ff; and my article "Las imágenes de Alejandro", in J. Álvarez and S. M. Blázquez (eds.), *Alejandro Magno. Hombre y Mito*, Madrid, Editorial Actas, 2000, pp. 15–31. I will return to this subject in Chapter III.

48 See R. Reitzenstein, *Poimandres*, Stuttgart, Teubner, 1966 (1st ed. Leipzig, Teubner, 1904), pp. 2 ff. On the Arabic continuity see pp. 172 ff. More details in our Chapter IV.

49 Op. cit., pp. 32 ff. See also N. Holzberg, ed., *Der griechischer Briefroman. Gattungstypologie und Textanalyse*, Tübingen, Narr, 1994 (it says very little about the novel of Alexander), and the articles by M. Grignaschi that I have already mentioned regarding an Alexander novel in letters that reached the Arabic period.

ander and the Gymnosophists. This, as I have explained, is the root of the theme of the slave Teodor debating with the sages, and also of the story of Aristotle and Alexander at the beginning of *Poridad*, except that here there is an inversion: Alexander appears as a learned man. The topic must be studied in more depth.

5. The intellectual and moral background of all these works is uniform. It has nothing to do with academic or Stoic philosophies, which were not cultivated by the gnomology, the fable or the novel, nor has it to do with Epicurean philosophy; the Epicureans quoted Socrates mostly to criticize him[50]. This background is the same as what I have studied elsewhere for the fable: to the earlier tradition it adds Cynicism (just as in the above-mentioned papyrus of the *Life* of Socrates) and then moralism and Christianity. What is fundamental is the Socratic line, to which the Byzantines added the Christian one. Perhaps the presence of the physicians in *Bocados* is the work of the Arabic translator al-Mubassir, who was a physician.
6. Still to be resolved, as I have said, is the question of the date of the "blending": the creation of *Buenos Proverbios* with the Alexander theme and certain gnomologies as a starting point, or of *Bocados* based on various gnomologies. Of course, to the Arabic translators must be attributed the initial prologues and the role of narrator in *Buenos Proverbios* and *Poridad*; we do not know whether the blending is ascribable to them as well. In any case, we have seen that they were capable of making additions and of reworking the material, as were Petrus Alphonsus and the Castilian authors.

But the Greeks already worked in this way; it is typical of sapiential literature, as I have said. Since Merkelbach we know of the progressive inclusion of diverse stories in the *Life of Alexander* (of course, the Arabs created other legends on the theme), and one outstanding case, Plutarch's *Banquet of the Seven Wise Men*, which I have studied in detail in a

50 See E. Acosta and E. Angeli, *Filodemo. Testimonianze su Socrate*, Naples, Bibliopolis, 1992 (cf. my review in *Emerita*, 63, 1995, pp. 146–147). Some exceptions must be made for the Stoics, see D. Gutas, op. cit., p. 451, but the Cynics were the ones who left their mark on the genre.

special work[51]. And the Greeks also added fables to their collections and maxims to their gnomologies, all of which I have studied.

These are considerations of a general character, which must be made more specific. And without doubt there will be things left pending, because, as I pointed out above, it would be necessary to have a computerized corpus encompassing all the maxims of the gnomologies, including those of our works, but this does not exist. In any case, with this work my intention is to open a field of studies that will require the efforts of many.

But I consider that, added to what has been said above, these considerations establish with certainty that if not the complete works in all cases, at least the elements they are composed of are Greek, Byzantine Greek, from the 6th or beginning of the 7th century at the latest, taken from the Byzantine world. These works have very uniform literary and doctrinal characteristics that fit exactly into this period. But at the same time they are heirs of an earlier tradition that dates from the classical era that then evolved throughout the Hellenistic and Roman eras and finally reached the Byzantine period. The doubts, the vacillation and, finally, the silence of the scholars of Arabic and Castilian literature are unjustified. What the Arabic translators say is true: they were translating from Greek.

51 See my "Géneros helenísticos en el Banquete de los Siete Sabios de Plutarco", in *Estudios sobre Plutarco: Aspectos Formales*, Salamanca, Ediciones Clásicas - Universidad, 1996, pp. 125–142.

Chapter 2

A Study of the Sapiential Tradition That Led to Our Works

I. Traditional elements and innovations in our four sapiential works

In the previous chapter the reader was informed of the compositive schemes that underlie our four sapiential works, either preserved in them exactly or altered and contaminated, the date of these changes being difficult to determine. The schemes, on the other hand, are to a great extent comparable to those of the *Philosophical Quartet (PQ)*[1] and other Arabic works of Greek origin that will be dealt with at the end of this chapter and in the following ones. For example, we have seen that in *Buenos Proverbios* the central scheme, fashioned around Plato, Aristotle and Alexander, has been subjected to insertions and the addition of maxims of various philosophers. And in certain chapters the scheme *Life* + maxims itself suffers alterations.

Thus, this same work relates (VI, pp. 55 ff.) how Aristotle was adopted by Plato as his disciple, next are his teachings, then (VII, p. 62) Plato's teachings, after that (XIII, pp. 83 ff., following some extraneous elements) the teachings of Plato again (with no biography); in XIV, pp. 93 ff. are the letters of Aristotle to Alexander, those of his mother, the mourning for her death, and also, at times, the "teachings" of Alexander: the biographical element surfaces here and there, but it does not precede the body of the work. In the insertions that I have mentioned there are maxims, some anonymous, some by Socrates, Diogenes, etc., without *Lives*. In short, the

1 D. Gutas, *Greek Wisdom Literature in Arabic translation* cited above. It is a recension of the work of al-Sijistani (end of the 10th century), *Siwan al Hikmah* ("The Philosophy Salon").

element *Life* + maxims has been somewhat marginalized compared with the ascetic and governmental elements, which include letters and lamentations.

Now, in *Bocados*, as we have said, there is a long list of *fechos* (acts) (or *Lives*) and maxims of certain philosophers but only maxims of others. And there is duplication with regard to *Buenos Proverbios*: specifically, there are *Lives* and sayings of Socrates, Diogenes, Plato, Aristotle and Alexander (among other philosophers). The comparison of details is another matter; in the case of Alexander, for example, the long biography, mixed with letters and laments, is followed by his *castigos*, or counsels. And if we now compare it with *PQ*, the *Life* of Socrates is very different. In short, *Bocados* is more or less the sum of different *Lives* + gnomologies and of gnomologies with no *Lives*: in part the work is dependent on *Proverbios*, in part it is not.

In *Poridat* there is a different treatment: here the biographical element, much Christianized, is quite diminished in comparison with the doctrinal element, expressed in a letter that, other things not considered, is organized thematically and contains abundant gnomic and protreptical works. The *Donzella Teodor* is yet another different model: there is an anecdote followed by questions (What is...?, What is the most...?) and answers classified thematically.

With this I repeat that the works we are discussing offer a modification of the traditional models, at times consciously and at times, in some cases, by means of secondary interpolations. An analysis reveals, among other things:

a) The mentioned model *Life* + maxims, and sometimes letters.
b) There are various *Lives* for the same person, markedly novelized, with adaptations at recent chronological levels.
c) The maxims are sometimes simple maxims in the indicative, sometimes protreptical imperative (or by questions), sometimes *khreîai* (situation + questioning + reply, including the type What is...?, What it the most...?), sometimes dialogues. There can be concatenation. And there are clear, although rather disperse traces of organization by themes, and of similes, fable-like elements, etc.
d) There are clear strata: pre-Socratic elements followed by elements that are Socratic, Platonic, Aristotelian, Stoic, Cynic, moralistic, Hermetic and Christian. They are also present in the *Lives*. There is a tendency toward a synthesis of all these elements that without doubt entered the successive phases gradually. And there is confusion of authorship, either

with regard to the identity of doctrinal conception (Socrates as a Cynic) or owing to accidents of transmission; more about this below.

e) Together with the model *Life* + maxims there is the model of the simple maxims, arranged arbitrarily or systematically; and that of an organization of the maxims by author (with or without a preceding *Life*) and, within each author, by themes.

f) This type of literature is clearly related to ancient poetry and prose, from which they draw constantly; to *Lives* or anecdotes + individual maxims, which it often incorporates; to symposiac literature; to the fable, which in the collections is preceded by the *Life of Aesop*; and to the story. This is the sapiential literature of which we have spoken. On the one hand, it is imitated by the later Romanic literature, which creates similar works that culminate in the picaresque novel, and on the other hand, just as it draws from all different kinds of elements, so it provides the narrative, preaching, etc. with material in the form of "examples" .

It is necessary, then, to find parallels for the elements mentioned, at times within new combinations: the chronology is not the most important thing; it is a matter of identifying elements that persisted over the centuries and in different literatures, and then comparing details a) within our four works, and b) between these works and the parallel elements that we know of in Greek literature and in others.

For we must not forget that we still have pending the when and the how of the amplification of materials in our works. Many features in these works may have come from Hellenistic or late Antiquity and later been lost; others may have been created in Syria in the Byzantine epoch, or in the Ommiad period, or even in the Arabic or the occidental Christian world, based on ancient pagan and Christian models. These, however, are themes that we will leave for later chapters.

It is necessary to distinguish between: a) the gnomologies with personal reference (*Life* or anecdote + maxims); b) the *gnômai*, *khreîai*, similes, fables, single anecdotes; and c) the collections of gnomologies both with an author and anonymous.

Maxims that are simply general or protreptical are sometimes "signed" by a specific author, though many of the later attributions can be erroneous or imaginary. Often the attribution is to a character of the traditional legend or a purely novelesque person; such is the case of Aesop in the ancient Orient and Egypt. But this also happens with Greek sages and philosophers, who thus enter a context at times distorted and novelistic, and frequently the attribution varies. Sometimes these works contain questions and answers or debates. The genre remained in use in the western Middle Ages and among the Christians, alongside the pseudo-epigraphs of imaginary attribution, no less imaginary letters, and other genres, "signed" but whose attribution can be more or less real, more or less fantastic.

Here, too, we find the presence of individual examples of the sapiential genre (fables, similes, anecdotes, maxims) in the context of other genres, giving rise later to the collections, especially in Greece.

But together with the collections that are "signed" or have "personal reference" are the anonymous ones, although the difference is really subjective, since the "signature", as I have just said, is frequently imaginary. These collections had already appeared in Mesopotamia; in Greece they did not appear until the Hellenistic period. There is osmosis between collections, and at times material is taken from them to create individual instances, including the "examples".

In this chapter I am going to present a general panorama of this whole literature, with certain restrictions, as in the following chapter I will discuss an important part of it, especially the novelistic literature centering on Alexander, his gnomologies and those of Aristotle, the letters, the literature of consolation and other points. On the other hand, in earlier publications of mine I have studied in detail certain themes such as the fable and the *Life of Aesop*, as well as the literature of Mesopotamia and Egypt. In those cases I give abbreviated references. But I feel that the presentation of a general picture is necessary; none has been made before, to the best of my knowledge. What I offer here will have to be completed with the reflection of all this literature in other languages only partially included here: Ethiopian, Armenian, Slavic, Latin, the Romance languages, etc.

I will emphasize, above all, the gnomologic literature and its relation to the more or less novelized *Lives*, which is what is fundamentally seen in the four Castilian works that are my point of departure. But all of this had to be placed in a general frame, a matter already cleared up, to a certain extent, in the previous chapter.

I will present only the more relevant examples, making reference when necessary to other publications, including my own and will indicate the character and organization of the collections when this is of interest. I will study successively the oriental models, the archaic and classical Greek ages, and the Hellenistic, Roman and Byzantine ages.

Naturally, this chapter will be followed by others that go into the themes in detail, especially the ideological theme. Here we will simply deal in general terms with the principal lines of the ancient gnomologies (with their oriental precedents and their Byzantine continuation), to see to what extent they coincide with our works and to what extent there is a gap or a rift which must be explained in some way.

II. Sapiential literature in the ancient orient

With respect to ancient Mesopotamia and Egypt I will commence by referring to my compilation of titles and summaries in *Historia de la Fábula Greco-Latina*[2], where I give the pertinent bibliography.

On the one hand, we have "Instructions" (by Suruppak, a Sumerian); also, in Babylonia, "Advice of a pessimist", "Advice to a prince", etc.; in Egypt, "Instructions" of Ptahhotep, of Merikare, and of Amem-Opet, among others. Normally, it is a king who gives advice to a son, but the advice can also be given by a friend or a person of prestige. All of this is literature "with reference to the author", imaginary in any event. Alongside these are the "Proverbs", numerous Mesopotamian collections composed of maxims, counsels, similes, jests, fables, etc., all anonymous. In Mesopotamia there are also dialogues, such as the *Babylonian Theodicy*, a dialogue between the man who complains about the injustices of the world and the friend who instructs and consoles him.

All the above does not take into account individual proverbs, similes, debates and fables, in Mesopotamia as well as in Egypt, India and the Bible. For the influence of all this on Greece and India, see my work cited above. As simple examples of these isolated texts, I can refer to the fable of the eagle and the serpent in the Akkadian *Etana* and numerous other ones in the Indian *Jataka*. In various works of these literatures can be found, too,

2 Vol. I, Madrid 1979, pp. 310 ff. (English translation in Leiden, Brill, 1999, with amplification of the bibliography). A good part of the Mesopotamian collections can be found in W. G. Lambert, *Babylonian Wisdom Literature*, Oxford, Clarendon Press, 1960. For the *Ahikar* see the translation of R. H. Charles, *The Apocrypha and Pseudepigrapha of the Old Testament in English* II, Oxford, Clarendon Press, 1971, pp. 728 ff.

isolated maxims and similes, as is the case of the Babylonian "debates" ("the tamarind and the palm tree", "the ox and the horse", etc.).

But, above all, there is the Assyrian *Ahikar*, which exerted a strong influence on Greece, and in which come together the themes of the advice of the secretary Ahikar to the king (Sennaqerib or Asharadon) and then to his own son. And there is a novelesque element: Ahikar solves a riddle and achieves the triumph of his king over the king of Egypt; he is slandered, and sentenced to death but is later saved[3]. Ahikar is at times the person who instructs the kings of Assyria and Egypt and solves their enigmas and problems, at times the one who, as a father, gives advice to his perverse son Nadan.

The sapiential dialogues of the Judaic tradition must also be recalled: dialogues between Solomon and the queen of Sheba (in *Kings* 10, 1–17) or between Solomon and Hiram of Tyre (in Josephus, C. *Ap*. 117). And all the sapiential literature of the Bible, the books of *Job* (God enlightens the rebellious Job), *Proverbs* (supposedly by Solomon) and *Ecclesiastes* (supposedly by Qoheleth, the son of David). The first of these books is believed to be of the 5th century B.C., the other two Hellenistic. Naturally, their influence on ancient and medieval Judaism and on the whole Christian culture was great, as was that of other Biblical books that are simple collections of proverbs, such as *Ecclesiasticus* and *Wisdom*. This not to mention the more or less sapiential books and books of maxims that appear all through the Bible in the mouths of various personages. This literature sometimes takes the form of a monologue, sometimes of a dialogue, and at other times of maxims and proverbs. There are popular sayings, *gnômai*, satires, enigmas, similes, parables, and fables.

We can recall the Indian fable, organized in the *Tantrakhyayika* and the *Pañcatantra* using the procedure of "framing": it begins telling the story of how the Brahman *Visnusarman*, with the help of fables, is going to educate the king's sons. But the first fable is interrupted in order for another, narrated by one of the characters, to be embedded in it, and so on successively; the same happens with the other nuclear fables that form chapters with their own themes. The fables usually end with a maxim. My theory is that

3 For the influence of the *Life of Ahikar* on that of Aesop see my "The Life of Aesop and the origins of the novel in Antiquity", *QUCC* N.S., 1979, pp. 93–112. On the *Life* in general see my *Historia* I, pp. 619 ff. (the English version, Leiden, 1999, gives the new bibliography).

the Mesopotamian fable, and then the Greek one, had an influence on the Indian fable (and on its philosophy and maxims). The Indian fable, in turn, in the Middle Ages, had an influence on the Byzantine and the western fable, and even on the creation of collections.

The sole objective of this brief account, which can easily be amplified, is to demonstrate the presence in the ancient Orient of elements that, by way of a long tradition, reached our Greco-Arabic-Castilian texts. Especially:

a) the theme of the knowledge that God, a king or a sage imparts to some inferior by way of a series of maxims etc., all cloaked in a mantle of legend;
b) the theme of the inferior character, such as Ahikar or the Brahman *Visnusarman*, who imparts this learning to a king or the sons of a king;
c) the combination of proverbial maxims, protreptical maximums, similes, fables and anecdotes;
d) the presence also of dialogue: questions or objections and answers;
e) the presence in the literatures mentioned of anonymous collections of proverbs, fables, etc., which grew out of the material discussed above, while the opposite also occurred. There were, too, maxims, fables, and isolated anecdotes present as "examples" in other works, for example, in the truly mythical ones, which I do not deal with here.

All of this is repeated in the Greek ambience in which the works we are studying were engendered and grew. Indeed, in Greece the genres with personal reference, the simple collections of anonymous maxims and the "examples" proliferated. There is evolution depending on the epochs, which I will attempt to outline.

III. Sapiential literature in archaic and classical Greece

I have discussed this literature in various publications of mine[4] and there are comments on it in the previous chapter of this book; here I merely want

4 In my *Historia* cited above, see especially for the "Life of Aesop" vol. 1, pp. 661 ff. (and pp. 647 ff. of the English translation, with abundant new bibliography). Also the "Life of Aesop" cited, and "Elementos cínicos en las *Vidas* de Esopo y Secundo y en

to bring it to mind and augment this information for the above-mentioned purpose of establishing the parallelism with our Greco-Arabic-Castilian works[5].

Of course, a few preliminary observations must be made. In Greece we frequently find two situations: that of the oral tradition (for example, the themes of Aesop and of the Seven Wise Men are, in their beginnings, oral) or of individual literary citations, and that of the systematic gathering into collections, which can have personal reference or not. This latter is the case of the maxims, similes, fables and protreptical works in various poets, from Homer on, frequently in connection with a situation or an anecdote followed by the maxim. They can be attributed to personages from historical to fabulous: Demetrius of Phalerum collected the maxims of the Seven Wise Men around 300 B.C.

Inverting the order of exposition, I will begin by making reference to the presence of isolated maxims, similes, fables, etc. in literature; they later pass into collections and, conversely, literature in general takes "examples" from all of these. In Homer, before the genre of the collection with personal reference, which originated with Hesiod, we already find isolated sapiential texts. And later they coexist with the genre of the collection in different authors and even in a single author.

Indeed, there is no need to refer to the well-known Homeric "similes", in which the animals intervene in an action that explains and instructs and have characteristics that later will be found in the fable. But there are also *gnômai*, such as that of the Odyssey that says that rule by many is not a good thing, or "let there be only one chief" (*Il.* 2.204), or Hectors' when he said (*Il.* 22.243) that the best augury is to fight for your country, or the instruction of Achilles by Cheiron (*Il.* 6.208). And the *gnóme* remained alive and vigorous in all genres.

For example, in the lyric: in Archilochus it frequently appears joined to some situation, or vice versa. Quoting from my edition[6] we see that in fr. 3, which opens the consolatory elegy for Pericles, it says "Fortune and Des-

el *Diálogo de Alejandro y los Gimnosofistas*", in *Homenaje a Eleuterio Elorduy*, Bilbao, Universidad de Deusto, 1958, pp. 309–328.

5 A good study of the Greek gnomological tradition, with an extensive bibliography that adds a number of things to what is said here can be found in the book by R. Mª Mariño and F. García Romero, *Proverbios Griegos. Menandro: Sentencias*, Madrid, Gredos, 1999, pp. 343 ff.

6 *Líricos griegos. Elegiacos y yambógrafos arcaicos* II, 2ª ed., Madrid, CSIC, 1990.

tiny give all things to men, oh Pericles"; fr. 7, which closes it, concludes, "Come then, be quickly resigned, abandoning womanish sorrow." Fragment 13 begins another poem with the words, "Glaucus, a mercenary is a friend while he is fighting." An epode opens (37) with the maxim: "The fox knows many things but the hedgehog knows a single decisive one"; another, that of the charlatan, ends with (66): "Among the gods Zeus is the most truthful soothsayer and on him depends fulfillment." It would be easy to continue.

And the same is true of the other poets. Sappho 16, the poem to Anactoria, begins with the well-known verses: "Sometimes they say that the troops mounted in chariots, sometimes those on the ships are the most beautiful thing on this black earth; but I say that it is what a person loves." This theme of "What is the most...?", which reaches our later collections, was typical of the banquet and of the poetry engendered there: it can be found in Tyrtaeus 8, in Xenophanes 2, in Theognis 699 ff. and in Solon 44, Bergk. Satirical themes can be related to symposiac poetry, as in *PMG* 892 ("Thus said the crab catching the serpent with its claw: a friend must be straightforward and not have twisted thoughts"), and various others like *PMG* 897 ("Comrade, knowing the story of Admetus, be a friend of good persons and stay away from bad ones, aware of the scarce gratitude that there is in ignoble men"), or *PMG* 903 ("Comrade, under every stone there is a scorpion. Be careful that it does not sting you: deceit accompanies what is hidden").

As we can see, animalistic themes (also the theme of "What is [...] similar to?"), including fables, find their place in symposiac literature and its literary reflection. And the fable is included in a long range of genres that extends from Hesiod onward in writers of iambics, comic poets and especially Socratics. Demetrius of Phalerum, the compiler of the Greek collection of fables, did nothing other than collect this material; I have studied this carefully elsewhere[7]. There are also, as I have said, various maxims that passed over into poetry, sometimes with the "signature" of their authors, sometimes with mythical references. But also found in this literature are maxims with reference to the Seven Wise Men and to Aesop that were only later gathered together in collections; the written text appears not to have

7 In my *Historia...* I, pp. 381 ff. (= English ed. pp. 367 ff.). Also G.-J. van Dijk, *Ainoi, Logoi, Mythoi*, Leiden, Brill, 1997.

existed until the 4th century B.C. All this is something that undoubtedly is connected with the theme of the *Ahikar*, as I have explained elsewhere.

We find this same background in the theater too: suffice it to mention the *Agamemnon* by Aeschylus with its "(Zeus) made it law to learn with pain" (177 ff.), its "there is no bastion of defense for him who satiated with riches, treads down with his foot the great altar of Justice" (381 ff.) and others that initiate the device of using a chorus to teach.

And the same occurs in prose works. The pre-Socratics sharpened their own maxims; Heraclitus, for example, wrote a long series of them. And there are some quite trenchant ones in Herodotus, as the one in IX 16 that says "it is impossible for a man to avoid what has to happen, if it is sent by a god" or, the greatest of sorrows is "while knowing about many things, not to have power over any of them".

It is this vein that we find later in Socrates and all of his school and that, indeed, formed the starting point for the Hellenistic collections. Everyone is familiar with "I only know that I know nothing" and with "life without examination is not livable" (*Ap.* 33d, 38a)[8]. And everyone knows many maxims in Plato, from "the beautiful is difficult" (*Hp.Ma.* 304e, actually a proverb) to the one about it being better to suffer injustice than to cause it (*Grg.* 509c).

In short, the prestige of the maxim as an abbreviated and decisive form of moral instruction was immense. The epigraphic maxims of the temple of Apollo at Delphi (later attributed to the Seven Wise Men: "know thyself", "moderation is best", etc.), and in the temple at Delos (the epigram later reproduced by Theognis 255–256: "The most beautiful thing is justice, the most valued is health and the most pleasant is getting what one wants") bear witness to this.

The scheme of the anecdote followed by a lesson is found early on, after poetry, in Herodotus, with its frequent theme of teachings imparted to the king by the wise man (to Croesus by Solon, to Xerxes by Artabanus, among other examples), which we have already seen in the Orient,

This theme of the maxim or lesson on the part of the poet or a more or less fictitious personage, frequently in specific contexts, went on to enter collections with personal reference, and also without it, in the Hellenistic

8 On the thoughts of Socrates in relation to his language and his literary attitudes see "La lengua de Sócrates y su filosofía", *Methexis* 5, 1992, pp. 29–52 (later in *Palabras e Ideas*, Madrid, Ediciones Clásicas, 1994, pp. 251 ff.).

period, where there developed what I have called "anthological genres", usually without personal reference: collections of diverse maxims, of myths, epigrams, glosses, oracles, fables, etc.; and also novels that join a *Life* or anecdote to a collection of maxims. The actual editing of the works of earlier poets, a Pindar or a Sappho, by the Alexandrian philologists based on the organization of these editions either by themes or by meter, comes from this same literary tendency.

It must be emphasized, on the other hand, that the enormous development of the Hellenistic gnomologies at the hands of the representatives of the Socratic school (Socrates, Plato, Aristotle, Aristippus, Diogenes, etc.) has its origin in the Socratic literature introduced by Plato, Xenophon and especially Aeschines. He created the genre of the Σωκρατικοὶ λόγοι or "Socratic Dialogues", which joined personal anecdotes and lessons of wisdom. From Xenophon's *Memorabilia*, for example, numerous anecdotes that ended with a reply by Socrates passed into later gnomologies.

Socrates was a very special master (he only knew that he knew nothing) in comparison with the other "wise men" of the literature we are studying, but he was soon placed at its center. Indeed, his satyric physical characteristics and his confrontation with the official "wise men", a Gorgias or a Protagoras, and his triumph over them make him the precedent of the Aesop, or the Diogenes or the Secundus of Hellenistic and Roman sapiential literature.

Thus were born in the Hellenistic period, in relation to the theme that interests us, collections of maxims that gather not only those of the Hellenistic sages (Diogenes, Menander, etc.) but also those of earlier sages (Simonides, Epicharmus, Anacharsis, Socrates, Plato, etc.), faithfully or not. And not without the oriental influence that we have mentioned, which is added to the classical and archaic anecdotes, maxims, similes and "examples". I will return to them: they already contain the germ of the model for the Hellenistic works and already have a connection with oriental genres.

Now, in Greece we do not encounter only collections of maxims and all the rest (protreptical sayings, similes, riddles, fables, etc.) that follow an initial anecdotic or biographical introduction, the Hellenistic genre comparable to other oriental genres that we are referring to; from the very beginnings of Greek literature we find, besides the individual use of the "examples", similar collections, but now with an anecdotal or biographical beginning. That is to say, this genre, which gained renewed impulse in the Hellenistic period, without doubt through the influence of oriental models, had appeared much earlier in Greek literature, already by then in connection with those models.

The first representative, as is known, is Hesiod, whose *Works and Days* offers a biographical framework (the injustices of his brother Perses and of the "kings" or nobles who protect him) followed by a series of fables, maxims, protreptical sayings, etc. addressed sometimes to the brother sometimes to the kings. The relation to the oriental genres has been alluded to repeatedly[9]. And something must be said about the organization of the *corpus*: we can point out an organization based on the *Stichwörter* or key words, which lead from one group of verses to another and which, interweaving with each other, make the theme evolve; and also, on occasion, a clearly thematic organization: for example, on work in the fields or on navigation.

But this is not the only case. The next most notable is that of Theognis: although the text that has reached us is, without doubt, a Hellenistic collection that has aggregated various materials that go from poetry of the 7th century to that of the 5th century B.C., the foundation is a collection of maxims that Theognis himself addresses to his young friend Cyrnus: it includes wisdom maxims, protreptical sayings, similes, fables and autobiographical elements followed by a commentary. It is the same material as always. It is difficult to decide to what extent the organization comes from Theognis or from the authors of the Hellenistic compilation. Attention both to the *Stichwörter* and to the themes is involved: at times there is a development of a single theme (fathers and sons, poverty, lineage, etc.) and at times there are oppositions between poems or doctrinal variants between them. The few maxims of Phocylides show traces of the same organization.

These collections of maxims with personal reference were also cultivated in pre-Hellenistic times by writers of prose such as Hippocrates *(Aphorisms)*, Democritus and Isocrates (to the kings of Cyprus: *To Nicocles, Nicocles*; *To Demonicus*, of doubtful authenticity; *Evagoras*, in the form of an encomium). And from there, later, Epicurus with his Κυρίαι Δόξαι or

9 See the bibliography and study of the composition in my "Las fuentes de Hesíodo y la composición de sus poemas", *Emerita* 54, 1986, pp. 1–36, and "La composición de los poemas hesiódicos" in *Emerita* 69, 2001, pp. 197 ff. See also J. A. Fernández Delgado, "La poesía sapiencial en Grecia y los orígenes del hexámetro", *Emerita*, 50, 1982, pp. 151–174, and *Los oráculos de Hesíodo. Poesía oral mántica y gnómica griega*, Cáceres, Universidad de Extremadura, 1986.

"Capital Maxims" and the collectors of the maxims of others: those of the Pseudo-Platonic *Horoi*, Aristoxenus, Demetrius of Phalerum and the others.

But let us go back. Really, all the pre-Socratics have a very important gnomic component, either traditional or of new creation. It is just that the vicissitudes of their transmission make it difficult or impossible to reconstruct the organization of their writings. Therefore, when M. Marcovich[10], for example, organizes the fragments of Heraclitus in groups under *logos*, fire, ethics, politics and the rest, with internal subgroups, this is a modern construction; the fragments have been transmitted to us individually. At other times, as in the case of Hippias, we lack sufficient information.

But there are more favorable cases, especially those of Hippocrates, Democritus and Isocrates. Others are less so: the only thing that is certain is that Critias wrote *Apophthegmata*. Let us look at these cases one by one.

For Hippocrates, the fundamental work in this respect is the *Aphorisms*, which have later been so widely edited, discussed and studied. We do not know exactly if they are a compilation of his principal doctrines done in his old age, but in spite of the repetitions and incoherencies, there is a clear structuring by themes with the aid of *Stichwörter* or key words. Words like δίαιτα "regimen" act as guides. There are sixteen numbers in the first section; and it is important in the second section, where the theme of prognosis is added. Then follows, in the third section, the theme of the influence of the seasons and the ages of life on illness. In the fifth there are as many as five thematic groups, well differentiated, and likewise in the two that follow[11].

The case of Democritus is similar. The gnomology transmitted by Stobaeus, *Ecl.* II, and collected (with some additions) by Diels-Kranz in his *Vorsokratiker*, together with some maxims confirmed by other sources, is revealed by its phonetics, its lexicon and its doctrine to be essentially authentic. Nevertheless, we cannot exclude the fact that there might be some additions of Epicurean origin or from other sources, for example, 219, on the appetites that create needs, and others of a type either traditional or Socratic (but not Platonic or Cynic). So then, there is a general organization that begins with personal themes (εὐθυμίη, pleasure, good and evil, justice, wealth, folly, πόνος or work), to go on to politics and then to themes about the family (returning at times to the theme of wealth, as in 204). Within all

10 M. Marcovich, *Heraclitus*, Mérida, Venezuela, Los Andes University Press, 1967.
11 See J. A. López Férez, *Tratados Hipocráticos* I, Madrid, Gredos, 1983, pp. 215 ff.

this, the *Stichwörter* give the tone: series on εὐθυμίη, ἡδονή, ἀγαθόν, the ἀνοήμονες or fools, φειδώ or thrift. Sometimes one of these words, previously abandoned, reappears: the theme of ἡδονή, pleasure, turns up every so often. Then arise themes of the πόλις, or city, of ἄρχειν, or command, of δίκη, or justice. And in the last section appear the themes of the woman (γυνή), children (παῖδες), etc.

The procedures are always the same: a mixture of system and conversational freedom: this is seen in Isocrates, in the discourse in which advice is given (in the imperative as prohibition and in the subjunctive) to Nicocles, king of Cyprus *(To Nicocles)* or to Demonicus; or that other one in which Nicocles gives advice to the people on how to be governed *(Nicocles)*. Really, they are variants of the genre of the "mirror for princes" which we will discuss: there are coincidences, in the first place, with the ancient traditional maxims of Theognis and Phocylides, secondly, with the Socratic moralists, and finally, with the pro-monarchic tendencies of the period. There are the beginnings of organization, after a prologue in *To Demonicus* (relation with god, with society, with oneself), but all this is infinitely disjointed, it is difficult even to identify clear *Stichwörter*.

The coincidences with the maxims of Aristotle and Alexander in our works translated into Castilian are important. Evidently in this period a morality between traditional and Socratic is developing, but with realistic touches regarding government, which is the basis of the later gnomologies that added, as we have said, Cynic and Christian elements, among others[12].

In all cases the organization is similar, to the extent that it can be known; this is not the case with Hippias, whose *Troikós* "Trojan Discourse" (advice of Nestor to Neoptolemus) and *Advice of Cheiron* (to Achilles) have been lost. In the first authors there are, as we have seen, beginnings of thematic organization, based on *Stichwörter*; sometimes with a prologue and even an epilogue, as in Hesiod, Theognis and Phocylides. Note that there is a link with the encomiastic genre and the genre of the "mirror for princes", already mentioned. This is seen in Pindar (advice to Hiero of Syracuse or to Arcesilaus of Cyrene), in the *Agesilaus* of Xenophon and in the *Evagoras* of Isocrates, which we have just mentioned. We can add, too, the *Pythagorean*

12 On the origin and orientation of the Isocratic parenesis, see W. Jaeger, *Paideia*, Spanish translation, Mexico, 1945, III, pp. 109–135 ("The education of the prince").

Maxims compiled by Aristoxenus of Tarentum, of which there remains a collection in Stobaeus, derived from an alphabetical collection[13].

To summarize, we already have, in the classical period and up to the Hellenistic period, examples of collections of maxims and the other writings by a poet or a thinker or a mythical personage addressed to a younger person or to a king or to the general reader. As for the prototype of the person of a lower social class who nevertheless prevails by reason of his intelligence and confidence, like Ahikar and the protagonists of the novels of late Antiquity, we do not find any yet except at the level of oral legend (as in Aesop) and in certain prototypes like Thersites, and Odysseus himself in Homer, poets like Archilochus and Hipponax, Homer himself in the *Vita Herodotea*, Anacharsis or "the good savage" of the *Vida de Anacharsis*, etc.[14] But this genre of *Lives*, including Aesop's and those that were placed as an introduction to the works of various authors or were composed separately, is from the 4th century B.C. The works come above all from the Peripatetic school (Dicaearchus, Demetrius of Phalerum, Satyros, Aristoxenus, Hermippus, then Sotion and others).

Now then, with regard to the classic period we are talking about monographic collections, maxims of one author or another attributed to himself or to some personage of the past: there are no anonymous collections, as far as we know. The link with novelesque episodes is rare or is limited to oral literature. Satirical elements comparable to those that later occur in the initial part of the combinations *Life* + maxims find their parallel in the iambics and the theater, above all, sometimes giving rise to isolated "examples" of anecdote + maxim or fable.

These collections bear a certain relation to the collections of "Memoirs" *(Apomnemoneúmata)*, in which the Hellenistic and later gnomologies drank deeply: there are those of Ion of Chios, now lost, and of Xenophon. They also bear a relation to the genre of the symposium or banquet, which is the foundation of much archaic poetry and was especially cultivated by Plato and the Socratics, and in later times as well. This genre was very important

13 See M. Timpanaro, *Pitagorici. Testimonianze e frammenti*, Florence, La Nuova Italia, 1964, III, pp. 272 ff.

14 See my "Hechos generales y hechos griegos en el origen de la crítica y la sátira", *Homenaje a Julio Caro Baroja,* Madrid, Centro de Investigaciones Sociológicas, 1978, pp. 43–63. See also the precedents of the Aesop of the *Life* in the classical period in J. T. Papadimitriou, *Aesop as an archetypal Hero*, Athens, 1997. On the Hellenistic *Lives* of the Seven Wise Men and Anacharsis, see my "Géneros helenísticos...", cited.

in the Hellenistic period, for example, in the origin of the writings about the Seven Wise Men[15].

IV. Sapiential literature in the Hellenistic age

1. General panorama

Naturally, we cannot do a complete study of the sapiential genres in the Hellenistic period here either. There is, of course, a factor of continuity in the form and the themes of sapiential literature. There continue to be "isolated texts": maxims, fables, etc., included as examples in different authors; the above-mentioned bibliography can be consulted for this.

And there continue to be authors who, like Epicurus, compose their own collections of maxims (the so-called *Capital Maxims*): their organization, based on *Stichwörter*, which are followed and interwoven to produce a series of themes (ἡδονή, φύσις, ἐπιθυμία, τὸ ἀλγοῦν, ἀσφάλεια, αἴσθησις, that is, pleasure, nature, desire, sorrow, safety, sensation), is practically the same as what we have already seen. His *Letter to Menoeceus* with its exhortative maxims can be added here.

This is the same procedure as we find in ancient "enlarged" collections, like that of Theognis, which we have mentioned. We must also recall the collection that was constructed from the initial nucleus of the *Palatine Anthology*: the "Garland of Meleager", an anthology of older poets and other more modern ones plus Meleager himself, to which was added the "Garland" of Philip of Thessalonica and later other collections[16]. The organization is thematic.

One problem is that frequently we cannot establish the date of these "enlargements". For example, the "Exhortations of Epicurus" edited by G. Arrighetti[17] contains some of his "Capital Maxims", plus others of Metrodorus, plus many without doubt from the lost Epicurus, plus others that

15 See my "Géneros helenísticos...", pp. 135 ff.

16 See the "Einführung" of H. Beckby to his edition of the *Anthologia Palatina*, Munich, *Tusculum Bücher*, 1957.

17 G. Arrighetti, *Epicuro. Opere*, Torino, Einaudi, 1975, pp. 141 ff.

are doubtful, some possibly Socratic. Who created the collection and when? It must have been one among various existing ones; in Seneca we find traces of gnomologies by Epicurus.

In any case, this points to a new situation: now there appear collections that are not assembled by the authors but rather by Hellenistic editors. To those mentioned must be added the collections of the above-mentioned ancient authors, with or without an authentic nucleus (Simonides, Epicharmus, etc.), and among them, naturally, those that we are going to study here, and the gnomologies in general. This is the great epoch of this genre, and the following one will be even more so. This is something really new.

And it is not the only thing that is new. We must also take into account the *Banquets* and the collections of pseudo-epigraphic *Letters*, already mentioned in the previous chapter, and the *Lives*, including the novelized ones, to which we have alluded. Among these last works we have mentioned those of Homer and Anacharsis, of Aesop (if our hypothesis that its written text comes from this period is true) and of Alexander, specifically the old strata of the Pseudo-Callisthenes and the *Life* of the Seven Wise Men, for which I refer the reader to my study on the work of Plutarch. To all this can be added debates such as the debate of Alexander and the Indian sages. And collections of fables, beginning with that of Demetrius of Phalerum: we know these only through their reconstruction based on later ones, as I have done in volume II of my *Historia de la fábula greco-latina*. All this does not keep fables, maxims and the rest from making isolated appearances, as examples, in various literary texts[18].

The most important thing for us, I repeat, is the appearance for the first time of anonymous collections of maxims and the rest; and of others whose reference is more or less exact or imaginary. This is the starting point for collections of the maxims of Socrates, Plato, Aristotle and Alexander in *Buenos Proverbios* and (with reference to the last two characters) in *Poridad*. And we know that *Bocados* contains a long series of gnomologies by different authors, of both classic and late Antiquity, Christian and pagan, including some that are difficult to identify, but all of them with the *terminus ante quem* of the 8th century A.D. In relation to Aristotle and Alexander we

18 See my *Historia...* II, pp. 339 ff. and van Dijk's book cited above. Also other publications of mine such as "Más fragmentos nuevos de poesía griega antigua", *Studi in onore di Adelmo Barigazzi*, *Sileno*, 10, 1984, pp. 1–10.

have found the combination *Life* (or anecdote) + maxims; at other times the first element is more reduced or nonexistent. In short, the works that we are studying amount to a series of gnomologies, without doubt with Hellenistic roots, that are sometimes different or partially different in the way they deal with the same author. They give the maxims author by author in approximately chronological order *(Bocados)* or they interpolate them arbitrarily *(Buenos Proverbios)*, or a single gnomology is composed *(Poridad, Donzella Teodor)*.

All this presupposes the existence of independent gnomologies (or combinations of *Life* + gnomology), author by author. And we have seen that we are dealing with literary pieces that contain very different strata, extending from the classic, through Hellenistic and Roman, to Byzantine (and perhaps to Syriac and Arabic and even to Castilian). What interests us here, since we are discussing the Hellenistic age, is to establish that the first gnomologies are Hellenistic.

This is the same period, I repeat, in which the *Lives,* including the novelized type, began to be written, and in which there began to be collected systematically, diverse maxims, old or newly created, in the context or without the context of these *Lives.* The oldest reference to Diogenes is by Metrocles, back in the 4th century. We will give more attention to these *Lives* before returning to the gnomologies.

The best-known work of this type is the *Life of Aesop*, which I have mentioned repeatedly. In my book I proposed the theory that it comes from the Hellenistic period: earlier, there is the legend of Aesop, influenced by the theme of the *pharmakos*, the abominable individual who is charged with all the sins of the collectivity. And later there is a written biography, placed by Demetrius of Phalerum at the beginning of his collection of fables (the Byzantine collections continued this procedure), just as occurred in the editions of Euripides and in others.

I have already pointed out that this is a fusion of ancient Greek elements influenced by the Orient and of new influences from the *Ahikar*, and, as I have explained in detail, of the Cynics.

In the *Life of Aesop* the biographical (or novelized) element predominates. Aesop is the prototype of the man from the lower classes, ugly and unconcerned with aristocratic values, wealth and power, who travels and satirizes a king like Croesus, is made a slave and satirizes his master Xanthos, his friends the philosophers and his wife too. He dies at Delphi, unjustly accused, but not without leaving evidence of his wisdom there as well. He solves enigmas, gives lessons in conduct, and tells jokes, all this through maxims, protreptical sayings, similes and fables. The biographical passages are followed by doctrinal passages.

In the previous chapter I alluded to the original Hellenistic elements in the *Life of Alexander*, included later in the work of the Pseudo-Callisthenes; the oldest episodes therein must go back to that time, as does the combination of the historic-novelistic element with letters and maxims, and above all, the *Dialogue of Alexander and the Gymnosophists*, which we have already discussed.

Here different Cynic concepts of Alexander come into conflict: now he is the king, the conqueror, who is beneath the ascetics, despisers of the world; now he has the attributes of generosity and wisdom. Then we have once again the dialogue of the powerful king and the sages who confront him in a wisdom debate. And we have, in one of the versions, the questions that the king asks the sages and their replies. And the theme of the journey, which connects the various episodes. This is a theme that was exported to India, where we have the Pali *Milindapanha*, the dialogue between the king Milinda (Menander) and the sage Nagasena.

These are Hellenistic genres that found an echo in the novelized *Lives*, together with maxims and the rest, of the following age. They can be compared with the genre to which belong the *Lives* and maxims of the Seven Wise Men compiled by Demetrius of Phalerum, and in which can be found the influence of symposiac elements (related of old to maxims, similes, anecdotes, etc.), various *khreîai*, etc.[19] And, of course, we must also mention the Cynic diatribe from the time of Bion and Menippus, best known particularly through its reminiscences in Lucian and Epictetus. All these genres are dominated by Cynicism, which does not exclude making use of the earlier wisdom of the Stoics and of simple moralism, together with the realism characteristic of the critical and popular origins of the genre.

Here must be added the anecdotes on the confrontation between the Cynics and the kings and other powerful figures overwhelmed by the moral maxims of the former: Diogenes before Philip, Antipater, Perdiccas, Alexander, the master to whom he is sold; Bion before Antigonus Gonatas; anecdotes similar to those referring to Aesop that we have mentioned and

19 See once again my "Géneros helenísticos en el Banquete de los Siete Sabios de Plutarco", in *Estudios sobre Plutarco: Aspectos Formales*, Salamanca, Ediciones Clásicas - Universidad, 1996, pp. 125–142.

to others of a later period. Independently of this current or not, the combination *Life* (sometimes just a few anecdotes) + maxims, which dominates the work of Diogenes Laertius and whose *disiecta membra* frequently reappear in the later gnomologies, and sometimes in earlier works, must be seen as dating from the Hellenistic epoch. Because these are, after all, materials coming at the latest from the Hellenistic period and sometimes before that.

Chapter I of Book I on Thales can serve as the model. It begins with biographical data which, according to what is said therein, come from Herodotus, Duris and Democritus. There follows a list of his books and doctrines, citing the authors that they include, especially Aristotle and various members of the Peripatetic school. There is a notable mention of biographers of the 3rd century B.C., such as Hermippus (biographer of philosophers), Lobon (of poets) and Apollodorus of Athens (2nd century B.C., author of a *Chronicle*). Next there is a list of maxims and ingenious replies to various questions: "Who was born first, the day or the night?, Who is happy?", etc. Finally, there are letters to Pherecydes and Solon. At other times (as in the case of Aristippus, Antisthenes, Diogenes, etc.) the material on maxims is extensive and the biographical material is minimal.

This confused material is often apocryphal, like the letters, and Diogenes Laertius himself says that others attribute some of his maximums to Socrates. And then there is the influence of the legendary tradition of the Seven Wise Men, on whom there was Hellenistic bibliography whose discrepancies Diogenes himself discusses.

The fact is that in the Hellenistic period there existed biographies of philosophers and poets in which were mixed real and imaginary details plus lists of doctrines, maxims, and δόξαι "opinions" about which the same can be said. They did not reach us: we have only echoes of them in authors like Diogenes Laertius, Eunapius, the Suda, etc., and also in anonymous *Lives* of Plato, Aristotle and others. But from the 4th to the 2nd centuries, apart from the more incredible *Lives* like those of Aesop and Homer, there was an important flowering of Bíoi or *Lives* of philosophers and poets (leaving aside the politicians for the moment). The principal names are Aristoxenus, Dicearchus, Neanthes of Cyzicus, Hermippus, Satyros (an important fragment of his *Life of Euripides* is extant), Antigonus of Carystus, Ariston of Ceos and Sotion, plus the epitomist Heraclides Lembus.

And alongside these were the collections of *khreîai,* anecdotes that ended with an ingenious saying, cultivated especially by the Cynics but that were frequently attributed to other authors. The oldest authors of Diogenes' collections of *khreîai* mentioned by Diogenes Laertius are Metrocles, from the 4th century and Hecaton from the 2nd; for the Seven Wise Men the collection of Demetrius of Phalerum must be cited and for the Pythagoreans, that of Aristoxenus. There are citations of lost collections of Crates and Ariston of Chios[20]. And there is the epigraphic collection of Cyzicus[21], transmitted by Sosiades[22], among other sources.

The biographies collected in the Βίοι or *Lives* sometimes became independent: for example, those of Socrates, Aristoxenus, Satyrus, Hermippus, Sotion and Heraclides Lembus[23]. The maxims and apothegms passed from the *Lives* to the collections and vice versa[24].

Now, the papyri offer us important remains of this flowering, which is at the root of these biographies followed by maxims (and of the maxims with no biography) in our collections, both the collections of the translations from Greek and from Greek into Arabic and Castilian and the collections known only from Greek or Arabic sources.

Italo Gallo's *Frammenti biografici da papiri*[25] includes the following works:

1. *Life of Philonides the Epicurean* (*PHerc.* 1044), attributed by some to Philodemus.
2. *Life and Apothegms of Socrates* (*PHib.* 182), which is believed to be from the end of the 4th century. It mixes biographical elements and other anecdotes, *khreîai* especially, which the editor Turner and then Gallo[26]

20 See P. Klauser and E. de Labriolle, *Apophthegma*, in *Reallexicon für Antike und Christentum*, I, 1950, cols. 545–550.

21 W. Dittenberger, *Syllogie Inscriptionum Graecarum*, 3rd ed., Leipzig 1915–24, no. 1268 (300 B.C.) = *IKyzikos*, ed. E. Schwertheim, *IGSK* 18, 1980, no. 2. This is an inscription that was somewhere in the temple of Apollo at Delphi (apart from the known maxims "know thyself" etc. that were on the columns at the entrance) and that has reached us through the inscription of Cyzicus (for teaching purposes apparently), the Miletopolis collection and by other means.

22 See RE Suppl. VII 1120, s.u. Sosiades. Transmitted to us by Stobaeus.

23 For the biographers of Socrates, see *Corpus dei Papiri Filosofici Greci e Latini (CPF)*, I 1***, Florence, Leo S. Oschki, 1999, p. 740.

24 See F. Leo, *Die griechisch-römische Biographie nach ihrer literarischen Form*, Leipzig, Teubner, 1901 (Hildesheim, Olms, 1965), p. 50 and Italo Gallo in the book cited immediately thereafter, p. 13.

25 Rome, Edizioni dell'Ateneo, 1980. Add also the *Corpus dei Papiri Filosofici Greci e Latini*, of which various volumes have been published. Those of *Autori Noti* form Part I; 1*** is from Florence 1992.

26 Op. cit., p. 183.

consider much Cynicized. He compares papyri with maxims of Diogenes and Simonides (more examples will be given later). The fact is that here we find the anecdote of Xantippe and the guests of Socrates (later in Diogenes Laertius 2.34, Maximus Confessor, etc.), and others on the theme of whether the philosopher should accept money or not (from Xenophon, Mem. 1.6.3) and the theme of control of one's desires (ἐπιθυμίαι) by habit and not by reason (with no exact correspondence anywhere).

Maxims of Socrates in other papyri are added, mixed with those of other philosophers: in *PBerol.* inv. 12311 from the 3rd century B.C. (the theme of "eat in order to live", known from many ancient texts); and *PFlor.* 113.2.19–38, from the 2nd century B.C. (a new anecdote: what Socrates teaches Alcibiades by day, others ruin by night)[27].

3. Various collections of *khreîai* by Diogenes (for whom Diogenes Laertius mentions numerous sources of the Hellenistic age). But those that have been preserved for us are post-Hellenistic, with one exception: that of the *PVindob.* inv. G. 29946, from around the middle of the 3rd century B.C., which contains no fewer than eleven *khreîai* or anecdotes, with dialogue in between[28].

Now before going on, something must be said about the concept of *gnóme*, *apóphthegma*, *khreîa* and the rest[29]. *Gnóme* is the term that refers to a simple maxim, of general scope, anonymous or having an author or included in various works (*Lives*, *Apomnemoneúmata*, etc.). But at the same time it has a general meaning: when we speak of gnomologies, we are referring to collections that include maxims in the strict sense, *apophthégmata* and *khreîai*.

Of these two sub-genres, which proliferated in the Hellenistic period and later, and with earlier antecedents, the former refers to maxims attrib-

27 These Socratic papyri are also collected and discussed in the *Corpus dei Papiri Filosofici Greci e Latini* cited above. They are indicated as T (testimonies), accompanied by others that are allusions to well-known Socratic themes (οἰκείωσις, mayeutics, δαιμόνιον, erotism) and they appear in commentaries on diverse books and in glosses. There is nothing to be gained from this work for the Socratic maxims and *khreîai*.

28 A more recent edition, with a good commentary, is that of the *Corpus dei Papiri Fiolosofici Greci e Latini (CPF)*, vol. I 1****, Florence, Leo S. Olschki, 1992, pp. 99 ff.

29 On this topic see K.-H. Stanzel, *Dicta Platonica. Die unter Platons Namen überlieferten Aussprüche*, Darmstadt, 1987, pp. 2 ff. as well as the bibliography given there. Also R. F. Hock and E. N. O'Neil, *The chreia in ancient Rhetoric*, I, *The Progymnasmata*, Atlanta, Scholars Press, 1985.

uted to someone: "So and so said...", generally without any context and with advice that has a certain incisive point. It does not differ greatly from the aphorism, which usually appears in series. But there are transitions with the *khreîa*, which includes a brief action in which someone (having been asked, having seen, having heard, in a certain situation) proffers a generally ingenious and sharp asseveration. There is frequently a reply to questions of the type "What is...? " or "What is the most...?". Sometimes a dialogue follows; sometimes there is a transition to the genre of the anecdote. It frequently happens that in the Hellenistic period and the following one ancient texts are reduced to these genres, which proliferated enormously.

Actually, the *khreîa* is a variant of the *apóphthegma*, which in turn is a variant of the *gnóme* in the broad sense of the word. But, as I say, there are transitions, and we speak of "maxims" and of gnomologies in a generic sense.

2. *More about the Gnomologies*

The essential thing, I repeat, is the new panorama represented, alongside the gnomologies written by the authors themselves, by others in which a writer compiles the maxims of some other author or of various authors, and even of anonymous collections.

In effect, there are numerous similar collections of various philosophers and poets, but almost all of them come from post-Hellenistic papyri, which we will discuss below. Nevertheless, there are some Hellenistic papyri apart from those mentioned. This material is continued later by material of the imperial period and finds an echo in works like that of Diogenes Laertius, or the Byzantine gnomologies, with the addition of Christian material, or in the works of the Arabs, which at times offer the same material, at other times new material which probably comes from the Greek models but sometimes, too, is reworked by them. This tradition is a topic that we will be studying in the following chapters, author by author, but we will say something more about it in this general presentation, specifically with regard to the Roman period.

In order to establish an indisputable starting point, I present here the gnomologies that appear in the papyri of the Hellenistic age; this will assist us in the difficult task of separating the gnomologies (in papyri or in manuscripts) of an age later than what is strictly Hellenistic. I will not consider the material relating to Socrates and Diogenes mentioned above. This is material that I will complete with what has reached us by way of manuscripts and in many cases is continued in papyri and works of later periods. I leave untouched various moral discourses (such as the one contained in *PBrol.* inv.12318, edited by E. Kühn, *Ber.Berl.Mus.* 42, 1920–21, pp. 102–104) and *excerpta* (such as *PHib.* 224) which can contain maxims.

- *PHib.* 7 (III B.C.): after a fragment of the *Electra* by Euripides and a text that seems to be lyric there are remains of four iambic trimeters, one of them a known maxim, perhaps by Euripides, perhaps by Menander[30]. In both cases we have a foretaste of the collections of monostichs by Menander (and others) and by Euripides in a later age.
- *PHeid.* inv.434 (III B.C.), edited by G. A. Gerhard in the *Sitzungsberichte der Heidelberger Akademie der Wissenschaften* 1912(13), and later by D. Young[31]: Maxims by Chares, an author from the end of the 4th century, in iambic trimeters, which are added to others transmitted by Stobaeus. A very interesting collection: various maxims coincide with the monostichs attributed to Menander; it is thought that this is secondary, that they are simply his source. The organization is by themes: honor due to the elderly and to the gods, the themes of friends, of avoiding wrong actions, of holding one's tongue, that it is better to suffer injustice than to cause it (?), falsehood and truth, behavior toward someone in adversity.
- *PHib.* 1 (III B.C.): maxims by Epicharmus. There are doubts about the authorship; they are usually edited (as in Diels-Kranz I, pp. 200 ff.) as pseudo-epigrams[32]. There must be an original nucleus to which have doubtless been added other elements, all in Doric, in catalectic trochaic tetrameters, with no trace of Hellenistic philosophies.
- *Hib.* 17 (III B.C.): Maxims by Simonides. They are mere *khreîai* that allude to his thrifty and miserly character.
- A. N. Oikonomides in *ZPE* 37, 1980, pp. 179–183 (III B.C.), with a good commentary: Delphic maxims. This deals with an inscription from the 3rd century B.C., from Miletopolis near Cyzicus, which coincides with "the maxims of Sosiades of the Seven Wise Men" in Stobaeus III

30 Φθείρουσιν ἔθη χρήσθ' ὁμιλίαι κακαί "bad company destroys good customs", cited in 1. *Ep. Cor.* 15.33: of Menander according to Jerome, of Euripides according to Socrates in his *Historia Ecclesiastica.*

31 In his edition of Theognis, Leipzig, Teubner, 1961, pp. 113 ff.

32 See the commentary of the editors, who allude to a certain Axiopistus, who according to Philochorus, collected them; Aristoxenus fr. 45. Wehrli cast doubt on its authenticity.

125–128. Furthermore, there is coincidence with a stele from Aí Khanum in Afghanistan and a papyrus of the University of Athens (no. 2782). These are, to be sure, copies of an inscription at Delphi, differing from the tradition we know from a later date, but which probably comes from the Hellenistic tradition and which attributes to each Sage a series of maxims. Here we find eight maxims preserved, each one of two terms forming an imperative ("follow god, obey the good man, save time", etc.), attributed collectively to the Sages.
- *POxy.* 4099: mythological lists followed by maxims similar to the previous ones, but not identical ("be benevolent with your friends [...] ask for what is possible...").

This is the material on papyrus that has reached us; we will add more from the manuscript tradition. But first some generalities must be explained.

We find ourselves before material that involves innovations with respect to the classical epoch, although because of the hazards of transmission the material is scant. It participates in the continuity of the previous procedures: collections of maxims written by the author himself, as I have said. This is the basis of later gnomologies: it is clear that the collections of monostichs attributed to Menander and that had such wide diffusion began to be formed in the Hellenistic epoch, just as the *Lives* are the basis of later *Lives*. And we must include collections of fragments or *excerpta* by poets, almost always with a moral theme, which often contain the same themes as the gnomologies and even coincide with them. The gnomologies are for didactic use; they have been attested to since Plato, *Lg* 811a[33]. As their purpose is to educate pupils, only the *Lives* and the collections of *khreîai* are meant to disseminate the doctrines of the philosophical schools.

With the confluence of the Greek classical tradition and the oriental influence, the bases are established for all later sapiential literature. To be sure, the collections of gnomologies dedicated to various authors are preserved very imperfectly, as I have said, apart from the fact that only the foundation is of the Hellenistic age. This base has been studied, for example, in various works on the origin of the *Lives* by Diogenes Laertius[34]; I

33 See H. Chadwick, *Florilegium*, in *Reallexikon für Antike und Christentum* 7, 1969, cols. 1131–1160.

34 Especially K. von Fritz, *Quellenuntersuchungen zu Leben und Philosophie des Diogenes von Sinope*, *Philologus* Suppl. Bd. 18.2, Leipzig, Dietrich, 1926; also A. Packmohr, *De Diogenes Sinopensis apophthegmatis quaestiones selectae*, Münster, 1913.

refer the reader once more to my above-mentioned study on the sources of Plutarch's *Banquet of the Seven Wise Men.*

What the modern writers of treatises do is gather all the anecdotes and maxims attributed to each philosopher, as has been done for the Socratics, even for Plato, and somewhat less for Socrates[35]. But without doubt they mix material from different gnomologies. And this surely had already happened in the Roman period. Now for the Hellenistic gnomologies the same thing occurs as for the fables of the same epoch: they have been lost, with rare exceptions, like the papyri mentioned above. What can be done is try to reconstruct what has passed from them into the gnomologies of the following period.

For the Hellenistic age represents a clear advance in sapiential literature: it is there that the roots of the later sapiential literature, including our treatises, are found. But it offers little material. From the imperial age we have more material, almost all with the same orientation.

I would say that for the Hellenistic age one must posit two classes of gnomologies (joined or not to a *Life*): the pre-Cynic and the Cynicizing. I will discuss this, adding to the material of the papyri mentioned other material that has reached us via the manuscript tradition that comes from Antiquity.

Because the Cynics invaded various genres, for example, the *Lives*, the parody, the fable, for their own propaganda. I have studied this extensively in my *Historia de la Fábula Greco-Latina*[36]. Note that the fable uses *gnômai* that are iambic trimeters or choliambics, perfectly comparable to the *gnômai* of

35 See G. Giannantoni, *I presocratici. Testimonianze e frammenti*, Bari, Laterza, 1969; id., *Socrate. Tutte le testimonianze*, Bari, Laterza, 1971; K. H. Stanzel, *Dicta Platonica. Die unter Platons Namen überlieferten Aussprüche*, Wurzburg, 1987.

36 See vol. I, 619 ff. = English edition pp. 604 ff. (among other places in the book). Also other works such as the above-mentioned "Elementos cínicos en las Vidas de Esopo y Secundo y en el *Diálogo de Alejandro y los Gimnosofistas*" in *Homenaje a Eleuterio Elorduy*, Bilbao, Universidad de Deusto, 1978, pp. 309–328, *Filosofía cínica en las fábulas esópicas*, Buenos Aires, Centro de Estudios Filosóficos, 1986, and "Política cínica en las fábulas esópicas", in *Filologia e forme letterarie. Studi offerti a Francesco della Corte,* Urbino, Università degli Studi di Urbino, 1987, I, pp. 413–426. It is strange that neither the scholars of the fable nor those of Cynicism have noticed something so evident. For poetry, including cynicizing poetry and philosophical poetry in general, there is a good overview, with abundant bibliography, in M. Fernández Galiano, "Poesía helenística menor", in J. A. López Férez, *Historia de la Literatura Griega*, Madrid, Cátedra, 1988, pp. 831–877.

various authors or anonymous ones. Thus, the final sentence of the fox in "The fox and the crow" (H.126) is: ἔχεις, κόραξ, ἅπαντα, νοῦς δέ σοι λείπει "You have everything, crow, but you lack imagination"; or the epimythium of "The farmer and the serpent" (H.62): δίκαια πάσχω τὸν πονηρὸν οἰκτείρας "I am suffering justly for pitying someone bad".

Of course, anecdotes and *khreîae* and gnomologies were used in Hellenistic times. We have seen that the *Life* of Socrates followed by maxims has a Cynic component, and the citations of Socrates in the post-Hellenistic gnomologies, with their recurring theme of Xantippe and the satire of women and various other themes, contain a strong Cynic element. The vacillation in attributing many of the maxims to Socrates or Diogenes should not seem strange[37].

But naturally, Diogenes is the one to whom the greatest number of gnomologies is dedicated, right from the 4th century, as we have seen; this is confirmed by the papyri. Without doubt they drank directly from his work and from the legend about his life, which he very probably fostered himself, and they added various Cynic elements. We cannot say exactly how many of the Diogenes *khreîai* of the Roman and Byzantine epochs come from the Hellenistic epoch, but a great number of them definitely do. And then there are the ones attributed to Bion, some of them his own, some compiled by his followers[38]. It was the Cynics who began to create these anthologies, even of authors who were not Cynics, like Socrates and Domocritus, whom they Cynicized. Nevertheless, we cannot be sure that all the *gnômai* by philosophers from this epoch cited by later ones come from Hellenistic gnomologies.

In any event, the Cynic influence in the attribution of *gnômai* in later gnomologies is enormous: we have seen this in *Buenos Proverbios* for Alexander and Aristotle; we will see it for Socrates, Plato and a long list of authors in the other works translated into Castilian. In the Byzantine gnomologies this can already be seen, as well as in those preserved only in Arabic like *PQ*: the works translated into Arabic and then into Castilian were in this line, which, I repeat, is not new, as it originates back in the Hellenistic age. Then in the Roman period more Cynic material was added: maxims of Epictetus and others, elements integrated in the Pythagorean maxims of

37 See A. Packmohr, op. cit.

38 See J. F. Kindstrand, *Bion of Borysthenes. A collection of the fragments with introduction and commentary*, Upsala, Almqvist, 1976.

Demophilus and the others. To be sure, at times the transition from the Socratic view to the Cynic and from here to the Christian one was easy.

Now, I wish to emphasize one point: in the Hellenistic epoch there were also created gnomologies that were not Cynic, that simply followed the line of the earlier ones, although at times they introduced the above-mentioned innovation of not giving an author's name. For example, the maxims of Demetrius of Phalerum[39], which we have in Diogenes Laertius, and the *Gnomologium Vaticanum* do not have a Cynic aspect, nor do the maxims of Anacharsis[40]. An exception, such as language as the best and the worst (in Diogenes Laertius I 105), can be one of the many confusions about various authors. And the theme of the barbarian by birth but not by conduct is common to all the Hellenistic philosophies and comes from a well-known passage from Isocrates.

This is not present in the above-mentioned maxims of the Seven Wise Men, and hardly even in the various collections of maxims that we encounter in Diels-Kranz and in Mullach, whose origin is in this period. Without doubt the oldest collection was that of Demetrius of Phalerum, as Diogenes Laertius says. To each sage is attributed a series of short phrases that end in an imperative or a prohibition + subjunctive. The truth is that the existence of many collections, some coinciding, others not, brings to mind various Hellenistic gnomologies. It is quite clear that they mix maxims of Delphi with others of an origin between traditional and Socratic: the cult of the city and the family, the themes of friends, of honoring the gods, of moderation, of restraining desire, of not trusting in ill-gained wealth or in fortune, of keeping silent.

I would like to point out here that in medieval Latin literature and in Castilian works derived from it there are various collections of "sayings" of the Seven Wise Men of Greece, the best known (but related to other older ones) being that of Hernán López de Yanguas (*Silva de varia lección*, before 1563), translated, according to the author, from Latin into Castilian; there is a later transcription in *Aljamía*[41]. It includes sayings of Bias, Periander, Pythacus, Cleobulus, Chilon, Solon and Thales.

39 In F. Wehrli, *Demetrios von Phaleron*, *Die Schule von Aristoteles* 4, Basel, Schwabe, 1968.

40 See J. K. Kindstrand, *Anacharsis. The legend and the apophthegmata*, Upsala, Almqvist & Wiksell, 1981.

41 See the edition of both by A. Galmés de Fuente, *Dichos de los Siete Sabios de Grecia*, Madrid, Gredos, 1991, whose prologue gives good information on this literature in Castile, but with regard to origins still speaks of Arabic and oriental sources. They are

It is perfectly clear that this Latin-Castilian tradition, which goes beyond the theme of this book, comes from the ancient Greek tradition beginning with Demetrius of Phalerum, since there are no indications of Arabic intermediaries. It is known through epigraphic texts, through Plutarch and through the collections of Diels-Kranz and Müller. It is included within the late tradition that we have been studying: the collections usually commence with references to God, then to parents. And apart from the old themes of moderation, knowing oneself, not being hasty, time as the wisest etc., it contains others, well known to us, on friends, keeping silent, the lack of desires as the greatest wealth, distrust in the woman, disregard of lineage, and loyalty to the king. All of this takes us back to the late Roman epoch, by then Christian.

The Hellenistic gnomologies also have other ancient features: in τὸ ἥμισυ παντὸς πλεῖον "Half is better than all" there are echoes of Hesiod (*Op*. 40), in τῷ δυστυχοῦντι μὴ ἐπιγέλα "Do not mock someone in adversity" reminds us of Archilochus (*Fr*. 209), in οἱ πλεῖστοι ἄνθρωποι κακοί "Most men are bad", Heraclitus (*Fr* 1), in δυστυχῶν κρύπτε "When you are wretched, do not show it", Theognis (259). And the form "What is the most pleasing (ἥδιστον) and this kind of *khreîai* are traditional. Very rarely does one encounter a Cynic touch, which in any case would be late Cynic. Nor is any found in the *gnômai* attributed to Simonides, or in those of Chares, or in those of the Pseudo-Epicharmus, or in those of Demetrius of Phalerum.

And, naturally, gnomologies of authors of different tendencies were compiled (if they were not works by the authors themselves). Thus, there is a long series of maxims by Zeno the Stoic in Diogenes Laertius[42]; he himself, according to Diogenes Lartius VII 4, had composed one on Crates. The collections of Ariston de Chios and the first Academy are mentioned. There is one by Cleanthes in the *Stoicorum Veterum Fragmenta*[43]; and Chry-

Greek and there is no mention whatsoever of Arabic intermediaries. The "mediate Arabic origin" that Galmés speaks of (p. 29) is not proved because some of the maxims are found in *Bocados de Oro* too; they are ramifications that descend from common Greek originals.

42 See the collection in H. von Arnim, *Stoicorum Veterum Fragmenta*, Leipzig, Teubner, 1964, I, pp. 56 ff..

43 Von Arnim edition, I, pp. 134 ff.

sippus systematically collected poetic *gnômai*[44]. And to change the topic, one would have to add the anthologies of epigrams; I have spoken above of Meleager's "Garland" in the 2nd–1st centuries B.C. Here I can add the anthologies of Posidippus, organized by themes, that were recently discovered in a papyrus.

In summary, for the Hellenistic epoch we must accept, in spite of the scarcity of papyrian documents, a widespread flowering of the gnomologies: some done by the authors themselves, like those of Epicurus or Demetrius of Phalerum; others edited by philosophers or anthologists who collected material from the previous age, although with little regard for fidelity (as is the case of the Seven Wise Men, Socrates, Epicharmus or Anacharsis). But at other times they directed their attention to contemporaneous material: the *khreîai* of Diogenes or the Cynic ones attributed to him, the maxims of Chares, and of the Stoics, etc. They might put together in a single collection maxims of more than one author or even add diverse didactic material.

Of a single author there were, apparently, many more or less similar gnomologies. And they introduced materials of various types: from ancient poetry, Socratic, Cynic, depending on the work. These gnomologies were preceded or not by a *Life*, again depending on the work. At times they took the form of maxims in prose or in iambic trimeters, and at others of the *khreía* that describe a situation and then continue with a question plus a reply with a "point"; a dialogue could sometimes ensue. And, as I have said, there were gnomologies organized by themes. Let us add, finally, those alluded to at the beginning which were organized around a novelized *Life* or *Dialogue*.

This, as I have already suggested, implies innovations with respect to the previous period, above all, the written *Lives* and the gnomologies of various authors, ancient or contemporary, collected with or without regard for fidelity by professional anthologists; and their organization, at times, by themes. These are innovations that will be extensively exploited in the following period. But things are missing here that we shall see in this next period: the anonymous gnomologies and those that are organized alphabetically, anonymous or otherwise, and as for the themes, an infinity of

44 See A. Elter, *De Gnomologiorum Graecorum historia atque origine commentatio*, Bonn, 1893–97.

things. And there will always remain the doubt about the point of departure of the *Lives* and gnomologies of certain authors.

A complicated panorama, not unlike that of the fable, which I have reconstructed elsewhere. A point of departure for the great flowering of this literature in the imperial Roman epoch and in the following one. What we can gather for a novelized *Life* like that of Alexander can be applied to the whole gnomological tradition.

In any case, the fundamental features of the *Lives* and gnomologies, which developed later, after their evolution in Roman and Byzantine times, and which reached our medieval works, are already present here in essence. The spectrum of the later age will be broader, but here are found the seeds of genres that will continue until the Byzantine and the Arabic-Castilian periods. And with the addition of the aforementioned genres of the *Life*, the dialogue philosopher or secretary/king, etc., they constitute the beginnings of a series of genres that we are already acquainted with. We have also seen in the Hellenistic age something that was normal later: the apocryphal maxims and the maxims of varying attribution. And the widespread Cynic ingredient, to say nothing of the pseudo-epigraphic literature, including the letters, which we will discuss in more detail in the following chapter.

V. Sapiential literature in the imperial age

1. *Papyri*

The panorama, as I say, is approximately the same, but much enlarged, partly by the progressive development of the genres, which required certain alterations in them, partly by the fact that we have a better knowledge of their sources.

We will begin with the papyrian material. Here we find first, *gnômai* in iambic trimeters; second, *gnômai* or *khreîai* attributed to a single author or a group of them (Epicureans, etc.); third, collections of anonymous *gnômai*. Almost all of it is material for didactic use. At times we have a collection, at other times one, two or three *gnömai* or *khreîai*; occasionally we have the example of the teacher and the copy done by the pupil: exercises of syllabication, mathematics, mythical or poetic *excerpta*, etc.

a) Gnômai in iambic trimeters

Frequently rediscovered in the so-called *Monostichs*, they are a preview of the collection of these trimeters in Byzantine manuscripts. They are attributed to Menander, but we can also include Philemon, Alexis and other comic playwrights, Euripides and also material of unknown origin. I give below the data of the principal material in chronological order:

- I A.D., *POxy.* 3004: trimetric monostichs by Menander new ones; *PRain.* 3.24 + 25; Monostichs + dialogue between a father and son (Menander?).
- II A.D., *POxy.* 3541: three trimeters, one perhaps by Theognis; *OBodl.* 2941 + 2942: trimeters against women, perhaps by Philemon; *PLit.Lond.* 253: a trimeter from the *Monostichs* and another by an unknown author; *OClaud.* 184: a monostich by Menander, perhaps from the *Kitharistes*; J. G. Milne, *JEA* 8, 1944, pp. 156–157: *gnômai* in trimeters, alphabetized, one of them from the *Monostichs*.
- I–III A.D., *PCair.* inv. 56227 (W. G. Waddell, *Etudes de Papyrologie* 1, 1932, pp. 16–18 no. 10): a new trimeter.
- II. A.D., *PSchubart* 28: trimeters on the theme of the slave, with quotes from Philemon and Antiphanes, 29: trimeters by Philemon and Menander plus others that coincide with *Monostichs*.
- II–III A.D., *ONarmoutbis* 130: some monostichs; *PRoss.Georg.* 1.12: they seem to be monostichs; *BKT* 9.69: a *gnômai* which is found again in the *Monostichs; Pland.* 77: *gnômai* "by Menander", there are verses by Alexis, Diphilus and others that are found again in the *Monostichs,* plus some new ones; *PGiss.Lit.* 4.9: two moralistic trimeters, one by Euripides and another from the *Monostichs*; *POxy.* 3005, an anthology by Menander, organized by themes (χάρις, ἀδοξία, εὐδοξία, ἐξ ἀπροσδοκήτου).
- III A.D., *PMil. Vogl.* inv. 1241 ue.: iambic monostichs, alphabetized; *PRoss. Georg.* 1.13: a trimeter, pupil's maxim; *POxy.* 966 descrip.: a corrupt trimeter; *POxy.* 3006, extensive collection of alphabetized trimeters, found again in the *Monostichs*; *POxy*, 2661: alphabetized collection of monostichs, more fragments of Menander, Philemon and Euripides.
- III–IV A.D., *PBrooklyn* 27: a trimeter, a *gnôme* for pupils.
- III–IV ad., *PKöln* 246: *gnômai* related to the monostichs, perhaps on the καιρός and alphabetized.
- IV A.D., *PBrooklyn* 30–31: waxed tablets on which, among pupils' exercises (syllabication, copy of texts), there are various moralistic iambic trimeters, some on the τύχη; *PGiss.Lit.* 4.9, *POxy* 1185, W. Froehner,

Annales de la Société Française de Numismatique et Archéologie 3, 1868, pp. LXVIII–LXIX: various didactic iambic trimeters; *PIFAO* inv. 172 (M. Papathomopoulos, *Recherches de Papyrologie* 2, 1962, pp. 113–116): three iambic distichs, the second one close to Euripides, *Medea*, the first and third perhaps by the same poet.
- IV–V A.D., *PSI* 280: three trimeters on the τύχη (Euripides?).
- IV–V A.D., G. Nachtergael, *Chronique d'Égypte* 66. 1991, pp. 221–225: a *gnôme monóstikhos* in Greek and Coptic; *PFreib.* 45: *gnômai* that include fragments of Menander and a monostich.
- IV–V–VI A.D., *OBodl.* 144: various monostichs with new maxims. Alphabetical order; *GDRK* 38: an anonymous maxim + mythical material.
- V–VI A.D., *Sammelb.* 14654–14655: a didactic iambic trimeter, mixed with school material, also found in other places; D. Hagedorn – M. Weber, *ZPE* 3, 1968, pp. 46–49: a long series of monostichs in Greek and Coptic.
- VI A.D., *BKT* 9. 175: antifeminist trimeters.
- VI–VII A.D., D. Hagedorn – M. Weber, *ZPE* 3, 1968, pp. 49–50: a maxim with its Coptic version.

It is quite clear that in the schoolroom they used the maxims of Menander, of other comic playwrights, of Euripides and from other sources in teaching the children. The Roman age did nothing more than amplify what was already being done in the Hellenistic age. Apart from the specialized use of some maxims, there were those that formed collections, some alphabetical, some thematic. This is a forerunner of the so-called *Monostichs* and the *Comparison of Menander and Philistion,* which appear in Jaekel's edition following the papyrian collections[45]. The papyri frequently offer us the same monostichs as these collections; but evidently there were multiple models and we constantly find new sequences, and others are missing.

These collections are heavily infiltrated by Cynic doctrine. On the relation of many maxims with the material attributed to Diogenes, see A. Packmohr (op. cit.).

45 See S. Jaekel, *Menander*, Leipzig, Teubner, 1974.

b. Monographic anthologies

These are almost always either monographic collections of prosaic maxims or collections of *khreîai* of one author or another. They are shown below in chronological order:

- I A.D., *CPF* 1.1.3: a collection of *khreîai* by Diogenes.
- I/II A.D., *BKT* 9.162: a collection of *khreîai* referring to Alexander (the last one to his mother apparently).
- II. A.D., *PBerol.* inv. 17154 (F. C. Görschen, *AfP* 22, 1973, pp. 115–131): the verse perhaps presents *gnômai* by Euripides.
- II. A.D., *PBerol.* inv. 16369 (*SIFC* N. S. 13, 1937, 267–281): Epicurean gnomology, in part known fragments of Epicurus and Metrodorus, in part other new ones; they are followed by a letter from Metrodorus and a *gnôme* by Epicurus.
- III A.D., F. G. Kenyon, *JHS* 29, 1909, pp. 29–31: Pythagorean maxim, copied as a school exercise.
- III–IV A.D., *POslo* 177, cf. *CPF* cited, p. 94: *khreîai* on Diogenes; Wilcken, *Ostr.* 1310: *khreîai* by Isocrates; Wilcken, *Ostr.* 1226: *khreîai* by Aesop.
- IV–V–VI A.D., *GDRK* 38: an iambic maxim + mythical material.
- V–VI–VII A.D., *PBaden* 111: a *khreía* by Anacharsis.
- IV/V A.D., *P57* 1348: juridical interpretations in Greek and Latin.

As can be seen, these gnomologies can be juridical or Epicurean, and added to this are collections of *khreîai* by Diogenes and other personages in the role of Cynics, of *gnômai* by Euripides and a Pythagorean maxim. There are clear traces of organization by themes.

c. Mixed anthologies

II A.D., *PHarris* 176: maxims of Philemon and Alexis on the φιλαργυρία. This is a thematic gnomology with alternation of the maxims of Philippides, Philemon and Antiphanes; *PMil. Vogl.* 263: two *khreîai*, one by Demosthenes and the other by Epaminondas; *PKöln* 63: an anonymous maxim, another by Antisthenes; J. G. Milne, *JHS* 43, 1932, pp. 40–43: a distich by Philemon and an antifeminist invective; *PRain* 3.32: a *khreía* by Diogenes.

- II/III A.D., *Fr.Biog.Pap.Phil.* pp. 433–445: Maxims by Aristippus and Aesop: A. Brinkmann, *Rh.M.* 71, 1916, pp. 581–584: *excerpta*, principally from the *ad Demonicum*; V. Bartoletti, *Atti XI Congr.Pap.* (1966), pp. 1–14: Euripides, Moschion, Menander, Antiphanes, Philemon, Potamon, all of them on πλοῦτος / πενία.

- III A.D., *PRein.* 85: Diogenes, Aristotle?; *BKT* 9.4 5 + 46: Euripidean gnomology on the theme of slaves and masters (as in Stobaeus 4.10), followed by a verse by Antiphanes on the same theme.
- III–IV ADD., B. Boyaval, *ZPE* 17, 1975, pp. 225–235: wax tablets with diverse material: Monostichs, comparison of Menander and Philistion, iambic distichs of a mythical-moralistic type, another by Thales, etc.: O. Plassberg, *AfP* 2, 1903, 217–224: Judeo-Christian maxims.
- IV A.D., *PSI* 120: maxims by Isocrates *ad Demonicum* + others that appear in Byzantine gnomologies.
- IV A.D., *PBouriant* 1: Diogenes, alphabetized maxims of Menander, Babrius.
- V A.D., *PLitPahu Rib.* 3 + 5: maxims by Sextus and from the Old Testament.
- V/VI A.D., D. Hagedorn-M. Weber, *ZPE* 3, 1968, pp. 22–45: monostichs, Euripides, maxims with no parallel. An alphabetic collection.
- VI/VII A.D., *Mon.Epiph.* 615: Christian proverbs + alphabetized monostichs, also Homer, Diogenes. It comes from instruction in a monastery; J. Sijpesteijn, *ZPE* 51, 1983, pp. 291–292: a paragraph of the *ad Demonicum* + a monostich.

The important thing to note is that in this epoch anthological collections proliferated, including, beginning in the third to fourth centuries A.D., the Judeo-Christian maxims; and thematic anthologies were already in existence, for each of whose themes there were maxims by various authors[46], for example Stobaeus and later Maximus Confessor. But there are also alphabetical collections[47].

Let us attempt to draw some general conclusions. In the first place, many of these gnomologies appear in papyri for scholastic use, together with exercises in grammar and mathematics. But others no: they are devoted simply to ethical or literary teaching. Their number increases from the first century A.D. on, their types being those mentioned above: anony-

46 On these anthologies see *Museum Helveticum* 24, 1967, pp. 70 ff.

47 See L. W. Daly, *Contributions to the History of Alphabetization in Antiquity and the Middle Ages*, Brussels, Latomus, 1967, p. 47, and K. Alpers, *Gnomon*, 47, 1975, p. 115.

mous, mixed, by authors and thematic. They are generally in prose, but there are also trimeters that come from the new comedy.

The number of mixed anthologies has increased, as have the anthologies of a single author. And Menander stands out especially, together with other playwrights like Isocrates, Diogenes and above all Euripides (also Socrates, already mentioned). Antisthenes, Aristippus, Domosthenes, Alexander, Aesop and others also appear, although infrequently. And there are collective anthologies of the theater, the Epicureans, the Pythagoreans and the Seven Wise Men. It is worthy of notice that the pre-Socratics, Plato, Aristotle and the Stoics do not appear, and the orators and historians only rarely. It can be said that the preferred line is that of Socrates and the Socratics, including the Cynics, with the Epicureans, Euripides and Menander. Simonides and the Pseudo-Epicharmus, known in the Hellenistic gnomologies, do not reappear.

Another point to note is the appearance, starting in the 3rd to 4th centuries A.D., of mixed anthologies of Greek authors and the Old Testament. This is the beginning of a phenomenon that culminated in the Byzantine epoch. And still in existence, although rare, are the anthologies by themes, which were very important beginning with Johannes Stobaeus. Also of importance from the beginning of the 1st century A.D. is the existence of gnomologies organized alphabetically; this is the system followed in Menander's gnomology (monostichs) transmitted via the manuscripts and various Byzantine gnomologies, evidently based on gnomologies of the imperial epoch.

To all this must be added the existence of various papyri of the same epoch as the *Life of Aesop* and of a papyrus (the *PRoss. Georg.* 1.17, of the 3rd century A.D.) of the *Life of Secundus*. This completes the outline of the Greek sapiential literature that has reached us by way of the papyri. It is very little, indeed, but it provides us with orientation to comprehend the panorama of the sapiential literature of the Roman and Byzantine periods known through manuscripts, which is much more abundant. Here we will give a general idea of this literature.

Nevertheless, what has been transmitted through manuscripts is not very much either, given that the Greco-Arabic-Castilian collections and the Greco-Arabic ones not translated into Castilian contain a great deal of material that we know only through these collections and that without doubt comes, for the most part, from Antiquity.

2. *The tradition that comes from medieval manuscripts*

What we deduced from the study of the papyri of the Roman period must be completed, in the first place, with the study done for the Hellenistic ones; we can be sure that even those authors and collections that do not appear now continued in circulation, and provide indirect conclusions: in the final analysis, the Byzantine gnomologies derive from others of the Roman age and, in their origins, from even earlier ones. And the *khreîai* and maxims in the *Lives* of Diogenes Laertius presuppose the existence of gnomologies "with an author". We consider that in line with this would be the gnomologies of Alexander, Aristotle, Socrates and Pythagoras which more or less altered, reached our Arabic-Castilian texts and the Arabic ones that were not translated.

Because what happens, with few exceptions, is that in the papyri we find material that is fragmentary and minimal, sometimes simple *gnômai* or *khreîai*. We must consider that the whole immense mass of material of, for example, the *khreîai* of Diogenes was at one time collected in various extensive gnomologies. And the same is true of the Seven Wise Men and others.

We should like to give a general view of the material that has reached us by way of medieval manuscripts and of its organization, a view that will complete what was obtained from the papyri. Although it might seem strange, as far as I know, no such overview has ever been offered. We will leave aside related genres such as the letter and the diatribe, which we have mentioned.

a) *Individual authors or those that form groups*

- Carmen Aureum. This Neo-Pythagorean poem, edited by D. Young[48], between a prologue dedicated to the gods and an epilogue dedicated to Zeus, contains groups of hexametric maxims on self-control, justice, lying, action, moderation, action again, the oath, etc.
- Epictetus. The *Gnomologium Epicteteum*[49] contains series of maxims on various themes (food, friends, the city, etc.); without doubt it comes from an anthology organized by themes.

48 In his edition of Theognis, Leipzig, Teubner, 1961, pp. 86 ff.

49 In H. Schenkl, *Epicteti dissertationes*, Leipzig, Teubner, 1916, pp. 478 ff. (by Stobaeus).

- Epicurus. We have a *Gnomologium Epicureum*[50] that combines citations from the philosopher's *Capital Maxims* with some by Metrodorus, plus various others. No classification criteria are evident.
- Aesop. B. E. Perry[51] has edited some *Proverbia Aesopi* that lack a clear organization.
- "Menander". We have seen repeatedly the appearance of iambic trimeters of a moralistic nature used in teaching. They are anonymous or attributed to "Menander". However, where it is possible to ascertain, we have seen that they include trimeters by Chares, the playwrights (Alexis, Diphilus, Philemon, Antiphanes), Euripides and others whose authors we are unable to identify. We already know that these anthologies began to take form in the Hellenistic age, but later they grew considerably.
  Now the Byzantine manuscript tradition has transmitted to us the so-called *Monostichs* of Menander and the "Comparison of Menander and Philistion"[52]. These are frequently the same verses as we find in our papyri, but not always. In addition, the monostichs, which number 877, are completely alphabetized. They probably began to be formed, based on earlier texts, in the 2nd century A.D. Their effect was enormous: there are translations in Coptic, Slavic and Arabic.

  One must suppose that they are one of the collections "by Menander" of the imperial epoch. Or perhaps earlier. There is little Cynic content (on ἔρως, πόνος, woman, but at times with a non-Cynic content). Most of it is religious and traditional morality, sometimes Socratic moralism with the themes of σοφία, ἡδονή, δίκη, παιδεία, σιγή, θυμοῦ κρατεῖν, λόγος, ἰατρός (wisdom, pleasure, justice, education, silence, control of one's appetites, reason, medicine). I am inclined to accept the idea of a Hellenistic thematic gnomology alphabetized later in the imperial epoch.

50 In G. Arrighetti, *Epicuro. Opere*. Turin, Einaudi, 1973, pp. 140 ff.

51 *Aesopica,* Urbana, University of Illinois Press, 1952, pp. 259 ff. (from the *codex Mosquensis* 239). I do not cite the *Aesopi sententiae,* collected by the author himself in various sources.

52 Its origen can be situated in the 2nd century A.D., see G. A. Gerhard, *Phoinix von Colophon*, Leipzig, Teubner, 1909, p. 276. For the monostichs of Menander, see Mariño-García Romero, cited, pp. 356 ff. This tradition is imitated in Latin by the so-called *Maxims of Cato*, believed to be of the 3rd century A.D.

- Moschion. Small collections of *Gnômai* and *Hypothékai* with a certain thematic organization[53]: friends, definition of the various virtues, etc.
- Pythagorean maxims. The case of the Pythagorean maxims attributed to Demophilus (alphabetical collection from the Vat. Gr. 743 especially) is of exceptional interest: it is a collection to which Syriac versions and citations by Stobaeus are related. This demonstrates the existence of an abundance of collections in Antiquity and of an interchange of ordering criteria. Alongside this there are non-alphabetical collections, also related, the so-called Sextus and Clitarchus collections (and the *Letter to Marcella* by Porphyry). Christian elements merged in this tradition, and there were translations into Syriac[54].

  Furthermore, and this is absolutely exceptional, many of these maxims reappear in Mubassir, in the *Bocados de Oro*: 43 maxims of Mubassir are in the alphabetical Greek collection, although he used a different Greek version, related to the one followed by the Syriac versions. He added maxims from Plato's *Phaedo*, Diogenes Laertius, the *ad Demonicum*, etc., which gives us an idea of Mubassir's working method and of his absolute dependence on Greek sources[55]. It also shows that there were variants in the Greek tradition, doubtless based on a common model.
- Plutarch. Next come the collections of apothegms compiled by Plutarch: the *Apophthegmata regum et imperatorum* contain, in approximately chronological order, maxims of the orientals, Greeks and Romans. The *Apophthegmata Laconicorum* contain first, in alphabetical order by authors, maxims by Laconian personages, then other anonymous ones. Here must be added, from the Pseudo-Plutarch or Pseudo-Caecilius, the *Apophthegmata romana*, with no recognizable order[56].
- Pseudo-Phocylides. A poem in hexameters with traces of Judaic doctrines organized with a prologue and an epilogue, having in the center a series of maxims and exhortations that develop various themes, with gaps, loops and returns: on parents, justice, life, love of money, love, envy, temperance, etc., always within the strictest moralism.

53 In H. Schenkl, *Epicteti dissertationes de Arriano digestae*, Leipzig, Teubner, 1916, pp. 493–496.

54 See H. Chadwick's edition of Sextus, Cambridge, University Press, 1959.

55 On all this see A. R. Sodano, *Le sentenze "pitagoriche" dello pseudo-Demofilo*, Roma, Accademia Nazionale dei Lincei, 1991.

56 Edited by E. Offenloch, *Caecilii Caleactini fragmenta*, 2nd ed., Stuttgart, Teubner, 1967.

- Porphyry. *Sententiae.* See Lamberz, E., Leipzig (T) 1975, pp. 1–51, *Sententiae ad intelligibilia ducentes.* A summary of his doctrine, presented in gnomic form.
- The Seven Wise Men. To the above-mentioned collection of Demetrius of Phalerum must be added others of a later date collected in Mullach[57]. They do not differ much from the previous ones, except that they frequently take the classic form of the *khreía*: "having been asked [...] he said". There is always the same traditional and common-sense wisdom.

Thus these gnomologies extend the panorama of the papyri, but in the same direction. There are some organized by themes, others alphabetical, and there are indications of transferences from one to another. Almost always, in contrast to what still occurred in the Hellenistic epoch, they are collections assembled by someone who was not the author, although naturally a follower of his ideas. Or these can be independent gnomic-type poems. A clear influence of Cynicism is not found here, but it is present, in various citations, in the confusion of attributions to Diogenes, Socrates, Menander, Democritus, Euripides and other authors.

It would be appropriate to complete this panorama with an allusion to the collections of *Horoi* or Definitions: by the Pseudo-Plato (Speusippus?), Aristotle, Theophrastus, Galen and others. The maxim, at one time an instrument for oral instruction, became a manner of introduction to the thought of, for example, Epictetus (in his *Manual*) or Porphyry (the *Sententiae ad Intelligibilia ducentes*[58] and the *Letter to Marcella*). Here, too, we have the same catechistic system of questions and replies, which will be discussed later.

Reference must also be made to the Hermetic gnomologies[59]. They are interesting because they provide a preview of things in the *Poridad* and *Bocados*, works which they reached starting from a Hermetic base, either ancient or residual in Arabic times; they also reached Armenian and Syriac.

57 W. A. Mullach, *Fragmenta Philosophorum Graecorum*, I, reedited, Darmstadt, Scientia Verlag, 1968, pp. 217 ff.

58 Edited by E. Lamberz, Leipzig, Teubner, 1975, pp. 1–51. These are Neo-Platonic themes relating to the soul, the body, God, nature, death, catharsis, the *noûs*, etc.

59 See *Textos Herméticos*, translation by Xavier Renau, Madrid, Gredos, 1999, pp. 309 ff. More details are given there, as well as passages of Hermetic works from which appear to have been derived the *gnômai* of the *Stobaei Hermetica* XI; in the same book, pp. 527 ff. are the "Armenian Hermetic Definitions", written in *gnômai.*

What we do not find are mixed Christian-pagan gnomologies: as far as we know, their roots in the papyri we have seen, in which the Old Testament is presented alongside the pagan authors, would have to wait to find continuation. But we do find diverse Christian gnomologies that will end up merging later with the traditional Greek ones.

A good example is the florilegium of Saint Basil, which is to occupy first place, after the Bible, in the Byzantine gnomologies. According to its editor, J. F. Kindstrand[60], it comes from a more extensive Christian florilegium organized by author's name.

The confluence of Christian and pagan thought, often expressed in maxims, has been well known since Saint Paul. One can cite, among others, Clement of Alexandria, the Pseudo-Justin, Lactantius, Didymus, Origen, Theodoret, Cyril of Alexandria and, of course, the Cappadocian fathers and Johannes Chrysostom. From Alexandria comes a *Theosophia* that contained sayings of the pagan philosophers interpreted as prophesies pointing forward to Christianity[61].

And we have other Christian texts from late Antiquity, for example the florilegium entitled *Doctrina Patrum de Incarnatione Verbi*[62]. On pages 249 ff. we find a series of definitions, beginning with that of ἀγαθόν, Goodness, in alphabetical order. And especially *The apothegms of the fathers*[63], in which we have the questions addressed to the monks of the Egyptian desert and their replies: in form (but not in content) it is the traditional Greek model, but with a greater number of questions and answers. So then, these collections of apothegms are either systematic (by themes: spiritual advancement, ἡσυχία, compunction, etc.) or alphabetical (by the names of the ascetics). And there is a constant passing of maxims from one to the other.

We can add, too, the apothegms of Macarius (Egyptian and Alexandrian, together with the Pseudo-Macarius), 4th century A.D.[64], those of Evagrius Ponticus (4th century A.D.)[65] and the various gnomologies in

60 "Florilegium e Basilio Magno ineditum", *Eranos* 83, 1985, pp. 113–124.

61 See S. Brock, "A Syriac Collection of Prophecies of the Pagan Philosophers", *Orientalia Lovaniensia Periodica* 14, 1983, pp. 203–246.

62 Edited by F. Diekampf, Münster, 1907.

63 See Jean-Claude Guy, 1st cent., *Les apophthegmes des Pères*, 1, Paris, Éditions du Cerf, 1993 (thematic collection). And the edition in *MPG* 65, cols. 71–134 (alphabetical collection).

64 In *MPG* 34, pp. 230–263.

65 In *Apoph. Patr.*, *MPG* 65.

verse of Gregory of Nazianzus. And also, from the epoch of the emperor Zeno, the group of *excerpta* from the *Codex Vaticanus gr.* 1431[66].

And again we emphasize the repercussion of all this sapiential literature in the languages influenced by Greek: Syriac, Armenian, Coptic, Ethiopian and Slavic.

b) Collections with the participation of various authors

These are an innovation of this period, and a brilliant future awaits them in the Byzantine age (and in our *Buenos Proverbios*). We have already encountered them in the papyri, where various philosophers or poets take part in the discussion of a theme. Apart from that, in the *Seven Wise Men* there is the opposite system: a series of maxims is attributed to each of them.

In the first place we must mention Johannes Stobaeus, with his organization by themes and, within each of these, the manifestations of different philosophers. There are four books of his: the first on natural philosophy, the second, chapters 1–6, on logic, the rest and chapter III on morals, and the fourth on diverse matters. Each book has chapters, each with successive themes and the opinions of various philosophers and writers on them. He did not invent this genre; Stobaeus is of the 5th century, and we have encountered the genre in papyri much earlier than that, and also in the sources that he cites, especially Aristonymus and Serenus.

We can add Orion, who toward the middle of the 5th century compiled another collection of maxims, of which only a brief summary remains. And the *Placita Philosophorum* or "Opinions of the Scientists[67]" should be added, in which, under titles such as "What is nature?", "What is the difference between the principle and the elements?", "How was the cosmos formed?", etc., the opinions of the different scientists are given.

There are traces of this form in the Byzantine gnomologies, as I have said, and also in the Arabic-Castilian treatises. It is easy to pass from one genre to another.

In summary, we know the great wealth of the ancient gnomologies only partially. For example, the very presence in the Byzantine gnomologies of authors who, like Jamblichus, are missing in the older ones is an indication

66 Edited by E. Schwartz, Munich, 1927.

67 In Plutarch, *Moralia* V. 2 (ed. J. Mau, Leipzig, Teubner, 1971). See also, with more sources, H. Diels, *Doxographi Graeci*, Berlin, de Gruyter, 1929², pp. 273 ff.

of the enormous losses that the latter have suffered. The Arabic-Castilian works have saved another part of this lost material for us.

c) Collections related to a Life

Finally there remains a theme already discussed in part: the theme of the connection of maxims and the rest with the more or less novelized *Lives*. At times this is a matter of simple anecdotes or debates at a banquet.

The boundary with the *khreîai* is flexible; they often appear alongside the maxims either in the indicative or in the imperative or subjunctive (advice); there is a mixture of definitions, replies to riddles, questions of the type "What is...?", "What is the best...?", etc. As we already know, these maxims normally deal with indoctrination by a parent or a philosopher or a religious man, very frequently someone of an apparently inferior status. And there is no clear line that differentiates them from the genres that we have seen (indoctrination by different philosophers based on *khreîai* or maxims or letters) or will see ("catechistic" genres, instruction using questions and replies).

I will not go into the Pseudo-Callisthenes in its various strata here; this will be discussed in the next chapter. In it we have themes such as the Aristotle/Alexander relation, Alexander/the Gymnosophists, the mourning for Alexander and the words of consolation addressed to his mother. The *gnômai* are constantly interwoven with the biographical narrative.

And we have already commented on the fundamental points of the *Life of Aesop* and its Cynicizing character, inserted into a traditional Greek framework, with the influence of the *Ahikar*. We have the slave Aesop defeating with his ingenuity his companions in slavery, his master and his master's philosopher friends, his wife, Croesus., the Delphians – and this with the enormous variety of genres that we know (maxims, solution of riddles, similes, fables, etc.). Always the same association of life and sapiential literature. The written prototype of the *Lives* of the Byzantine era (recensions G and W) that has reached us is from the first century A.D., although it derives in turn, I believe, from one from the Hellenistic epoch. It is a text that was strongly influenced by versions in Latin, Armenian, Syriac, Ethiopian and various other languages.

We usually situate in the following century, the second century A.D., the *Life of Secundus*, another "inferior" wise man, whose cynicizing character I have emphasized in my writings: the lack of knowledge about this on the part of so many commentators, for example, the editor of the work, B. E. Perry[68], only goes to demonstrate the lack of philosophical training of some eminent philologists.

Disillusioned with women's virtue, including his mother's, Secundus decides to maintain silence. And then comes the scene where the emperor Hadrian wants to ask him questions via a *speculator*: he refuses to speak in spite of being threatened with death; he is admired and pardoned by the emperor. He then answers the questions in writing. The themes are: the wickedness of women, the dignity of the philosopher, the emperor's admiration of him.

Unlike the *Life of Aesop*, in which the maxims arise from a series of incidents, here, after the prologue, there is a series of "What is...?" questions followed by the replies. Questions are asked about the existence of the cosmos, the ocean, God, the day, the sun, the moon, the earth, man, beauty, woman, friends, etc. An order not very different from the Φυσικῶν δόξαι, with maxims tinged with Cynicism and, at times, Stoicism.

I bring in now, a series of dialogues from the Jewish *Haggadah* in which the sage and the religious man always triumph; these have been discussed previously[69]; I remind the reader of some Jewish themes discussed above. Here we have dialogues between Alexander and the Jews or the Indians; between Ptolemy and Eleazar or the Seventy-two interpreters (put to the test, they triumph); Hadrian and Aquila; Turnus Rufus and Aquila (Why are there indigents?); a Roman emperor and Gamaliel (the omnipresence of God); a Roman emperor and Joshua. The model was, then, widely used and later passed to the Middle Ages.

And important, too, in Antiquity is the presence of the theme in the realistic novel related to the *Life of Aesop*: Apuleius' *Golden Ass* and the version attributed to Lucian, and Petronius' *Satyricon*. Always the humble character (the ass and the parasites) ridiculing those in high positions and teaching them a lesson).

68 B. E. Perry, *Secundus the silent philosopher*, Ithaca, New York, Cornell University Press, 1964. Cf. my "Elementos cínicos...", cited, pp. 317 ff. Nor do I exclude the presence of Stoic elements.

69 See "Literatura sapiencial antigua en la Haggadah y en Pedro Alfonso", in *Illinois Classical Studies* 18, 1993, pp. 229–236.

We must mention too the *Altercatio Hadriani Augusti et Epicteti philosophi*[70]. This apparently is no later than the 3rd century A.D. It is imitated more or less in the *Disputatio Regalis et Nobilissimi Iuuenis Pippini cum Albino Scholastico*: again the philosopher (Alcuin) teaching the son of the king (Pepin, the son of Charlemagne), and in the Provençal text about the *enfant sage*, who defeats everyone with his wisdom.

Returning to Antiquity, let us recall what has been said above about the wise maiden Tarsiana in the *Vita Apollonii* or about the dispute between Solomon and Hiram of Tyre in Josephus (Hiram was unable to solve Solomon's enigmas and had to pay him). The theme of the virgin and martyr Catherine of Alexandria, who according to the medieval legend defeated the sages convened by the emperor Magentius to oppose her in a wisdom debate. And the evangelical theme of the child Jesus among the doctors.

In this context we must also mention the theme and organization of *The Thousand and One Nights*: Scheherazade has the same role before the Sultan as the humble wise characters who defeat the proud king with their wisdom. This is a work with Sassanid and even Indian roots, augmented later in Fatimid Egypt, but diffused with Greek themes, as I have demonstrated elsewhere[71].

Finally, let me remind the reader that this line, beginning either in Greco-Latin Antiquity or in India and arriving by way of the Latin Middle Ages or by the Arabic route, yielded new fruits in the European Middle Ages. In the *Sendebar*, also called the *Libro de los engaños y asayamientos de las mujeres* (the title of the 13th century Castilian version), the philosopher, who is the main character, manages to save the king's son by arguing with the king's wife, who had maligned the son, and convincing her. Mention can also be made, without the antifeminist element, of the *Speculum Stultorum* by Nigel de Longchamp (end of the 12th century), and the adventures of the ass Burnellus accompanied by satire, fables and dialogue. And in the 14th century, *El Conde Lucanor* by the Infante D. Juan Manuel, in which the preceptor Patronio teaches the king's son with fables and stories of wisdom.

In short, the continuity of the old Mesopotamian theme, present in archaic and classical Greece, is perfectly clear: the sage who gives lessons to

70 Edited by L. W. Daly and W. Suchier, Urbana, 1939, with an important prologue, from which come various facts given above.

71 "Documentacíon suplementaria de la fábula greco-latina", *Euphrosyne* 18, 1990, pp. 213–226.

the powerful by the traditional means of the maxim and the fable, all in a novelistic medium. Back in archaic Greece, Solon, a historical figure, played the same role with respect to king Croesus of Lydia in the well-known passage from Herodotus. And so very many later philosophers were seen in the same light, at times preserving their own characteristics, at times with a literary touch, from the Socrates who finds himself, ironic and only apparently insecure, before pompous personages like Protagoras or Gorgias, to Cynics like Diogenes or Bion, and to Epictetus and the rest.

It was usual, beginning in Hellenistic times, to publish the writings of poets and philosophers with a preceding short biography; I have given examples from the Hellenistic age. This later became common practice. Now then, along with this usage there was another, related to the previous genre of the novelized biographies studded with *gnômai* and the rest, i.e. writing the lives of the philosophers, with accompanying, more or less authentic *gnômai* and *khreîai*. We have seen this, with respect to Socrates, in a papyrus from the 3rd century B.C.; for Plato the existence of a florilegium of citations has been proposed, doubtless preceded by a biography[72]. And we have already seen the collections of *khreîai* by Diogenes, which combined (fantastic) details of his life with his doctrine. The same is true of the Seven Wise Men and others. Of course gnomologies without a *Life* and *Lives* with no gnomology were written too, as we have already said.

But we have more examples that fit into this context perfectly. Such is the case of Lucian's *Life of Demonax*, which is the life of this eclectic Cynic of the 1st–2nd centuries A.D. There follows a series of *khreîai*: *bons mots*, frequently ironic, in his confrontations with the Athenians, with Favorinus, with an athlete, a Roman senator, Peregrinus Proteus, Herodes Atticus, the ex-consul Cethegus, etc. Throughout all of these his feelings, cloaked in irony and compassion, are evident: scarce religiosity, hope, fear, simple joking.

This is the model of the *Life* that Diogenes Laertius undoubtedly followed most frequently in his *Lives of the Philosophers*; I have already spoken about the precedents of this work and about some of the *Lives* contained therein. All of them should be studied in detail from this point of view. *Lives* like those of Socrates or Aristippus, not to mention that of Diogenes, are replete with short anecdotes or *khreîai* of the type that we know, to-

72 See H. Chadwick, art. "Florilegium", in *Reallexikon für Antike und Christentum* 7, 1969, col. 1142.

gether, of course, with references to different sources and to doctrine. This is less the case in some others, such as Xenophon and Plato. Frequently, lists of works, pseudo-epigraphic letters, etc. are added; but we can suspect that the nucleus is here in this model of the *Life*.

Then too, we must at least allude to the genre, related to this one, of the question and answer (or catechistic) dialogues between a master and a disciple, which reached a high degree of development. There are burlesque ones, like the medieval *Ioca monachorum*, but they were also important in the teaching of Medicine, Grammar, and Theology. Sometimes these are real debates (between the values of the Old and New Testaments or of Jewish and Christian values, for example; sometimes they were simple "catechisms"). They were important in indoctrination and education[73].

Finally, it must be remembered that this type of literature goes far beyond the limits of Greek, finding its echo in Latin, Slavic, Syriac, Ethiopian, etc.

VI. Conclusions for the Arabic-Castilian and Arabic works of Greek origin

In view of all this, we can repeat what was already announced in the initial chapter of this book regarding the ancient structural elements of our Arabic-Castilian works: they are Greek. And this is also the case of other Arabic works not translated, especially the Philosophical Quartet, which contains the combination *Life* + maxims of Pythagoras, Socrates, Plato and Aristotle. Since we have given the essentials about our four works, we can identify the principal types of organization of the maxims in them. They are types that coincide with those that we have seen in Greek literature:

a) Anonymous maxims (at the end of *Bocados*).

73 See the Introduction to the Daly-Suchier edition of the *Altercatio*, pp. 25 ff. See examples of various medical catechisms in M.-H. Marganne, *La chirurgie dans l'Égypte gréco-romaine d'après les papyrus grecs,*, Leiden, Brill, 1998. Dionysius of Thrace was one of the grammatical texts reduced to this form, which was perpetuated in Catholic catechisms and in traditional teaching methods.

b) Maxims with an author: in *Buenos Proverbios* (maxims on the sashes of the philosophers; maxims of Socrates, Plato and Aristotle, with no *Life*); in *Bocados* (counsels of various philosophers, with no *Life*: Tad, Çagalquius, Homer, Assaron, Logines, etc.); In *Poridad* (maxims on various themes; Aristotle is always the speaker). Also, of course, in the *PQ*.
c) Maxims by various authors on the same theme: in *Buenos Proverbios* in the initial *ayuntamientos*, above all on the theme of wisdom, and in the final ones, especially on the theme of death. And in the *Donzella Teodor*, with the confrontation of the sages and the maiden on various themes, with the frequent "What is...?" and "What is the most...?" questions.
d) *Lives*, in another case, leading the maxims. And sometimes there is the traditional theme of the person, apparently inferior but wise, who triumphs: Aristotle in *Buenos Prov*erbios, Teodor *in Donzella Teodor*.

Now then, all these types area clearly the same as those we have encountered already in the Hellenistic epoch, but especially in the imperial Roman period. Other points still need to be developed (which will be done in the following chapters): the form of the maxims and *khreîai*, their organization, the doctrines encountered. We have already said that, just as happened in the final Roman epoch, a synthesis of diverse philosophies has been arrived at, basically along the line of the Socratics, the Cynic-Stoics, the moralists in general and the Christians. More details will be given in the following chapters.

But there is a problem. I have already said that the existence of the combination *Life* + gnomology and even of simple gnomologies is, in the case of many ancient authors, a deduction of our own; these works have not been preserved. We consider that in the Arabic-Castilian texts there has simply been preserved, greatly Christianized, much of what was lost in the rest of the works of the tradition. So I must emphasize the condition, marked by a profusion of lacunae, in which the Greek gnomologies have come down to us and also the possibility of increasing our knowledge of them through our Arabic-Castilian texts. For they contain a sector of the oldest Byzantine literature that did not find other routes of transmission.

Consider that, in effect, the progress of the Greek gnomologies halted in the 5th century; later authors were not admitted, not even when a new epoch opened for the gnomologies in the 9th century. And so, for example, no Byzantine gnomologies before the 9th century are preserved that put the pagan Greek authors side by side with the Christian ones, even though examples of Biblical and pagan gnomologies existed in papyri. And there were also Christian gnomologies.

Not until the 6th and 7th centuries, when the versions preserved in Damascus and Alexandria were done and were translated into Syriac and Arabic, was there a modernization, in a Christian direction, of the works we are dealing with, those that combined a *Life* and a gnomology. It seems clear that the texts that were the basis of those that the Arabs found in the Orient had undergone considerable reworking, which, without doubt, was unknown in Constantinople. The Greek, or even the Syriac communities of the Orient, were, very probably, responsible for these changes[74]. But the essential line was not altered.

It must be accepted therefore, that the Greek texts that are the base of our Arabic-Castilian ones, and of some that are only in Arabic, were founded on the earlier tradition in the Orient: in Damascus and perhaps in Alexandria. Damascus fell in 636; it is known that the Ommiad caliph Omar (r. 717–720) took the Greek manuscripts from Alexandria to Antioch. And we know of translations of Greek texts into Syriac and Arabic (sometimes into Arabic by way of Syriac, as in the case of *Poridad* and perhaps of *Bocados*). These Greek texts were, without doubt, from the 6th and 7th centuries, and were found in the Orient by Christian translators, but not until the 9th century, with the Greek renaissance and better relations, could texts from Constantinople be imported.

It is not strange, then, that there is a discontinuity: modifications of the previous tradition, especially as regards monarchy and Christianity, more radical in the Orient than in Constantinople; and the conservation of texts that were lost here in the iconoclastic period. This can be proven literally in some cases, as in the legend of Alexander: a Greek epistolary novel, of a very Christian cast, has been preserved only in Arabic; it comes from a Greek collection of letters, which will be discussed in the next chapter. And

74 See in our Chapter IV the part pertaining to the Syriac gnomic collections of the Pythagorean type, to the extent that we can know them. For other collections of Greek origin but apparently distanced from the Greek ones (although this would have to be re-examined), see N. Zeegers-Vander Vorst, "Une gnomologie d'auteurs grecs en traduction syriaque", in *Symposium Syriacum 1976, Orientalia christiana analecta*, 205, Roma, Pontificium Institutum Orientalium Studiorum, 1978, pp. 163–177. And also S. Brock, "A Syriac Collection of Prophecies of the Pagan Philosophers", *Orientalia Lovaniensia Periodica* 14, 1983, pp. 203–246 (the author indicates Hermetic and other sources).

the Christian image of Aristotle and Alexander is more advanced in our works (and in the Syriac and Ethiopian traditions) than in Constantinople, as we shall see.

Note that his occurs not only in Arabic works translated into Castilian, but also in those that were not translated. This is the case of the *Philosophical Quartet* and other Arabic sources (such as al-Sijistani and Ibn Hindu), which, furthermore, are considered by Gutas[75] as depending fundamentally on Hunayn, although with the addition of other sources.

An important Arabist, G. Strohmaier, has emphasized[76] that the markedly ascetic tone of many of the maxims attributed to Socrates and other ancient sages, the tendency to see them as ascetics, has no parallel in Greek; it has a distinctly monastic tinge that suggests the Christian communities of Syria, the Nestorians among others, and even, he believes, Muslim asceticism. He cites as an example the maxim of Socrates in the mausoleum of Tamerlane's sister in Samarkand (this also appears in Mubassir): "Man is tormented in this world in all his circumstances; he cannot live from the means of subsistence that are his lot; he can seldom be congratulated on the pleasures he finds in it; what remains for him is the choking feeling in his throat when his loved ones leave him in it".

In any case, the synthesis of the old moralism (Socratic-Cynic-Stoic, plus Neo-Pythagorean, Neo-Platonic and Hermetic elements) with Christian moralism was already under way in Antiquity; our treatises do no more than move a step forward in this direction without our being able to find exact parallels in Rome or Byzantium. As for theme, we will look at this in detail with reference to each treatise. And a third element must be added: Hermetism. We have already alluded to its ancient gnomologies and also to its presence in some of the Arabic-Castilian treatises.

The Arabic gnomologies, to the minimal extent to which they are published, coincide with the Greek ones most of the time and also with Mubassir and Ibn Hindu, but it also happens that no model is found for some *gnômai*. This is the case in Ibn Durayd[77]: of his 74 maxims there are 14 (11,

75 Op. cit., pp. 436 ff., 450.

76 "Ethical sentences and Anecdotes of Greek Philosophers in Arabic Tradition", in *Actes du Ve Congrès d'Arabisants et d'Islamisants, Correspondance d'Orient*, 11, Bruxelles, 1971, pp. 436–471; "Die arabische Sokrateslegende und ihre Ursprünge", in P. Nagel (ed.), *Studia Coptica*, Berlin, Akademie Verlag, 1974, pp. 121–136.

77 See F. Rosenthal, "Sayings of the ancients from Ibn Durayd's *Kitab al-Mujtana*", *Orientalia* 27, 1958, pp. 2–54, 150–183.

18, 31, 35, 36, 40, 42, 47, 48, 49, 56, 68, 69, 71) that do not appear in the Greek sources. It is clear that elements reached the Arabs that have been lost in Greek or were never published, although sometimes there can be new creations also. But in general the maxims are Greek. Even their gross errors, like Socrates in the barrel, are in Greek.

VII. Sapiential literature in the Byzantine age

As I said before, gnomological literature appears again in Byzantium in the 9th century, but this literature offers no gnomological material later than the 5th century. The developments that there may have been in the 6th, 7th and 8th centuries can only be known from the comparison of the Greek gnomologies since the 9th century with the old ones and from the Arabic texts that we have been discussing. One might ask, then, what interest there is in studying this other, more recent Byzantine literature. The reply is to have one more bit of information for the reconstruction of the gnomology of the imperial Roman period and even earlier, from which the Byzantine literature derives, and which, of course, is at the base of the Arabic texts that we know of: both the four that were translated into Castilian and the others.

On the other hand, we must always bear in mind that we are dealing with a literature that is difficult to study. The greater part of more than a thousand Byzantine collections is unpublished, and of those published, some are very badly done[78]. Nor is there an up-to-date comprehensive survey[79].

But the following is clear: sapiential literature reappeared, through the copying or reworking of ancient texts that were found in the libraries, beginning in the 9th century during the renaissance promoted by Photius. This is the same epoch in which there was a parallel movement in Bagdad

78 For the so-called Maximus Confessor see M. B. Phillips, "Some Remarks on the Manuscript Tradition of the Maximus Florilegium", *Illinois Classical Studies* 7, 1982, pp. 261–270, and M. Richard, see below.

79 The best one is "Florilèges grecs", in *Dictionnaire de Spiritualité*, Paris, 1962, cols. 475–512, by Marcel Richard.

under the Abbassids, with the translation of Greek books found in the libraries and the search for others.

But this movement was limited. The ancient sapiential literature was reduced (save special genres, such as the fable) to gnomologies of various types, with no initial *Life*. That is why the gnomologies, often with an initial *Life*, of our Arabic-Castilian, or simply Arabic texts were apparently left aside. They clearly preserve something ancient that was lost in Byzantium.

These gnomologies are sometimes profane, sometimes sacred-profane, sometimes monastic. We will attempt to give an idea of each group.

1. *Profane gnomologies*

The most important ones are: the *Gnomologium Vaticanum* edited by L. Sternbach in 1887 and 1889 and reedited by O. Luschnat in 1962. It comes from the *Cod. Vat. Graec.* 743[80], and contains a long series of Greek and Latin non-Christian authors, arranged alphabetically by the first letter. The edition points out the correspondences with regard to other gnomologies and the different attributions of each *gnôme* in them. There is no clear order in the sections on each author. More than *gnômai*, these are *khreîai*. The first citation gives the name of the author (Aristotle, etc.), the following ones say ὁ αὐτός, or "the same" (which results in errors); then follows a circumstance ("inquiring", "seeing", a genitive absolute, etc.); and it concludes with an expression having a *verbum dicendi*, such as "he said". The selection reaches as far as the Hellenistic epoch, no farther.

It is evident that this is a Byzantine collection, but its roots are ancient, even Hellenistic: it was used in an ancient period by writers like Stobaeus, Diogenes Laertius and Plutarch, and there are parallels in Seneca, Philo, Clement of Alexandria, Gregory of Nazianzus, etc.[81]

A collection from an Oxford manuscript[82]: 42 maxims ordered neither by authors nor by themes, although there are traces of a possible source with ordering by themes. It only contains authors up to the Hellenistic age.

80 There are various related collections. Cf. J. F. Kindstrand, "A collection of Apophthegmata in an Oxford Manuscript", in *Greek and Latin Studies in Memory of Cajus Fabricius*, *Studia Graeca et Latina Gothoburgensia* 54, ed. by S.-T. Teodorsson, Gothenburg, 1990, p. 142, note.

81 See H. Chadwick, art. "Florilegium", cited, col. 1137.

82 Published by Kindstrand, see note 80.

But notice must be taken, above all, of the fact that the various gnomologies dedicated strictly to personages of the pre-Christian world, which we have discussed above, come, with the exception of the papyri, from the Byzantine manuscripts. Others must be added that were not mentioned before because they contribute very little to the documentation of Antiquity: the *Gnomologium Byzantinum* by A. Wachsmuth, Berlin, 1882, reprinted in Osnabrück in 1971 (Democritus-Isocrates-Epictetus, ordered by themes), the *Gnomica Homoeomata* edited by A. Elter, Bonn, 1902–1904; another *Florilegium* edited by H. Schenkl in *Wiener Studien* 1889, etc.[83] There are also the gnomologies that arrived by the Arabic route, with no citations of Christian authors.

These gnomologies bear witness to the continuing presence in Byzantium of gnomologies of classic authors from Antiquity, whom we may or may not know, depending on the case: some are monographic gnomologies, others mixed. We have seen many of the *gnômai* in Antiquity in various sources. This is a tradition that without doubt penetrated the one initiated by Johannes Damascenus (see below) but that maintained its vigor even without him.

The very fact that in these gnomologies there frequently appear series with maxims of one author (sometimes with his name, sometimes with the indication "by the same person"), shows that there were monographic gnomologies that were later fused together. And the repetitions within a single gnomology plus the gaps in some with respect to others can be interpreted in the same way.

2. *Sacred-profane gnomologies*

These contain citations of both ancient Greek and Christian literature. Their starting point, as is generally recognized, is found in the confluence of ancient gnomologies with that of the *Hiera*, a Christian gnomology by John of Damascus that cites in the first place the Old and New Testaments and then Basil, followed by the other Fathers. But we have already indicated the antecedents: the presence of texts from the Old Testament together with pagan ones in papyri from the 3rd century A.D., the appearance

83 See M. Richard, "Florilèges spirituels grecs", in *Dictionnaire de Spiritualité*, XXXIII–XXXIV, Paris, 1962, p. 488.

of diverse Christian elements in the gnomologies. The contact was close from an early date: from the time of Saint Paul there are clear indications of the use of gnomologies in authors whom we have mentioned, such as Gregory of Nazianzus (who rebelled against Julian's prohibition against the Christians studying the old Hellenic works).

One can therefore understand the frescoes of the Byzantine age in which Christian saints and Greek sages appear together, as in the Georgian Monastery of the Iberians on Athos, in the Church of the Nativity in Arbanassi (Bulgaria) and in the Cathedral of the Annunciation in the Kremlin.

Then too, at an early date there appeared anthologies by Origen, Basil (one, cited above, has reached us), and Gregory of Nyssa. The true synthesis, however, does not appear to have begun before the 6th century, although it was Johannes Damascenus who gave it its great impulse, as I have said[84].

Note that in the gnomologies of our Arabic-Castilian texts there is a considerable Christian element but only one explicitly Christian gnomology, that of Gregory in *Bocados* (possibly one by Basil also). There are no Christian authors in Ibn Durayd's Arabic gnomology.

Characteristic, then, of the Byzantine age beginning with Photius is this flowering of the sacred-profane gnomologies based on the *Hiera*, which I will explain: this is a work known only from various extracts, with a first book, alphabetized by authors, on God, a second one, also alphabetical, on man, and a third one, this time organized by opposing themes, on virtues and vices[85]. Now the generally accepted theory today is that Maximus Confessor (an apocryphal name, of course) from which derive almost all later gnomologies, comes from the fusion with the *Hiera* of an extensive gnomology, drawn from earlier ones, preserved in the 14th century manuscript *Paris. Gr.* 1168[86].

84 On all this see the cited art. "Florilegium" by H. Chadwick, col. 1145 ff., and M. Richards' cited article also. In the *Clavis Patrum Graecorum* 3, Turnhout, Brepols, 1979, pp. 511 ff. and *Supplementum*, 1998, pp. 462 ff. can be found a complete listing of the works of John of Damascus that have been preserved.

85 In M. Richard, op. cit., col. 480 ff., can be found a long list of gnomologies derived from the *Hiera*.

86 See M. Richard, op. cit., col. 489.

This is what Gutas calls the *Corpus Parisinum (CP)*, which remains inedited[87]. It probably represented an attempt to create a complete gnomology of the wisdom of the ancients (although other partial ones survived, as has been said), of collections that, in the final analysis, have their origin in the Hellenistic age. It was organized by themes and, within these, by authors, as was later the case of Maximus and Antonius, based on the precedents that we are familiar with.

For Gutas[88], from the *CP* must have come an archetypal *gnomologium*, the source in turn of Maximus and Antonius, among others, although the *CP* must itself have included other sources, namely *excerpta* of orators and maxims by Philistion, Isocrates, Democritus and Menander. Maximus added the Christian maxims of the *Hiera*.

The opinion of P. Odorico, author of the most complete study of the said *Corpus*[89] (although it is still only an outline) is different and more nuanced. He considers that after a period in which there were some religious and some profane gnomologies, whose sources he investigates to a certain extent, the *Corpus Parisinum* represents a fusion of both types and from it come Maximus and other later gnomologies. As for the Christian maxims, besides Johannes Damascenus other sources were used, just as Maximus uses, in turn, other sources besides the *CP*. A detailed study of the enormous tangle of Byzantine gnomologies, many, like this one, unpublished, is still pending.

The fact is that the principal derived work and the Byzanatine gnomology most widely disseminated is the one falsely attributed to Maximus Confessor: a gnomology without doubt from the 9th century with a revised edition in the 10th, plus other abbreviated ones, very badly edited to be sure. We continue to use Migne's edition. And what has already been said of other gnomologies must be said here: the text shows traces of the use of monographic collections of the different philosophers.

So then, from Maximus come the *loci communes* by Antonius Melissa, which add things from the *Hiera* and other gnomologies. And from Maximus come several more Byzantine gnomologies: the *Baroccianum* gnomol-

87 See Gutas, *Greek Wisdom Literature*, cited above, pp. 11 ff., where this manuscript is analyzed in detail, giving its content.

88 See the table on p. 34 of his book

89 P. Odorico, "Il 'Corpus Parisinum' e la fase costitutiva dei florilegi sacro-profani", in *Studi Bizantini e Neogreci, Atti del IV Congresso Nazionale di Studi Bizantini*, Galatina, Congedo, 1983, pp. 417–429.

ogy, the *Laurentianum*, the *Mutinense*, the gnomology of Georgides (alphabetical, sometimes with an indication of the author), etc.; not the *Atheniense*, which is independent, although it, too, is sacred-profane[90]. Writers of a later date than those cited by Maximus appear. The extensive collection of Arsenius Apostolius can be added. And we must bear in mind that the Greek tradition of *paroemia*, or proverbs, which has a long history[91], finds frequent points of contact with the gnomological tradition.

We must also add the collection of *Anekdota* of the so-called Georgides[92], an alphabetical collection that includes the origin of the maxims in the entries: "from Basil, from Gregory, from Plato, from Aristotle", etc.

Thus, in Maximus, Antonius and the other Byzantine gnomologies we find maxims derived from and coinciding with the ancient gnomological tradition, and other patristic ones from Christian gnomology and other sources. We can, therefore, find maxims that also appear in the Arabic-Castilian and Arabic texts, and this by reason of these ancient sources. But they belong to a branch that split off and became autonomous in 9th century Byzantium, just as, I believe, the branch we find in the texts I am studying split off and became anonymous in the 7th–8th centuries in the Orient.

3. *Monastic gnomologies*

This is a genre that flourished on the base of the ancient antecedents that we have studied, adding multiple instances of *excerpta* and *catenae*; we cannot enter into detail here. The most notable are the *Questions and Replies* (we have spoken of the genre already) by Anastasius Sinaita (7th century), the *Doctrina Patrum de Incarnatione Verbi*, of the same date. And in the 11th century, the great *Synagoge* of ascetic doctrines of the Fathers, the work of Paul Evergetis[93].

90 See M. Richard, op. cit., col. 294 ff.

91 Published (except for several later items) in the *Corpus Paroemiagraphorum Graecorum* by E. L. von Leutsch and R. G. Schneidewin, Göttingen, 1838 (reedited Hildesheim 1965), 2 vols. See Mariño-García Romero, op. cit., pp. 9 ff. (with a translation of the most important items).

92 In J. F. Boissonade *Anecdota Graeca*, I, Hildesheim, 1962, pp. 1 ff.

93 See M. Richard, op. cit., col. 499 ff., and H.-G. Beck, *Kirche und Theologische Literatur im Byzantinischen Reich*, Munich, Beck, 1959, pp. 442 ff. and 587 ff.

But even before that we find the *Ekthesis* of Agapetus addressed to Justinian: a collection of maxims to educate the king, with influences that come from Isocrates, Basil (his *Homily* on the thirteenth anniversary of the coronation of Constantine), of Philo, etc.[94]

Once again, there is nothing that says that a part of this material, the oldest, might not have entered our texts, although this is difficult to see without a databank of the entire Greek gnomology. And it is not very likely, because our texts, as I have said, contain ancient wisdom, as well as Christian, moral and ascetic, but not theological, wisdom, attributed with a single exception, to the ancient Greek sages or given anonymously.

VIII. Conclusion

Ancient sapiential literature, especially the sub-genres, intimately bound to each other, of *Lives* and gnomologies, and the genres of the novel and pseudo-epigraphic letters, entered Byzantium in the 6th and 7th centuries, under an ever-increasing Christian influence. There was also a clear influence of Neo-Pythagorism and of Hermetism. Traces of all this remain, but they are scarcer in European Byzantium, where the iconoclastic movement played havoc with this literature. There are remains of the literature on Alexander, and ancient gnomologies were saved in the libraries. But when literary activity was resumed in the 9th century, everything was reduced to gnomologies and specialized genres such as fables and letters.

In their conquest of the Orient, however, it seems that the Arabs found a series of Greek works (and translations of them into Syriac) which, although they had the same roots, differed in that

a) they preserved to a considerable extent the scheme *Life* + gnomology, which promoted the creation of new novelesque *Lives*;
b) in these works the impact of Neo-Pythagorism and Hermetism, which continued under the Arabs, seems greater;
c) the impact of the Christian religion, with the conception of the ancient sages as ascetics and almost saints, was also greater.

94 See P. Henry III, "A Mirror for Justinian: the *Ekthesis* of Agapetus Diaconus", *GRBS* 8, 1967, pp. 281–308.

So, if I began by pointing out the Greek origin of our works (which should never have been in any doubt), and if the existence of enormous parallels in Greek sapiential literature is evident, then it is clear that in our works there is a somewhat "special" Greek genre, derived from earlier works and related to what we have seen in Byzantium, but special all the same. This is the genre of Greek sapiential literature contaminated with Pythagorism, Hermetism and Christianity from late Byzantine Syria and Egypt, which the Arabs conquered.

Now, to document the maxims of our treatises (and the Arabic ones that were not translated) is an uncertain undertaking. This is because we lack an instrument like a great databank, as I have said. And furthermore because it is quite possible that in many cases we could be dealing with new creations built on Greek, Pythagorean, Hermetic or Christian foundations. All these cultural areas need to be explored in order to find exact or close parallels. But the general lines are clear.

In the following chapters we will attempt to situate in the cultural panorama that we have presented some of the gnomologies and the combinations of *Life* + gnomology from the works we are studying. A complete study cannot be expected of all the authors or of any of them exhaustively, but we do believe that a certain approximation can be attained within the guidelines given.

Because if our first chapter established the Greek, or more precisely the late Greek character of the sapiential works that were translated into Arabic, and many into Castilian, and here we have added certain facts on their origin in the Byzantine and Syriac Orient around the 7th century, in the following chapters we are obliged to provide further information.

Chapter 3

The Greek Models for the Themes of Aristotle and Alexander

I. Aristotle and Alexander in our treatises

1. Overview

We do not have the Greek originals of the three treatises, *Buenos Proverbios, Poridad* and *Bocados*, nor of the *Donzella Theodor*, only the translations in Arabic and the Castilian translations of the Arabic ones, in both cases in texts not always supported by the entire tradition. Nevertheless, we maintained in the first chapter of this book that, if not the complete works themselves, elements of these works, later combined in them, come precisely from Greek. And based on these works, the original texts can, to a great extent, be reconstructed.

Two prior cautions should be kept in mind. First, that we are doubtless dealing with works from the first Byzantine period, between the 6th and the early 8th centuries, judging from a series of characteristic features and from the very fact that some of the Arabic translations are from the Ommiad period, the rest from the 9th century and later. Secondly, that these works are, nevertheless, the final phase in a process of accumulation of strata and revisions that began in the Hellenistic period (and even earlier), and continued throughout the entire Roman epoch, as we have seen, and into the Syriac, Arabic and Castilian epochs.

The ideal situation would be to be able to reconstruct those accumulated layers and the process of their formation, as regards both the contents that were gradually added and the literary forms used. There would still remain, of course, the problem of the when and how of the organization of these elements in our works. And the problem of the possible, at times certain, later elements already mentioned: the Byzantine, Syriac, Arabic and

Castilian elements. All of this has been discussed at length in the preceding chapter, and now the time has come to deal with each work in detail.

We shall begin with the study of the two closely related themes of Alexander and Aristotle. They have their own structure within some of the works. I have already given a general idea; now I shall add more precise details, in order to consider, in a second phase, the question of their Greek origins, comparing what appears in our treatises with what we know from other sources. And comparing, too, the conception of Alexander with the various conceptions existing in Greek literature.

We shall study, one by one, the three treatises in which our theme appears. It is necessary to analyze them and establish certain previous conclusions prior to entering upon our real theme: the search for the Greek elements in the three.

2. *Buenos Proverbios*

There are three sections which interest us and which we will call "Education and wisdom of Aristotle" (I), "Education and wisdom of Alexander" (II) and "Aphorisms and letters of wisdom on the death of Alexander" (III). These sections, which could be linked together in a continuous whole with a *Life* of Alexander, are nevertheless preceded (before Section I), separated from each other (between Sections I and II) and followed (after Section III) by various sapiential elements.

On the other hand, all narration of the conquests of Alexander is missing; we only have allusions to his wisdom and good governance. It is perfectly clear that the Alexander theme must be considered sapiential literature; it is far distanced from the theme of wars and heroic deeds and from the many criticisms of his exploits and conduct.

1. Education and wisdom of Aristotle. There is an entire narration, which begins in VI (after the "seals of the Philosophers", their "meetings" and teachings and the "lessons and counsels of Socrates and Plato") when, after the failure of Nitaforius, son of the king, Aristotle demonstrates his wisdom, that is, his maxims. In VII, he is chosen by Plato as his disciple and becomes "a wise man and philosopher and one who knows all these ten arts." There follows, after VII, a sapiential interlude.

   VI begins with a novelesque element: the king creates a school for his son Nitaforius and makes Plato his teacher. But Nitaforius was "of little understanding and did not learn anything." On the other hand, Aristotle, Nitaforius's *sergente* or page, was *"moço pequeño sin padre y sin madre y pobre"* (a small boy with no father or mother and poor); he listened to the lessons and learned, he was *"mucho entendido y mucho agudo"* (very skilled and very keen).

The moment of the examination came, in the palace with royal pomp: Nitaforius was unable to *"fablar una palabra de quanto avie oydo de su maestro"* (to repeat a word of all he had heard from his teacher). Plato then asked whether any of those present wished to come to the dais and recite the doctrine that he had taught; and Aristotle came forward.

For the second time Aristotle's poor physical presence is mentioned: *"subio mal arropado e mal vestido y començo de fablar que semejava una calandria"* (he came up badly cloaked and badly dressed and began to speak like a lark), but he demonstrated all the wisdom of Plato, so that Nitaforius was not made king and, instead, favors were granted to Aristotle, with whom everyone was very pleased.

The narrator Johaniçio (Hunayn, see our first chapter) then says that Aristotle gave thanks and praised the great man to whom he owed his philosophy. And there follows a series of maxims. The first are given below:

> *Con el pensamiento agudo alcança omne consejo a las cosas graves.*
> (By thinking shrewdly, one attains advice on serious things.)
>
> *Mansamente puede omne mejor aver las cosas que demanda.*
> (With gentleness one can best obtain the things he asks for.)

Justice, gentleness, moderation, health, friendship, suffering, thinking, truth, fear of God are the themes; greed and hypocrisy are rejected, the immutability of nature is taught: the typical Socratic-Cynic philosophy with nothing really Aristotelian. It all culminates in VII with the instruction in the ten arts at the side of Plato, who accepts Aristotle as his disciple: *y fue sabio y philosopho y sabidor de estas diez artes* (and he was wise, a philosopher and proficient in these ten arts).

What is notable about this part is the novelesque opening: the great celebration before the palace of the king of the Greeks, the examination on wisdom. We have the king and the philosopher who is going to teach his son, and the son fails; and there is the young page who becomes a disciple of the philosopher. The origins of this theme will be discussed below. For the moment, we take note of the majestic luxury in a royal setting, but above all, of the opposition Nitaforius/Aristotle, the former, the son of a king but with little intelligence, the latter a poor page, unkempt, but open to learning. We shall see the traditional elements with which this narrative was constructed.

2. Education and wisdom of Alexander. The preceding part is merely a prologue: after a series of chapters (from VIII to XIII) with a sapiential theme (meetings of philosophers, maxims of Socrates and Plato, with some of Aristotle's mixed in) that situate the foregoing within the general framework of philosophy, especially Socratic-Platonic philosophy, the narrative continues. Curiously enough, the teachings of Aristotle are not mentioned, they are taken for granted, just as Alexander's conquests are.

   In XIV to XVI there are three letters from Aristotle to Alexander, in which the conquests of the latter are implicitly understood. The first two are reported; the third is literal. It recommends to Alexander los *"saberes ondrados"* (the honest arts), and above all to do good to the people, not to treat them as slaves, *"vencer con el bien"* (conquer by good treatment), in order to be loved, to achieve fame *"de tu alteza y tus buenos fechos"* (for your greatness and your good works).The third letter ends with an explanation of the appellation *"señor de los dos cabos"* (lord of the two horns) given to Alexander. In XVII Alexander demonstrates that, as Aristotle said, sadness destroys the heart, a demonstration of the master's wisdom.

   We are clearly in the presence of an epistolary novel in which Aristotle teaches Alexander good governance. It is followed by a chapter of dialogues (XVIII): Alexander consults Aristotle about how to choose *"omnes que me fagan servicio"* (men who will serve me well); then come questions that Alexander answers wisely. There are dialogues of Alexander with his confidants, among which has been inserted a question to Plato about government (reply: *"comedir y pensar de noche en pro de su pueblo y de día mandarlo fazer"* [reflect on it and think about it at night for the good of your people and by day have it done]). It concludes with the dialogue between Alexander and the gravedigger who, living in the cemetery, finds no difference between the bones of kings and those of slaves. And Alexander confesses that he cannot give him what he wants: youth without old age, wealth without poverty, joy without sorrow, health without sickness. This is a theme that comes from the *Dialogue between Alexander and the Gymnosophists*, in the Pseudo-Callisthenes.

As can be seen, there is a mixture of themes here: advice to Alexander about government, aphorisms of wisdom from Alexander, and a Cynic dialogue on death and the limitation of human power. Without doubt this is in preparation for the third part, on the death of Alexander, which commences directly thereafter in XIX. Alexander has become a learned man in matters of government, of human life and of death. But if he sometimes asks for advice and other times gives it, in the end we have the Cynic sage as opposed to the king. There is also a mixture of various traditions. But the moralizing of Alexander the king continues, as does the censure of the adverse versions of the Cynics and various other thinkers that will be discussed later.

3. Aphorisms and letters of wisdom on the death of Alexander. XIX. This transcribes the letter of consolation sent by Alexander to his mother when he learned that he was to die from the poison that he had been given to drink by order of Antipater. It is placed between the receipt of this news and the reception that Alexander's mother, following his instructions, organizes after his death. It is the recognition of the fact that everything grows and then wanes, of the example of so many fallen glories, of the wise man's capacity to be consoled. In XX there is another letter of consolation, in poetic tones: no reign endures forever, the grasses wither, nothing is everlasting except the coming century. In XXI the mother replies that she will soon follow him.

   XXII narrates how they placed Alexander in the golden casket and took him to Alexandria, to his mother; her words (*"buen vivo fuestes e buen muerto sodes"* [you were a good man in life and you are good in death]), expressions of grief by her ladies. XXIII, which follows, goes back to a meeting of philosophers in Babylonia: the eldest speaks and asks the others to express words that would be of consolation for those who are good and an example as well as a punishment for those who are bad. Ascetic-Cynic words on death: everyone envied Alexander; now everyone grieves for him; he came poor and he departs poor; in life he must have had great need for this intelligence and this silence; he hid his gold and now he is hidden by gold, etc. The wife of Alexander speaks, as do his steward and other functionaries. On arrival at Alexandria, another scene of mourning, in which the mother participates, followed by "others", ending with the mother. In XXIV, Alexander is buried in the presence of a congregation of philosophers; the mourning of the philosophers alternating with the mother's.

XXV. After the funeral we have the letter of consolation from Aristotle to the mother ("the lord of the whole earth is powerful"), followed by the mother's words and, when she retires to her chamber, the maxims of the philosophers. In XXVI, the mother replies in a Christian tenor: we must thank God for what he has given instead of lamenting what he has taken away.

It is interesting to note that this whole part follows immediately upon the previous one with no mention of Alexander's deeds: we go from his education and his wisdom directly to his death and the letters and maxims of Aristotle, to the mother, her ladies, the officials of the house, the philosophers. But it is not a matter of there being anything missing. All that interests the author is the wisdom of Plato, Aristotle and Alexander, and the lesson of Alexander's death. After this there is an added passage, secondary without doubt, with aphorisms of Diogenes and Pythagoras, just as there are before I and between I and II.

Apart from this, the composition of the whole seems to be unified, proceeding in III just as in I and II. We have the following elements:

1. Brief comments by the narrator, which bind the other elements together.
2. Letters: two from Alexander to his mother, one from the mother to Alexander, one from Aristotle to Alexander's mother and, closing the collection, her reply. In total, five letters.
3. Repeated manifestations of grief on the part of the philosophers and the others, and finally on the part of the mother. All this takes place in various acts: when Alexander is placed in the tomb (the court ladies); in Babylonia (the philosophers, Alexander's wife, the officials); on arriving in Alexandria (mourning of the mother and "others"); at the funeral (the mother and the philosophers); after the funeral and the letter from Aristotle (the philosophers).

These three elements are perfectly combined in a crescendo; they give the impression of reproducing exactly an ancient novel composed in part of letters, in part of aphorisms, about family and home (Alexander's mother and his wife, the court ladies, the functionaries). It would seem that the author is imitating the funeral rites of Hector in the *Iliad*, but with the addition of the philosophers, who can almost be said to have the role of monks or Christian men of the church. Because this whole funerary part, the grief because of death and the ensuing consolation, together with an undeniably Cynic background, has an equally undeniable Christian character. I do not believe I am wrong in attributing it to the first Byzantine period, but the themes and literary forms are older. Beginning with the Pseudo-Callisthenes, a remarkable effort was made in eliminating some elements, reinforcing others, thereby creating a harmonious whole. I will return to this theme.

3. Poridad de Poridades

I feel that this treatise has been discussed sufficiently in the first chapter. Nevertheless, I must emphasize that we are dealing here with something that is, without doubt, an Arabic text well differentiated from the so-called oriental version, which was translated into Latin with the title *Secretum Secretorum*. Basically, the latter contains numerous accretions which are added to those proposed for a previous phase, Syriac or perhaps Ommiad Arabic, common to both versions.[1]

Not to be excluded either are additions to the occidental version, which was translated into Arabic by the Nestorian Christian Yahya ibn al-Batrik, John son of Patrick. Certain coincidences with *Buenos Proverbios* can be the result of having been borrowed by the author of that translation, Hunayn; but they could also be from a common source. One certain addition to the *Poridad* is, as I have said, the *Lapidarium*[2].

The Alexander/Aristotle theme is inserted in this work in connection with the exterior prologue of the book, by the translator ibn al-Batrik, though supposedly composed by Aristotle. Following the narration of how the caliph charged the translator with finding the book by Aristotle, it consists of the following elements:

1. The narrator, evidently the translator, talks of the old age of Aristotle, who had been made a governor by Alexander, of his humility and his

1 See L. Kasten, "Poridat de poridades. A Spanish Form of the Western Text of the Secretum Secretorum", *Romance Philology* 5, 1951–1952, pp. 180–190. See also the papers by M. Manzalaoui and M. Grignaschi cited below.

2 Besides the bibliography given in my first article, see M. Manzalaoui, "The pseudo-Aristotelian Kitāb Sirr al-āsrār", *Oriens*, 23–24, 1974, pp. 147–247.

love of justice and truth, and of his death. He also speaks of Alexander's conquests.

2. He transcribes two letters: Alexander wants to kill certain rebellious Persian lords, but he asks Aristotle for advice. Aristotle's rely is not to kill them but, on the contrary, to treat them well so that they will truly love him. Narration: Alexander does this and Persia is well-governed.
3. After relating the discovery of the book (in the temple of Homer the Greater or Hermes Trismegistus), the narrator goes on to say that in the book he found there was a letter from Aristotle that answered a previous one from Alexander in which the latter had requested his presence and his help. As that is impossible, Aristotle sends his advice in this letter, counsels which must be kept secret so that nothing evil will happen to him. What follows is the letter, actually a book on government.

In this way different elements are skillfully combined:

1. An exterior prologue, the conventional theme of the discovery of the book, which introduces the theme of the secret, thereby anticipating what Aristotle will say later. This is clearly the work of al-Batrik.
2. An outline of the life and death of Aristotle, the great philosopher.
3. A set of two pairs of letters (one of them is only alluded to), linked by the narrator's account. Aristotle appears as the good counselor, Alexander as the faithful disciple.
4. A real doctrinal treatise presented as a letter, all of Aristotle's second one, after the introduction.

There are differences and similarities with *Buenos Proverbios*. Aristotle's entry into philosophy is not discussed; there is, however, a brief summary of it. And the relation teacher/disciple is reduced to an epistolary exchange after the conquests, in a setting provided by the narrator. All of this presupposes the dialogues of *Buenos Proverbios* XIV; they are two versions of the same thing: the theme of the good philosopher and the good king. What happens is that *Poridad* has abbreviated Aristotle's letters and the advice given in *Buenos Proverbios*, leaving them as a mere anticipation of the following treatise, but there are notable coincidences:

Buenos Proverbios	*Poridad*
Enseñorate sobre los pueblos haciendoles bien y merced y avras su amor, que mas durable sera el tu	mas avet los con bien fazer et amar vos an de coraçon, que el uuestro

señorío con facerles algo y merçet	bien fecho uos dara mas
que el señorío que fuere con fuerça	su amor que non uuestra braueza
Y sepas que quando los pueblos	que el pueblo, quando
pueden dezir, pueden fazer	puede de dezir, puede fazer

(*Buenos Proverbios:* Rule over your peoples treating them well and favoring them and you will have their love and your rule will be longer if you do something for them graciously than if your rule were by force and know that when the people can speak, they can act.)
(*Poridad:* But keep them with good treatment and they will love you from the heart, because your good actions will give you their love more than your harsh ways because when the people can speak, they can act.)

I consider that the epistolary novel of *Buenos Proverbios,* with its prologue on the education of Aristotle, is the older. See below for more on this novel. Here we have made a very brief initial summary: a picture of Aristotle, his life and death, plus a few brief citations of his advice given by letter. And this has been used for the authentic innovation: the letter-program for government, a real "mirror for princes". And something more has been added: from the theme of the secret doctrine, which, as we shall see, has an ancient tradition, was derived, in Antiquity or in the Arabic epoch, the inclusion of the Hermetic tradition. All of this is, without doubt, a work from the late Greek epoch on the theme of royalty, but with older Greek foundations. It presupposes the original of *Buenos Proverbios*, but the central ideas are maintained and a new literary form has been created.

And actually, in the body of advice to Alexander a new content has been created which brings together the teachings that I would call Socratic-Cynic, the Christian teachings and those addressed to royalty, that is, those that are appropriate for a sovereign in a Hellenistic, Roman or Byzantine court. From the theme of the moderate and just conduct of the king the text goes on to the themes of body and soul and of the administration of the kingdom and the command of the armies. To give some examples (using page numbers from Kasten's edition):

In the first treatise (pp. 33 ff.) the dominant theme is "give" to whoever needs it when he needs it; the king must not "demand" of his people more than what they can give, as this causes rebellion and death. Then follows the theme of "sense" or understanding: this is where truth comes from and from truth comes the fear of god. There is the criticism of the "desires" or passions: one must not satisfy them because in that way man acquires a bestial and covetous nature. This whole moralizing ethic continues in the second treatise (pp. 36 ff.) with the criticism of *"sanna"* or wrath, and preaches a return to "sense" or reason and obedience to the law.

But this same treatise passes on to a different current: the king should dress well, not speak overmuch, allow himself to be seen only at a distance and surrounded by his men; the people will enjoy seeing him like that. At the same time he should favor them economically and not impose tolls, causing wealth to increase (and the king's rents to increase also). Then the treatise returns to the restrictions that the king must impose upon himself in eating, drinking, sleeping, avoiding fornication, "which is of the nature of the swine" (it debilitates the body and makes a man dependent on women).

The text returns again to the advisability of the king's sometimes eating with his confidants and nobles in order to keep them friendly. He should be sedate and not laugh. The king should only promise what he can fulfill. And he should care for his soul, which is noble and celestial. And he should study astronomy, this is the most curious point.

The third treatise (pp. 42 ff.) speaks of justice: it is the "image of the mind"; the laws rule and the people obey them through justice. Next comes the fourth treatise (p. 44) which emphasizes the idea that true understanding comes from philosophy. God made the mind and then the soul and put them in the body of man; the mind is like the king, the soul like his governor. The treatise goes on to a Hermetic context (νοῦς and ψυχή). And when it gives a definition of what a governor or a minister should be like, the skills of understanding and wisdom combine again with those of the body. The fifth treatise (pp. 49 ff.), about manners, opens with a definition of man, comparing him with qualities of animals: he is strong as a lion, cowardly as a hare, villainous as a crow, etc. – a comparison of popular wisdom that is found again in *La Donzella Teodor* (p. 40 Mettmann).

The counsels continue on clerks, rent collectors, the envoys of the king, the good knights, battles and armies. The people are the treasure of the king; no one must be permitted to commit "any harmful or arrogant act" against them. And advice is given for the battlefield: how to insure the defense of one's own army, frighten the opponent, maintain the king's safety.

The author, at times covering one theme in the manner of the gnomologies, at other times mixing several themes, has managed to combine moral wisdom of the Socratic-Cynic type (control of reason, self-control, asceticism, justice) with that of the benefit granted to the people, in material matters as well, and the organization of the court and the army. What appears to be the underlying doctrine is that of virtue: besides being valuable in its own right, it is politically advantageous. The book adds some curious prejudices to this, such as the belief in the maidens of India who kill with their sweat or that one must avoid naming blond governors (because of the Goths, so greatly feared after their victory at Hadrianopolis in 378?). And there are misogynous echoes (Cynic or simply popular), together with other Hermetic ones (Hermes is quoted, p. 45, as well as in the prologue) and Christian ones, as I have said, but passages like the following one (p. 41) can also be mentioned: *"Guardat uuestra alma que es noble et çelestial, et la tenedes acomendada, et non seades de los torpes que non se quieren guardar"* (Guard your soul, which is noble and celestial, and you have it placed in trust, and do not be one of those fools who do not want to be guarded). From time to time there are added to the parenesis illustrative "figures" or similes, plus constant references to India and Persia.

A work between learned and popular, well organized as a whole, chaotic at times, combining the Alexander theme with various parenetic ones; all of it, in the end, depends on ancient models and themes like those of the popular wisdom of the *Lives* and sapiential works that have a Cynic orientation. On hypotheses regarding Arabic reworking, see what is said below with reference to an article by M. Manzalaoui.

4. *Bocados de Oro*

The scheme is different: we have several *"Fechos de Aristotiles"* (deeds of Aristotle) (pp. 98 ff.) followed by *"Castigos de Aristotiles"* (counsels of Aristotle) (pp. 101 ff.); then *"Fechos de Alixandre"* (deeds of Alexander) (p. 117 ff. Crombach), followed by *"Castigos de Alixandre"* (counsels of Alexander) (pp. 133 ff.). Here we have the fusion of a *Life* of Aristotle not too far removed from the facts plus a series of his maxims and a novelesque narration of the life of Alexander derived fundamentally from the Pseudo-Callisthenes, but with a great deal of innovation, plus a series of maxims that come from the Greek gnomologies. The result is one more unit within the extensive gnomology that forms the *Bocados*, as we have seen. In any case, the innovations are significant and deserve to be studied at the opportune time.

I will indicate the most important "deeds", citing by Crombach's page numbers, in order to be able to discuss the characteristics of the Greek model translated:

a) Aristotle's Deeds

P. 98. Birth of Aristotle, genealogy, arrival in Athens "land of the sages", his defense of grammarians and versifiers; he hears Plato in the Academy and becomes head of it when Plato goes to Sicily for the second time.

P. 99. After Plato dies, Philip has Aristotle return to Macedonia; and when Alexander goes to Asia, he returns to Athens but has to go back to Stagira for fear that they might do the same to him as they did to Socrates at the instigation of one of the priests, because *"non adorava los idolos"* (he did not worship the idols). He gave alms and benefits and provided Stagira with laws; and the citizens wanted to be close to his bones: this made their understanding more acute.

P. 100. There is a reference to his disciples ("kings and sons of kings") and his books, some words by Plato and a physical description.

As can be seen, from a few minimal historical details and the cognizance of the phrase attributed to Aristotle to the effect that he did not want the Athenians to sin against philosophy for a second time, without mentioning many details but including the teachings imparted to Alexander, the author turns Aristotle into a kind of Christian saint who gives alms and performs works of charity, does not worship idols and leaves his bones almost as relics; but a saint who gives "intelligence". The physiognomy is typically Byzantine.

b) Aristotle's Maxims

Their origin will be discussed below; simply an idea of them will be given here. Let me point out the following:

1. They are often addressed to Alexander. They are of the moralistic type that we are familiar with, frequently connected with the theme of the kingdom: 37 the people should not be considered an inheritance but rather friends and relations, 40 good people obey *"por el bien fazer"* (to do what is right), 41 his anger should be neither very strong nor very weak, 42 (letter) it is the duty of the king to promulgate fine laws, and conquer and populate uninhabited lands, 43 he must excuse mistakes, 46 (and also 12) achieving good results in a lasting rule, 77 the king must be gentle, 78 he must want to be the master of slaves and not of free men.

2. At other times they are addressed to his disciples or are simple maxims, sometimes quite long, as much as half a page, very frequently on the theme of the king. There are the themes of avoiding greed and lying (8, 10, 93, 95, 122, 123), of the wise man (16) and wisdom (20, it is the weapon of the soul and the mirror of the mind, cf. 50, 64, 115), of rule and truth (22), of the law (27), of justice (38, 39 "if the king is not just, he is not the king"), of speech and maintaining silence (61, 72, 75), of love (82 "the best love is the oldest", cf. 117), of understanding (14 no one is without defects, one must pardon for the sake of the goodness that there may be) etc. We find typically Socratic themes like "death is better than performing ugly acts" (105) or "the diminishing of knowledge is the reason for evil" (106). Present also is the theme of the body and soul joined to divine fortune (98, 99) and to wisdom (84, 85), and the typically Cynic theme of saving from a shipwreck what is floating along with one (58, cf. Phaedrus 4,23 *mecum mea sunt cuncta*, said by Simonides in a shipwreck), and the *amicus Plato* (52), and a quote from the *Celumundi*, that is, from the Pseudo-Aristotelian *De caelo* (128).
3. There are also Christian elements: emphasis on how transitory this world is and how long-lasting is the other (4, 6, 30, 35, 36), the king should make his reign the vassal of his faith, not vice versa (22), piety, law and fear of God are combined (27), God favors who loves Him and wisdom both (112), in exchange for what God caused him to win, Alexander should pardon what He wants to take from him (114). Disdain for wealth to gain other riches (spiritual, is understood of course) is illustrated in 60 with an anecdote (the philosopher neglects his estate) traditionally attributed to Anaxagorus.

In short, there is the same atmosphere, between Socratic-Cynic (of the "education of princes", of Alexander and in general) and Christian (of *Poridad*). And the theme of the secret that must be kept by the king (24). And there are almost literal coincidences, like the theme of the *"buena nombradía"* (good name/fame) of the king in *Poridad*, p. 35 and *Bocados* 1 (also in *Buenos Proverbios*, p. 97); the theme of the relation between the king's "giving" and merits and opportunity in *Poridad*, p. 33 and *Bocados* 19; the figure of the world as a garden, its wall is the kingdom, it is defended by the laws, which the king establishes, etc. (with variants, in *Poridad*, p. 43 and *Bocados* 129). In *Buenos Proverbios* there are more coincidences: the saying that he who has the power to speak, has the power to act (p. 94), the one about not being the lord of slaves (p. 95), the aphorisms against cruelty and wrath (p. 96).

But literal coincidences are rare and one gets the impression that the version of *Bocados*, much shorter and more exact in examples like that of the figure of speech describing the world as a garden, comes from gnomologies that were in turn the source of *Poridad.* In *Buenos Pröverbios* the same maxims are found in letters: they may have passed from there to the gnomologies or vice versa. Nevertheless, the form of *Poridad* is original, while the presence of Aristotle and Alexander in the gnomologies and letters is older.

It is evident that *Bocados* takes elements from an Aristotle gnomology centering on the theme of the kingdom and advice to the king; it has added, at the beginning, a *Life* that fits in badly, and has put at the end another combination of *Life* + gnomology. This combination is the one intimately related to Alexander, but which, nevertheless, has a very different orientation in the *Life* part.

c) Alexander's Deeds

P. 117. Taus (Attalus; Pausanias in the Pseudo-Callisthenes), enamored of Olympias, Philip's wife, tries to murder him. Olympias tells Alexander to kill Taus and Alexander wounds him, but Philip, who is still alive, is the one who finally kills him. Philip gives Alexander to Aristotle as a disciple.

P. 118. With Philip dead, Alexander addresses the people: I am *"vuestro desengañador e vuestro amador"* (the one who reprimands you and loves you), fear God and take as your king *"a el que mejor piensa del pueblo e al que mayor piedat aya de los vuestros pobres"* (the one who best thinks of the people and the most compassion has for your poor). They raise him up as king.

P. 119. A letter from Alexander to the governors of his kingdom: God is my lord, let him who has *"seso e conoscimiento"* (intelligence and understanding) not adore idols, images made by the hand of man. He addresses his peoples by letter, everyone admires him. And he refuses to pay the tribute to Darius: the goose that laid the golden eggs is killed.

P. 120. He was the first to cause all Greeks to have a king. He departs for Egypt. A letter from Darius to the Tyrians calling Alexander a thief; a letter from Darius to Alexander, "the thief", saying that the king of heaven made him king of the earth, that Alexander crowned himself;

this is the "madness of the Greeks"; he must take the crown off. He adds other insults.

P. 121. Alexander wants to decapitate the messengers because they call him a thief and he wants to *"fazer fecho de ladron"* (act like a thief). But he pardons them so they will see his mercy *"so cercano del omildoso e alongado del sobervioso"* (close to the humble and far from the proud) (does this recall Virgil, *Aeneid* VI 853?). He writes to Darius: *"no tengas que eres dios, mas eres ome arrufado"* (don't think you are god, you are just a braggart). He adds words of mockery.

P. 122. Conquests of Alexander. The Tyrians say that they did not open the gates to him because they feared Darius; he tells them to open the gates, that he will not enter. Victory over Darius, capture of his family.

P. 123. Darius writes to Alexander begging for mercy. Two of his generals wound him with their swords, Alexander weeps for him.

P. 124. Darius kisses his hand and tells him not to trust this world. He entrusts his women to Alexander. Darius dies and Alexander buries him and puts his assassins to death. He burns the books of the gentiles and their temples, and he founds cities.

P. 125. A letter from his mother: she wants to know how many treasures Alexander has accumulated. He orders the list to be given to her; she only wants to know the amount. A letter to Porus, king of India saying that he should pass into the service of his god, the creator of both of them, and he should send his idols to Alexander. Porus sends him a reply that is *"dura e brava"* (hard and fierce).

P. 126. Stratagem in the campaign against Porus; duel between Alexander and Porus, who turns around on hearing a supernatural voice and is killed.

P. 127. A visit to the Brahmans. When Alexander asks them what they want from him, they ask him to make them live forever. And as the Macedonian replies that he cannot do this, they ask the reason, then, for so many short-lived conquests. Alexander says that he obeys God, who has sent him. A reference to the letter to Aristotle on the marvels of India.

P. 128. The king of Çuy gives him fabulous treasures, he makes conquests. Anecdotes: Alexander incognito at a trial, another about the city where there was no judge.

Pp. 129–130. The warning of the astrologers; Alexander must dismount from his horse and learns that the hour of his death has come. He dictates a letter of consolation for his mother: all things must return to matter; on the day of his death his mother should invite many men from Libya, Greece, Macedonia and Asia to dine.

P. 131. They place him in the golden casket. The sages and princes carry him on their shoulders; the oldest expresses his grief and asks each sage for a maxim.

P. 132. They arrive in Alexandria: the mother's weeping and aphorisms of the sages (not reproduced literally). The banquet. Summary of the life of Alexander; a physical description.

This *Life* invites comparison with that of the Pseudo-Callisthenes in its various versions, something that has not been done, to my knowledge. It is, in essence, a summary of the oldest version with a few additions of its own (see below). To the *Life* have been added aphorisms imitating the combination *Life* + aphorisms (see below also); actually, it summarizes *Buenos Proverbios*. Of course it has undergone a process of Christianization and of elimination of the fantastic and novelesque elements. And it contains nothing about the relation with Aristotle, a theme apparently considered exhausted in the previous chapter

d) Alexander's Maxims

This is a gnomology of brief maxims: presented either individually in the manner of aphorisms or as replies to questions or reactions to certain incidents *(khreîai)*. They are of the ideology we are now familiar with, but with little Christian influence (though in 1 and 2 we do have: to fear God and to obey God is better than sinning).

References to the theme of the kingdom are found, cf. 6 (Alexander does not consider as a day of his reign the day in which he performed no beneficial act), 12 (the king should think at night and order it done by day), 13 (what pleased him most about being king was giving awards), 14 (how to choose his men), 16 (not to be a king of slaves), 22 (win the love of men by doing good), 26 (have many friends and do good to your enemies, cf. 45), 38 (the obedience of the people and the justice of the king keep the kingdom in order, cf. 33). They are an echo of aphorisms that we already know, and, as always, the themes of mind and knowledge (37, 46) and of doing good (40) dominate. Cynic aphorisms are added, for example, against women (8, 20, 39), against greed (43), that it is better to have good sense than good clothing (9), disdain toward nobility (35), the theme of the person who could not distinguish the bones of kings from the others (we have already seen this in *Buenos Proverbios*), etc.

What is notable is that among these maxims some stand out that are well known from the Pseudo-Callisthenes, such as 14 (Alexander's reply to Aristotle in I 16), 20 and 39 (Alexander's conduct with Darius' women and the Amazons), and others from the gnomologies (for example 10, if the beggar does not deserve money, Alexander deserves to give it); 18, the superiority of the teacher over the father). We will return to this. The impression is that *Buenos Proverbios* has reworked its sources to a lesser extent, that there are fewer additions and more traditional material.

5. *First conclusions on the Greek models for the Aristotle/Alexander theme*

We have before us three Greek works of the Byzantine epoch but based on older Greek texts. What the translators of *Buenos Proverbios* and *Poridad* say should not be doubted, nor does anyone believe that *Bocados* is not a translation. A different matter is that these works should contain certain Syriac or Arabic additions which, on the other hand, within the Greek tradition represent an accumulation and reworking of earlier elements.

Arabic additions, without doubt, are the external prologues of *Buenos Proverbios* and *Poridad*, in which the translators, following a widespread tradition, relate in a rather novelistic form the discovery of the original works that they are translating.

To the Arabs must surely be attributed the inclusion in *Buenos Proverbios* of previous (before VI), intermediate (from VII to XIII) and final (XXVII to XXIX) sapiential elements which, furthermore, are Greek, although it is not impossible that this unification, secondary in any case, was already present in the Greek manuscript that Hunayn copied. The same possibility exists for the inclusion in *Bocados*, together with the material on Aristotle and Alexander, of other sapiential material, Greek also, of course. This is the case of the story of Anchos in *Buenos Proverbios* I: the cranes caused the murderers of this poet to be punished, a story derived from Ibycus's legend of the cranes. And the same is true of the Hermetic elements of *Poridad* and *Bocados*, which might have been added by the Arab translators but could also have been present in the Byzantine model. In any event, they are Greek, from a school that flourished from the 2nd century on, especially in Egypt.

As for minor additions, Arabic or Castilian, they do not seem to be important and in any case, they are not easily detectable with the knowledge we have at the present time. For on the one hand, the Greek models are known to us only indirectly, leading into a vicious circle, and on the other hand, the Arabic text of *Buenos Proverbios* has not been published, only the text of *Bocados* (Badawi 1958) and the "long version" of *Poridad* (Badawi 1954). And numerous other problems remain, as will be seen below.

But I must repeat that aside from the above-mentioned external prologues, there is hardly anything left in the treatises that is Arabic or Muslim; or in our version of *La Donzella Teodor* either, but in other versions there is. As for the Castilian references, as far as we can see they are limited to details of the vocabulary and to institutional adaptation, since the royal and Christian setting comes from the Byzantine model.

This is what must be reconstructed for the three works with the Aristotle/Alexander theme, and from there, their oldest Greek sources. The exclusion of ancient Greece and the monarchical and Christian background lead us, in effect, to Byzantium and specifically to its ecclesiastical circles. A maxim like 22 of *Bocados* (the king must subject his kingdom to his faith, not vice versa) illustrates their thinking. We have already discussed the phenomena of the "Byzantinization" of earlier literary texts in a previous chapter. We will see the details of this process in a comparison with an old source such as the Pseudo-Callisthenes, although it is quite possible that the Christian elements increased in an intermediate Syriac phase (see below).

As for the date, it is clear that if the translations into Syriac and Arabic began in the 7th and 8th centuries with the Ommiads and the first Abbassids, the Greek texts must be from the 6th, or no later than the early 7th century, as I said above. I remarked that the reference to the fact that "the moors paint in their mosques" (*Buenos Proverbios*, p. 55) points to the Ommiad epoch. And in *Bocados* the obsession with idols, *"imajen de mano fecha"*, (an image made by hand), the religious books and the sanctuaries of fire (see pp. 119, 124, 127) take us to the epoch of the iconoclasts and of the Abbassids, beginning in the middle of the 8th century, and to Greek manuscripts of the area: Syria and Egypt.

For *Poridad*, whose translator speaks of Greek and Syriac phases of the work, M. Manzalaoui[3] has proposed an origin in the Hellenism of Syria and even of the Persia conquered by the Arabs, and also for an epistolary novel

3 M. Manzalaoui, art. cit., pp. 160 ff.

which is reflected in our works. M. Grignaschi[4] has proposed Ommiad and early Abbassid phases, with the attribution to al-Batrik being secondary: from this work would come, after various revisions, the "long" or oriental version (whose Arabic text Badawi published in 1954) and the short or western version. All this will be discussed below.

Returning to the date of the Byzantine originals: if they cannot be later than the 7th century or beginning of the 8th, neither can they be earlier. The 6th century, the century of Justinian, is still a cultured period with Greek Antiquity still relatively close, but the Christian circles of Syria were a different world. The 7th and 8th centuries are the period of cultural decadence in Byzantium, where, nevertheless, sapiential literature continued to be cultivated. From this literature come, for example, various versions of the Pseudo-Callisthenes, the *Barlaam*, the Vindobonense Collection of Aesop's fables and the gnomologies that combined pagan and Christian material (but only material up to the 6th century) and that continued later in the 9th and 10th centuries. Here we can also include the Pseudo-Ammonius, with biographical details about Aristotle.

On the other hand, we have found coincidences within all the treatises we are studying, coincidences in conception, regarding moralistic intention and royal and Christian government, and specific coincidences in the maxims. They all drank from the same sources and profess the same ideas. And they all belong to the same type of literature, between popular and doctrinal, with a background part Cynic, part Christian. They are, without doubt, ecclesiastical work that attempts to influence the people and even the emperors. Aristotle appears as the defender of grammarians and versifiers!

Thus, what we have, in the end, are three works of the early Byzantine epoch, but works derived from a previous tradition. In Syriac Christianity they suffered additions and reworking of a doctrinal type, and others, not doctrinal, in the Arabic period plus some minor ones in the Castilian epoch. The same is true in the case of *La Donzella Teodor*, which we will study separately.

Now then, what interests us is to reconstruct the original models of the Aristotle/Alexander theme, which either the Byzantines or their Syriac or Arab continuers augmented in certain cases, clearly with Byzantine elements also. This model is, for *Buenos Proverbios*, a sapiential work on Aris-

4 See his works cited in note Ch. 1, note 14.

totle and Alexander to which were added initial, central and final elements, as I have said; for *Poridad*, the entire text except the external prologue and perhaps the Hermetic elements; for *Bocados*, the parts about Aristotle and Alexander, augmented with gnomological elements of the same antiquity and orientation.

Presented below are several schemes that could have been the models for our three treatises:

a) The model for Buenos Proverbios

The introduction is a novelette on the education of Aristotle and Alexander; the choice of the former as a disciple of Plato is followed by a series of his maxims. Then a narrator strings together:

a) a series of letters from Aristotle to Alexander, giving him advice on governing;
b) a series of *"enseñamientos de Alixandre"* (lessons of Alexander): he asks Aristotle and Plato for advice on governing, proffers maxims and answers various of his nobles and other people;
c) a series of letters between Alexander, his mother and Aristotle, the last one a letter of consolation on Alexander's death. They are connected in turn with a series of scenes in which the philosophers, the mother, the wife, household functionaries and relatives pronounce words of wisdom on the themes of death, of all that is transitory, of all that is human and of the power of God.

The historical or pseudo-historical narrative element that can be found in the Pseudo-Callisthenes has been reduced to a minimum: Alexander as the disciple of Aristotle (the relation of the latter and Plato is added), the conquests as a background, the omen of death, the poisoning, the golden casket, the removal to Alexandria, the burial. This is a work that is well organized but of a different character. It is not a biography but rather a doctrinal treatise composed in a form that is between novelistic, epistolary and aphoristic, quite within the literary tendencies favored by the Cynics: see, for example, Plutarch's *Banquet of the Seven Wise Men*. It shows us the king-philosopher and speaks at length of death.

Almost nothing remains of the oldest Pseudo-Callisthenes except the figure of Alexander, and genres like the consolatory letter and the maxims of Socratic-Cynic-Christian philosophy are intermingled. The work is the culmination and synthesis of various traditions. We will return to this.

b) The model for Poridad

My comments are limited to our text, the western, or abbreviated version.

Leaving aside the introduction, we have a well-composed work that summarizes the biographical element (a note on the life of Aristotle and his relation with Alexander) and the element of letters of advice from the preceptor to the king; there are two letters (Alexander asks for advice/ Aristotle replies), plus a reference to another letter from Alexander and Aristotle's long reply – a true doctrinal treatise.

The whole thing gives the impression that the traditional material has been reduced to the minimum, transforming the old epistolary novel into a letter-treatise, and to do this it presents the picture of an elderly Aristotle, unable to give advice directly. Of the old material there remain only the two letters mentioned, where Alexander is shown accepting the lessons of his teacher, all of which produces good government in consequence. We will see its reflection in Arabic works, and I have already said that successive reworkings and additions of Syriac and Arabic origin have been suggested.

The theme of good government is the link that remains with *Buenos Proverbios* and with the tradition from which both works are derived. Starting here, there was created a very personal work, evidently influenced by the genre of the epistolary novel, by the "mirror for princes", to which we must return, and by the gnomologies. I have already pointed out coincidences with the other works that we are studying which we attribute to common sources.

The material relating to the Hermetic theme, of which I have already spoken, must be added here. Whether it was added by the Syriac or Arabic translator or was already present in the Byzantine model, it is clear that it coincides completely with the title, and with what Aristotle says at the beginning of his long letter (p. 32 Kasten): *"onde conjuro a uos, rey, como conjuraron a mi, que lo tengades en poridad, ca el que descubre su poridad non es seguro que mal danno no le uenga"* (whereby I entreat you, King, as I was entreated, to keep this secret, as he who reveals his secret cannot be sure that evil harm may not come to him). The theme of the secret it also found in *Bocados* 24 and reflects both the general theme of "maintaining silence" in the three treatises and the tradition regarding the secret among the Pythagoreans and the Aristotelians.

In this respect I refer to the letter from Alexander to Aristotle and the latter's reply in Simplicius, *In Physicorum* I 1 (also in Plutarch's *Life of Alexan-*

der): Alexander criticizes Aristotle for having published his acroamatic works, asking "how are we different now from the others?", and Aristotle replies that he has published some and others no, but that "they are only comprehensible for those who have heard us."

The imperative of the secret reached the Hermetics, to whom there are references in *Poridad*, both with regard to these philosophies and to the mysteries and to various Hellenistic religions. As is known, they flourished beginning in the 2nd century A.D. The most probable conclusion is that in the Byzantine treatise that we are discussing this assimilation of Hermetism and Aristotelianism had already appeared.

c) The model for Bocados de Oro

Still pending here is the matter of the moment of the synthesis of the two segments *Life* + maxims that interest us here (those of Aristotle and Alexander), and of the others. In any case, their characteristics are the same as in the other treatises: their interest is in morality and government, their orientation is Socratic-Cynic-Christian, their setting and date early Byzantine. As for their originality, the combination *Life* + maxims is ancient, it had already appeared in the 4th century applied to Socrates and Diogenes.

But, there are still the details. The *Life* of Aristotle seems to be a creation of the Christian type, whose parallels must be found. Alexander's *Life* depends basically on the Pseudo-Callisthenes: here the process of reworking and the degree of originality can really be studied. In this the treatise differs from the others, although the maxims sometimes coincide. As for the gnomologies of Aristotle and Alexander, they should be compared with what is preserved of the Greek and Arabic gnomologies to see whether, along with their dependency, which is great, there is anything original, added by the author or from sources that are not available to us.

After this study of the material on Aristotle and Alexander in the three treatises, there still remains the study of the gnomological material not contained in them, which we have pointed out, and of course, the *Historia de la donzella Teodor*, with its novelistic and sapiential elements.

II. Aristotle and Alexander: ancient and Byzantine precedents

1. The images of Alexander in antiquity

I think that before investigating the prehistory – sources and composition – of the three Byzantine texts we have studied, texts that have been selected from the broader category of Arabic translations and their Castilian versions, it would be helpful to describe the image of Alexander that they offer and situate it within the tradition related to him: a brief introduction to the various images of Alexander in Antiquity and those described here as well. But after that, in a second phase, it will be necessary to compare the image of Alexander in the old Pseudo-Callisthenes and some of its medieval versions with that of our treatises. We shall be able to see what lines they reject, what lines they follow, what new things they contribute.

On this subject I have written an article cited above (Ch. 1, note 47). Based on this and other bibliography[5], I give an outline of the theme from the point of view that interests us here. Only by working from the different ancient views of Alexander can we situate those of the Pseudo-Callisthenes, those of the other writers, those of the gnomologies and those of our treatises.

But these diverse views or images, in turn, can only be understood if we consider the image that Alexander himself tried to promote and the negative impact that the reality of his life had on it.

I will discuss the matter briefly as I do not want to repeat myself. But the fact is that in Athens there were reservations and resentment (which led

5 See the abundant bibiography that I cite in that chapter, as well as my "Aristoteles en la Atenas de su tiempo", *Estudios Clásicos* 108, 1955, pp. 43–55, also with bibliography. An overall view can be found in the article by P. Hadot, "Fürstenspiegel", *Reallexikon für Antike und Christentum*, VIII, Stuttgart, 1972, pp. 582 ff. On the position of the Cynics, my "Elementos cínicos ..." and my "Géneros helenísticos ..." cit., as well as "Política cínica en las fábulas esópicas", in *Filologia e forme letterarie. Studi offerti a Francesco della Corte,* Urbino, Università degli Studi di Urbino, 1987, I, pp. 413–426. Also the unpublished thesis of Juan Pedro Oliver, *Los diálogos entre el rey y el sabio en época helenística*, Murcia, 1988, whose original the author has kindly permitted me to consult. And for the Middle Ages, the book by G. Cary, cited above repeatedly, and my "Alejandro, Plutarco y las gnomologías griegas", in *Plutarc a la seva època: paideia i societat. Actas del VIII Simposio Internacional de la Sociedad Española de Plutarquistas*, Barcelona 2005, pp. 33–50.

to armed rebellion, as is known) against the Macedonians in general and against Philip and Alexander in particular and against Aristotle as well. And this for a number of reasons: they were all disapproved of because they were Macedonians and the two kings because they were rivals of Athens, representing, besides, a political system abhorred in Athens: the monarchy.

Faced with this inimical situation, Alexander reacted on the one hand, by making political gestures in favor of Athens (for example, returning the statues of the tyrannicides that he recovered in Persia), and on the other hand, by creating his own image. He surrounded himself with a group of writers or philosophers (like Callisthenes, the nephew of Aristotle and author of a panegyric history, Eumenes, who wrote his *Ephemerides*, Anaxarchus and others) and artists like Apelles, Pirgoteles and Lysippus, who had the "exclusive" on portraits, engravings and sculptures. The image sought for was that of his heroic virtues, his generosity, his sense of friendship, his justice, his holding to the rules and not taking advantage of the circumstances to "steal a victory", his benevolence toward the conquered: Darius, his women, the Persians in general.

It should be noted that in Athens itself, even then, in the 4th century B.C., a pro-monarchic ideology was emerging which combined in the king the ideals of peace and unity, good government, justice and morality; this can be seen in Plato *(Politicus)*, Xenophon *(Agesilaus, Cyropedia)* and Isocrates *(Evagoras, To Demonicus, To Nicocles, Nicocles, Philip)*. In a worn-out century, Alexander had awakened the imagination, he was a second Achilles, and he wanted to make the idea of monarchy palatable using this romanticism accompanied by a more or less diffuse Socratism. Actually, it was the official ideology of the Hellenistic monarchs, also of the Roman principality and even of contemporary India[6]. Alexander is always the model, imitated and copied (sometimes grotesquely) by Caesar, Augustus, Caligula, Nero, Titus, Trajan and Caracalla, not to mention the medieval and renaissance monarchs.

Now in the case of Alexander the official image was soon shattered, after the battle of Gaugamela in 331, because of his pro-Persian policy that neither the Macedonians nor the Greeks could support beyond a certain limit. They did not accept the *proskýnesis* or adoration that was accorded to the Persian monarch; they viewed with a critical eye his pretension to be the

6 See my *Asóka. Edictos de la Ley Sagrada*, 2nd ed., Barcelona, Apóstrofe, 2002, pp. 65 ff.

son of Ammon; they accepted unwillingly the Persian wives that Alexander gave them (only Seleucus kept his).

Thus the Peripatetics distanced themselves, as Alexander did not follow Aristotle's advice (in Plutarch, *De Alexandri fortuna* 6) to treat the Greeks like a leader and the barbarians like a master. And there was a conflict with Callisthenes, dead, at Alexander's orders, in unclear circumstances, which cooled his relation with Aristotle. There followed more sanguinary acts: his father's old generals and his friends were murdered: Philotas, Parmenio, Clitus, the pages. His image was tarnished because of these deaths and because of his excesses and drunkenness, but of course the Pseudo-Callisthenes spreads a veil over all this.

This is why Alexander's image is irremediably split in two: that of the hero who is at the same time a good king, even a philosopher-king, and that of the conqueror by fire and sword, the man who respects nothing. It is quite clear that the Pseudo-Callisthenes and our treatises reflect the first image and that this was the model in the writings of Aristotle addressed to him, the *On ruling* and the *Alexander or on colonization.* From the former comes the phrase "Today I did not govern because I performed no beneficial act" that appears in *Bocados* 6 (and is attributed to Titus in Suetonius, *Titus* 8, and other sources).

But what has been said above is not sufficient if one does not take into account the position of the Cynic school, where the open attack on power was traditional. In the Cynic collections of *khreîai* we find harsh anecdotes about the confrontations, more supposed than real, between Cynics and kings or tyrants, with the acid words of the former. In my publications already cited I have mentioned them: Diogenes confronting Philip, Antipater, Perdiccas and Alexander; Bion opposing Antigonus Gonatas; Aesop challenging his master, Croesus, and the Delphians. The Cynics also attack Sardanapalus and the oriental despots. And hence a thousand debates between the philosopher and the king: Nagasena and the king Milinda in India, Secundus and Epictetus against Hadrian in Rome, Niloxenus and Amasis in Egypt (in the *Banquet of the Seven Wise Men*), sages and Jewish rabbis before powerful Greek, Roman and Jewish figures in the *Hagaddah.*

With respect to Alexander, then, we have in later literature the hostility that we have seen and that is reflected in well-known anecdotes, but there was also another position that saw in Alexander the good king, the philosopher king that some representatives of the Cynic sect, Dion Chrysostom is the best known, advocated. This favorable position is attributed to Onesicritus, who accompanied the conqueror. No doubt he saw points in common with the doctrine of the sect and Alexander's behavior: his freedom in the face of prejudices, his efforts in the service of men, his feeling that the unity of men is more important than nations or social and family origins.

Consequently the position of the Macedonian is ambiguous in the familiar tale of Alexander and the Gymnosophists, which is in the Pseudo-Callisthenes and has left its imprint on our treatises. Without entering into the complexity of variants and sources, in the old Pseudo-Callisthenes, whose basic story is considered to be from the 2nd century B.C., the position of Alexander is, I repeat, ambiguous (cf. III 6). With the Gymnosophists he plays the traditional role of the king or the person in power before the sage. They tell him that his business is to make war, theirs to philosophize; they speak to him of death, they say that man is the most destructive animal, that monarchy is "an unjust power".

The main Gymnosophist, Dandamis, does not stand up before Alexander, nor does he salute him as king; he speaks of his simple life, says that he is mortal and criticizes Alexander's conquests. And nevertheless, Alexander admits that he, too, is mortal. His defense is providence, which moves the world. He takes his leave amicably.

All this comes, in one way or another, from Onesicritus, a disciple of Diogenes, who wrote a work, *How Alexander was educated*, which is, without doubt, at the bottom of the favorable view of Alexander on the part of one sector of Cynicism. It is perfectly clear that the disdain for necessities, wealth and institutions made the Greeks identify the Indian Gymnosophists or "naked ascetics" with the Cynics. Thus, in certain versions of the story we are discussing Onesicritus was sent by Alexander to the Gymnosophists Calanus and Dandamis (Strabo 15.1, 63–67, Plutarch, *Alex.* 65) asking them to come to him, as he wanted to hear their wisdom. The former acceded to the request, astonished at the existence of a philosopher-king. The fact is that there is a certain agreement, and in the versions in which there is a confrontation with a threat of death, Alexander comports himself generously in the end[7]. But the Pseudo-Callisthenes suppresses these threats and others in Strabo, not wanting to ruin Alexander's reputation.

7 See "Elementos cínicos ...", cit., pp. 321 ff.; Merkelbach, op. cit., pp. 51 ff. and 104; and (with much more detail) Pedro Oliver, *Los diálogos entre el rey y el sabio en época helenística*, unpublished doctoral thesis, Murcia, 1988. As Merkelbach says, our Pseudo-

Note that in the medieval version of *Bocados* (p. 127) Alexander justifies himself because he is obeying the will of God, who has sent him. And that in this work p. 133, and in *Buenos Proverbios*, p. 104, there is an echo of that version in the story of Alexander and the man who lived in the cemetery and could not distinguish the bones of kings from those of other people. The Cynic resonances are preserved.

Something similar happens with the theme of Nectanebus, the pharaoh-magus who, disguised as Ammon, managed to deceive Olympias and engender Alexander. Although it comes, to be sure, from the sacred Egyptian legend about the origin of the pharaohs, there is no doubt that this is a Cynic response to Alexander's pretension, so hateful for the Greeks, that he was the son of Ammon[8]. This character has been completely eliminated in the medieval versions. And earlier, in the Pseudo-Callisthenes, an inversion of the theme takes place: it is Alexander who causes the death of Nectanebus; he pushes him into a hole while he is contemplating the stars. He justifies himself with the words, "Without knowing what there is on earth, you study the heavens."

I have explained elsewhere[9] that this is a theme that the Cynics took from Plato, *Tht.* 174a (an anecdote about Thales, who fell into a well because he was looking at the stars): they criticize pure science and astrology; they attend to the things of the earth. Alexander plays the role of the Cynic opposing the astrologer. There is, at the same time, the punishment of the magus, who receives honorable burial just the same. In short, the theme of Cynic hostility to Alexander disappears. What is interesting is that in our treatises there appear traces of the image of Alexander as an astrologer characteristic of a later date.

To sum up, both in the Pseudo-Callisthenes and in the works derived from it that were the model for our medieval texts, the image of Alexander

---

Callisthenes has greatly abbreviated the original narrative, which is preserved in other sources, papyrological among others (it is reconstructed in H. van Thiel's edition, *Leben und Taten Alexanders von Makedonien*, Darmstadt, 1974, pp. 242 ff.). It has eliminated the "wisdom debate" where Alexander threatens with death the Gymnosophists who answer his questions incorrectly and everyone else for that matter. In spite of the fact that the narrative ends with Alexander's magnanimity, our version has taken a more radical direction, suppressing any threats, like the version mentioned in the text.

8 On these coincidences with the Egyptian legend of Tinufis see Mª Paz López Martínez, *Fragmentos papiráceos de novela griega*, Alicante, Universidad, 1998, pp. 254 ff.

9 *Historia de la fábula greco-latina*, III, 1987, p. 64 (67 of the English edition).

as king and philosopher prevailed. Later we will see details; here we simply point out that this is an image created by Alexander himself in the context of a specific line of thought, and that it was an image propagated by the Cynics, among others. Therefore, we have the association of Alexander with their doctrine, understood in the very broad sense that we have explained.

In the historians in general and in the echoes of his name in the ancient and medieval epochs there are, naturally, many more variants. Plutarch admires him, kings and emperors imitate him. But other historians express doubt, like Arrian and Quintus Curtius, who cannot conceal his excesses. The philosophers and moralists like Cicero and Seneca excoriate him as do many medieval writers. None of this passed into the current that we are dealing with here: it was strictly censured; this is also true of the other Alexander, the hero of the marvelous adventures of the Byzantine, Jewish, Arabic and medieval European tradition.

It must be pointed out here that the figure of Alexander the philosopher reached its culmination in the Cynic-Stoic tradition, perhaps beginning with the *How Alexander was educated* and was already clear in Plutarch's *De fortuna Alexandri*. Actually he did nothing more than provide the model for the tradition of the "mirror for princes" in Isocrates, Xenophon and other authors already mentioned, among them Aristotle himself in two lost works (*On reigning* and *Alexander, or on colonization*). Plutarch saw as the key moment in Alexander's career the time when he refused to follow Aristotle's advice about different treatment for Greeks and barbarians, with the result that from then on the idea of a king of the world, a *Kosmokrator*, who should unite men, a true representative of God, was attached to the figure of Alexander[10].

Really, in authors like Aristotle, in the *Letter of Aristeas* and various Hellenistic writings, the *Monumentum Ancyranum*, in Diotogenes, Philo, Seneca, Musonius, the Roman and Greek panegyrists, the rhetor Menander, Plutarch, Dion Chrysostom, Marcus Aurelius, Julian, Themistius, and Christian writers such as Synesius, Eusebius, Augustine or Agapetus we find the idea of the good king as a compendium of all the virtues, a true representative

10 On all of this see P. Hadot, art. cit., pp. 582 ff., and M. Grignaschi, "La figure d'Alexandre chez les arabes et sa genèse", *Arabic Sciences and Philosophy* 3, 1993, pp. 205–234. Actually, in his time Isocrates demanded of the kings, as the best service to the gods, the cultivation of justice; their real virtues are love of men and of the city *(A Nicocles)*.

of God, an idea that contributed to the conception of Alexander as a monotheistic, or even Christian saint in the following epoch[11]. See more on this topic in Chapter IV, and also in ancient Hermetism[12].

Nevertheless, going back, Alexander is, for the line of the Pseudo-Callisthenes that we are following, only an example of government that is just and beneficial for the people, because, I must repeat, there was added to this moralistic line the theme of his skills of government that bring prosperity to the nation. These are complementary matters: our texts are explicit in the sense that just government (and the fear of God in the Christian amplification) brings prosperity and success.

2. *Aristotle and Alexander in the old Pseudo-Callisthenes*

As is known, we normally call the author or compiler of the novel of Alexander that we have been discussing "Pseudo-Callisthenes": an Alexandrian author who, probably in the 3rd century A.D., more or less stitched together preexisting elements, namely: a narrative of the deeds of Alexander, very probably from the 1st century B.C., written in choliambics, a popular meter; a novel in letters, most probably from the 2nd century A.D., from which he selected certain of them (we know of more from other sources); a text on Alexander's final days, from shortly after the death of the Macedonian; and a letter from Alexander to Aristotle about the marvels of India. The encounter with the Gymnosophists is of earlier origin[13].

"Callisthenes" is the name of Aristotle's nephew, a historian who accompanied Alexander, a name which the anonymous compiler appropriated for himself. The work is one of many pseudo-authored texts of the late period. Doubtless the compiler took this name because the *History* of the real Callisthenes, which went as far as the year 330 (he died after his con-

11 See P. Hadot, art. cit., pp. 587 ff.

12 See M. Grignaschi, art. cit., p. 212.

13 On all of this see Merkelbach, op. cit. L. Bergson, *Carmina praecipue choliambica apud Pseudo-Callisthenem reperta*, Stockholm, Almqvist, 1989, has reconstructed, as far as possible, the choliambics of the *Life of Alexander* put into prose by the compiler. In my *Historia de la fábula greco-latina*, I, Madrid, 1979, pp. 551 ff. (pp. 538 ff. in the English translation, Leiden, 1999), I explain that this meter was usual in the popular literature favored by the Cynics and related circles in the Hellenistic epoch.

frontation with Alexander regarding the theme of the *proskýnesis*), was a historical panegyric, as was all the material included in his work.

It was widely disseminated in the Middle Ages in Greek recensions and translations in various languages. But for the moment we will look at the oldest known version in order to define more closely its relation to the theme of Alexander: we have already said that it is a true panegyric. We know the oldest version through a Greek recension called *a* (it has lacunae and errors) and from two traditions closely related to it but not exactly the same: the Latin version by Julius Valerius and the Armenian one[14]. There has been no attempt to reconstruct a prototype.

I begin with recension *a*, pointing out only a few key moments, and then explain that it is a fabric of deeds and prophecies, plus mythical and fantastic elements, all to the greater glory of the hero. Rather than present the life of Alexander systematically, it emphasizes individual incidents, small or great, true or false, and attempts to attract the reader with the marvelous and with feats of bravery and generosity. Naturally it makes no mention of the tragic confrontation between Alexander and his generals and friends or of the political problems in general. We have already seen how it changes the sense of the episode of Nectanebus and how it criticizes the episode of the Gymnosophists. All this is common to the narrative, originally in choliambics, and to the letters, and it will be accentuated in the Byzantine version that was translated into Castilian. We will also see how other medieval versions treat the topic.

One can point out important moments such as Alexander's birth when the cosmos reaches its plenitude or others in which there are prophecies of greatness, victories and then death for him; or in which he bravely presents himself before Darius, Porus or the Amazons, disguised as a messenger from himself; and dreams, marvelous places, monsters never seen before. Already as a child he teaches his schoolmates (I 13); and soon thereafter shines in his military exercises (I 14); he tames Bucephalus (I 15), and triumphs in the Olympic Games (I 18). He refuses to pay tribute to the Persian (I 23), fights for the freedom of the Greeks (I 25), severs the bridge over the Euphrates so there can be no retreat (II 9), does not accept compromises as he might if he were Parmenio (II 17).

14 Recension *a* was published by W. Kroll, Berlin, Weidmann, 1926. For Julius Valerius there is B. Kubler's edition, Leipzig, Teubner, 1888. For the Armenian version, A. Raabe, Leipzig, 1896 (reprinted Columbia University Press, 1969).

But above all, he is just and at the same time generous: this is true in the case of Nectanebus, as I have said, and also in the marital problem of his parents, whom he reconciles (I 22). His filial piety can also be seen when he makes Philip himself be the one to kill Pausanias, who had tried to assassinate him. He rejects the arrogance of Darius and Porus (I 37, III 2), admits he is a mortal man, not a god (III, 2, 6). He is clement, as with the Athenians (II 5) and with Darius' women (II 12); he feels pity for Darius himself and punishes his assassins (II 21). He has received the teachings of many wise men (I 13); he is already wise as a child in his reply to Aristotle (I 16) when he points out the power of fortune, and later on several occasions before the Asian despots (the defeated Darius accepts this, II 20). He seeks peace, as he tells the Trojans, whom he conquers by persuasion (I 35), as he does the Amazons (III 27). He is just: he leaves the Persians their possessions (II 21). He loves poetry and science: in Troy at the tomb of Achilles he recalls Homer (I 42); in Thebes he respects the house of Pindar (II 46); in Athens he desired to greet the masters, he was not going to wreak vengeance on the theater of liberty (II 5).

There is, then a synthesis of the noble and valiant king and the man who is just and generous, a scholar of ancient philosophy and one who knows the limitations of mortal man. This explains the devotion of the man of the common people who approached his death bed and said, "Now you will abandon us and it would be wonderful for us to die with you." The story continues, "Alexander broke into tears and stretched out his right arm in a gesture of consolation" (III 32).

This is the new image of Alexander, coinciding with that program of his which, in the face of diverse circumstances, failed: the good king, the liberator of his nation, just and accommodating, wise, of a rather Cynic nature. This is the starting point for the much reworked version that was translated into Arabic and then into Castilian.

Not much can be added from the other ancient testimonies of the Pseudo-Callisthenes. That of Julius Valerius adds nothing essential. The Armenian translation adds the exchange of letters with an educator Zeuxis, Philip and Olympias, and Alexander and Aristotle (pp. 36 ff.): Zeuxis complains about Alexander's liberality; Alexander, with all due respect for everyone, defends his freedom. It is not clear whether this comes from the 3rd century A.D. text or if it was added in the 5th century.

3. Aristotle and Alexander in our Byzantine Pseudo-Callisthenes

Now let us pass on to the Byzantine tradition: the tradition that came to us directly in Greek and the one we know through other sources, Syriac, Arabic, Slavic, Ethiopian, etc. We will begin with Greek

These are recensions that derive from *b* (*e*, *g* and *l*) and come from the 5th to the 8th centuries, although there are Byzantine derivatives from the 13th century[15]. In some of them we see an increase in the mythical and legendary component (the theme of Gog and Magog, the entrance into Jerusalem, Alexander the emperor of Rome, the conquest of the West, the victory against the Scythians, etc.) developed more fully later in the Arabic and the medieval Christian tradition.

Of more interest to us is the emphasis on the education of Alexander by Aristotle: he finished all of his instruction and then taught his schoolmates one by one (rec. *g*); he learned quickly, Aristotle is amazed, the children envy him. He asked his mother to let him study astrology under Nectanebus and she did; he becomes the chief of his 200 classmates (rec. *e* and the medieval rec. of Lolos, according to which he learned "writing and Homer"); there is a tribute to his virtues "of soul and body" *(g)*, of his "moderation, valor, fortune" *(e)*. Alexander sets up Aristotle as regent in Macedonia, the same as in *Poridad (g)*, he competes in the chariot races in Rome, where his reception is magnificent (they even make him emperor according to recension *g*!).

All of this is with a very Byzantine ambiance and language and with notable errors. And there is constant reference to "divine providence", to "the decision (νεύματι) of providence from above", and to the cosmic forces that favor him. The tenor is clearly Christian when in *g* III 33 Alexander, in a letter to his mother, remembers that "I invoked the Lord God of the

15 On the relation between the various recensions see, especially, Merkelbach, op. cit., pp. 61 ff., as well as the prologues of the editions. For the Byzantine Pseudo-Callisthenes, see, especially, J. Trumpf's edition of *E* (Stuttgart, Teubner, 1974); of *Γ* (by von U. Von Lauenstein - H. Engelmann and F. Parthe, Meisenheim, 1962–69); of *Λ* with the ms. *L* (edited by H. van Thiel, Darmstadt, 1974 and translated by C. García Gual, *Vida y hazañas de Alejandro de Macedonia*, Madrid, Gredos, 1977). They all come from *B*, a late Antiquity derivative of *a*, the oldest text that we have considered above. Two medieval collections, edited by A. Lolos and V.L. Konstantinopoulos, *Zwei mittelgriechische Prosa-Fassungen des Alexanderromans*, Königstein, A. Hain, 1981–83, also related to *B*, can be added.

Heaven and the Earth" to ask his help against the peoples of Gog and Magog.

In these recensions the number of letters increases: in *l* are added those exchanged with Demosthenes, I have already mentioned those in the Armenian translation, and Merkelbach had already pointed out, with the help of the discoveries of the papyrologists, that the letters in recension *a* of the Pseudo-Callisthenes were only a selection.

Worthy of attention, too, is the treatment of the death of Alexander. It differs from the version of *Buenos Proverbios* and *Bocados*, but it is along the same lines, with extensive passages that are consolatory (I have mentioned above the letter from Alexander to his mother) and threnetic: the Macedonians and Persians weep for him, there are the poignant lamentations of his wife Roxana, he dies reciting verses, leaning on Charmides, with his horse Bucephalus at his feet, and the horse kills the slave who had poured the poison. The Byzantines apparently considered the mourning for Alexander in the Pseudo-Callisthenes insufficient.

And there is no doubt that there were Byzantine sources for the final part of *Buenos Proverbios*, the theme of the death of Alexander, with letters and lamentations of philosophers and family. As I have said, there were some points of departure in the old Pseudo-Callisthenes: the prophecy, the poison, the weeping of the unknown Macedonian, the golden casket. In I 33 is added (only in ms. *L* and recension *l*, both Byzantine) the letter from Alexander to his mother, which is an abridged version, one might say, of the two letters in *Buenos Proverbios* XIX and XX[16].

With this we come once again to the theme of the letters. We can say that the falsely attributed letters and the epistolary novels come from the ancient tradition, from the 4th century B.C.; we will return to this matter. And we have already seen that for the theme of Alexander and Aristotle, the letters, from whatever period they may be, were much more numerous than what the Pseudo-Callisthenes leads us to believe: *Buenos Proverbios* is not alone, by any means, in this multiplicity of letters.

The topic of the letters relating to the death of Alexander is partly ancient, partly Christian; they reflect both the old consolatory letters and the

16 Also in ms. *O* of the Spanish *Libro de Alexandre*, see the edition of J. Cañas, Madrid, Cátedra, 1988, pp. 583 ff. The presence of these themes in Petrus Alphonsus and certain Arab authors is due in part to the Arabic original of *Buenos Proverbios*, but without doubt to other sources as well.

Christian ones. Actually, this whole subject has become a Byzantine ceremonial: the philosophers are almost a kind of Christian priests. But I repeat, the translator Hunayn must have found all this in his Byzantine Greek model, possibly with its Christianization heightened in the Syriac versions.

For one of the letters, Alexander's to his mother before his death, the Byzantine model has been shown quite clearly, as has likewise been made clear for other moments in the life of Alexander (correspondence of Philip, Olympias, Alexander and Zeuxis; of Alexander and Aristotle; of Alexander and Demosthenes). Actually, in Antiquity there was already in circulation a large collection of apocryphal letters between Alexander and Aristotle, of which only a few have come down to us[17]. No doubt in the Byzantine epoch others were added. See what is said below about the Arabic tradition, which preserves even more letters, translated in Damascus.

But this is not only a matter of the letters. The aphorisms and lamentations of the mother, the relations and the philosophers coincide with Cynic and Christian philosophy about the vanity of ambition, power and life: read, for example, Lucian's *Dialogues of the Dead* or certain Christian funeral laments[18]. But this is not only the ancient Byzantine ecclesiastic tradition: even today the funeral lamentation remains alive in Greek popular customs. We know the popular laments, on the part of the mother and the women of the family, even of outsiders who answer as an antiphon as the body is carried from the house to the tomb, during the burial and after it[19]. It is a continuation of the funeral lament in Homer and the tragedy, in the "funerary discourses" of Thucydides and the others. The structure of the lyric dialogue and themes like the eternity of death, the praise of death, the light that goes out and the vegetation that withers are repeated. In short, the mourning for the dead Alexander must be understood within the Byzantine tradition.

And that is not all. The aphorisms of the philosophers and the others who mourn for Alexander in a Cynic-Christian tenor (the universality of death, the nakedness with which one comes to the earth and leaves it, the end of suffering, the passions, the deceptions, the nearness of life and death and the example for everyone), all this is not far removed from what is said

17 See C. Huit, "Les épistolographes grecs, *REG* 2, 1889, p. 161.

18 See M. Alexiou, *The ritual lament in Greek Tradition*, Cambridge, University Press, 1974, p. 33.

19 M. Alexiou, op. cit., pp. 36 ff.

in the consolatory letters of Christian authors like Basil and Gregory of Nazianzus[20], letters that were also heirs of the ancient consolatory tradition.

The sorrow and the sympathy are there, the consolation and the exhortation, at times even in the form of a monody. There is a constant repetition of the theme of the universality of death, the Universe itself is mortal; the theme of the respect for divine will and for Providence; that of the escape from the sorrows and afflictions of life; the theme of "the Lord giveth and the Lord taketh away." And as an example they give the pagan philosophers who abhorred meat, like Anaxarchus, Epictetus and Socrates: the two philosophies meld.

In close connection with all this is the treatment of Alexander in the Byzantine gnomologies. Based on ancient sources, the Byzantine gnomologies (and the Arabic ones derived from them as well as the Castilian ones that we are familiar with) attribute to Alexander the philosopher a series of maxims, not many but much repeated, within this tradition. See below.

In summary, the medieval versions of the Pseudo-Callisthenes introduce and develop elements that come from the epistolary novels to a greater extent than the old version; they promote the image of Alexander as king of the world, favored by divine providence, a model for governors, who is loved by the people; they also give prominence to that final threnetic moment. All of this is oriented in the same direction as the Byzantine works that we know from our Castilian treatises, but without coinciding exactly. I consider that we are dealing with the two branches that I mentioned in the preceding chapter.

4. *Aristotle and Alexander in Byzantine sources known indirectly*

But the Greek versions preserved are only a small part of those that existed. This can be seen from versions in other languages that accentuate on the one hand, the legendary aspect[21], and on the other, and this is what interests us here, the theme of Alexander's wisdom and virtue.

20 See J. F. Mitchell, "Consolatory Letters in Basil and Gregory Nazianzen", *Hermes* 96, 1968, pp. 299–318.

21 I will not go into this point. I direct the reader, apart from other bibliography, to G. Cary, op. cit., pp. 18 ff., E. García Gómez, op. cit., pp. XXI ff. and Manuela Marín, "Legends on Alexander the Great in Moslem Spain", *Graeco-Arabica* 4, 1991, pp. 71–89.

They are based, of course, on Greek sources: in part on the Pseudo-Callisthenes, in part on other texts which are lost today. They are various Arabic versions, at times coming from Greek via Syriac, which I have already mentioned. We can now study them in more detail.

For the life of Aristotle, specifically, we must consider a lost work by Ptolemy Chennos (from which details passed to Hunayn and from there to other Arab writers, and other details to a Pseudo-Ammonius of the 8th century A.D., which had a similar influence), and a *génos* or short biography preceding some works, which, again, had a like influence. Echoes of all this can be found, besides in Hunayn, in Ibn al-Qifti, Ibn Abi Usaibi'ah and al-Mubassir, especially. A. Baumstark and M. Brocker have studied this subject[22].

The fact is that to Ptolemy (who otherwise gives correct biographical details) are attributed the supposed phrases of Plato to the effect that he would begin his explication "when the people arrive" or "when the *noûs* arrives", referring to Aristotle. That Alexander was entrusted to Aristotle was due, according to him, to an oracle at Delphi. From this first source, or from the Pseudo-Ammonius derived from it, comes the story that in Athens the hierophant Eurimedon accused Aristotle of sacrilege because he did not honor the idols (which corresponds with *Poridad*); and the one where in recognition of what he did for the people, a stele was dedicated to him on the Acropolis; it was later destroyed by a certain Himeraios, who for this deed was condemned to death by Antinous (Antipater?).

Here there are, quite clearly, antecedents of the conversion of Aristotle into a kind of Christian saint. This is not the case in the *génos* referred to above, which distinctly does not mention Aristotle in Macedonia and alters the dates considerably. All of this, I repeat, belongs to a Byzantine tradition from which comes, then, this image of Aristotle as a sage and practically a Christian saint in the treatises that we are dealing with.

It is clear that the treatises have sources of the same kind, but more explicit on the theme of Plato/Aristotle/Alexander in its doctrinal-novelesque version. In the Syriac and Ethiopian tradition, which is Byzantine in origin, of course, Alexander was already a pious sovereign, guided in his actions by

22 A. Baumstark, *Aristoteles bei den Syren vom 5. bis 8. Jahrhundert.* Leipzig, Teubner, 1900 [= Aalen, Scientia-Verlag, 1976 (reprint)], especially pp. 36 ff. and pp. 105 ff.: M. Brocker, *Aristoteles als Alexanders Lehrer in der Legende*, Bonn, 1966, cf. pp. 26 ff. on the *Lives* of Hermippus and Ptolemy and their Syriac and Arabic versions.

the Holy Spirit. In the Ethiopian *Novel* his letters begin "from Alexander, servant of God"[23]. In the Arabic *Nihaya* of the 9th century Alexander was nothing more than a plaything in the hands of God; he could not escape his destiny: to roam the world, wage war and collect useless treasures[24].

The coincidence between Ethiopians and Syriacs takes the Christianization of the topic back to the Byzantine epoch, although it is quite possible that the Syriac Christians accentuated it, just as they added so many Christian themes. The Alexander figure as a servant of God, diffuser of monotheism, Christian, Jewish or Muslim saint, combined at times with marvelous deeds, has its origin, then, in late Antiquity and the Byzantine world[25]. From there, via the Arabs, its repercussions reached our Castilian works.

Actually, the conception of Alexander as an imitator of God, who imparts well-being is based on the Christianization, promoted by Basil and his followers, of the "mirror for princes" theme that we have seen ever since Isocrates and even much earlier. It finds its culmination in the one written for Justinian, shortly after he began his reign in 527, by Agapetus, Deacon of Hagia Sophia[26]. The king imitates God by means of good works; he answers only to him, as he is his servant; his reign is a stairway to eternal glory. He controls his passions and cultivates *sophrosýne*. This was the Christian-pagan ideology regarding the empire that dominated in the 6th century A.D., the same ideology as we find in the now familiar versions of the life of Alexander.

But to complete what we know, directly or indirectly, about the Byzantine tradition of the theme of the life and death of Alexander, with its ancient roots of course, and to reconstruct it insofar as possible, it will be helpful to add more arguments taken from the tradition that extends from Greek to Arabic.

23 See S. Alvarado, "Paralelismos entre la literatura etíope clásica y las antiguas literaturas eslavas", *Boletín de la Asociación española de Orientalistas* 34, 1998, p. 328; and E. A. Wallis Budge, *The Alexander Book in Ethiopia*, London, 1933. On Aristotle and Alexander as believers in the Syriac and Arabic tradition, see M. Brocker, op. cit., pp. 79 ff., 83. Also, on the Syriac Christianization of the Alexander legend, S. P. Brock, "The laments of the philosophers over Alexander in Syriac", *Jounal of Semitic Studies*, 15, 1970, pp. 205–218 (especially 216).

24 See M. Grignaschi, "La figure d'Alexandre ...", p. 211.

25 See more details in M. Grignaschi, "La figure d'Alexandre ...", cit., pp. 213 ff.

26 See P. Henry III, "A Mirror for Justinian: the *Ekthesis* of Agapetus Diaconus", *GRBS* 8, 1967, pp. 281–308. The loans from Philo and the coincidences with the *Barlaam* are notable.

To be more specific, I want to take as a basis the epistolary novel studied by M. Grignaschi to which I have alluded above[27]. It is of extraordinary importance for our subject.

This is a text of Greek origin, our author insists repeatedly, a text from the 6th or 7th century, written by a Greek from Egypt or Syria greatly influenced by Hermetism, the Arabic translation of which he attributes to Salim Abu-'l-Alah, a secretary of the caliph Hisham Ibn-Abdel-Malik toward the end of the Ommiad period, in the 7th century. Once again we come upon the oriental Greek tradition and the Syriac one.

It consists of an introduction, various letters (a selection) between Alexander and Aristotle, narrative passages regarding Alexander and maxims spoken at the time of his death. Its point of origin is the Greek Pseudo-Callisthenes, recension *g* (there are coincidences, for example, in the expedition against the Scythians) and perhaps *l* (a letter from Alexander to Olympias). And it contains elements that are clearly gnostic, some Arabic, especially in the letter to the Arabs, which replaces an earlier one preaching monotheism.

I cannot give the contents in detail. The introduction speaks of the work of translation and of the later discovery of the "Letter from Alexander to his mother" which, in effect, is found in various Arabic sources before Hunayn, together with the maxims of the philosophers[28].

The letters comprise a strange mixture. For example, XI and XII enlarge upon the topic, already seen in *Poridad*, of Alexander's question to Aristotle about whether or not to kill the Persian nobles and Aristotle's reply. There is Philip's request that Aristotle instruct Alexander and his reply (I, II and III). There are added letters from Aristotle to Alexander congratulating him on his conquest of Scythia and Anfisan (Babylonia?). Letter IV, from Aristotle to Alexander, emphasizes the need for education. XV is an interces-

27 "Le roman épistolaire classique conservé dans la version arabe de Sālim Abū-l-'Alā", *Le Muséon* 80, 1967, pp. 211–264; and "Les *Rasā'il Aristātālisa ilā-l-Iskandar* de Sālim Abū-l-'Alā et l'activité culturelle à l'époque Omayyade", *Bulletin d'Études Orientales de Damas* 19, 1965–66, pp. 7–83. Cf. the critical comments of G. Endress in *Oriens* 21–22, 1968–69, p. 414.

28 See M. Grignaschi, "Le roman ...", pp. 234 ff. Also M. Brocker, op. cit., and the review by G. Endress in *Oriens*, cit., pp. 411 ff. (especially 414 ff.). F. Rosenthal, *The Classical Heritage in Islam*, London, Routledge, 1975, pp. 126 ff. translates these maxims from another Arabic source, with the names of many Greek philosophers (Plato, Aristotle, Diogenes, Ptolemy, Apollonius of Tyana, etc.) where Hunayn does not give names.

sion in favor of a certain Arhsadis (Arxadis?). XIV, on the nature of the world, is a summary of the Aristotelian *Peri Kósmou* or *De mundo*. Others are elaborations of the medieval versions of the Pseudo-Callisthenes. Grignaschi insists that the letters are a selection: letters alluded to are missing and there are more in other Arab authors.

Through the letters there is a return of themes such as Alexander's duty to conquer Persia and, as *kosmokrátor*, to restore the old monotheistic divine law in the whole world, and also of Hermetic themes, as I have said. And once again we have the problem of whether there is a Syriac intermediary.

In the Arabic works themselves from which the Castilian works are derived, the epistolary novel appears mixed (along with themes like the war against Scythians, Corasmians and Turks) with frequent maxims that constitute recommendations on government, laments on the death of Alexander and ascetic themes. This is part XVI, which, moreover, contains errors such as placing Rufus (1st century A.D.) at the funeral rites of Alexander or having Aristotle converse with Hippocrates. We are accustomed to these errors in the popular Byzantine literature in the period of cultural decadence (in Maximus Confessor Alexander converses with Socrates). Furthermore, Grignaschi has certain doubts about whether the combination formed by the letter to Olympias (missing from our collection) and the funerary maxims belong to the epistolary novel. He also brings up the theme of Aristotle as a magus in letters unrelated to our treatise, for example two in a Syriac manuscript (Vaticanus 209). This coincides with one branch of Hermetism.

I feel that knowledge of the Arabic texts derived from the Alexander literature of the Byzantine age, derivatives with no echo in the West, is very important in order to judge those other derivatives that did pass into Castilian literature. We see that in both cases there is a remote origin in the Pseudo-Callisthenes and other ancient writings (the epistolary novel, the death of Alexander), there are tendencies similar to those of the Byzantine Pseudo-Callisthenes, but there is also testimony of other developments: Byzantine elaborations, lost there but preserved in the Arab world, some passing into Castilian, others, those we are looking at now, no. Unfortunately, we cannot compare them more closely, because there are no translations of this last group of texts, only references in Grignaschi's articles.

As regards the lamentations of the philosophers on the death and burial of Alexander, we have encountered approximations in Greek but no exact models. Nevertheless, they must have come from Byzantine literature; I believe I have demonstrated the verisimilitude of this.

A version that brings us closer to this lost Byzantine one is a version in a different line from that of Hunayn and independent of it, possibly older. This version gives the lamentations in Arabic of Eutichus, patriarch of Alexandria, and in Syriac of Al-Makin and Abu Shakir, from around the year 900[29]. There is some kinship with those of Hunayn but they are, I repeat, independent; both must have come from Byzantine sources now lost: provincial Egyptian sources.

This is, admittedly, a selection of those maxims. Now what is interesting about the collection is that it gives the names of some of the philosophers who proffer them: Aristotle, Theon. Lotas (Philotas?) Metron (?), perhaps Polemon; it also sometimes simply says "another person".

This makes clear the connection of these lamentations with the gnomologies from which most of the Arabs' knowledge of the ancient philosophers was acquired. From the gnomologies also come certain "Sayings of Alexander" in a 7th–8th century manuscript edited by Sachau[30], as well as the Socrates legend in general[31], and so much more, as we shall see. We know the Byzantine gnomologies, at least in part, and also the Arabic texts derived from them. Someone used them to compose these "lamentations", without doubt close to the time of the collections of letters that ended up in the Arabic sapiential works.

All of this is important; it rescues our Castilian texts and their Arabic models from their isolation and incorporates them into a line of literature that has not been preserved for us in Greek, although we do have considerable information about the literary, philosophical and Byzantine religious background that produced them. It is evident that the popular literature about Alexander was abundant and of various kinds: novelesque, moralistic, Cynic, Hermetic, and later Christian. The Syriac and Ethiopian versions are other works derived from the same background, as are, of course, the Arabic ones and, based on these, the Castilian ones.

As an appendix to this, let me present another Arabic testimony already mentioned in the previous chapter: the gnomology that its editor[32], who

29 See S. P. Brock, art. cit.

30 See S. P. Brock, art. cit., p. 16. See also M. Grignaschi, "La figure d'Alexandre ...", art. cit., pp. 205–234.

31 See G. Strohmaier, "Die arabische Sokrateslegende und ihre Ursprünge", in P. Nagel *(ed.), Studia Coptica*, Berlin, Akademie Verlag, 1974, pp. 121–136.

32 D. Gutas, *Greek Wisdom Literature in Arabic Translation. A Study in the Graeco-Arabic Gnomologia*, New Haven, American Oriental Society, 1975. This is a recension of the

translated and published it for the first time, entitles *Philosophical Quartet.* It contains the *Lives* and sayings of Pythagoras, Socrates, Plato and Aristotle, the same scheme as we are already familiar with and that we know of from ancient tradition. And in both *Lives* and maxims there is a resonance of ancient themes that we are also familiar with. Others found in *Buenos Proverbios* and *Poridad* are not repeated here, but it is interesting to point out the parallels.

For example, anecdotes about Aristotle in Plato's school where Plato places Aristotle in the doorway at first ("as befits your age") and later in a lofty seat ("as befits your intelligence"). The likewise familiar themes of calling Aristotle "the people" and "the intellect" are added also, as well as other anecdotes about Plato being irritated or about the man who called him stupid. This in itself shows us the free play of the anecdotes that proliferated around the philosopher.

In this line of tradition, the inclusion of Plato in philosophical theism is clear. When Plato asked what demonstrated the existence of God, Aristotle answered him: "Every part of Creation." At other times we have the ancient gnomological tradition: various maxims are derived from it; others may be, although we have no other testimony.

The same can be said of *Bocados de Oro.* M. Manzalaoui's study to which we referred above alludes again and again to Byzantine and earlier texts that are the basis of the Arabic work. Its translator, Mubassir, was a Syrian from Damascus; it has been suggested that he might have translated from Syriac. We will deal with this work later.

In short, although we do not have Byzantine texts on Alexander and Aristotle translated specifically into Arabic, without doubt sometimes to Syriac first, we do have sufficient indications of them. To what extent the Christianization of Alexander and Aristotle had advanced by then and to what extent it progressed in the Syrian milieu before the Arabic translations is hard to say, but the beginnings are, in any case, Byzantine.

And consider that if this literature began to be translated and reworked in the Ommiad period, it means that these are Greek manuscripts that the Arab conquerors found in Syria (Damascus fell in 636) or took from Alexandria (the caliph Omar reigned in 717–720) or from other places in the Orient: manuscripts from the 6th or 7th centuries, no later. Because then

---

work of al-Sijistani (end of the 10th century), *Siwan al-hikmah* ("The Philosophy Salon").

came the dark epoch of Byzantium when manuscripts were no longer copied, and besides that, communication was interrupted.

It was resumed with the great translating movement in Abbassid Bagdad, which coincided with the resurgence of the copying of manuscripts in Byzantium around the year 800 A.D.[33]. Until that time the translators had to be satisfied with local Greek manuscripts, although other similar ones might have reached Bagdad in a second period, in this case from Constantinople.

I consider, then, that basically the legend of Aristotle and Alexander, in the contexts of wisdom and government, must have existed in Byzantium around the year 600, although it could have been subject to some reworking at the hands of the Syrians, and to a lesser degree with regard to the wisdom aspect, at the hands of the Arabs.

5. *Aristotle and Alexander in the Byzantine gnomologies. Generalities*

I have already touched on the subject, but when we discuss the gnomologies in more depth in the following chapter, we shall see that they come from the 4th century B.C., taking some materials from earlier literature and adding others. All this material tends to be contaminated in a single ideological line: Socratic-Platonic-Aristotelian-Cynic. And we shall see, too, that there is the model of the pure gnomology and of the gnomology that follows a brief *Life*, with transfers from one to the other.

All this material, biographical and strictly gnomological, reached the Byzantine epoch. It is, as I have said, more or less authentic, depending on the case. I mentioned above something about an Aristotelian gnomology in an Arabic text edited by D. Gutas. This author analyzes very carefully the extent to which the maxims attributed to Aristotle come from the real Alexander himself or from this confused tradition that I have been discussing: sometimes they coincide exactly with gnomologies preserved in Greek. To sum up, the initial *Life* comes from Ptolemy Quennos via Arabic texts derived from it. There are extracts of the master's *Metaphysics* and Eudemus, derivations of the epistolary novel of which we have spoken, and, espe-

33 On this movement see the important book by D. Gutas, *Greek thought, Arabic culture. The Graeco-Arabic translation movement and early 'Abbāsid society (2nd–4th/8th–10th centuries)*, London-New York, Routledge, 1998.

cially, maxims that coincide, as I have just said, with the Greek gnomological tradition that reached Byzantium; and other maxims coinciding with Arabic gnomologies and not always present in the Greek gnomologies that we know, but whose existence, allowing for exceptions, must be supposed in other lost ones. There are many coincidences, notably with *Buenos Proverbios* and *Bocados.*

But let us return to the gnomologies that were the model for the works that we are studying here. Without going into detail, we can recall that those we saw in the previous chapter, constructed basically in the Socrates-Plato-Aristotle-Diogenes line (at times also the line of Alexander, at times of Hippocrates, Plutarch, Galen etc., at times, too, of Hermes and his followers), reached the Byzantine age enlarged and with the addition of maxims by Basil, Gregory Nazianzus and Johannes Chrysostom. The compilations were closed, then, in the final period of Antiquity and were copied and altered in the Byzantine age. The collections of Diogenes Laertius, Johannes Stobaeus, the paremiographs and other Biblical and Christian collections continued.

The point of unification of all this material and its transmission to the Byzantine epoch lies, it is thought, in Johannes Damascenus' lost *Hiera*, of the 8th century[34]. Later Byzantine gnomologies come from here, as we have seen; if we mention them again it is only because they are a testimony of earlier ones, either preserved or lost. But all this is of a later date; our treatises clearly worked with older gnomologies, as did the "Sayings of the ancients" from Ibn Durayd's *Kitab al-Mutjana*[35].

34 See P. Hadot, art. cit., pp. 615 ff; M. Richard, "Florilèges spirituels grecs", *Dictionaire de Spiritualité*, 5, 1964, pp. 476 ff.; H. Chadwick , "Florilegium", in *Reallexikon für Antike und Christentum*, col. 1143 ff.; M. B. Phillips, "Some remarks on the manuscript tradition of the Maximus Florilegium", *Illinois Classical Studies* 7, 1982, pp. 261–275; G. Strohmaier, "Ethical sentences and Anecdotes of Greek Philosophers in Arabic Tradition", in *Actes du Ve Congrès d'Arabisants et d'Islamisants, Correspondance d'Orient*, 11, Bruxelles, 1971, pp. 436–471.

35 Editions, respectively, of L. Sternbach, Berlin, 1963 (first ed. 1887); J. F. Kindstrand, Upsala, 1991; J. F. Kindstrand, "Florilegium Baroccianum and Codex Hierosolymitanus Sancti Sepulchri 255", *Byzantion*, 54, 1984, pp. 536–550; S.-T. Teodorsson, "A Collection of Apophthegmata in an Oxford Manuscript", in *in S.-T. Teodorsson (ed.), Greek and Latin Studies in Memory of Cajus Fabricius*, *Studia Graeca et Latina Gothoburgensia* 54, Gothemburg 1990, pp. 141–153; F. Rosenthal, "Sayings of Ancients from Ibn Durayd's *Kitab al-Mutjana*", *Orientalia* 27, 1958, pp. 29–54; G. Strohmaier, "Ethical Sentences and Anecdotes of Greek Philosophers in Arabic Tradition", art. cit., pp.

Now, what must be said here is that in these collections there are maxims by both Aristotle and Alexander, all within the ancient Socratic tradition. I have already indicated that these gnomologies contributed greatly to creating the image of the two that was transmitted by works like those translated into Castilian in the 13th century. And further, that they were used to create these works, although it must be pointed out that their authors offer numerous maxims that do not appear in the gnomologies that have been preserved: either they come from other lost gnomologies or, at times, from maxims whose attribution fluctuates, or they might have been created by the authors themselves within the line of thought that we have tried to describe.

In any case, the gnomologies furnished a basis for transforming Aristotle and Alexander into practical "philosophers" of a moralistic type. The authors of "sapiential novels" like the ones we are studying did no more than continue along this road.

It would take too long to recall all these gnomologies; see the bibliography in note 34. We must add the paremiographs, who very frequently include the same maxims. I give a list of the most important works and of the "sayings" of the philosopher and the conqueror in these gnomologies, many coming from earlier Greek literature, but not without pointing out that the Greek ones have been published only partially and that their relations are not always clear, and that the attribution of maxims changes from one to another. And further that the number of gnomologies in the Arab domain was also large; here we cite only the one by ibn Durayd, but those of Ibn Hindu and the *Siwan al-hikmah* by al-Sijistani at least should be added.

In any case, as we pointed out above, with respect to Alexander, there is a small number of maxims, some of ancient tradition, others that appear for the first time in the gnomologies, almost all of which refer to ethical and moralistic themes. We described them briefly above. It is possible that they were invented because of the scarcity of old ones and because of this same lack in the Pseudo-Callisthenes. They do not show much originality within this moralism[36]. As for Aristotle's maxims, they too are inserted in the mor-

---

436–471 and "Die arabische Sokrateslegende ...", cit.; Y. M. Manzalaoui, art. cit., pp. 195 ff.

36 For exact details see M. Grignaschi, art. cit., p. 207.

alistic tradition; they hardly touch the theme of government, and that of metaphysics etc. even less.

The citations are by the numbers in the respective editions, except for Maximus Confessor and Antonius Melissa, a name given to two Byzantine gnomologies of the 10th century or later, which are cited by pages (there can be more than one maxim attributed to our authors on a single page):

L. Sternbach, *Gnomologium Vaticanum* (reed. Berlin 1963): 49, 50, 51, 52, 53, 54, 55, 56, 57, 58, 59.

J. F. Kindstrand, *Gnomica Basileensia* (Uppsala 1991): Alexander: 9, 15, 18, 24, 25, 33, 42, 58, 59; Aristotle: 11, 16, 17, 18, 26, 34, 35, 41, 45, 46a, 60, 61, 62,65, 66.

J. F. Kindstrand, *Florilegium Baroccianum* (*Byzantion* 54, 1982): Aristotle: 17, 39, 40.

Teodorsson, *Oxford Ms.*: Alexander: 2, 6, 36, 40; Aristotle: 20.

Ibn Durayd (ed. Rosenthal, *Orientalia* 27, 1958): Aristotle: 18, 20, 21, 22, 23, 25, 26, 27, 29, 30, 31, 32, 33, 34, 35, 36, 37; Alexander: 8, 10, 11, 12, 14, 16.

Maximus Confessor (ed. Migne): Aristotle: 748, 780, 796, 797, 817, 824, 833, 840, 848, 853, 860, 873, 896, 916, 936, 957, 961; Alexander: 742, 745, 748, 764, 773, 812, 833, 860, 948.

Antonius Melissa (ed. Migne): Aristotle: 804, 819, 936, 957, 964, 992, 998, 1008, 1048, 1085; Alexander: 748, 984, 1005, 1185.

6. *More information on the Byzantine, Arabic and Arabic-Castilian gnomologies*

I have culled out a few details, by way of example, from the above-mentioned Byzantine and Arabic gnomologies (abbreviated as GV, GB, FB, OM, ID, MC and AM); to these must be added the Arabic-Castilian ones of our treatises, from which I have given examples above.

I have divided the study, which is not exhaustive, into several sections. I must repeat that very often the sources, when they exist, attribute the maxims to various authors: Diogenes, Isocrates, Philip, Aristippus, Anaximenes, Antigonus, etc. This is habitual in the gnomologies, whose practice of introducing many maxims with ὁ αὐτός "the same person" was the cause of numerous errors on the part of the copyists. Nevertheless, sometimes the other attribution is without doubt the original one; thus, ID 38, in which Aristotle called "the people" to hear him, comes from Diogenes searching for "a man" with a lamp (but it was later attributed to Aristotle, as we have seen).

The maxims can consist either of a direct affirmation or of a *khreía* that is a response to our protagonist's having seen (ἰδών), having been asked (ἐρωτηθείς ...). All this in accordance with the ancient gnomic tradition of principally Cynic origin.

a) Origin of the maxims

There is very little that comes from the real Aristotle; of him I only find *GB* 11 (θυμός, passion does not allow the use of διάνοια, reason, cf. *FR* 108), *GB* 46a (against envy, from *Rh.*), *GB* 60 (everyone knows he will die, but not the moment, from *Rh.*), *ID* 32 (the sweetest thing is what one desires, from *EN, EE*). Material from the Pseudo-Callisthenes is also scarce, all of it related to Alexander: *GV* 78 (the theme of Alexander and Homer), *GV* 94 = *OM* 2 = *ID* 16 (the theme of the Amazons, it is not honorable to defeat women), *GV* 98 (Alexander covers the dead Darius, the theme of fortune).

But there are certainly maxims that refer, although not literally, to the Platonic or Aristotelian philosophy, for example, those that speak of παιδεία or education as an ornament and a refuge (*GV* 50), of not being ashamed of injustice as the worst wrong (*GB* 66 = *MC* 916), of doing good as the closest thing to God that man has (*GV* 53), of the person able to suffer injustice as most worthy of friendship (*AM* 819): maxims that are repeated in various gnomologies.

In contrast, there are numerous maxims that have passed into the Byzantine gnomologies (and sometimes into the Arabic ones) from a long line of ancient authors: Isocrates, Plutarch, Stobaeus, Arrianus, Valerius Maximus, Diogenes Laertius, Themistius, Libanius, Theon, etc. For Alexander there are some that come from the ancient Cynic tradition that opposes him to Diogenes, as in *GV* 91 ("I would like to be Diogenes if I were not Alexander"), *GV* 97 = *GB* 9 = *MC* 833 = *AM* 984 (Alexander and Diogenes in the barrel: a barrel full of intelligence"), *GV* 104 (It is not kingly to give a drachma or Cynic to beg for a talent), *ID* 8 (Alexander the great king and Diogenes the dog that bites), *ID* 10 (Alexander: "Are you afraid of me?" Diogenes: "Are you good or bad?"). There is also, as I have repeated, a great quantity of Cynic material in general; I will come back to this.

But there are also many maxims in the Byzantine gnomologies (in the gnomologies that are the sources for the ones that I cite), and that pass on occasion to the Arabic gnomologies, including those of our Castilian texts. I will cite a few examples:

Aristotle: *GV* 49 (Aristotle seeing a youth fond of entertainments said to him: "Lest you not have anything worth seeing"), *GV* 55 (The uneducated walk among the living like cadavers), *GB* 17 = *ID* 20 (The most difficult thing is not to say what should not be said), *GB* 21 = *MC* 853 (The person who explains what is evident is like someone who illustrates the sun by using a lamp), *GB* 23 (The son is the slave of the father), *GB* 61 = *MC* 957 (One must leave life as if leaving a banquet, neither thirsty nor inebriated), *GB* 62 (against the person who does not make a will until death is near), *MC* 936 (The root of education is bitter, the fruit is sweet).

Alexander: *GV* 74 (Alexander conquered so many lands so as not to put off decisions), *GV* 75 = *GB* (His mother charged him a high rental for the nine months), *GV* 76 ("My sons are my triumphs"), *GV* 88 ("The lost cup will always be ours"), *GV* 898 (He does not wish to be called an executioner instead of a king), *GV* 95 (The old man should dye his knees, not his hair), *GV* 98 (Do not wait to make conquests lest you lose your boldness). One can see how the gnomologies add material of a moralistic nature, between Socratic and Cynic.

Now, it seems remarkable that Maximus Confessor and Antonius Melissa, false names without doubt, behind which are concealed the most extensive and most widely disseminated Byzantine gnomologies, contain maxims of Aristotle and Alexander that for us are new. Thus we have:

Aristotle: *MC* 780 ("Whom many fear let him fear many"), *MC* 797 = *AM* 804 (Cynic maxims on wealth, excess, nature, the desires), *MC* 817 (It is better to be reprimanded than praised), *MC* 961 (On the effeminate youth and the one who abuses), *AM* 964 (Better than receiving honors is to consider oneself worthy of them).

Alexander: *MC* 773 (Alexander sends talents to Socrates, who refuses them. "Don't you have any friends?"), *AM* 948 (Alexander does not believe the accusations, which is why he drinks the poison).

The anachronisms and the invented character of these last two maxims, foreign to the ancient tradition, let us see the progressive growth of the gnomologies: either more new maxims were anthologized or they were simply invented[37], but always within the same moralistic line.

These maxims, both the old and the recent ones, appear in the Arabic gnomologies, not only in *ID*, but also in others whose parallels can be found in Rosenthal's edition. The authors either had access to Byzantine gnomologies that have not come down to us, or else, within the Arabic tradition, they created new maxims with a basically similar orientation. I have made note of some of these new maxims, a list which by no means pretends to be exhaustive.

Aristotle: *ID* 18 and other Arabic gnomologies – the observation is also valid for the citations that follow – (The need of intelligence is worse than the need of money), *ID* 26 ("Intelligence makes life miserable", which contradicts the usual doctrine), *ID* 35 (How can a rich man and a poor man be friends?), *ID* 36 (If you cannot bear the effort of studying, you will have to bear the misery of ignorance).

Alexander: *ID* 11 (against the uneducated person who was wearing a ring of gold).

It should be noted that many of these maxims, of whatever origin, can be found in our Castilian treatises. Thus, a number of the maxims of *ID* appear in them: 8 *(Bocados)*, 11 (id.), 12 (id.), 20 *(Buenos Proverbios)*, 21 (Mubassir, not the Castilian translation), 22 *(Bocados)*, 25 (id), 27 (id.), 29 *(Buenos Proverbios)*, 35 (both collections), 38 *(Bocados)*.

Naturally, an exhaustive comparative study must be made of all the gnomologies and our treatises. To do this, it would be necessary, as I have said above, to have a complete databank for all this material. In any case, the original source of the Arabic-Castilian treatises and the constant growth of the maxims are clear. Some of them may have been created, based on earlier models, through Arab or Castilian initiative (it is not possible to carry out a comparative study of details in both groups of texts).

b) Fundamental features of the maxims

The first thing one must know is that there are two types of Greek gnomologies: those organized alphabetically (like *GV* and *GB*) and those or-

37 On the two possibilities see G. Strohmaier, "Ethical Sentences and Anecdotes of Greek Philosophers in Arabic Tradition", *Actes du Ve Congrès International d'Arabisants et d'Islamisants, Correspondance d'Orient* 11, Brussels, 1971, pp. 436–471.

ganized by themes (Maximus Confessor and Antonius Melissa, among others). Nevertheless, it must be added that among the first group there are, at times, traces of organization by themes, as in *OM*[38]. The same thing happens in our Arabic-Castilian treatises, as we shall see.

If we turn now to the themes of the Greek and Arabic gnomologies that we have been referring to, we note, also, that maxims of the same theme appear, following each other in order: no doubt some gnomologies specialized by authors derive from other general ones. But putting aside the question of origin, what I want to emphasize, even at the risk of repeating things already said, is the matter of themes.

The themes are more limited for Alexander: his royal condition, which implies courage, benevolence toward his subjects, friendship, moderation, sense of honor, rejection of tyranny. Many examples have already been given. For Aristotle there are more: there is the theme of παιδεία or education opposed to ἄνοια, uncouthness, stupidity; the theme of resisting passion, insatiability, intemperance; that of the criticism of wealth, women, effeminacy and luxury, injustice, the insults of the fool, physicians; the themes of not speaking, work (πόνος), benefit (εὐεργετεῖν), praise of the father and the teacher (with vacillation in the respective evaluations); the reminder of the life's vanity and of death. It is not difficult to infer the presence of numerous Cynic themes, especially in Aristotle, and, I repeat, the predominance of the moralistic theme over those of government and royalty.

The comparison with our Castilian treatises is enlightening. To be sure, as I have said, this cannot be done in an exhaustive manner yet, but it is certain that these treatises add elements foreign to the gnomologies, especially in the theme of government but also in others. A maxim like the one attributed to Aristotle in *Buenos Proverbios*, p. 60, "he who hurries more than he should, deceives himself", is the σπεῦδε βραδέως "hurry slowly" of the Delphic maxim; ibid. "Everything in the world can be changed except what is natural" corresponds to all the Hellenistic philosophies; on p. 59 "The fear of God is the apparel of wise men" is Christian, as is, on page 60, "He who places himself in great danger puts his soul at risk." Note that in our texts we encounter *khreîai* that are not in the gnomologies we are familiar

38 See J. Kindstrand, "A collection of Apophthegmata in an Oxford Manuscript", in *Greek and Latin Studies in Memory of Cajus Fabricius, Studia Graeca et Latina Gothoburgensia* 54, ed. by S.-T. Teodorsson, Gothenburg, 1990, p. 142.

with, but that are found in the *Life of Aesop*; for example, there are several against women in *Buenos Proverbios*, pp. 138 ff. No doubt they reached our text via gnomologies that we do not have: the phrase about the hanged woman "Would that all trees bore such fruit", attributed to Aesop in the *Life*, is attributed here to Diogenes.

What I want to make clear is that the themes, if additions like those cited are removed, are the same ones we know from the Byzantine and Arabic gnomologies. In *Buenos Proverbios*, indeed, there are, as we have seen, the themes of the funerary lamentation on the brevity of life, etc. And limiting ourselves to the maxims attributed to Aristotle and Alexander, since we will return later to other gnomologies present in our works, we find themes and maxims that are familiar to us. For example, to Aristotle are attributed maxims on knowing how to keep silent, moderation, the mind, *"el bien fazer"* (doing good), suffering meekly, truth, friendship, good teaching, the law; and against greed, hypocrisy, wrath, wanting too much. On page 93 he gives advice fitting to a philosopher speaking to a king: *"enseñorate sobre los pueblos faziendoles bien y merced y avras su amor"*, (rule over the people treating them well and mercifully and you will have their love), not unlike others in the gnomologies. On p. 96 maxims like this one are strung together with others against wrath and in favor of the mercy that makes the kingdom prosper. And the same can be said of the maxims of Alexander on pp. 101 ff., the ones that end with the theme of the gravedigger who does not see any difference in the bones of kings, a Cynic theme that we have already seen. More examples have been given above.

The organization of the maxims by themes, just as in the gnomologies, is seen in all the treatises, where from time to time Christian maxims are intercalated. These are the themes of the intellect, maintaining silence, meekness and wisdom.

There are specific classifications, by chapters, in *Poridad* and *La Donzella Teodor*: we have seen the main themes. Then, too, we reencounter the traditional formulas of the Greek gnomologies: "and Alexander said," "and he said," "and they asked Alexander," "and he asked," "and he saw a man", whose Greek originals are well known to us. And we find, in Maximus, for example, an organization by chapters of the same type: "On virtue and vice", "On temperance and advice", "On purity and chastity" (almost all of them Christian maxims), "On justice", "On friends and love of brothers", "On giving alms" (Christian), "On valor".

Collections like these without doubt came out of the gnomologies devoted to one single philosopher, with an organization of themes that is a model for ours, which preserve the old scheme of *Life* + maxims. It is no wonder that in these mixed collections what refers to one philosopher or another should be enlarged with the maxims of someone else, even Christian maxims: we have already seen the constant changes in attributions. The cases of Aristotle and Alexander are no exception, although here there was a previous underlying fabric: the Pseudo-Callisthenes and other ancient works, either about the philosopher or about the king.

This, as I have said, is not a complete study; that would require all of the materials to be collected in a computerized databank, which, at the present time, we lack. Even so, it is clear that it is in the sphere of the gnomologies (and of the old *Life* + maxims scheme) and in related genres like the epistolary novels, the "mirrors for princes", the consolatory writings or the sapiential debates that we will find the roots of the Arabic-Castilian treatises, specifically those that deal with the Aristotle/Alexander theme, namely *Buenos Proverbios* and *Poridad.* They are two ramifications of the same theme and with the same precedents.

They are Byzantine roots, extended, although minimally as regards gnomological material, by the Arabs (and possibly the Syrians), but whose more remote origin in Hellenistic and imperial Greece, and even earlier, we shall see in the following section. At certain times the ancient works underwent the additions and transformations to which I have alluded. This entire complex, I repeat, is preserved more faithfully in our works than in the Byzantine literature later than the 9th century.

III. The process of the creation of the three works beginning in Greek antiquity

1. *The works of late antiquity (2nd or 3rd centuries). A model for the Byzantine works*

On attempting to investigate the Greek originals of the three works that we are studying, insofar as they relate to Aristotle and Alexander, we find a complex panorama. In the first place, the Aristotle/Alexander theme was included (except in the model for *Poridad*) in more extensive works, and received additions that are without doubt Byzantine but were incorporated perhaps in the Byzantine epoch, perhaps in the Syriac and Arabic epoch. And there were minor additions, either Arabic (especially the "external prologues" of two of the works, as we have seen), or possibly Syriac. We have, then, three works of late Antiquity on the Alexander/Aristotle theme, but that must be separated from the additions, the "wrapping" (above all in the case of *Buenos Proverbios* and *Bocados*).

But secondly, these nuclei that we extract with more or less precision present all the symptoms of having undergone a process of Christianization and Byzantinization parallel to that of the Pseudo-Callisthenes and the *Barlaam*, for example. This process has partially masked originals that were, without any doubt, of late Antiquity. We can compare them with other works of that period that also underwent the processes of amplification and diversification in ancient and medieval times, such as the *Life of Secundus*, the *Altercatio* of Hadrian and Epictetus and the *Life of Apollonius King of Tyre*. They, too, belong to sapiential literature, which, as we know, was subject to these processes within that open tradition.

And this sometimes began at an even earlier date: I believe that the *Life of Aesop* is Hellenistic, and likewise Hellenistic are the central component of the Pseudo-Callisthenes and most of the sources of Plutarch's *Banquet of the Seven Wise Men*, as I have said above and as we shall see in more detail.

In our case, too, many of the elements of the three works on Aristotle and Alexander are of Hellenistic date: we have found them in *Lives* of Aristotle, in the Pseudo-Callisthenes and in maxims attributed to philosophers of that period or earlier. But the originals that we are studying and that later were Byzantinized and amplified are not Hellenistic; they come, as I have said, from late Antiquity. For in them we find a great increase in the biographical and gnomological elements and a change of orientation toward the purely ethical and in the teaching of government, based on the new image of Alexander. Furthermore, the comparison with the works of late antiquity cited above points to the 2nd century A.D. or, at the latest, the 3rd century as the date of origin.

We must acknowledge, then, the existence of true creators who wrote three well-organized works that have reached us as the extended and revised nuclei of later Byzantine works:

1. *Buenos Proverbios.* The introductory novella about Aristotle and Alexander is followed by maxims by Aristotle, letters from him to Alexander,

teachings of Alexander, letters between Aristotle, Alexander and the latter's mother as his death draws near and the mourning of the philosophers when the death occurs.

This is an assemblage of a short biographical novel with maxims, letters and philosophical laments, all perfectly organized and intended to present a philosophy of moralism and government with a Cynic orientation. The image of ragged Aristotle, who triumphs nevertheless, is comparable to that of the Cynic philosophers like the Aesop of the *Life*.

2. *Poridad.* This, too, is a short biographical novel, followed, in this case, only by letters: Alexander asks for advice, Aristotle gives it to him in a long letter that introduces the theme of advice to the prince *(Fürstenspiegel).*

   The elements are, in part, the same, the organization and the purpose are similar, as are the use and the image of the figures of Aristotle and Alexander.

3. *Bocados de Oro.* The Aristotle/Alexander theme that we obtain from a much more extensive compilation consists of two parallel series of Life + maxims, first of Aristotle, then of Alexander. The anecdote of Anchos and the cranes, of Greek origin, opens the whole composition. And the Life of Aristotle has been much reworked, acquiring Christian features. Once again we have the same elements and the same intent, once more based on a moralistic and Cynicizing image of Aristotle and Alexander.

The three works belong to the same ideological orientation and work with similar literary elements. The same is true, as we shall see, of *La Donzella Teodor.* This is always a matter of popular literature that combines the biographical novella with a philosophy of morality and government. The two protagonists are now stereotyped, and traditional narrative elements such as the maxim and the letter are used. All of this corresponds to the Cynic biographical tradition, which combines novelistic elements, elements of entertainment and doctrinal ones (with sapiential dialogue that includes "What is...?" questions, "solutions" to problems, etc.)[39]. It is not surprising that all this should be adopted by the Christian moralism of the Byzantines for identical purposes.

39 On this see *Historia de la fábula greco-latina* I, pp. 661 ff. (= pp. 673 ff. of the English translation, Leiden, 1999).

But if, looking forward, it was an open literature that experienced the evolution that we have indicated, looking back at the past, it was a crystallization of ideological and formal tendencies that came from Antiquity, at least from the Hellenistic period, and even farther back (Socratism, monarchical moralism of the 4th century, biographies from the same century).

Therefore, we must examine these elements, if only summarily (some things have already been said), and establish parallels regarding how they were used in the first and 2nd centuries A.D. to create new works, works of which only a minimum part has reached us and which were enlarged and reworked in the medieval epoch. In our case it is only the medieval Arabic and Castilian tradition that remains; we must reconstruct the Greek Byzantine tradition and from there the Greek tradition of late Antiquity.

This is what we have attempted, and we must conclude that these are works which, within the same ideological and literary orientation, are no less important than others that have been preserved and have been repeatedly mentioned here.

2. *The Hellenistic and ancient models for our works*

I have already said that the scheme that provides a short novel, generally biographical, and a sapiential dialogue or else a series of maxims, is of oriental origin. Here we have the variant that includes the philosopher and the king or the future king. In the Orient we have encountered it in the *Ahikar*, the *Pañcatantra*, and the dialogue of Solomon and the Queen of Sheba; in Greece it commences with the dialogue of Solon and Croesus and continues with the debate of Alexander and the Gymnosophists, the Lives of Aesop and Secundus, the *Altercatio* of Hadrian and Epictetus and with various examples in Josephus (Solomon and Hiram of Tyre in *Ap.* 1.17), in the *Haggadah*, in Plutarch's *Life of the Seven Wise Men*, etc. There are Christian variants in the gospels (Jesus before the doctors), in the debate of Saint Catherine and the Philosophers (and others in which a woman takes part, as in the cases of *The Thousand and One Nights*, *Sendebar*, and *La Donzella Teodor*).

The author of the works that we are discussing simply adapted to this scheme, no less than did Plutarch and also the author of the work that has been preserved in Arabic and that we have mentioned above under the name of the *Philosophical Quartet*. In order to do this, he needed a little information about Aristotle and Alexander and a lot of imagination. For what follows he fluctuated between maxims, the "What is...?" questions and "solutions" to problems, letters and the rest, just as in the other works. He left out the fables (they appear in the *Life of Aesop* above all) and the banquet (in Plato, Plutarch, the Deipnosophists of Athenaeus, etc.).

We shall emphasize later that our anonymous authors are not the only ones to use this scheme for their creations. Apart from that, the use of the biography for moralizing and exemplifying purposes, which we have already seen in the Pseudo-Callisthenes and in the Alexander tradition, had become widespread[40].

The second part of these works, the doctrinal part, employs the various resources of doctrinal literature of a moralistic type: a line that incorporates Socrates and his successors and culminates in the Cynic-Stoic philosophy. Basically it is propaganda partly Cynic, partly moralistic, that considers as its own the previous philosophy, to which it frequently attributes its maxims. As I have already said, Christian moralism was incorporated later.

In order to simplify a bit, I will consider as one the different literary forms of this moralistic literature: forms that frequently interchange their content: the maxims and the rest pass from the *Lives* to the gnomologies, which, inversely, penetrate the letters, fables, etc.

1. In the first place we have the maxims contained in gnomologies, collections of apophthegmata, florilegia, etc., which, as I say, pass to the *Lives*, and vice versa. Their attributions vary, as I have also said, the Cynic element that is inserted in those attributed to Socrates and the Socratics being especially characteristic.

   Byzantine gnomologies have been preserved that include material from the imperial epoch and earlier, something that has already been studied. There are also collections of apothegms and florilegia that are frequently equivalent in essence[41]. But apart from the old material contained therein, of which we have spoken, we conserve a little material, some fragmentary, some complete, that is strictly from Antiquity. We have already provided the principal details.

40 See, for example, A. Dihle, "Zur antiken Biographie", in *La biographie antique, Entretiens sur l'Antiquité classique* 44, Geneva, 1998, pp. 125 ff.

41 I direct the reader, after the above-mentioned bibliography on gnomologies, to T. Kluser, "Apophthegma", in *Reallexikon für Antike und Christentum*, Stuttgart, 1950, cols. 545–550; H. Chadwick, "Florilegium", ibid., 1969, cols. 1131–1160.

There were also, let me remind the reader, florilegia by Plato that have left their mark on later literature, and florilegia by Aristotle as well. But especially important are the papyri, partly biographical, partly gnomological, from the 3rd century B.C., especially on Socrates and Diogenes. *PHib.* 182 contains apothegms of a Cynicizing type by Socrates, connected without doubt to a *Life*: in *PFlor.* 113.2.19–38 there are *khreîai* by Socrates and Antisthenes. This is a tradition that goes back to the 4th century, some of whose maxims reached the Byzantine gnomologies. It is here that the mixture of Socratic and Cynic ideas begins that culminated in the Arabic epoch, as we have seen[42]. We also have gnomologies for Diogenes (together with biographical aspects) from the 3rd century B.C., where maxims are very often attributed to him that sometimes are attributed to other authors, as we have seen[43].

What is interesting is that in these testimonies we find the same fusion of *Life* and maxims and the same moralistic, Socratic-Cynic vein as we find in our treatises (and in the *Philosophical Quartet*). Remember, also, that some works cited, of the same kind and the same orientation, go back to Antiquity, both Hellenistic and imperial (the *Lives* of Aesop and Secundus, the *Altercatio* of Hadrian and Epictetus, Plutarch's *Banquet of the Seven Wise Men*, etc.). And that the existence of gnomologies of Aristotle and Alexander can be inferred from the presence of their maxims in the later mixed gnomologies (some of them, as we have seen, coming from the Hellenistic period). This is a tradition that continued in the sections on important philosophers in *Bocados*, for example.

This is, then, the main source that the authors of our treatises drank from. The maxims, the "What is...?" questions, the "solutions", which, furthermore, sometimes go back to the classic epoch (Sappho, Theognis, Cleobulina), also come from this source[44]. As I have said, there is a constant interchange between *Lives* and *gnômai*, and also, the conservation of this scheme in our works makes them at the same time more ar-

42 For all this see I. Gallo, *Frammenti biografici da papiri,* II, Rome, Edizioni dell'Ateneo, pp. 169 ff.

43 See A. Packmohr, *De Diogenis Sinopensis apophthegmatis quaestiones selectae*, Münster, 1918; G. Giannantoni, *Socraticorum reliquiae* II, Rome, 1983, pp. 409 ff.

44 On its frequent presence in philosophy, grammar, medicine, etc., and also in theological writings and diverse medieval works, see L. W. Daly and W. Suchier, *Altercatio*, cit., pp. 25 ff.

chaizing than anything that can be found in the Byzantine literature of the 9th century and later.

One must add, as I have already mentioned, collections of *gnômai* (sometimes preceded by a *Life* or by diverse anecdotes) of the Neo-Pythagorean and Hermetic tradition: they come after the sections dedicated to "Pythagoras" and to "Hermes" and other Hermetic sages in *Buenos Proverbios*, *Bocados* and the *Philosophical Quartet* (among other Arabic works), apart from their influence on *Poridad*.

2. Secondly, we have the pseudo-epigraphic letters. Pseudo-epigraphic literature is abundant beginning in the 4th and 3rd centuries B.C. and is very frequent in the case of letters. As examples we can mention those attributed to Socrates and the Socratics[45]. Especially well known are those of the Seven Wise Men, those of the *hetairai* of Alciphron, etc. But there are many more pseudo-epigraphic letters[46]. Letters were used for different purposes, very often for instruction: such were the letters of Plato, Isocrates, Aristotle, Epicurus, Seneca, Saint Paul, etc., many of them pseudo-epigraphic.

A variant is the letter of consolation, in Cicero, Panaetius, Posidonius, Seneca *(Ad Marciam de consolatione)*, Plutarch, etc.; we have already mentioned those of the Christians[47], continued, as we have seen, in *Buenos Proverbios*. I repeat that the theme of consolation passes from the maxims to the letters and vice versa.

Another very frequent use of the pseudo-epigraphic letter is to represent it as a novel. We have seen it included (only partially) in the Pseudo-Callisthenes and in the most extensive collection that we have

45 See J. Sykutris, *Die Briefe des Sokrates und der Sokratiker*, Paderborn, Schöningh, 1933; J.-F. Borkowski, *Socratis quae feruntur epistolae*, Stuttgart, Teubner, 1997.

46 See J. Schneider, "Brief" in *Reallexikon für Antike und Christentum*, Stuttgart, 1954, p. 573; J. Sykutris, "Epistolographie" in *RE*, Supplb., V, col. 210 ff.; R. J. Gallé Cejudo, "La carta ficticia griega y el diálogo", *Excerpta Philologica*, 4–5, 1994–95, pp. 41–51. But in cases like Plato's and in that of Aristotle, who we know published a collection of letters in eight books, the problems of authenticity are difficult. On the letter in general, see C. Hutt, "Les épistolographes grecs", *REG* 2, 1889, pp. 149–163; E. Suárez de la Torre, "La epistolografía griega", *Estudios Clásicos* 23, 1979, pp. 19–46. A good list of pseudo-epigraphic letters can be found in A. Beschorner, "Griechische Briefbücher berühmter Männer" in N. Holzberg (ed.), *Der griechischer Briefroman. Gattungstypologie und Textanalyse,* Tübingen, Narr, 1994, pp. 169 ff.

47 See J. Sykutris, art. cit., col. 202 ff., and for the Christians, the above-mentioned work of J. F. Mitchell.

traces of in early Arabic translations. The letters of the Seven Wise Men are another epistolary novel, and there is the novel of Chion of Heraclea (a conspiracy of Platonic philosophers to overthrow the tyrant Clearchus of Heraclea). And more[48].

Thus the use of pseudo-epigraphic letters in *Buenos Proverbios* is traditional in origin. In this treatise, Alexander's second letter is also an example of another traditional genre: it is a "mirror for princes".

3. This is the third traditional genre used in our treatises, blended with the doctrinal letter and, of course, with the maxim, as can be seen. There is a long list of works that, from the work of Theognis and even earlier (Hesiod, Pindar), are devoted to the teaching of princes: poems, letters, orations, treatises and, of course, maxims and fables[49]. They have a moralistic orientation related to Socratism and the 4th century B.C. monarchical tendencies influenced by him, as I have mentioned. To this was incorporated the "image" of Alexander that he himself promoted and that later tradition favorable to him propagated. To this tradition belong both the Pseudo-Callisthenes and the works that we are studying here even more so.

The tradition has an important moment with Isocrates in his three Cyprian orations: the best service of kings is Justice, they must love men and love the city. In the same line are Xenophon's *Cyropedia*, Plato's *Letter VII* and innumerable works of the Hellenistic, Roman and Byzantine (including the Christian) periods. This includes lost works of Aristotle ("On royalty", "Alexander or on colonization") and Onesicritus ("How Alexander was educated"), Plutarch's *de Alexandri fortuna*, etc. As I have said, in this tradition Alexander is the philosopher king, the ideal ruler in the service of Cynic-Stoic moralism; the beginnings seen in the Pseudo-Callisthenes have developed in our treatises.

Without doubt the authors of our works had access to an extensive bibliography, orations or treatises that were often entitled "On the kingdom"

48 See the book *Der griechische Briefroman*, ed. N. Holzberg, Tübingen, Narr, 1994.

49 There is a good general overview in P. Hadot, "Fürstenspiegel", *in Reallexikon für Antike und Christentum*, cit., col. 568 ff. For the fable (absent here except that of Ancos and one in the Pseudo-Callisthenes) see my "Política cínica en las fábulas esópicas", in *Filosofia e forme letterarie. Studi della Corte*, Urbino, Università degli Studi di Urbino, 1987, I, pp. 113–126 and "Filosofía cínica en las fábulas esópicas", Buenos Aires, Centro de Estudios Filosóficos, 1986.

(Zeno, Sphaerus, Ecphantus, Diotogenes and then Johannes Chrysostom and others). Works with the same intent, of this period or later, are, among others, the *Letter of Aristeas*, and those of Philo, Musonius, Rufus, Seneca (especially the *de clementia*) and Themistius. This is the official ideology of the Hellenistic monarchs as can be seen in inscriptions and papyri and can be deduced from their own official titles ("benefactor", "pious"). It is also the ideology of the *Res gestae divi Augusti*, of the Roman panegyrists (for example, Pliny's *Panegyric of Trajan*, which speaks of his *humanitas*, *liberalitas*, *benignitas*, *fortitudo*, of his example) and of the Greek panegyrists like Synesius (in honor of Arcadius) or Procopius (in honor of Anastasius).

There is, then, an uninterrupted tradition going from Plato to the Byzantines, which promotes the model of the king-philosopher, strong and humane, a devotee of justice, a benefactor of the people. This is the model that was exemplified by Alexander (and also, for the Cynics, by Heracles and other prototypes of virtue).

The only thing that the authors of our treatises did, then, was to develop, using the Pseudo-Callisthenes as a base but going beyond that, the ideology of the beneficent, humane monarchy, opposed to tyranny, in the service of justice and good. All of this is expressed mainly through maxims and letters and is made attractive thanks to the biographical-novelistic frame that presents the virtues of the philosopher and the king-philosopher.

This is an ideology that later takes on a Christian tinge, but that at the time that our treatises were written represented a moralist synthesis that did not differentiate Socratism, Cynicism and Stoicism: the more technical or disturbing features of the different schools were simply removed.

Such are the principal elements that the composers of the three treatises on Aristotle and Alexander used to write these new versions of their lives: the technical aspects of Aristotle's philosophy and Alexander's feats of war were eliminated. In this way edifying works were created in a lively and entertaining style, in accordance with the literary ideal of the Cynics[50]. They are three works (one of them, *Poridad*, falsely attributed to Aristotle) that, with all their differences, are literarily and ideologically akin; the similarity increased later in the Byzantine epoch. They were important works within a popular style that eschewed great ideological and formal novelties.

50 On Cynicism and biographical genres see my *Historia de la Fábula Greco-Latina* I, pp. 687 ff. (pp. 673 ff. of the English translation, Leiden, 1999).

These three works grew up on the base of ancient literary forms and an earlier moralist concept of government. They took all these elements and doubtless more (specific things on the organization of the government, Hermetism), but what was created was something new that had the good fortune to prosper in a later period, becoming contaminated at times with other works of the same orientation (in the case of *Buenos Proverbios* and *Bocados*). It found its way to Arabic and then Castilian texts and then to all of Europe. But its ancient Greek roots and its later extensions, Greek and otherwise, are undeniable. Although an exact reconstruction is impossible, it is perfectly possible to have a general idea of its different phases.

But these are different from the type of novel on Alexander that was developed in Byzantium; there are coincidences, but the conversion of the theme into an edifying text of moral advice with a Christian inclination went much further. Once again, I repeat, this points, more than strictly to Byzantium, to the Greek and Syriac Christianity of the Orient.

In our Castilian works Greek ideas and forms survive that matured and evolved over a millennium before the creation of the works of the 2nd century A.D. and were later developed further. They were adopted by Byzantines, Syrians and Castilian Christians as well as by Muslims. To these cultures they brought Greek moralism in its personal, social and political aspects. They are a testimony to the synthesis of the diverse ancient philosophies, and of Christianity and Islam.

3. *Parallel examples of literary creations of late antiquity*

Considering what has been said, the creation of literary works beginning with a series of themes and preexisting formal elements, or the linking of biographical-novelistic elements with specifically sapiential ones should not come as a surprise. Note that, on the one hand, in the Hellenistic and imperial Roman epochs, the Greek novel flourished, and within that genre, the epistolary novel. And on the other, the sapiential gnomologies also flourished and, within this Cynicizing literature, works of a complex type such as the Pseudo-Callisthenes or the *Banquet of the Seven Wise Men.*

But before we come to these works, we must emphasize that the combination novelized *Life* + *gnômai*, debates and sapiential letters is traditional and continued to prosper, especially in the Orient in my opinion. It appears in *Bocados*, not only as it relates to Aristotle and Alexander, something that we have already seen, but also for another series of philosophers. For each of the most famous of the authors that it cites it begins with a chapter on the "acts" (of Hermes, Solon, Hippocrates, Pythagoras, Socrates, etc.) followed by their "sayings" or "words of advice".

And neither is this exclusive to *Bocados*; it reflects a scheme that is followed, more or less, as I said above, in the Arabic *Philosophical Quartet* (of Greek origin) that I have mentioned: before the sayings of Pythagoras, Socrates, Plato and Aristotle there is a brief introduction, partly biographical, partly description of the doctrine.

I have already pointed out that this is a Greek tradition from the 4th century B.C. It is found again in sapiential papyri on Socrates and Diogenes, which we have adduced, and also in Diogenes Laertius. When Demetrius of Phalerum put the *Life of Aesop* at the front of his collection of fables[51], he was simply following the tradition. And in relation to this, we could compare the procedure of the Alexandrian philologists when they precede their editions of the classic figures with a *Life* of that person.

Note that in these novelistic introductions we can expect considerable originality on the part of the author, who tries to attract attention, even in a bizarre way, as in the case of Aristotle's admission to Plato's school according to *Buenos Proverbios*, or in that of the misogynous anecdote in the *Life of Secundus*. This gives rise to a tradition that reaches Petrus Alphonsus, *El Conde Lucanor*, etc. There might also be, consciously or unconsciously, some innovation in the attribution of maxims and all the rest to one philosopher or another; we have seen that in the gnomologies many were interchangeable. But the assemblage of *Life* + maxims is purely traditional.

Nevertheless, for the literary spirit of the period this was not enough, and sometimes more complex works were undertaken, in no less than in the case of the novel. I should like to make reference to two of them.

One is the oft-mentioned Pseudo-Callisthenes which, while it depends on earlier elements, probably Hellenistic from the 2nd century B.C., is a synthesis of these same elements. Reinhold Merkelbach, in a book that we have mentioned repeatedly, established some time ago that this is the creation of one author, "an uncultured and ignorant man" of the 3rd century A.D.[52] who used diverse materials: a Hellenistic text (actually a poem in

51 See my *Historia de la fábula greco-latina* I, pp. 664 f. (pp. 650 f. of the English translation, Leiden, 1999).

52 See Merkelbach, op. cit., pp. 56 ff.

choliambics), extracts from an epistolary novel, Alexander's letter to Aristotle on the marvels of India, the *Dialogue of Alexander and the Gymnosophists* and a text on the last days of Alexander.

He added various inventions of a novelesque type and his own interpretations of episodes such as the one involving Nectanebus. The work is, then, a concoction of various materials, but his intention is clear: to give a particular picture of Alexander and to envelop his conquests in a novelesque atmosphere.

Even clearer, if possible, is the secondary character of the personal recreation of ancient themes, genres and motifs in Plutarch's *Banquet of the Seven Wise Men*, to which I have devoted a study[53]. I will not repeat the details here, but I want to touch on certain points.

There is no strict parallel with our works; everything centers on a banquet (a feature present in the *Life of Aesop*, among other works), and at the end there are some Platonic elements. But there are many elements that do coincide, as we know: the opening and the novelesque setting, namely the banquet of the sages and information about them; the use of the letter (Niloxenus brings one from King Amasis of Egypt), which leads to the debate; the confrontation of king (Amasis, Periander) and wise men, especially Thales; the use of the enigma (how can one drink up the sea?), of the "What is...?" (What is the oldest thing?); the debate on government, followed by another on the economics of the home and the order of the world. There is the alternation of dialogue and narrator and abundant maxims. And the literary composition is good.

With a different novelistic scheme, that of the banquet and the seven sages, and using the letter, the maxim, the "problem" and its "solution", the themes of government are discussed. All of this has a clearly Cynic orientation, although Plutarch imposed a Platonizing end.

Of our three works the one that presents the most complex literary structure is *Buenos Proverbios* (the Aristotle/Alexander part, later embedded in other sapiential themes). Literary devices that go from the letter to the mourning of the philosophers are wisely used in a perfect dramatic climax.

On the other hand, what *Poridad* has done is join to the biographical and epistolographic elements another, the "mirror for princes", whose exact source is unknown. Curiously, one of the letters that we have in Arabic includes the doctrine of the pseudo-Aristotelian *de mundo*: in *Poridad* is in-

53 "Géneros helenísticos en el *Banquete de los siete sabios* de Plutarco", cit.

cluded a letter of the moralistic type we are familiar with, but also of the practical type dealing with government. But *Bocados* is only a series of sequences of a *Life* (or "acts") + maxims or teachings (sometimes the *Life* is missing, sometimes a physiognomic description is added to the *Life*): Aristotle and Alexander are only two sequences among many others.

We are referring here only to the Aristotle/Alexander theme. There is no doubt that in the 2nd or 3rd century it crystallized in the three works we have been studying, which were written by popular, moralistic, not very cultured writers. Their main interest was in the subject of government, which they developed using the device of the two great historical figures, whose image in these works is unilateral and considerably deformed. And this was continued and exploited later along lines that were sometimes Hermetic, sometimes Socratic-Cynic-Christian.

4. *Conclusion*

If we wanted to summarize our conclusions, we would give the following chronological scheme of the literary treatment of the Aristotle/Alexander theme, by phases:

I. From the 4th century B.C. to the 1st century A.D.: precedents in relation to Aristotle/Alexander (biographical-novelistic narratives, letters, maxims, a poem in choliambics – always with a moralistic image).

II. 2nd or 3rd century A.D.: the composition of three works that are the remote model for *Buenos Proverbios*, *Poridad* and *Bocados de Oro.*

III. 6th or 7th century: amplification of these works using other Greek sapiential elements. And Byzantinization: novelesque themes, other Christian ones, imperial Byzantine setting. This is something especially cultivated in the eastern provinces of the empire.

IV. 7th or 8th century: Syriac translations (of all or some of the works) with Christian and Hermetic reworking, unless this is from the previous phase.

V. From the 8th to the 11th centuries: translations into Arabic, with slight reworking, in the Ommiad, Abbassid and Fatimid periods.

VI. 12th and 13th centuries: after several fragmentary translations into Latin, translations into Castilian, with slight reworking.

VII. 13th and following centuries: translations from Castilian into Latin and other languages; imitations.

As can be seen, it is a very complex history, which cannot be dealt with in two lines as our treatises on Castilian literature do. And these works cannot really be understood, in spite of their Byzantine and Christian characteristics and their passage through the Arab world, without knowing their origin in that Greek literature, between novelistic and sapiential, with its imprint, Cynic and moralistic in general but later, in the Hellenistic and imperial Roman periods, also Neo-Pythagorean and Hermetic.

Naturally, the subject remains open with regard to a series of details, and the definition of the works in the different phases at times is not absolutely clear-cut. But the fundamental lines have, I think, been established.

Chapter 4

Our Works within the Ancient Sapiential Tradition: Recent Strata

I. Overview

I feel that the moment has come to situate precisely, within ancient sapiential literature, the place occupied by the works that we have been studying, namely, the Greek-Arabic-Castilian works and the Greek-Arabic works that were not translated into Castilian. That they grew out of that particular soil has, I think, been amply demonstrated. And we have also given a general idea of this ancient sapiential literature, something that was, to be sure, more than necessary.

This is a matter, then, of explaining succinctly to what extent our works correspond to what we know of that sapiential literature and also to what extent they add to our knowledge, because something that we have pointed out time and again is how insufficient that knowledge is. Our works help to fill it out for a specific geographic area and, especially, a specific temporal period.

To begin with, the concept of sapiential literature is rather vague. It comprises genres like the fable, the epistolary novel, the "mirror for princes", the *khreîai*, the diatribe, the novelized *Lives*, all this combined with a profusion of maxims or *gnômai* that are also transmitted to us in separate collections of the various types to which we have made frequent reference. Furthermore, there is a constant osmosis between the philosophical treatise, Christian preaching, and Hermetic and Gnostic writings on the one hand and the maxims on the other. From those writings maxims were extracted (at times by the authors themselves), and, in turn, the collections of maxims were used to write new treatises, back and forth from the popular to the most elevated genres of wisdom.

But, as I repeat, our knowledge is incomplete. What we know of Hellenistic sapiential literature proves this. The papyri provide gnomological and biographical material for Antiquity that later diminishes or disappears completely; curiously enough, our Arabic-Castilian works sometimes provide this material. And they also provide a continuation of themes and genres of the oriental and classical Greek literature studied here as precedents of Hellenistic literature, which later sometimes fell into disuse. In any case, we have in our works examples of maxims, of the combination *Life* + maxims, of the novel followed by a dispute on wisdom, and of the "mirror for princes" joined to the epistolary novel, which are all examples of genres with ancient roots, existing in Antiquity, although no exact testimonies of this have come down to us. They constitute a new item within a common general program.

Sapiential literature had a double function in Antiquity: on the one hand, maxims, fables and all the rest were widely used in the schools; this is well documented. On the other, the Cynics and the Stoics, but especially the former, used this literature freely for proselytizing purposes, giving a rather falsified version of earlier doctrines (those of Socrates, Democritus, Isocrates, etc.) and continuing with *khreîai* of their own cultural or anti-cultural heroes: Diogenes, Bion, Crates, Zeno, Cleanthes, Chrysippus; diatribes, "mirrors for princes", novelized lives, collections of fables, epistolary novels, and wisdom debates all served the same purpose. These genres existed in a constant state of osmosis.

This literature advanced in the imperial Roman epoch. As regards form, diverse gnomologies were created in iambic trimeters, hexameters and especially in prose, and were added to the Hellenistic ones. Alphabetic and also thematic collections were created in which various authors took part. And there was a decline in genres like the *Life* followed by a collection of maxims, decline, that is, to our knowledge, because in the works we are studying they are perfectly in evidence. Not only that, we find combinations of *Life* + maxims or simply maxims of authors who are not especially well treated in this respect in the tradition that we preserve. And also anonymous maxims, of course.

As for the content itself of the maxims in our treatises, I have already remarked that we reencounter many of them in our tradition, but others no. Either they are an addition, a new creation, or our search instruments are insufficient (the lack of a databank, as I have said).

Added to this, new schools made use of popular literature to disseminate their doctrines: Porphyry's Neo-Platonism, the Neo-Pythagoreans, the Hermetics and the Christians. Either they attributed their doctrines to the most diverse authors (as the Cynics had done before, from Hellenistic times) or they created their own independent collections (but not lacking in a great variety of material, which they appropriated). Once again we find this osmosis between doctrinal writings and the popular gnomological collections.

I repeat that the works that we are studying here provide new data on this, and so they help to complete our knowledge. I remind the reader that this knowledge was already being augmented by the Byzantine gnomologies beginning in the 9th century A.D., which proves the existence in Antiquity of maxims and collections of maxims (alphabetical or thematic) that we do not have direct knowledge of and that sometimes changed the names of the authors of the maxims erroneously. They demonstrate the growing symbiosis of the ancient tradition with the Christian one.

In our works we find traces of the following:

a) The novelistic tradition, ancient, as we know, that deals with the themes of Aristotle, Alexander, the cranes of Ibycus, the story of Teodor, that of the discovery of the lost Greek originals.
b) The Socratic-Cynic-Stoic-moralistic tradition in general, disseminated from Hellenistic times. It is present, with the names of Socrates, Plato, Aristotle and Alexander, in *Buenos Proverbios*, *Bocados* and the *Philosophical Quartet* (edited by D. Gutas), and it is also present, with no names given, in all four of them.
c) The maxims in which philosophies such as Neo-Pythagoreanism, Neo-Platonism and Hermetism (sometimes contaminated with Gnosticism) were propagated, basically beginning in the 2nd century A.D., sometimes earlier. All this appears, especially, in *Buenos Proverbios*, *Bocados*, *Poridad* and the *Philosophical Quartet*.
d) The Christian tradition, which in our works, with two exceptions, Gregory and Basil (Tesileus, possibly also Silus = Basil in *Bocados*), who are expressly mentioned, was disseminated by Christianizing all the other philosophies, beginning mainly in the 2nd century A.D. It appears in all four works.
e) Various combinations of *Life* + maxims or else maxims with a specific author: in Chapter 1, note 30, I have given a long list of the Greek authors in *Bocados*, to the extent that they can be identified. They go from Homer, Simonides and Solon to Melissus, Pindar and Democritus, Xenophon, Crito, Philemon, Plutarch, Apollonius of Tyana, etc. They

bear good witness to the popularity in late Antiquity of *Lives* and gnomologies known only from this source.

Considering all this, our four works can be situated within the framework of late Antiquity, whose sapiential literature they represent and complete. But, as we have insisted, there also exist early Byzantine traces (the court, the palaces, the union of Christianity and the empire) and an ascetic and hagiographic view of ancient philosophers and of Alexander that seem to take us to the eastern part of the Byzantine empire, to Syria and Egypt, in the moments prior to the Arab invasion. This is without doubt where the Greek originals of our works come from and where they began to be translated into Syriac and Arabic at an early date.

The Neo-Pythagorean-Hermetic and Ascetic-Christian background (themes of the transitoriness of the world, death, body and soul, salvation, the beneficent monarch as the representative of God) which dominates in our works, forming a stratum that crowns earlier, basically Socratic-Cynic ones, is, in effect, reencountered in this sector from the time of its Christianization, and also, with variants of course, among the pagans of Harran at the height of the Arab epoch. A Greek collection of maxims[1] refers to the proselytism that was directed at them in an earlier period. These are environments that seem to us to have blended.

It is indeed interesting to review what has been said about the presence of gnomologies and other Greek sapiential material in translations of our works into the languages of various bordering countries, especially into Syriac, but also into Coptic, Ethiopian and Armenian. And this applies as much to the *Life* of Alexander as to the Syriac gnomologies, Neo-Pythagorean or not (some with a Christian intention), and also to the Armenian Hermetic *Definitions* and related Coptic texts.

In synopsis, we find the following in our works:

1. *Buenos Proverbios*. A novelized life of Alexander has been converted into a "mirror for princes" with the help of an epistolary novel: the maxims of Alexander and Aristotle and the laments on the death of the former (the Ascetic theme of death) predominate. There are insets (we do not know when they were included): maxims of various philosophers, of Socrates, Plato, Diogenes and Pythagoras.

1 See S. Brock, "A Syrian Collection of Prophecies of the Pagan Philosophers", *Orientalia Lovaniensia Periodica* 14, 1983, pp. 203–246.

2. *Bocados.* A long series of the combination *Life* + maxims and of maxims of many different authors. Apart from the Socratic and Cynic authors, as we have said, there are numerous Greek sages plus Neo-Pythagorean doctrines attributed to Pythagoras and other Hermetic sages (Hermes, Sed, Tat, Escalibus or Çagalquius = Asclepius) and Christian ones (I have already mentioned Gregory and Basil). And there are maxims of other infrequent authors and some anonymous ones that could be of the tendencies mentioned.
3. *Poridad.* Another work derived from the novelistic Aristotle/Alexander theme. Added to this is a "mirror for princes" presented with the help of an epistolary novel.
4. *Donzella Teodor.* A short novel followed by a wisdom debate.
5. *Philosophical Quartet.* Four combinations of *Life* + maxims: Pythagoras, Socrates, Plato and Aristotle. It is preserved only in Arabic and has been edited by D. Gutas[2].

As can be seen, these works are notable literary creations, something new based on existing traditions: two "mirrors for princes" aided by novelistic elements and letters; two groups of gnomologies or combinations of *Life* + gnomology; and a short novel followed by a wisdom debate. This apart from the insertions in *Buenos Proverbios*: ancient elements of the same gnomological tradition, but added secondarily by Greeks, Syrians or Arabs. And all within the same ideological syncretism that we are now familiar with and also within a Byzantine atmosphere from Asia.

I feel that all this definitively identifies our works as a special case within a sapiential tradition that is being investigated here in its entirety for the first time. This is the case of the syncretism referred to, centered on ascetic Christianity and the image of the Christian monarch of Byzantium. I consider that all of this was created in Syria in the 6th and 7th centuries A.D. and translated into Arabic (sometimes via Syriac) without great changes and from there into Castilian[3] (except in the case of the *Philosophical Quartet*).

2 D. Gutas, *Greek Wisdom Literature. A Study of Graeco-Arabic Gnomologia.*, cit.

3 On the influence of the Greek gnomologies on Syriac literature, add to what has already been said N. Zeegers-Vander Vorst, "Une gnomologie d'auteurs grecs en traduction syriaque", *Symposium Syriacum 1976, Orientalia christiana analecta*, 205, Rome, Pontificium Institutum Orientalium Studiorum, 1978, pp. 163–177; S. Brock, "From Antagonism to Assimilation: Syriac Attitudes to Greek Learning", in *East of Byzantium. Syria and Armenia in the formative period, Dumbarton Oaks Symposium 1980* (eds.

What is of note is that the ideological background of the treatises makes them enormously apt for incorporation into the circle of ideas of the Court of Alfonso the Wise, which promoted a kind of wisdom that united the Christian and pagan worlds and without doubt adopted the idea of the empire that underlay the works on Alexander: an empire that was really Byzantine, a model for the empire of Charlemagne and his successors, which Alfonso wanted to renew for himself, though he was unsuccessful. This is the reason for the imitation of these works in later Castilian literature, and even in earlier literature; they were already known in the reign of Ferdinand III.

I am referring, mainly, to the *Libro de los doze sabios o tratado de la nobleza y lealtad*, the *Flores de Filosofía* and the *Libro de los Cien Capítulos*, in the reign of Alfonso X and to the *Castigos de Sancho IV* in that of his son Sancho IV at the end of the century[4]. They are all "mirrors" or "regimens for princes" that add the theme of the salvation of the soul, which the king achieves thanks to the benefits that he confers on his subjects. The setting varies: in *Doze Sabios* Fernando III convokes the sages at the beginning of his reign to have them advise him (although it seems that the work was completed in the time of Alfonso X); in *Castigos* it is the king who advises his son; the other two works are gnomologies divided into chapters, but always centering on the themes of the king, God and the salvation of the soul.

The obligations of the king and his relationship with God, the obligations of his subjects, the *mind* as the norm of conduct of the knight, and nobility as goodness are themes that are constantly heard. They all derive from the religious, political and human philosophy that we have learned to recognize in the Greek treatises that we are studying in translation. The notable syncretism, the long history that this represents, is no longer detected in the works that were derived from it in Castile: to their authors and readers and almost to us it seemed something perfectly unitary. But it came from the synthesis of Socratic tradition and other various ancient traditions with the Christian tradition and the empire in the Byzantium of the 6th and following centuries.

N. Garsolan et al.), Washington D.C., 1982; S. Brock, "A Syriac Collection of Prophecies of the Pagan Philosophers", cit.

4 On these works see, apart from other bibliography cited there, F. Gómez Redondo, *Historia de la Prosa Medieval Castellana* I, Madrid, Cátedra, 1998, pp. 242 ff., 262 ff., 425 ff., 913 ff. Also H.O. Bizarri, "La estructura de castigos e documentos del rey Don Sancho IV", *Incipit* 17, 1997, pp. 83–138.

I did not want to omit an allusion to this point: the reason for the reception of our works in Castilian literature alongside others that I have already mentioned such as the *Sendebar*, the *Calila* and the *Barlaam*, besides the fables, all of them works with a related moral and political intent, though not so clearly defined or so Christianized.

But naturally, this is not the central point of this book. I will continue with the analysis of the contents of our works, of the various strata which melded in them, adding certain things to those already mentioned. And I will proceed by inverse chronological order, dealing with the recent elements first: the Neo-Pythagorean, Hermetic and Christian elements especially. Then, with the great traditional Socratic line, Socrates and his continuers, Diogenes and the Stoics, moralism in general. Another chapter will complete all this with diverse elements: anonymous maxims or maxims attributed to various authors. And two more must be devoted to special complementary matters regarding *Poridad* and *Donzella Teodor*. Their novelesque elements, which I feel have been sufficiently studied in the case of *Buenos Proverbios*, will be dealt with there and, of course, the elements concerning the content.

II. The Neo-Pythagorean elements

In Chapter II we have already commented on the Neo-Pythagorean elements introduced into our works under the name of Pythagoras (or Fayágoras), but there are more things to be added. We are dealing, as I said, with an exceptional case.

For not only in the Greco-Arabic-Castilian works do we find maxims (and sometimes a *Life*) of Pythagoras, that is, Neo-Pythagorean maxims, but we also encounter independent collections of them in Antiquity, collections that, furthermore, were translated into Syriac and Latin. Of course they are contaminated with the ancient moralistic and Christian traditions, and at times it is not easy to distinguish them from the Neo-Platonism of a Porphyry or a Jamblichus[5].

5 For Porphyry we have already cited E. Lamberz's 1975 edition of the *Sententiae ad intellegibilia ducentes*; add W. Pötscher's edition, Leiden, 1969, of the *Epistola ad*

These collections are a continuation of a pseudo-apocryphal Pythagorean literature from Hellenistic times, works attributed to Pythagoras, Timaeus, Architas and Ocellus Lucanus, usually in Doric. Then, beginning in the 1st century A.D., there appear in Alexandria and Rome Neo-Pythagoreans like Eudorus and Nigidius Figulus, who connect with the Platonic school. And this continued in the 1st century A.D. with Moderatus of Gades, with his ascetic practices and vegetarianism, and Apollonius of Tyana, who preached drawing near to God, occult science and purity. In the 2nd century came Numenius, a predecessor of Plotinus, and Nicomachus of Gerasa, these last two cultivators of magic. In the same century Porphyry and his disciple Jamblichus, both Neo-Platonists, considered themselves Neo-Pythagoreans as well: it is difficult to distinguish the difference with Neo-Platonism. But going on to the gnomologies and leaving aside those of Porphyry already mentioned, we have basically the following works:

1. The *Golden Verses* of the Pseudo-Phocylides.
2. The *Pythagorean Maxims* of Sextus and its Latin translation by Rufinus[6]. There are 451 maxims, followed by two appendices, which bring the total to 610. The authorship is in doubt; in any case, the attribution to Pope Xystus, Martyr, is incorrect. Chadwick proposes a pagan collection with Christian additions widely circulated among the Christians, which had already been cited by Origen. It has a rich manuscript and papy-

Marcellam; for the *Treatise on the* Soul by Jamblichus see A. J. Festugière, *La révélation d'Hermès Trismégiste,* Paris, Les Belles Lettres, 1981, III, pp. 177 ff.

6 See the edition of H. Chadwick, *The Sentences of Sextus*, Cambridge, University Press, 1959, with an important introduction and notes. It is better than A. Elter, *Sententiae Pythagoreorum*, in *Gnomica Homoeomata* 5. Bonn, 1904. It also includes the editions of Clitarchus and the Pseudo-Demophilus. For translations into other languages see J. Bouffartige, "Du grec au latin. La traduction latine des Sentences de Sextus", in *Études de Littérature ancienne*, Paris, Presses de l'Ecole Normale Supérieure, 1971, pp. 81–95; P. Poirier, "À propos de la version copte des Sentences de Sextus", *Laval Théologique et Philosophique* 36, 1980, pp. 317–320, and "Le texte de la version copte des sentences de Sextus", *Colloque International sur les textes de Nag Hammadi*, Québec-Louvain la Neuve, Presses de l'Université Laval, 1981, pp. 383–389; A. Carlini, "Le Sentenze di Sesto nella versione di Rufino", *Studi forogiuliense in onore di C.G. Mor*, Udine, Arti Grafiche Friulane, 1984, pp. 109–118; H. Kaufhold, "Die Überlieferung der *Sententiae Syriacae* und ihr historischer und literarischer Kontext", *Akten des 26. deutschen Rechtshistorikertages*, Frankfurt am Main, Klostermann, 1987, pp. 505–518.

rological tradition which I will discuss later. From this collection, in one phase or another, come:

a) The maxims of Porphyry's *Letter to Marcella*, derived from a phase in which the collection had not yet been Christianized, but it was alphabetically ordered. It adds Epicurean maxims.
b) Clitarchus' collection, which is also an extract (144 maxims), probably from a pre-Christian phase. The maxims are in the same order as in Sextus.
c) The *Pythagorean Maxims*, known as the Pseudo-Demophilus, from the *Vat. Gr.* 743, another extract (45 maxims), this one alphabetical, which is secondary, in any case[7]. Note that the original alphabetical collection, transmitted by other sources also, especially manuscripts D and P, was more extensive.

These maxims, as I said, found widespread dissemination together with translations into Syriac and Coptic in the Orient, and in the West, translated into Latin. For the Pseudo-Demophilus, specifically, Sodano has done a careful study that demonstrates the existence of an old alphabetical corpus from which are derived the citations from Stobaeus and ms. D, the Syriac translations, *Vat. Gr.* 743, and ms. P. Therefore, the Syriac texts depend on Greek texts not exactly identical to ours. And the original alphabetical collection was closer to Sextus than to Porphyry: it had elements that were more clearly Christian. Furthermore, in *Bocados*, as I have said, there is a derived Arabic version that comes from a Greek text close to the one used by the Syriac versions, but not identical[8].

For once we find Greek texts close to the maxims of our treatises, specifically, as I have just said, to *Bocados*. Add to this the fact that the Pythagoras section of *Buenos Proverbios* comes from the *Golden Verses*, and that we also have, in the *Philosophical Quartet*, Pythagorean maxims that come from the ancient tradition.

Perhaps before continuing, it would be helpful to say something about the content of these maxims.

Chadwick demonstrates clearly that the Christian elements are especially notable at the beginning of the collection but do not offer external features

7 See, besides Chadwick's edition, that of A. R. Sodano, accompanied by an extensive study (*Le Sentenze "pitagoriche" dello pseudo-Demofilo*, Rome, Accademia nazionale dei Lincei, 1991). Also F. W. A. Mullach, *Fragmenta Philosophorum Graecorum,* I, pp. 485 ff.

8 See Sodano, op. cit., pp. 87 ff.

that are especially characteristic: they do not speak of Christ, the Church, the Virgin, the kingdom of God. Doubtless, there was an attempt to create a synthesis valid for everyone. But the themes are Christian: faith, the man of God, sin, the power of God, the wise man who needs God, etc., as well as adultery, salvation, the uncertainty of the world, etc.

Other themes such as temperance, death, the pleasure that leads to injustice, etc. cover a broader domain. They can be considered as much Christian as Pythagorean, as can the ideal of imitating God, faith as the starting point to know God, the body as inferior to the soul but also its image, the refusal to want possessions, the generosity of giving alms. There is the wise man, recognized by few but elevated to the knowledge of God, who practices the renunciation of transitory possessions; and the themes of prudence and silence are also present. Part of all this comes from Socratism, for example the "know thyself", the Delphic maxim elaborated on by Socrates.

All this, as I say, ended up in a considerable part of our treatises. Gutas's work is the most in-depth study of the subject[9]. He has demonstrated without doubt that Hunayn (that is, *Buenos Proverbios*, pp. 32 ff.) comes from the *Golden Verses*[10]. But they have lost their pagan features: Zeus is replaced by God and his angels, for example.

He has also studied the Pythagorean tradition in the *Philosophical Quartet* and related literature: he takes it back to the Pythagorean collections of Antiquity through a long series of confusions and false attributions that he believes come from the Arabic epoch; they hardly exist in al-Hindi. And he has studied the tradition in Mubassir *(Bocados)*, a subject also treated by Sodano[11].

In *Bocados* our maxims are preceded by a *Life* in which features are mixed that could just as well be Pythagorean as Christian (reject the world, serve God, sanctify your senses, love all men, fast, know that the soul has a reward or a punishment) and others more strictly Pythagorean such as keeping silent and investigating the nature of things. Then, as for the maxims, of the 103 of the Arabic text and the 87 of the Latin one (derived from the Castilian text, as we know) there are 41 that come from the Greek alphabetical collection (19 of them are in the Pseudo-Demophilus). To these

9 In his above-mentioned 1975 book , pp. 62 ff. and 268 ff.

10 For other Arabic translations of this see F. Rosenthal, op. cit., pp. 118 ff.

11 Op. cit., pp. 61 ff.

Mubassir (or better, his source) adds diverse material of Greek origin, according to E. Franceschini[12], from Plato's *Phaedo*, from Diogenes Laertius, from Isocrates' *Ad Demonicum* and from the *Liber Ethicorum*[13]. They more probably come from various ancient gnomologies.

In the Chadwick and Sodano editions, on the other hand, we have the *loci paralleli* of Mubassir and the different Pythagorean collections plus references to Porphyry's *ad Marcellam*, Jamblichus' *Vita Pythagorica*, earlier gnomologies that some of the maxims come from (for example, the *Menandri Monostichi*) and Byzantine gnomologies, like that of Maximus, where some of them end up. But to see the depth of the doctrine, one has only to open *Bocados* to confirm the frequency of the themes of God, the pure soul that must return to God, doing good works although they receive no thanks, death and sleep (death is better than allowing the soul to darken), freedom and goodness, the vanities of the world, lying on a wooden bed believing in God and not on a golden one doubting Him, moderation, continence and fear of God, knowledge and keeping silent, the person who errs in word though clothed in fine stuffs.

Pythagoras is a teacher seated in a chair who preaches temperance and justice. Sometimes maxims of various provenances are joined, like the one about the old man who was ashamed to learn, which reminds us of Solon and Socrates, or the one that says that the sweetest thing is what man covets (Sappho). In short, a long tradition passes through Pythagorism and Neo-Platonism to end up in a Christianity that is as ancient as it is medieval. It often touches on the familiar theme of the king: the much-repeated "it is in the interest of the king", a translation, without doubt, of a πρέπει τῷ βασιλεῖ that asks of him that he care for his kingdom, that he teach the laws, abolish greed, beware of beautiful men and women. It introduces the theme of the "mirrors for princes", which appears confluently here.

In summary, for once this is not simply a hypothesis: from other sources we know at least a part of the old Pythagorean texts and of others assimilated into them, which, under the name of Pythagoras, entered a number of our medieval texts.

12 "Il Liber philosophorum moralium antiquorum", in *Acta della regale Accademia dei Lincei, Classe di Szienze morali, storiche e philologiche* 3, 1930, pp. 355–399.

13 An Alexandrian-Arabic compendium of the *Ethics to Nichomacus*, ed. D. Marchesi, Messina, 1904.

Nevertheless, it should be helpful to make a few comments on the type of Neo-Pythagorism cultivated in our gnomologies, in those preserved in Greek and in those of the Greco-Arabic tradition. They refer, insofar as they are really Neo-Pythagorean, to the Pythagorean kind of life, a religious asceticism not easily separated from the Neo-Platonic and Christian sort, although the most extreme feature of this asceticism, namely vegetarianism, is lacking, as are certain aspects of Christian dogma. And missing, too, are the speculation on the One (present in Moderatus, for example), the mathematical theories derived from it and magic. We have the impression of a syncretism in which the most extreme and shocking aspects of each doctrine were eliminated, and morality was given preference over dogma and speculation.

III. The Hermetic elements

Throughout this book, in the previous chapters and in this one, we have presented information on the presence of Hermetic elements in at least three of our treatises: in *Poridad*, with the tale of the discovery of the book in the temple of Homer the Greater (Hermes Trismegistus), plus the theme of the secret and internal allusions; in *Bocados*, with the "acts" and "sayings" of Hermes and the sayings or *castigos* (counsels) of Sed (Set), Tad (Thoth) and Çagalquius (Asclepius, that is, Imuthes, called Escalibus on p. 168 Crombach). But I have also mentioned the collection of Greek letters on the theme of Alexander identified by Grignaschi, who discusses their Hermetic elements.

And I have alluded, as well, to the presence of Hermetic elements in Syriac and Arabic literature[14]. And aside from our *Corpus Hermeticum*, a Byzantine selection, we have a Latin *Asclepius* (which Lactantius still consulted in Greek), Stobaeus' *excerpta Hermetica*, the Hermetic texts from Nag Ham-

14 See also B. P. Copenhaver, *Hermetica*, Cambridge, 1994, pp. XLIV ff., also on western Hermetism in the Middle Ages and Renaissance. For the Arabic tradition see, also, L. Massignon, "Inventaire de la littérature hermétique arabe", appendix to J. P. Festugière, *La révélation d'Hermès Trismégiste*, vol. I: *L'astrologie et les sciences occultes*, Paris, Gabalda, 1944 (reed. 1981), pp. 384–400 (reproduced in L. Massignon, *Opera Minora*, vol. I, Beirut, Dar al-Maaref, 1963, pp. 650–666).

madi and the Armenian *Definitions*[15]. Hermetism was widespread, probably since the 2nd century A.D. (and possibly before that), especially in the Orient; Clement of Alexandria, around 200, cites 42 treatises. He and Lactantius are witnesses to the intimate contact between Hermetic and Christian texts that culminates in our works.

In earlier pages I have left in doubt whether the Hermetic elements in our texts come from ancient writings (from the imperial or Byzantine period) or rather from the Syriac or Arab translators, although I incline toward the former hypothesis. I continue to believe this, as in *Poridad*, and also in the novelized Letters on Alexander, both elements are intimately combined. In order to accept a different hypothesis for *Bocados*, one would have to defend the idea that not only the "Hermetic" chapters, but all of them were independent and were put together into a collection in Syriac or Arabic times. This is hardly credible.

Now something similar to this must be said about the Neo-Pythagorean elements: the Hermetism of the treatises is one thing and our Hermetic texts are something else. It is advisable, then, to say something about the latter. The *excerpta* of Stobaeus, the texts from Nag Hammadi and the Armenian *Definitions* are treatises of Byzantine transmission.

Nowadays we have been disabused of Festugière's affirmation that Hermetism is a Greek philosophy, a kind of Platonism. After the discovery of the Coptic texts from Nag Hammadi (found in 1946, but made accessible much later), we must return to the Egyptian origin that Reitzenstein defended, even if it had a veneer of Platonism. Hermes is Thoth (τρισμέγιστος, "thrice great" comes from the Egyptian invocation *"aa aa"* [very great]); this identification is already present in Herodotus. And to the Egyptian pantheon belong the other two gods mentioned above (plus Isis and Ammon, who also appear). Furthermore, in these works, which are offered as a revelation to mortals, an attempt to overcome the opposition

15 For Hermetism in general, besides Reitzenstein's *Poimandres* and the above-mentioned books by Festugière and Copenhaver, see the edition and translation of the *Corpus Hermeticum* by A. D. Nock and A. J. Festugière, *CUF*, vols. I–IV, Paris, Les Belles Lettres, 1946–54; J. P. Mahé, *Hermès en Haute Egypte*, I–II, Québec, Université Laval, 1978–82; X. Renau Nebot, *Textos herméticos*, Madrid, Gredos, 1999, with a good introduction. For the form, see A. D. Nock, "Diatribe Form in the Hermetica", in *Essays on Religion and the Ancient World*, Oxford, Clarendon Press, 1972, pp. 26–32. See, in general, the recent update by R. Goulet, art. "Hermetica", *Dictionnaire des Philosophes Antiques*, vol. III, Paris, CNRS, 2000, pp. 641–650.

between life and death, the whole atmosphere is Egyptian. And much of the cosmogony and the eschatology are Egyptian, as well as the whole aura of magic, alchemy and astrology that hardly appears in the treatises but is noticeably present in the Greek and Demotic papyri on magic.

But this Egyptian starting point, which must be situated within the broader setting of the mystic, miracle-loving oriental religions, in the Roman Empire was enveloped in a Neo-Platonic interpretation of God, the world and the fate of the soul. The treatises look for salvation and union in God through knowledge, and in connection with this, purity in life. But Hermetism in its entirety cannot be understood if we do not take into account the whole atmosphere found in the religion of Isis, the "potter's oracles", the Chaldean oracles, the "oracles of Baalbeck" or of the Tiburtine Sibyl, the pseudo-Orphic poems, Gnosticism, etc.[16] Here we can add the pagan maxims interpreted in a Syriac work as prophetic, which have been mentioned above. And from very early on, there is the contact of the Jewish religion with the Christian one; it is impossible to go into details here.

Apart from this, there are various treatises of different orientations: the dualism between the divine and the worldly, the theme of souls as divine sparks that must be liberated. Actually, for certain treatises the pessimistic version of the world is the central point; however, for others, the world, a work of God, is perfect. Still others attempt a sort of indoctrination of the initiates (although there does not seem to have been a Hermetic church, at the most groups and communities). There are others too, as we have said, that are gnomologies taken from Hermetic works: number XI of Stobaeus' *excerpta*, the Armenian *Definitions* and perhaps, within the *Corpus*, treatise XVI *(Definitions)*. Notable also is the passage from the *excerpta* of Stobaeus XXVIII, in which Thales, Socrates and Hermes reply in succession to the question, "What is God?". Mahé considers that the gnomologies were probably the beginning of the Hermetic writings[17].

Now then, if the treatises preserved transmit only a part of the Hermetic doctrine, and not entirely coherently, they are, as has been said, "cultured" treatises as opposed to popular writings: here we must investigate their content in relation to that of the Hermetic gnomologies in the texts we are studying. And also the content of the Hermetic gnomologies alluded to,

16 See B. P. Copenhaver, op. cit., pp. XXIII ff.

17 Op. cit., II, p. 409.

which are nothing more than catechisms or summaries the better to master the doctrine, the same device as we have seen used by the pagan authors, or by their epitomizers. "If you keep these maxims in your mind, you will easily remember the things that I described in detail for you in numerous discourses," says the *excerpta* from Stobeaus XI[18].

This situation is different from the one we have encountered in the case of the Neo-Pythagorean maxims. There our treatises collected at least part of the exact maxims of the Neo-Pythagorean gnomologies of Sextus, the Pseudo-Demophilus and the rest. Here no; the maxims attributed to Hermes and the other Hermetic figures coincide only to a rather limited extent with the Hermetic gnomologies, that is, with Hermetic doctrine, which now appears greatly modified in an ethical sense akin to Christian ethics. Furthermore, the treatises preserved contain discourses by Poimandres (to an unnamed faithful person), Hermes (to Tat and Asclepius) and Isis (to Horus). The two gnomologies mentioned give the maxims without the author's name. However, in our treatises there appear, as I have said, discourses by Sed, Hermes, Tat and Çagalquius. So the form varies.

And the content also. The gnomologies cited, to be sure, omit the mythical, cosmological, eschatological and astrological elements of the treatises, but they insist on the hierarchy God-cosmos-man, the oppositions body/soul, mortal/immortal, heaven/earth, good/evil, the unengendered/the engendered and corruptible, as well as the theme of silence. The definition of God as an immovable monad, the invisible cosmos, the hierarchy of the living, the theory of the *logos* and the *noûs* occupy a great deal of space in the texts.

Man knows God and can become a god, while God "adopts human form" (surely a Christian concept). Praise of man is emphasized, the greatest marvel of Creation, capable of knowing God, and without whom as a witness the cosmos "would not exist," "he can become God". "There is nothing inaccessible to thought, nothing that cannot be expressed in words." "By maintaining silence, you understand." All these are nothing more than extracts of doctrines that are found in the treatises, as I have said. But missing is almost all the moral exhortation, which is only indirectly deduced from the theme of the need to do good, of raising oneself to God as the soul is liberated from the body.

18 P. 314 of X. Renau's translation.

The Arabic-Castilian treatises accentuate the elements of advice and guidance for the soul, just as the Neo-Pythagorean doctrines do, in the form of maxims of the gods or Hermetic figures mentioned, addressed to the initiate or simply to the reader (except 110, addressed to Ammon by someone whose name is not given). In only one case is this indoctrination preceded by a *Life*, in accordance with the scheme we are familiar with: this is the "acts or deeds" of Hermes, previous to his "sayings", as I remarked above. But the very fact that the Hermetic maxims, with or without a *Life* and attributed to one person or another, appear in *Bocados* on an equal footing (or better, taking preference, as they open the book) beside those of Homer and the long line of Greek sages (Pythagoras also), proves that this new wisdom was already being assimilated on the one hand into the traditional Greek wisdom and on the other, into the Christian wisdom by the end of Antiquity and in the first Byzantine epoch.

Hermes was born in Egypt; he is considered the equivalent (as in other places) of the Hebrew Enoch and his genealogy is shown within a line that begins with Adam. Hermes (continuing the tradition of the Egyptian Tot, who, in the *Corpus*, strangely enough, appears as his son) traveled about the world founding cities and teaching the Sciences, especially all about the stars. He encouraged men to follow the law of God and abhor the world, to pray and fast, to avoid eating the meat of the swine, the zebra and the camel, to abstain from drinking wine. He established holy festival days and sacrifices in relation to the movement of the sun and the moon, specifically sacrifices of plants and beverages.

It is interesting that as in the case of Pythagoras, *Bocados* inserts a *Life* before the maxims, following an ancient model familiar to us, and that this *Life* combines features of these ancient philosophies (or, rather, religions) with the Christian ones. Really, with some exceptions, they try to find features that can be reconciled. What is most severely Hermetic and Pythagorean is avoided. And it all centers on the moral theme in accordance with the model of the Greek gnomologies: there are hortatory maxims, maxims in the imperative, and a few *khreîai* with dialogue (*Bocados* 62, 63, 105, 106). Although in this case, unlike the former one, we have only preserved the old models partially, it is perfectly clear that they must have existed, for example, the combination *Life* + hortatory gnomologies with an orientation between Hermetic and Christian.

Let me point out some features of the gnomologies preserved in the translations into Arabic and Castilian. You can guess what my conclusion is: we must go back to the syncretic Greek gnomologies that select Hermetic material compatible with Christian material and annex the latter, together with still other material. All of the content can be explained by the currents that came together at the end of Antiquity and in the first Byzantine centuries, as can the form of the maxims and *khreîai* mentioned above. It is often possible to reconstruct the Greek parent formula: thus, the frequent "it is in the interest of the king" is without doubt πρέπει τῷ βασιλεῖ.

Let us look at the maxims of the successive Hermetic gods or sages.

Sed. Curiously, the evil god Sed or Seth, the enemy of Horus, who does not appear in the *Hermetica*[19], does appear in *Bocados* before Hermes, with a collection of maxims, (and he appears as the son of Adam, and consequently as older than Hermes or Tat).

This collection of thirty-five maxims is not very important. It begins and ends with the theme of the believer in God and of service to God respectively, the composition like that of the hymns. In the center there are Hermetic themes like keeping silent (18), wisdom (the "wise one", "sapience", 22 ff.) and others, also Christian, like the rejection of the world (35), doing good works (32) and alms (33). But what stands out is the long list of recommendations to the king (2 ff.), who should know himself, be for his people as the soul is with the body. He should follow the model of *"buen facer"* (correct comportment) and guide his people in it, and they will be obedient. There is also the theme of friends.

These are topics that fit in with the Hermetic mentality, but they come from the "counsels for the prince" of the Greek tradition that we are familiar with. In *Poridad*, they appear likewise in the Hermetic context as mentioned above, and they reappear in the maxims of the other Hermetic sages. With no connection to this doctrine, but definite connection to the Christian doctrine, they appear in *Buenos Proverbios* (the Alexander theme), as we have seen. Evidently the ancient Greek tradition of giving counsels to the king connects, on the one hand, with the Christian tradition and on the other, with the Hermetic tradition. It is clear that this did not enter the *Hermetica*, which proves that it is not the only source of our gnomologies.

19 He only appears, with his perverse characteristics, under the name of Tiphon in Stobaeus' *excerpta* XXV 8. However, he appears repeatedly under the two names in the magic papyri, where his help is requested. See J. L. Calvo's translation of the magic papyri, *Textos de magia en papiros griegos*, Madrid, Gredos, 1987.

Hermes. This is the fundamental collection: 119 maxims after the *Life*. Once again it opens with the theme of God, but, it seems to me, with a strong Judaic-Christian influence: the fear of God, prophets, commandments, prayer, etc. The theme is recurrent, but its close relation to the theme of wisdom ("sapience") is essential: this is Neo-Platonic and Hermetic, not Christian. It is wisdom that allows one to know God, to save one's soul (25: "the life of the soul lies in wisdom, and wisdom is to believe in God and keep the law"), 31, 40, 41, 45, 46, 47, 50, 66, 68 ("the sages ... who descend to the depths of the seas"), 112 ff. It is accompanied by praise of truth and of man (94: *"la mejor cosa que Dios fizo en este mundo es el ome. E la mejor cosa que es en el ome, es el seso"* [the best thing that God made in this world is man. And the best thing that there is in man is his mind]). On the other hand there is little about the soul and salvation.

The asceticism that we have seen also appears: not eating the "wrong viands" (13), fasting, giving alms, performing good works (31: in this way the soul is cleansed, one is following God), chastity (69); and disdain for the world (76, 103).

There are also maxims that are more specifically Christian: not harming someone who has harmed us; making a friend of one's enemy (48), taking pity on fools (52); and those that have been added from earlier traditions, for example, the king who should do good, while the people should obey him (19, 110), or the nobleman who is noted for his justice (111). And there are more that in some way or another have been included here: the one that recommends the old man not to marry because he cannot even manage himself (80), the *khreía* (63) that asks why the sages come to the door of the rich men and not the other way around (wise men know the advantages of wealth but the rich do not know the advantages of wisdom).

Tad and *Çagalquius*. They do not add much to the above. Tad (13 maxims) repeats the themes of wisdom and the king; he does not speak of God, the soul or salvation, or of the world either. The last maxim, the inscription on his seal, is important: "I hold to the first cause". In this way the theme of God enters.

In the ten maxims of Çagalquius or Asclepius, the son of Tad, we do have God as the creator. Man must guard against the wrong viands, abandon the world and serve God; the maxims speak of faith and keeping silent. Under the name of Escalibus, as I have said, there is another maxim in Crombach, p. 168, in the form of a *khreía*: a man with a great heart *"non le puede conplir ninguna cosa si non el paraíso"* (can be satisfied with nothing except paradise).

This is more or less the panorama. We must take as a starting point Hermetic gnomologies with the most mythical and abstract parts expurgated and reduced to the ethical and ascetic, though there are allusions to salvation. There remains a great deal that is Neo-Platonic-Hermetic, especially in the theme of wisdom. And Christian and other common themes are added plus still others of ancient origin, more or less adapted to the new environment.

Our treatises are, then, (we must add certain things when we look at *Poridad* and *Donzella Teodor*) a source for the reconstruction of lost gnomologies of the Greco-Byzantine tradition and even the gnomologies of the neighboring oriental peoples' traditions. We know or suppose their origins, but it is only here that we preserve their texts more or less intact.

IV. The Christian elements

I am not going to do a study here parallel to those done for the Neo-Pythagorean and Hermetic elements, partly because this has been done in the previous chapters, and partly because it is better to do this later in relation to the diverse gnomologies. The beginnings have already been seen: the syncretisms pagan/Jewish and pagan/Christian from the time of the 3rd–4th centuries A.D., the creation of Christian gnomologies parallel to the others and the subsequent mixing of both.

In the preceding chapters we have already seen:

a) Socratic maxims continued by other Cynic maxims and these by others that are simply moralistic. As I have said, the Socratic maxims and *khreîai* were infiltrated by the Cynic doctrine and were frequently attributed to Diogenes (or vice versa), and also to other authors. It is evident that there were multiple points of contact (self-control, virtue, knowing one's self, etc.) that were enlarged upon. And strictly Cynic themes such as antifeminism were attributed to Socrates, who, in our gnomologies and in the Greco-Arabic ones, is an ascetic or saint with Christian leanings[20].

We have already mentioned Aristotle as a saint and Alexander as the force behind a Christian empire, an echo, really, of the theories of the Christian empire that had been being formulated from the time of Basil and that culminated in Agapetus. We will continue with this theme, giving more precise details, when we discuss Socrates and the other Socratics.

b) We have studied the themes of death and Christian consolation within the Aristotle/Alexander theme in *Buenos Proverbios*, in Chapter III. The philosophers, the relatives, the mother, both in letters and in the funeral mourning, all develop this theme amply, with Christian accents. We know of a Greek epistolary novel, translated into Arabic, in which the theme appears and also Byzantine and Syriac works of the 9th century in which it reappears. And there is the theme of the "mirror for princes" or counsels that, coming from Isocrates and even earlier, acquired a Christian tint (goodness, imitation of God). We have already seen that there are those who consider that all this comes from a Syriac Christianity that is reflected in the Arabic texts. In any case, the process of Christianization of the Alexander/Aristotle theme began in the Byzantine epoch.
c) We have just seen the fusion of Neo-Pythagorean and Hermetic themes and maxims with Christian ones.

With some exceptions (the mention of Christ and the Virgin in *Donzella Teodor*, for example), a neutral situation was arrived at in which the least conflictive Christian themes and also the least conflictive themes of the other philosophies were sought. And what was cosmological, magical and astrological was omitted to concentrate on what was ethical and religious. This is what constitutes the backbone of our gnomologies. It is present in the various personal gnomologies, that of Socrates and those of the other sages.

20 G. Strohmaier, "Die arabische Sokrateslegende und ihre Ursprünge", in P. Nagel (ed.), *Studia Coptica*, Berlin, Akademie Verlag, 1974, pp. 121–136; and "Ethical sentences and Anecdotes of Greek Philosophers in Arabic Tradition", in *Actes du Ve Congrès d'Arabisants et d'Islamisants, Correspondance d'Orient*, 11, Bruxelles, 1971, pp. 436–471.

Thus, in each of the following studies on the different ancient philosophers we will try to discover the Christian elements that were added to the earlier ones.

Naturally, to distinguish between the Socratic, the Platonic, the Aristotelian, what is attributed to Alexander (pure fantasy) and generalized moralism is no easy task. The maxims of each one of these authors are infiltrated by this other philosophical wave, which consists of none other than the Neo-Pythagorean and Hermetic maxims. And the other way around: where they might least be expected, we find, for example, purely Socratic elements. Furthermore, apart from the existence of all kinds of contradictions, we must take into account, as I have said, the fact that we do not have a database to orient us.

Then, too, I must emphasize the Christianization of the sapiential genres that we are not studying here, for example the fables of Aesop in the Syriac collections[21].

Using the CD-ROM of the *Thesaurus Linguae Graecae* and certain indices, I was able to find the Greek originals of some of the maxims in our treatises. Of course, we must start from the Castilian maxims in order to find the Greek prototypes, which sometimes is easy. Earlier I spoke of the πρέπει τῷ βασιλεῖ; there are other groups of words that permit the reconstruction of phrases with, for example, μὴ πιστεύετε τῷ κόσμῳ "do not trust the world", ἰατρὸς τῆς ψυχῆς "Physician of the soul", ὁ αἰώνιος κόσμος "the eternal world", φύλαττε τὰ ἀπόρρητα "guard you secrets", εἶπον τῷ Σωκράτει "they said to Socrates", ἀγάπη τοῦ κόσμου "love of the word", etc. More details are given throughout the book.

21 See my *Historia* ..., II, Madrid, 1985, pp. 393 ff. (pp. 426 ff. of the English translation).

Chapter 5

Socratic and Post-Socratic *Lives* and Gnomologies. I. Socrates

I. General comments

We shall connect here with matters discussed in previous chapters, especially Chapter 2: the Socratic-Cynic-moralistic philosophy, contaminated with Christian and also Neo-Pythagorean and Hermetic philosophy, is what dominates the Greek and Byzantine gnomologies and also the gnomologies that passed into Arabic and in some cases into Castilian.

Of our texts, *Bocados* and the *Philosophical Quartet* are the ones that preserve a combination of *Life* + Socratic gnomology; in *Buenos Proverbios* there is only a gnomology, whose relation with that of *Bocados* we shall study. I believe that this continues an old tradition and that, therefore, our treatises contribute something new to the knowledge of ancient sapiential literature, although without doubt in its final phase, that of early Byzantine Syria. But it was nothing more than a continuation of previous phases.

Indeed, we have seen the existence, in *PHibeh* 182, of this same combination, with a number of maxims and *khreîai* that by then had a Cynicizing character. And we have seen that from an early date there were biographies of Socrates: those of Aristoxenus, Demetrius of Phalerum and Phaenias, among others. No other philosopher is more cited, sometimes with praise, sometimes with criticism (as in the Epicurean citations given in E. Acosta and E. Angeli[1]). In any event, as far back as the 4th century B.C. there are the biographies that we have mentioned, then the above-mentioned papyrological texts, the chapter regarding Diogenes Laertius, and many citations.

Nevertheless, the combination *Life* + gnomology was abandoned, or rather, it did not reach us, with the exception of Diogenes Laertius. But, as

1 *Filodemo. Testimonianze su Socrate*, Naples, Bibliopolis, 1992. See my review in *Emerita*, 63, 1995, pp. 146 ff.

I say, the Arabic and Arabic-Castilian texts are proof of the fact that it continued to exist.

And the different Socratic citations, both from Antiquity and from the Byzantine gnomologies, bear witness to the existence of ancient Socratic gnomologies. It is evident that when in a gnomology by authors, such as the *Gnom. Vat.*, there is a section dedicated to Socrates, this is a continuation of an old gnomology. And when in a gnomology ordered by themes, such as Maximus Confessor's, there are in each theme three or four maxims by Socrates one after another (with his name or, after the first mention, with "by the same person"), then we have a second trace of the gnomologies by Socrates. And we are talking about more than one gnomology, because in authors like Maximus Confessor, there are repetitions, and because in comparing certain gnomologies with others, we find maxims in some that are missing in others, so that the authors used gnomologies that coincided only partially.

And without doubt there were maxims that did not leave any trace in these Greek gnomologies, because in *Bocados* and *PQ* we find maxims that exist nowhere else, the same, or different ones in the two treatises.

This is, then, a matter of inserting the content of these two works into the ancient Socratic tradition. Ideally, the following would have to be done:

a) Establish a complete collection of Socrates' maxims and *khreîai* in ancient and Byzantine authors and gnomologies. We will attempt this here, although not exhaustively. After that we will try to shed some light on the Socratic gnomologies.
b) With this starting point, see what there is new (compared with other authors and gnomologies) in *Bocados*, + *PQ* + Ibn Durayd, or in any one of these works.
c) Situate each one of these two works, *Bocados* and *PQ*, within the entire tradition.

But to go on from here, it would be necessary to do an in-depth study of the Socratic tradition in general and in each work: truly Socratic elements and also accretions of the different philosophies and religions that we have seen. This has been done in part, especially when we spoke about the Cynic and Christian strata, but it should be done more thoroughly.

Of course we cannot do a complete study of all this here, but we can establish the principal lines. We are going to treat Socrates quite thoroughly in order to draw the major lines in the evolution of the gnomologies from the ancient up to the Castilian ones. Those of other authors will be treated more summarily so as not to make this book interminable. In any case, what interests us is to draw the major lines of the evolution.

II. The *Lives*

It will be best to commence with the two treatises, *Bocados* and *PQ*, since they are the central theme of our study, and to begin with the *Life*, which offers a panorama of how Socrates was seen by the authors of our works or by their predecessors.

Now then, we have already mentioned Strohmaier's observation that the view of Socrates as an ascetic, almost as a saint, with its themes of renunciation of the world and the rest, goes beyond what was said about him in the Greek world, and suggests a Syrian, and even Muslim asceticism. In any case, it is asceticism with a Byzantine base. This is the same panorama as we have presented in relation to Aristotle and Alexander.

The *Lives* in our two works conform to this scheme exactly (as do the maxims that follow them). The shortest is the one in *PQ*, transcribed below in its entirety (Gutas, p. 85):

> With him Philosophy first appeared and from him it issued; his are the well-known proverbs and the useful sayings of universal application. Like a breath of fresh air when it blows, and like relief for the afflicted, so are his words to the hearts; and like the effect of water in the sultriness of midday heat, so is his effect upon the minds and thoughts. He was an ascetic man, practising austerities, who never ate his fill of bread. (Selected maxims follow.)

So we have Socrates the ascetic: all discursive argumentation is missing, as is the search for new rational definitions or the political theme or the theory of knowledge or the confrontation with the Sophists. The maxims are meant to edify the faithful, nothing more. As can be seen, this is the same scheme as we have encountered for the Neo-Pythagoreans and the Hermetics.

Now, if we go on to *Bocados* (p. 45), we have a much longer *Life*, one that introduces us to a Christian Socrates. He was condemned for wanting to “get rid of the idols”, he enjoined men to “pray to the One, the Lasting, the Creator, the Wise Man, the Powerful". Delos is "the house of the idol". On dying he wants to *"facer oración"* (pray), *"endereçar a vuestras almas"* (set your souls to rights).

What is interesting is the concurrence of notable errors that bespeak the Byzantine age (the text mentions the "king" of Greece, and that Crito proposes that he go to Rome, that the eleven judges of Athens condemned him, that he died at the age of eighty, that he left twelve thousand disciples), showing a considerable knowledge of Plato's principal dialogues. The defense of living thought as opposed to wisdom on parchments comes from the *Phaedrus*; the long description of death and the dialogue with Simias (Sumes) on "the fact of the soul" from the *Phaedo*; the discussion with Eclitón (Crito), who wants him to escape from prison, from the *Crito*; the decision that "I will never cease to protect the truth and oppose falsehood", from the *Apology*.

The author, unless he had read Plato's dialogues, very probably had read a biography of Socrates, one oriented in a Christian direction evidently, but also, before that, toward Cynic reasoning, because the *Life* begins with the theme of Xantippe (*"la más fuerte muger e la más nescia que había en su tierra"* [the strongest and most stupid woman in the land]). Socrates endured her stupidity and that of men in general.

It is important to say this because it gives some orientation about the maxims that follow. In order to judge them, it will be useful first to offer, as a setting, the Socratic maxims and *khreîai* of the gnomologies, then those of *Bocados* and of *PQ*, to show their relation to each other and to the preceding ones and to those that are new, and also those of *Buenos Proverbios*. Finally, we will try to establish a stratification of the content of our collections of maxims.

III. List of *gnômai* and *khreîai* attributed to Socrates in the gnomologies and Greek authors that have been preserved

In order to establish the list of Socratic *gnômai* in the Greco-Arabic-Castilian and Greco-Arabic works it is necessary first to establish, as a term of comparison, a list of the Socratic *gnômai* in the Greek gnomologies that have been preserved. I remind the reader that there are frequently variations of attribution: Socratic *gnômai* attributed, at times, to Diogenes and other ancient authors. I will give an account of them, though only briefly. I omit those attested to by Plato and the Socratics that we have already seen.

I enumerate below the *gnômai* or maxims that are attributed to Socrates. They have been collected by me, but I add maxims from the second edition of G. Giannantoni (*Socratis et Socraticorum reliquiae*, 1990, pp. 99 ff.)[2].

Neither will I attempt to give complete data and bibliography on the tradition of each maxim: the data I give can be completed with the editions of the gnomologies, which provide good material. Also, the maxims are given in abbreviated form.

I will begin with the *gnômai* (or *khreîai*) in the *Gnomologium Vaticanum*, the most extensive collection, and also in other related gnomologies, when the *GV* fails. I give the essential details about the presence of these maxims in other gnomologies, the rest can be found in Sternbach's edition. I consider that these maxims come from ancient gnomologies that reached the Byzantine epoch and were recorded there, independently of the collection (identified with the *Corpus Parisinum*) that reached the hands of Maximus Confessor and Antonius Melissa, among others. We also find many of them in the imperial epoch, others no, but without doubt they already existed in gnomologies of that period, including those that were collected, more or less completely, in our Greco-Arabic-Castilian and Greco-Arabic works. When we allude to these gnomologies collectively, we call them "A". Sometimes the attribution to Socrates is in doubt.

I continue with a supplement of other ancient gnomologies: of papyri (already seen), especially of Diogenes Laertius and Stobaeus, with the necessary references for each maxim: that is, I list the maxims that are not in the *Gnomologium Vaticanum* but that, nevertheless, were cited in Antiquity, likewise, I believe, from various gnomologies. Some did not reach the Byzantine period, or at least were not recorded then, but they may have reached the tradition that we are studying here. I also point out some maxims of doubtful attribution. I classify these maxims and *khreîai* as "imp." (imperial): they go from even earlier, from Cicero, to the 5th century (Johannes Chrysostom, Libanius, etc.).

2 There also exists a collection of papyri that refer to Socrates in the *Corpus dei Papiri Filosofici Greci e Latini (CPF)*, 11***, Florence, 1999. It contains abundant *kreîai* and *gnômai*, as well as a good study of the biographical tradition. I use all this in another place in the book.

Finally, I give a collection of maxims in Maximus Confessor (MC) and Antonius Melissa (AM), as the main representatives of the *Corpus Parisinum*, which blended with the tradition of Johannes Damascenus, as I have said. The purpose is to see to what extent this tradition comes from gnomologies disregarded by the above-mentioned ones and to what extent they coincide with those that have reached us via the Arabic route. When I allude to these maxims collectively, I refer to them as *CP (Corpus Parisinum).*

In each case, I indicate the presence of these maxims in the principal Arabic collections but not in collections that are only derived from them. The lack of this indication signifies the absence of the maxims in question in the Arabic gnomologies.

I have numbered the maxims consecutively. There is a total of 280. One asterisk indicates direct derivation from Pl. or X.; two, presence in Antiquity. For further details, see Sternbach.

a) Maxims from the GV (Sternbach's ed.) and related gnomologies (A)

Other documentation is added, namely: other Greek gnomologies or citations (selectively), the Arabic ones and (in parenthesis) documents that bear witness to the existence of the maxim in Antiquity (imp. and/or *CP*, plus diverse authors).

1**. 37 (Aristippus). Intelligent people should address unintelligent ones as physicians address sick people, (cf. D.L. 6.1.6: Antisthenes), MC (Romulus); ID, Mub., Ibn Hindû (S).

2**. 169 (Diogenes). The prodigal son who ate olives. (D.L. attributes it to Diogenes, MC to Plutarch and Plato; ID, Ibn Hindû, *Boc* 123 (S.).

3**. 470. What is the most pleasing thing? – Education (*paideía*) = J.D., MC, AM; (Stob.); Boc. 125, ID 57.

4*. 471. What possession is the most useful? – A reliable friend = *CM* (cf. X. *Mem.* 2.4.1, 7); cf *Boc.* 127, *PQ* 38.

5*. 472. The person who can dominate his passions is king. Cf. X., Pl. (Plu., Stob. 2.8.29, 4.7.26, MC, AM (Isocrates); *PQ* 2.

6**. 473. If the poor man could see what happened to the rich under the Thirty, he would repent of having suffered (D.L., Ael.).

7. 474. I love you, someone said. – You are the one responsible, not I. (*VG* 1144).

8**. 475. Who can keep a secret? – The person who can keep a live coal on his tongue = *FM* , VG 742; (Stob. 3.41.5); cf. *Boc.* +.

9**. 476. Who is the richest? – He who is satisfied with the least = J.D., MC, *FM* (Stob. 3.5.31, cf. Epicur.).

10. 477. It is just as wrong to give to those to whom you should not as not to give to those to whom you should = *VG* 1144, *FM,* MC (Alexander); cf. *Boc.*, ID 477.

11**. 478. Socrates condemned to be thrown over a cliff, dialogue with Xantippe < X., MC (cf. D.L., Stob., Theo, Tert., V.M.).

12**. 479. Others live to eat, S. eats to live (*PBerol.* inv. 12311, D.L., Stob. 3.17.21., Ath., Plu. 2.21e, Mus.); MC (Zeno); *PQ,* v. Strohmaier, *Die arabische...*, p. 127: Arabic sources attribute it to Plato, Aristotle, Hippocrates and Galen.

13*. 480. It is better to live with a violent woman; it is like breaking in a wild horse. Cf. *Symp.* 2.10, MC (Pythagoras or Aristippus, others ascribe it to Anacharsis and Diogenes), (Plu., D.L., Chrys., etc.); cf. *PQ,* ID., Ibn Hindû, Hunayn, but some speak of "youths", D.L. of Xantippe.

14**. 481. Someone insults S. – Why? – He does not insult me but rather the person to whom this matters = *VG* 1144 (D.L.), also to Antisth.; cf. *PQ* (+).

15. 482. How can one speak without making mistakes? – By not speaking of what one does not know well = *VG* 1144, cf. *Boc.*, *PQ.*

16. 483. A slip of the foot is better than a slip of the tongue = MC, AM, others give it as a common saying. The coincidence with *Ahikar* is quite notable.

17**. 484. The ignorant rich man like a golden sheep = J. D., MC, *VG* 1144 and 742; (Stob. 2.31.46, others attribute it to Isocrates, Diogenes or Demosthenes, cf. Packmohr 23, or they speak of the "golden slave").

18**. 485. Envy as a wound of the truth (Stob. 3.38.48: of the soul), others attribute it to Democritus, Anacharsis or Dion Chrysostom.

19*. 486. S. does not accept gifts, dialogue with Xantippe. Cf. X. *Mem.* 1.6.3 (*PHib.* 122, Sob. 3.3.50, also 3.17.16); cf. *Boc.*, *PQ.*

20*. 487. You have been condemned to death by the Athenians – They have been condemned by nature. Cf. X., *Ap.* 3.27, MC; (D.L., Stob.); cf. *Boc, PQ.*

21. 488. S. excuses the person who spilled the wine; that way he won't be harmed. Various gnomologies assign it to Diogenes.

22**. 489. Is the world round? - I have not looked to see (cf. Tert., *ad nat.* 2.1., of Diogenes).

23. 490. Things belong to those who know how to use them = *VG* 1144.

24**. 491. Xantippe thunders – Soon it will rain = *VG* 1144 (D.L., Sen., cf. Epict., Ath.).

25**. 492. To someone who does too many favors: You make harlots of the Graces = Arsen.; (Stob.); MC and others attribute it to Democritus.

26**. 493. To Aristippus, richly dressed: You are wearing the *himation*, you are not being worn by it.

27**. 494. The movement of a dolphin, not of a man (D.L. of Aristippus).

28**. 495. S. will not go with Archelaus as long as the *cheonix* of barley costs three bronzes. (He does not want to go with Archelaus: Lib., D.L., Chrys.; other replies: Arist., M. Ant., cf. also D.L. 2.5.25).

29*. 496. I do not know the happiness of Archelaus because I do not know his culture (παιδεία. This comes from Plato (*Grg.* 470d–e), cf. D. Chr., Theo, Themist., etc. Cf. 302 (Anax.). On the happiness of the king of Persia, see Theo, *Prog.* 5, p. 98, Arsen., p. 437.

30**. 497. Pleasure does not go hand in hand with wealth (Stob.).

31. 498. Against the person who likes to hunt, neglecting everything else.

32** 499. What is not written is easier to sell than what is written, *PQ*.

33**. 500. If a donkey kicked me, I would not sue it. (D.L. 2.5.21, attributed to Demetrius, cf. Plu. 2.550f), cf. Diog.

34*. *OM* 3. It is difficult to be a good man and stay that way: envy, deceptions, fortune oppose this (from Sim.).

35**. O? *(Oxford Manuscript)* 8, Anytus is speaking badly of me? – Let him strike me when I am not present (D.L., *GV* post Dem.), MC 10.20. Cf. Packmohr 64.

36**. *FM (Florilegium Monacense)*, *VG* 743. To keep men away from evil is a sufficient benefit of education (Stob. 31.68 attributes it to Antisthenes); MC (to Romulus); ID, Mub. Ibn Hindû (anon.).

37. *FM* 239. What does the liar get out of his lie? – That they do not believe him even when he tells the truth.

38. *FM* 247. As a man's nature is, so is his *lógos.*

b) Maxims not in GV or in related gnomologies

To the citations from the basic collections we add those from the papyri and documents from the imperial epoch. These will be catalogued under the headings of Diogenes Laertius and Stobaeus, complementing what has already been given, and following that, under the headings of Maximus Confessor and Antonius Melissa (the tradition of the *CP*).

In papyri

39. Gallo, p. 184, *PHib.*: Xantippe and the guests (= D.L., J.D., MC, Damasc., etc.).
40. Gallo, pp. 191 and 212, *PHib.*: the ἐπιθυμίαι or desires controlled not through reasoning but through habit; more about the passions, satiating oneself. Not found in our gnomologies, although there are vague parallels in Plato.
41. Gallo, p. 227, *PFlor.* 113, II 19–38, s. II d. C.: two unknown anecdotes of S. and Antisth. What S. teaches Alcibiades by day, others invalidate by night.

In various authors

42. Cic. *De fin.* 2.28.90. The condiment of food is hunger, that of beverages, thirst.
43. Cic. *Tusc.*; Ath. 157e. S. was taking a walk and in reply to someone's question said that he was gathering condiments for his supper.
44. Ath. 186d. Seeing someone who was using too many condiments (or accompaniments with his bread), he asked who of those present used his bread as a condiment and the condiments as bread.
45. Plu. 2.124d. Avoid meals that are eaten without hunger and beverages that are drunk without thirst.
46. Plu. 2.470f. To someone who said that the city was expensive because of the price of wine, honey, crimson cloth, etc., S. replies that it was cheap, adducing the price of barley, olives and inexpensive clothing.
47. Cic., *Tusc.* 5.32.91, cf. D.L. 2.25. Seeing the quantity of gold and silver that was worn in a procession (or before the innumerable goods in the market place), S. said: "What a lot of things that I do not need!"

48. X., *Ep.* 4. A lesson of S.: "Measure wealth by its use."
49. Plu. 2.550f. It is better to drink turbid water than to take vengeance with a turbid soul full of wrath.
50. Sen., *De ira* 3.11.2. S. was struck and said that it was unfortunate that men did not know when they had to go out with a helmet.
51. Plu. 2.10c. If a donkey kicked me, would you want me to kick it in return?
52. Plu. 2.106b. If we were to put all of our misfortunes together to distribute them equally, most would take their own and leave.
53. Plu. 2, 486e. It is better to have Darius as a friend than a *dareico* (a Persian coin).
54. Ael. *VH* 9.29. To the person who said that it was wonderful to achieve one's desire, he replied: "It is better to have no desires at all."
55. Plu. 2.141d, Stob. 2.31.98. He recommended youths to look at themselves in the mirror saying that the ugly ones should with virtue recompose themselves as handsome, and the handsome ones should not make themselves ugly with vices.
56. Ath. 20f. Dancing is gymnastics for all members of our body.
57. Ael. *VH* 2.36. Old and ill, S. said that he was feeling well, because "if I live, I will have many who envy me and if I die, many who will praise me."

In Diogenes Laertius (1.33, 2.5; at the end, 2.6)

58. D.L. 1.33, Favorin., *Fort.* 17. Socrates said that he was grateful to Fortune that he was a man and not an animal, a male and not a woman, Greek and not barbarian.

59**. D.L. 2.21. (He was investigating) what is done right or wrong in the house (= *Od.* 4.392, also cited by Plu. 2.1063d and Stob. 2.31.126).

60**. D.L. 2.22. What I understood of Heraclitus is excellent and, I hope, what I did not understand also, but one needs a diver from Delos.

61**. D.L. 2.25. If I should be in need of shoes and you (Alcibiades) offered me leather to make some, it would be ridiculous of me to accept.

62**. D.L. 2.30. O Euclid, you and the Sophists may understand each other but you and men cannot.

63*. D.L. 2.31. He praised leisure as the most marvelous boon. This comes from X., *Smp.* 4.44.

64**. D.L. 2.31. There is only one good thing, knowledge, and only one bad one, ignorance.

65**. D.L. 2.31. Wealth and nobility from birth bring no dignity, but, rather, cause misfortune.

66**. D.L. 2,31. Did you imagine that such a noble man (Antisthenes) could have been engendered by two Athenian parents?

67**. D.L. 2.32. To the old man who wanted to learn to play the lyre (philosophy *FM*): Are you ashamed of being better at the end than at the beginning? (cf. Stob. 3.29.68); cf. ID, *PQ*, Mub. (PL, not in Castilian).

68*. D.L. 2.32. He said that a demon predicted his future, cf. Pl. *Ap.* 40a, etc.

69**. D.L. 2.32. He said that he knew nothing except that he knew nothing. From Pl. *Ap.*, also MC, AM.

70**. D.L. 2.32. He said that knowing how to obey is no small thing and it is conquered little by little.

71**. D.L. 2,32. He said that those who bought unripe fruit at a high price had no hope that it would reach maturity.

72**. D.L.2.32. What is virtue in a young person? – Not to go beyond the limits.

73**. D.L. 2.33. It is ridiculous to search for a slave who cannot be found and allows his virtue to be lost.

74**. D.L. 2.33. To marry or not? - You will repent in either case, cf., Val. Max. 7.2.

75**. D.L. 2.33. The young should look at themselves in the mirror in order to match their character with their beauty and so that those who are ugly can disguise their ugliness with their good character. Sob. 2,31,98.

76**. D.L. 2.34. To accept the masses is like rejecting a false tetradrachma but accepting a large number of them as genuine.

77**. D.L. 2.34. Aeschines: I consider myself nothing at all. I give myself to you. – S.: Don't you realize the greatness of that gift?

78**. D.L. 2.34. To someone who was complaining about not having been taken into account during the government of the Thirty: Isn't there anything else that bothers you?

79*. D.L. 2.35. To Aeschines: In three days I shall die (because of a dream, *Il.* 9.363, from Pl. *Cri.* 44b). Stob.

80**. D.L. 2.35. To Apollodorus: Why, if my cloak was good enough in life, will it not be good enough in death?

81**. D.L. 2.36, To Antisthenes: I can see your vanity through your cloak (speaking of the rips in it).

82**. D.L. 2.36. One must allow himself to be criticized by the comics: if they point out our defects they correct us; if they do not, it does not concern us.

83**. D.L. 2.37. To Alcibiades, who said Xantippe was unbearable: I have become accustomed, I hear her like the sound of a pulley. Don't you put up with the sound of the geese? – But they produce eggs and chicks – And Xantippe children.

84**. D.L. 2.37. My friends want me to beat Xantippe: yes, in order to cheer for one or the other.

85**. D.L. 2.40. To Lysias, who wrote a defense for him: your address is beautiful but it does not satisfy me, – Then why not adapt it? – Beautiful cloaks and beautiful shoes are not adapted either. Cf. Stob. 3.7.56 (Lysias adds that S. will die if he does not defend himself in this way. S.: I am to die in any case).

86*. D.L. 2.42. For my services I ask to be kept in the Prytaneum at public expense. Cf. Pl. *Ap.* 36d.

87**. D.L. 2,42. Paean of S.: Hail Delius Apollo, and you, Artemis, illustrious progeny.

88**. D.L. 2.42. Fable. Aesop once said to the citizens of Corinth: do not judge virtue by the measure of the wisdom of popular trials.

89. D.L. 6.19. S. defined beauty as a short-lived tyranny.

90**. D.L. 6.35. (Diogenes). The most valuable is sold most cheaply, as happens with a statue and a χοῖνιξ of barley (cf. *GV* 495, supra 28). For the attribution, see Packmohr 65 a.

91**. D.L. 6.63. (to Diogenes) Citizen of the world, according to Cic., *Tusc.* 5.108. Cf. Packmohr 67 a.

In Johannes Stobaeus

92**. Stob. 1.1.29. What is God? - The immortal and eternal = *Stobaei Herm.* XVIII.

93. Stob. 2.1.18. Wisdom is not a thing of humans.

94**. Stob. 2.4.13. In war iron is better than gold, in life *logos* is better than wealth.

95**. Stob. Like a good sculptor *logos* gives the soul a beautiful form.
96**. Stob. 2.15.37. Whose *logos* is the strongest? – It belongs to those who follow it in action.
97**. Stob. 2.31.44. Culture is a celebration for the soul, it provides performances and recitals.
98** Stob. 2.31.45. For the runners in the stadium at the end there is victory, for those who work in old age is reserved the prize for wisdom.
99**. Stob. 2.31.54. Bring up your children with education, then teach them to deal with whatever may happen and distribute your wealth to them so that they do not become enemies.
100**. Stob. 2.31.75. What is the heaviest thing that the earth bears? – An uneducated man (attributed perhaps to S., MC to D., others to Demonax). For the attribution see Packmohr 68.
101*. Stob. 2.31.79. What is science? – Caring for the soul. Where do bad people come from? – From bad up-bringing and bad company. From Pl. *Ap*. 29 e.
102**. Stob. 2.31.99, p. 828. What is the most pleasant thing? – Education, virtue and knowledge of what is not known. MC.
103**. Stob. 2.31.101. S. to X., who knew in what part of the market the fish and vegetables were: where are the fine and good ones?
104**. Stob. Against *polymathia* one must leave a space between the trees and, in the soul, between the things that we know.
105**. Stob. 2.31.103. Like good earth, culture produces everything good.
106**. Stob. 2.31.104. Philosophy brings good advice to the young. (Socrates?)
107**. Stob. 2.31.105. As on a long journey, in life one needs a good rest (Socrates?).
108**. Stob. 3.1.23. It is advisable to deal with the powerful as little as possible or very pleasantly. Also MC.
109**. Stob. 3.1.73. Only to the *logos*, as to a prudent administrator, should one entrust life and youth.
110**. Stob. 3.1.74. Shoes and life, when they adjust to use, cause less trouble.
111**. Stob. 3.1.84. You cannot tell a thoroughbred horse by its trappings but by its nature; and a man is not someone with great possessions but a person of noble spirit.
112**. Stob. 3.1.85. When a wise man opens his mouth, like the door of a temple, one can see, like the statues, the beauty of his soul.

113**. Stob. 3.1.86. In navigation one must obey the pilot, in life the one who reasons best.
114**. Stob. 3.1.87. Neither a banquet without conversation nor wealth without virtue give pleasure.
115**. Stob. 3.1.88. One must choose the smoothest path and the life most lacking in sorrow.
116**. Stob. 3.1.89. All parts of life, like the parts of a statue, should be beautiful.
117**. Stob. 3.1.90. A statue must stand firmly on its base, a man on his fine choice of life.
118**. Stob. 3.1.104. A ship should not be anchored with one single anchor nor should life be anchored on a single hope. Cf. III 2.45.
119**. Stob. 3.1.180. In life as in a drama, the main part should be played not by the wealthiest but by the wisest.
120**. Stob. 3.1.181. It is good that the fire be bright in the home, and good sense *(noûs)* in misfortune.
121**. Stob. 3.1.182. Just as troublemakers must be expelled from a well-governed city, so must the *noûs* inclined toward iniquity be expelled from the soul.
122**. Stob. 3.1.185. A horse cannot be used without reins or wealth without judgment.
123**. Stob. 3.1.186. Like a musical instrument, life is more pleasant if it is tuned with both relaxation and tension.
124**. Stob. 3.1.187. One must dedicate incense to the gods and praise to the good.
125**. Stob. 3.1.188. Those who use ill-earned profits for good purposes are like those who perform acts of piety with sacrilegious means.
126**. Stob. 3.1.189. One must defend those who have a reputation of being unjust, and praise those who are notable for some good reason.
127. Stob. 3.1.190. One must extol what is produced following the precepts of art.
128. Stob. 3.2.45. Entertaining hope with insufficient thought is the same as holding a ship in place with a weak anchor.
129**. Stob. 3.3.44. What is *phronesis*? - The proper adjustment of the soul.
130**. Stob. 3.3.56. Just as those who sail in a calm have everything prepared for the storm, so those who are sensible, in a period of good fortune, have made preparations for misfortune.

131**. Stob. 3.3.61. As with an empty boat, one must take on the ballast of reason.

132**. Stob. 3.3.62. The wise man takes for the journey of life not the most valuable provisions but the most indispensable ones.

133**. Stob. 3.4.55. The coward betrays his country, the ambitious person his paternal wealth.

134**. Stob.3.4.56. Deserters are afraid, although they are not being pursued, fools feel anguish although they suffer no misfortune.

135**. Stob. 3.4.57. The stupid are delirious in their drunkenness, fools are delirious in their good fortune.

136**. Stob. 3.4.58. Those who are not musical cannot adapt to the instruments nor can the uneducated to the blows of fortune.

137**. Stob. 3.4.59. In the life of the uneducated, as in the actor's, there are many traces of arrogance.

138**. Stob. 3.4.60. Any small pretext is enough for fools, like children, to cry.

139**. Stob. 3.4.61. Foreigners go astray on the roads, uneducated persons in their actions.

140**. Stob. 3.4.62. Giving good fortune to the uneducated is like putting a burden on someone who is ill.

141**. Stob. 3.4.63. Neither is it safe when sailing to anchor out of harbor nor is it without danger to live one's life against the law.

142**. Stob. 3.4.64. Proteus changes his form, the uneducated change their souls constantly.

143**. Stob. 3.4.65. Just as happens with the sick, the great number of things at their disposal causes harm to many fortunate people.

144**. Stob. 3.4.107. The incontinent are difficult to care for in sickness, and fools in misfortune.

145**. Stob. 3.4.114. The coward has weapons for himself, the fool money.

146**. Stob. 3.4.115. Sour wine is not good to drink nor is a rough character good to deal with.

147**. Stob. 3.4.118. Neither are the arms of Achilles suitable for Thersites nor the wealth of fortune for the fool.

148**. Stob. 3.4.119. The diet of the sick man and the good fortune of the fool have much that is unpleasant.

149**. Stob. 3.4.120. Thunder frightens children, threats frighten fools.

150**. Stob. 3.5.30. One must flee from pleasures as from the Sirens if one wants to hold virtue as his homeland.

151**. Stob. 3.5.32. What must one abstain from most? – From shameful and unjust pleasures.
152*. Stob. 3.5.33. It is a characteristic of God not to need anything. From X. *Mem.* 1.6.10 (Stob., *Fl.*).
153**. Stob. 3.5.34. The αὐτάρκεια, a short and not very tiring road = *Corp. Par.*, Demoph.
154**. Stob. 3.5.35. One must find pleasures by relying on oneself.
155**. Stob. 3.6.14. It is impossible to conceal fire in a garment and a shameful fault in time.
156**. Stob. 3.6.15. Wind drives away fire, custom drives away love. MC.
157**. Stob. 3.6.16. Adulterers do not drink from running water but from water that is deep and stagnant.
158**. Stob. 3.7.15. What is strength? - The movement of the soul in union with the body.
159. Stob. 3.7.56. Lysias gives S. a defense speech which he rejects, although it is beautiful. He said that roses were also beautiful, but that that crown did not suit him. In that case, you will die, replied Lysias. S.: I will die in any case, although it may not be now.
160**. Stob. 3.10.46. Who are avaricious? – Those who look for corrupt profits and scorn their friends.
161**. Stob. 3.10.54. The dregs of wine is the sediment, of the miser, meanness.
162**. Stob. 3.10.55. One does not seek conversation from a dead person or gratitude from a miser.
163**. Stob. 3.13.61. The pleasure of frankness, like that of youth, is at the opportune moment.
164**. Stob. 3.13.62. Neither a dull knife nor frankness without success.
165**. Stob. 3.13.63. Do not take the sun from the world or frankness from education.
166**. Stob. 3.13.64. One can have good health with a skimpy blanket and frankness with poverty.
167**. Stob. 3.14.21. The favor of the flatterers flees from misfortune as if in a defeat.
168**. Stob. 3.14.22. Hares are caught with trickery, most fools with praise.
169**. Stob. 3.14.23. Wolves are similar to dogs and flatterers to friends, but they are looking for different things.
170**. Stob. 3.14.24. Praise is like a painted panoply: it is pleasing but has no use.

171**. Stob. 3.16.27. The life of misers is like a funeral banquet: there is no one who rejoices in it.

172**. Stob. 3.16.28. The wealth of misers, like the sun that sinks into the earth, makes no one happy.

173**. Stob. 3.17.27. ἐγκράτεια is to dominate the pleasure of the body.

174**. Stob. 3.17.30. How to get rich? Be poor in desires.

175. Stob. 3.21.9. S. on being asked why he did not write, replied: "Because paper is much more valuable than what is going to be written on it."

176**. Stob. 3.22.33. To Alcibiades: Why are you so proud of your possessions, which you cannot even find on the map?

177**. Stob. 3.22.35. In an unconscious delirium, as happens to a bad sculptor, it is impossible to see the images of things.

178**. Stob. 3.22.36. Superstition obeys unconscious delirium as one would obey a father.

179**. Stob. 3.22.37. The wind inflates wineskins, belief inflates fools. MC.

180**. Stob. 3.23.8. At an announcement in the theater, cobblers and their like and everyone would stand up if someone asked those who were prudent and just to do so. Everyone feels he is.

181**. Stob. 3.22.38. Who are vulgar? – Those who scorn their equals.

182**. Stob. 3.24.13. Who live without worry? – Those who have a clear conscience. MC, AM (S.), on the attribution see Packmohr a 3 a.

183**. Stob. 3.34.18. As with salt, joking must be used with moderation.

184**. Stob. 3.37.26. Clothing covers ugliness, benevolence mistakes.

185**. Stob. 3.38.34. The beauty of glory is soon consumed thanks to a sickness called envy.

186**. Stob. 3.38.35. Those who walk in the sun are accompanied by the shade, those who walk swathed in glory by envy.

187**. Stob. 4.1.47. The enjoyment of good fortune should be common to those worthy of it, the same as political conversation.

188**. Stob. 4.1.82. What city is governed best? – The one that lives according to the law and punishes the unjust. MC.

189**. Stob. 4.1.83. What city lives with a lack of laws? – The one in which the magistrates are named in the *"heterias"*.

190**. Stob. 4.1.84. What city is the strongest? – The one that has good men.

191. Stob. 4.1.85. Who should be given the magistracies? – Those who were educated well as children and as adults did not betray their childhood.
192**. Stob. 4.15a.16. Etymology of Amalthea: "not lazy" in relation to the horn of the ox, an animal that works.
193**. Stob. 4.22.59. What men repent? – The married ones.
194**. Stob. 4.23.58. Men should obey the laws of the city, women the habits of their husbands.
195**. Stob. 4.25.42. An incomprehensive father must be endured like a strict law.
196**. Stob. 4.26.22. A father's reproach is a sweet medicine because it does more good than harm.
197**. Stob. 4.27.20. A man: I will die if I don't take vengeance on you. - S.: I will die if I don't make a friend of you.
198**. Stob. 4.29a.20. What is nobility? - A good mixture of soul and body.
199**. Stob. 4.29a.23. We do not think that the most beautiful field produces the best wheat nor do we consider a kind and serious friend the one from an illustrious family but rather the one with the best character.
200**. Stob. 4.30.12. Criticized by a wicked nobleman, he said: my ancestors are an insult to me, you are an insult to yours.
201**. Stob. 4.31c.83. Garments that reach your feet are a hindrance for the body, as excessive wealth is for the soul.
202**. Stob. 4.31c.90. Wealth does not go hand in hand with happiness.
203**. Stob. 4.31d.107. Wine changes with the receptacle, wealth with the character of the possessor. MC, AM.
204**. Stob. 4.31d.108. A bed of gold is of no use to the sick man, nor glorious fortune to the fool.
205**. Stob. 4.31d.129. The finest sweat comes from the gymnasium, and the finest wealth from one's own effort.
206**. Stob. 4.31d.130. One must direct wealth to fine actions like a strong friend who makes no pretexts.
207**. Stob. 4.32.18. Poverty is a slight temperance.
208**. Stob. 4.34.69. The gods always laugh when they see human vainglory, because everything human being small, it finds no like desires.
209**. Stob. 4.35.35. How can one live without pain? – It is impossible for one who lives in a city and has contact with men not to feel pain.
210**. Stob. 4.36.9. What is sickness? – Turmoil of the soul.

211**. Stob. 4.37.20. One must avoid the foods that incite one to eat without hunger and beverages that incite one to drink without thirst. Plu.

212**. Stob. 4.39.18. What is happiness? – Pleasure without regret.

213**. Stob. 4.39.19. Who are happy? – Those who have a mind that is clear and who keep their word. For the attribution see Packmohr a 4.

214**. Stob. 4.41.58. It is the same to boast about success as to run a stadium on a slippery path. MC.

215**. Stob. 4.44.74. When it was announced to him that his son had died, he said: Let us comply with what is customary in honor of Sophroniscus.

216**. Stob. 4.44.83. There is no guarantee of obtaining anything from what is lent to one's friends and children.

217**. Stob. 4.45.9. It is not fair to take someone to court who has beat us in a gymnastic competition nor to reproach fortune; one must know the rules of the contest of life.

218. Stob. 4.46.21. Bad expectations lead to sin, the same as bad guidance.

219**. Stob. 4.46.26. A woman does not engender anything without a man nor does a fine expectation without effort.

220**. Stob. 4.48b.31. For the sick, one must recommend physicians, for the unfortunate, friends.

221**. Stob. 4.50c.93. A storm requires a refuge, old age the absence of pain.

222**. Stob. 4.51.23. One must not be cowardly or weighed down with tears and lamentations; one must bear what is the fate of a good man.

223**. Stob. 4.53.39. As in the theater, in life one must stay on until the sight of the events is pleasing.

224**. Stob. 4.56.39. Life is like a game of draughts, one must put down his draught, it cannot be picked up or taken away.

From various gnomologies

225. Io. D. 2.12.34, Apostol. 468. Doing favors for a wretch is like putting perfume on a corpse.

226. Io. D. 2.12.34. Doing favors for a villain is like feeding a snake.

227. Apostol. 1.27. They are quick to see the wrong in others, but when we do the same, we do not realize it.

228. Apostol. 15.95. What is above us does not concern us. Do not attempt what is beyond your strength.
229. Apostol. 18.15. Our eyes are useless if they are not in agreement, and likewise our hands and our feet.

c) New maxims, in Maximus Confessor

I add those corresponding to Antonius Melissa where there are any.

230. MC 1.47, cf. Arsen., p. 437. To an important man who insisted on his statue looking like him, S. said: You demand that this stone look like you, but you are not concerned to make yourself the same as stone.
231. MC 6.43, cf. Arsen., p. 438. Those who neglect friendship, although they escape the punishment of the offended, do not avoid the punishment of God.
232. MC 6.44. To love inappropriately is the same as to hate.
233. MC 6.45. Croesus, having been asked what the best thing about royalty is, replied: "punishing one's enemies and helping one's friends." And S. said to him, "How much more pleasing it would be if you brought the former into your friendship."
234. MC 10.21. Do not listen to a slanderer, it is not out of kindness that he reveals to you what others keep hidden; he will tell others what is said about you in the same way.
235. MC 12.47. He compared the money of the rich and libertine to the fig trees in the ravines whose fruit is not picked by men but by crows and hawks; the fruit of the money of such men by harlots and flatterers.
236. MC 13.19. It is better to have tranquility of spirit with little money than to be unfortunate with a great deal.
237. MC 15.21. One should not dominate things on the basis of words but rather words on the basis of things, for things are not born of words but vice versa.
238. MC 33.11. Good men should have a character that is more dependable than an oath.
239. MC 33.12. Accept swearing an oath for two reasons: to avoid an accusation or to save friends from grave dangers.

240. MC 33.13. Do not swear before God because of money, not even if what you swear is true, because to some you will seem a perjurer, to others a miser.
241. MC 54.31. Many speak well of the dead at their burial though through envy they have caused them pain in life.
242. MC 55.24. He who voluntarily suffers misfortune with good expectations enjoys his suffering. Comfort and the pleasures of the body do not give health to the body nor do they provide any worthwhile knowledge to the soul.
243. MC 72.22. There is nothing pleasant or unpleasant by nature, everything occurs through custom.
244. MC 72.23. Choose the life that is most excellent; custom will make it pleasant.
245. p. 728. Take care that in cultivating your field you do not let your soul become uncultivated.
246. p. 745. Do women live here?, S. on seeing the doors of Corinth closed.
247. p. 753. Do not do what you do not want others to do to you.
248. p. 761. Those who leave their brothers and look for other friends are like those who leave their own land and cultivate that of someone else.
249. p. 816 (S.?). The *logoi* must be deduced from the facts, not vice versa.
250. p. 824. What animal is the most beautiful? – The educated man.
251. p. 824. I am barbarous (discourteous) in my words, you in your character.
252. p. 824. What is the best way to learn? – By forgetting what is bad.
253. p. 833. In the home the brightest fire is beautiful, in misfortune the *nous* (the intellect)
254. p. 833. Incontinence is difficult to cure in sickness, as are fools in success.
255. p. 833. What harms good men? – The success of bad ones. AM.
256. p. 833. He whom fortune abuses finds whips even in the meek.
257. p. 856. Those who abuse are like the birds that drink and some drown, and others disposed to drown follow them.
258. p. 860. The wife criticizes him for not attending to his son; he responds: he is mine but useless.
259. p. 901. Prefer to die beautifully than to live shamefully. AM.

260. p. 916. Do not use an impudent tongue, sometimes it will break your own head. AM.
261. p. 928. What is good and beautiful grows not because of its visible beauty but because of its virtue.
262. p. 928. One must avoid the kisses of the beautiful as he would the bite of poisonous snakes.
263. p. 965. He who suffers with patience has good hope; in the midst of sorrow he rejoices in hope.
264. p. 969. The feverish lose their appetite and strength, those who frequent the palaces lose their intelligence and good customs if they do not repeat to themselves the "know thyself." From the Delphic maxim in Pl. *Prt.* 343b.

d) New maxims, in Antonius Melissa

265. 1.29.32. He who renders services to the rich man is no different from one who pours water into the sea.
266. 2.34.45. When your wife says that she misses you and loves you, fear worse things from her than what she says.
267. 2.34.49. On marriage: like fish around the nets, the ones on the outside want to enter and those inside want to get out.
268. 2.75.14. No one sees what is bad in himself, but if someone else acts wrongly, he will see it clearly.
269. p. 849. Do not fear a true friend.
270. p. 946. Do not listen to the gossiper, he will gossip about your affairs in the same way.
271. p. 961. S. would hang himself if they loved him as they do the dissolute youth who criticizes him.
272. p. 769. Some pay with lovely sepulchers for the harm done to others when they were alive.
273. p. 1092. I am made of three misfortunes: of grammar, poverty and my terrible wife.
274. p. 1092. To those who asked him if they ought to marry: like fish near the nets, those on the outside want to enter and those on the inside want to get out.

275. p. 1092. Seeing Xantippe dressed up as if to go to the theater: woman, you are not going out to see anything, you are going out to be seen.
276. p. 1123. Occupy yourself with voluntary tasks so that it will seem that you are resisting involuntary ones.
277. p. 1156. Good men should have a character stronger than an oath.
278. p. 1156. Swear an oath to avoid an accusation or to save a friend from danger.
279. p. 1156. Do not swear before God because of money, as it will seem that you are committing perjury or that you are doing it out of greed.
280. p. 1169. It is arrogant to say everything and not want to listen.

IV. Analysis of the preceding Socratic material: conclusions

We intend to use the Socratic material as a guide to forming a concept of the history of the gnomological material in general in the Hellenistic, Roman and Byzantine periods, thus completing, with a concrete example, what was said in Chapter 2 about gnomologies in general and in Chapter 3 about those related to Aristotle and Alexander. This is worthwhile, as there is abundant material[3].

Socrates is, naturally, a special case. His gnomologies are not included among those compiled by the authors themselves or their disciples, nor are we dealing with gnomologies by authors of the classical period that were augmented (Simonides, Democritus, Epicharmus, although Epicharmus might be considered as close to this case). Socrates did not write, but there was a Socratic literature about him and, later, Hellenistic biographies. These were the starting points: from ancient times they took data and maxims of the Socratics, especially from Plato and Xenophon; and the process was

3 It is in Giannantoni, op. cit. (in which many of the maxims that we cite below are lacking). In the same work, pp. 21 ff., there are also compilations of testimonies, see also Acosta's book cited above. For Plato there is the book of K. H. Stanzel, *Dicta Platonica. Die unter Platons Namen überlieferten Ansprüche*, Würzburg, 1987, and that of A. Swift Riginos, *Platonica. The Anecdotes concerning the Life and Writings of Plato*, Leiden, Brill, 1976. For Diogenes and the other Socratics see G. Giannantoni, *Socraticorum Reliquiae*, Rome, Bibliopolis, 1983.

repeated time and again as new gnomologies were created, as in the case of Diogenes Laertius and Stobaeus (or, rather, their sources). Thus, as we have said, as far back as the end of the 4th century we have in the *PHib* 182 a combination of *Life* + gnomology which, first of all, connects with the Socratic tradition, secondly, offers *gnômai* accepted in the later gnomologies, and thirdly, already includes Cynic material.

This papyrus is important because it indicates the antiquity of these works on Socrates. It shows that there is continuity in them, but there are also losses (material from this and other papyri that is not present later). We have already pointed out traces of continuity in the genre *Life* + aphorisms or *khreîai*, which likewise has rarely been preserved (though it was in D.L., etc.). Nevertheless, it is a necessary presupposition in order to understand the Greco-Arabic works in which the process was kept alive.

We, and scholars in general, consider that the initiative of the genre, following earlier precedents, is in the Cynics. But between Socratism and Cynicism there are transitions, many maxims can be ascribed to one or another of the authors of the group, even to the Epicureans, and also to Plato and Isocrates. This explains the constant differences of attribution to which we have referred: to Socrates or else to Plato, Isocrates, Democritus, Aristippus, Antisthenes, Diogenes, Demonax, or Epictetus. Actually, the whole Socratic line has common elements; it really represents, with variants, Greek moralism, which merged, as I have said, with Christian moralism. Nevertheless, it is difficult to detect elements that are strictly Christian in the Socratic gnomologies that have come down to us and that we have studied (though perhaps in the maxims referring to oaths).

Thus of Socrates we have, in the first place, maxims that come from Plato on education, the "I only know that I know nothing", virtue, the law, etc. From here on there is an amplification, sometimes moralistic, sometimes strictly Cynic: themes of culture, knowledge, maintaining silence, reason, true nobility, disdain for wealth, friendship. Added to these are the themes of frankness, antifeminism (and anti-eroticism in general), asceticism, fleeing from pleasure, and those of delight in the accurate mind and word, noble death. The limits of what is Socratic and what is Cynic are fluid; at times there is an outlook that is more human or more realistic, perhaps Epicurean.

In summary, Socrates was, also in a vital sense, a precursor of Diogenes and even of Aristippus. His life is full of anecdotes, at times combined with *khreîai*, as anyone knows who has studied it through the ancient texts. Because many of the anecdotes are old, they are in Plato and Xenophon. Later others, true or not, were added following the same line. In these anecdotes we find characters like Xantippe, Alcibiades, Antisthenes, Aristippus, Archelaus, Xenophon, Aeschines or Apollodorus. I should add that the very manner in which Socrates expressed himself, which included comparisons and similes, anecdotes and myths, the fable, the parody, irony, the paradox and all kinds of popular elements, made him apt for inclusion in gnomologies similar to those of the Cynics[4].

Far from being a philosopher who revealed his truth almost *ex cathedra*, like Heraclitus or Parmenides, Socrates doubted and argued; he was, really, the inventor of the *khreía* and the diatribe, before the Cynics. But he also used maxims and adages as we have seen: there are some of each genre in his gnomologies. And to the original material of the Socratic tradition other material was added little by little, different in nature but not completely foreign to it (Cynic, Epicurean). We have seen this beginning back in the 4th century.

Formally, the Socratic gnomologies are no different from the others. We have, as I have said, the maxim and the *khreía* (which at times leads to a debate). In the *khreía* the anecdotes are normally presented in the usual formulas: "when asked (ἐρωτηθείς) ... he said ...", and also "having seen" (ἰδών, θεασάμενος). And the traditional questions "What is ...?", "What is the most ...?" are plentiful, as are, of course, similes, allusions and ironic touches.

With the confluence of all these streams the Socratic gnomologies gradually grew. For example, the role of Xantippe as a non-philosophical woman increased steadily. And also the strictly Cynic and the practically Epicurean material. More on this below.

The fact is that even though the Socratic gnomological material preserved in specific gnomologies, papyrian or not, is scarce, the gnomologies that we have designated as "A" (with regard to the *VG*) and the texts that we have designated "imp." (imperial, although some may be older, they actually go from Cicero to the 5th century), prove to us that there was a proliferation of Socratic gnomologies. And the same is true of the *CP (Corpus Parisinum)* and its derivatives, MC and AM.

4 For the language of Socrates, see my article "La lengua de Sócrates y su filosofía", *Methexis* 5, 1992, pp. 29–52 (and *Palabras e Ideas*, Madrid, 1992, pp. 251–278).

I believe things are much more complicated, at least for Socrates but also in general, than what Gutas proposes[5]. For him, certain (lost) *Apophthegmata Philosophorum* would be the source of *GV* and related gnomologies. These and others must have been, in turn, the source of the *Corpus Parisinum* of which we have spoken. When this was combined with gnomologies of Isocrates, Menander, the historians, etc., an *Archetypal Gnomologium*, the source of MC and AM, would have been created.

On the contrary, I believe that in *GV* and other gnomologies various ancient ones have come together, that D.L. and Stob., among others, are based on gnomologies partially independent of the earlier ones, and that the *CP* is partially independent of all of this.

The proliferation of Socratic gnomologies can be deduced from an internal analysis of the sources mentioned. But before doing this, we must point out certain information. For example:

Stobaeus transmits maxims that come from Serenus and Aristonimus, so he was not the first one to undertake this task. And not only do we have a Socratic gnomology like that of *Bocados*, which clearly derives from Antiquity, we shall see this in detail later, but there are preserved in Greek not only D.L. but also, in gnomologies organized by authors such as the *GV*, series that are purely Socratic. Naturally, in the gnomologies by themes, the monographic ones were subsumed as secondary, as we shall see in detail.

We have seen the monographic gnomologies proliferate from the time of the classical age (constantly augmented, to be sure, with various materials, as in the case of Menander) and then in the Hellenistic and the imperial periods, in which "mixed" gnomologies and those organized by themes appeared for the first time. But the existence of personal gnomologies is undeniable. Actually, some represent a school more than a thinker, for example the Hermetics, the Pseudo-Phocylides, the *Golden Verses*. Socrates' case is not very different.

The multiplicity of these Socratic gnomologies can also be deduced from the analysis of the material previously presented.

If we analyze list A (GV and related material, which can be augmented), we find the following noteworthy facts:

1. 31 is found only here.
2. 1–20 offer the following distribution variants: types A-imp., A-*CP*, A-ar. appear; also *CP*-ar., A-imp.-ar. The compiler followed one or more

5 Op. cit., p. 34.

gnomologies that were, in turn, available to the writers of the imperial epoch, to those of the Byzantine *Corpus Parisinum* and to the Arabic writers. There may have been intermediate phases with fragmentations, and the other way round, entrance of imp. material in A.

3. 21–35 do not appear at all in the Arab texts or in the *CP*, though they are found at times in imp. So the model is an independent collection not accessible to Byzantines or Arabs.

A (*GV*, etc.) has its roots in ancient times: in a collection (or various collections) widely circulated and in another one that was soon abandoned. At the very least it is based on two collections. A study of the content also certifies its antiquity, as will be seen below.

As for D.L., we have already seen that he sometimes uses the same collections; at times he coincides with A, *CP* and ar.; at others I believe that he draws directly (or through his sources) from Plato and Xenophon. More frequently still, these are maxims and *khreîai* that only appear here and that often signify an amplification of the contents. It is evident that he uses one or various collections only partially related to those that form the base of A. He, or one of his sources, is sometimes derived from the ancient originals, as in 45, 50, 67.

Similar to this is the case of Stobaeus, who coincides at times with the other collections, but more often is alone. Note that it frequently happens that the Socratic material on one theme or another appears in sequence, even organized by themes: 113 ff. the uneducated (ἀπαίδευτοι), 138 ff. frankness (παρρησία), 144 ff. flatterers (κόλακες), etc. There are traces of alphabetization and in any case there are Socratic "blocks" that betray a gnomological source. There is also access to the ancient Socratic sources, as in 80, 81. In any event, there is a source, or sources, that escaped the other gnomologists.

And something similar must be said about MC and AM, which derive from the *CP*. This collection was not unrelated to some of the other gnomologies, but it had access to some other sources as well, doubtless recent ones. I think that they were basically Socratic gnomologies, whose existence we have shown to be probable.

I do not believe, then, in Gutas's idea that certain lost *Apophthegmata Philosophorum* are the fundamental base of the *GV* and related gnomologies and that from their fusion came the *Corpus Parisinum*, the source, in turn, of MC and AM, together with certain marginal sources (Menander, Isocrates, the

Historians). The whole thing is much more complicated: in the interim between the multiplicity of collections of Antiquity, monographic and mixed, thematic and alphabetical, and our gnomologies, I cannot see that there should have existed complex collections. For Socrates what happens is that there have come down to us only the *disiecta membra* of a series of monographic gnomologies, used later in the mixed and alphabetical ones that flourished starting in the 3rd century.

Of our collections, A, represented above all by *GV*, is the one that presents the most archaizing panorama, after the collection of the *PHibeh* 182, which already had some of the features of Cynicism. Apart from the Socratic features whose ancient sources we are familiar with, here we find the traditional Socratic themes: on culture (παιδεία), αὐτάρκεια, friends, science, the control of passion, eating to live, breaking in a wild horse, not reacting to insults, not speaking of what one does not know, the philosopher-physician; and the criticism of the uneducated rich man, of the person who "is kept" instead of keeping and of luxury, and the disdain for power.

In A there appear three anecdotes about Xantippe that come from the ancient sources (11 adds the Byzantine error of the sentence to die by being thrown over a cliff), added to the one that says Xantippe thunders so it will soon rain (24). This theme of the non-philosophical woman was much cultivated by the Cynics; added to that are the disqualification of love (7), of natural science (22), of hunting and sports (27, 31). Nor is there an absence of touches that we might call Epicurean on the pleasant life (ἄλυπος) and happiness, although they are combined with moralism.

This is, after all, the Socratic culture that developed into a common patrimony, accentuated in some of its points by the Cynics, Stoics or Epicureans. The confusion of attributions (to Socrates, Aristippus, Antisthenes, etc.) is not surprising.

The gnomologies that reached the hands of D.L., Stob. and the writers of the empire in general, placed more emphasis on the Cynic features. They continue with the old themes, to be sure, and criticize philosophers like Heraclitus and Euclid, but they add, for example, themes like that of nobility of birth (εὐγένεια), which is disdained, attacks on matrimony and women, the theme of life as a game, and also that of effort or πόνος. The theme of foolishness (ἄνοια, ἀναισθησία) is perhaps Stoic and also that of fortune. And the themes of pleasure have an Epicurean flavor, but always in a moralistic context: one must abstain from shameful pleasures (127), and also that of the simple ἀλυπία or absence of pain.

There is no Christian atmosphere except for the moralism that constantly opposes the good and the bad. The mentions of God are either Hermetic (1) or of Socratic origin.

As for the *CP*, represented for us by MC and AM, we find the customary Socratic themes, some Cynic ones (against women, love and matrimony, in favor of πόνος, etc.) and others of rather traditional morality: praise of the family, masculine pride, disillusioned morality (see 207 ff.). It seems to me that there is a certain Christian tint in the themes of not doing to others what we do not want them to do to us (199) and of oaths (225 ff.).

We can see, then, the scene in which the gnomologies were circulating around Byzantium when the Arabs arrived in Syria. Of the ones that the Arab writers composed, most of which are unpublished, one at least, Ibn Durayd's, comes directly from this context. Others, as we have said, offer an added stratum of Christian asceticism that has become familiar to us through the themes of Alexander and Aristotle. We have attributed it to an evolution of this same material in the Christian Orient beginning in the 5th century. But it was necessary to emphasize the Greek precedents in order to be able to see where they coincide and where they differ.

V. The Greco-Arabic gnomologies: Ibn Durayd

F. Rosenthal's edition of Ibn Durayd[6] offers us a unique opportunity to become familiar with an Arabic gnomology fairly close to the Greek ones that we know or can suppose existed. It derives from some of them, but not exactly from those that have come down to us. In most cases the same maxims are in other Arabic works, among them those that we will study next, and generally there is attribution of the maxims to the same philosophers. The eleven maxims that Ibn Durayd attributes to Socrates are distributed as follows:

a) Maxims also in the *GV* with the same attribution to Socrates (I give Ibn Durayd's numbering and my own, where it exists): 57 = 3 (the most beautiful thing is education); 60 = 10 (do not give to someone who does

6 F. Rosenthal, "Sayings of the Ancients from Ibn Durayd's Kitab al-Mutjana", *Orientalia* 27, 1958, pp. 29–54.

not deserve it etc.); maxims with a different attribution: 1 (*VG* to Aristippus, the theme of the horse that is hard to tame); 2 *GV* and D.L. to Diogenes (the theme of the olives); 58 (Stob. to Antisthenes: education turns one away from wrong); 62 (to Aristippus and Antisthenes, address a fool as the physician does the sick person).

b) Maxims in other Greek sources, with attribution to Socrates: 59 = 49 (Stob., the old man who begins to study late); 61 = 222 (marriage and the fish); with a different attribution: 5 (D.L. to Metrocles, we do not know whether a person is rich if we do not know if he knows how to use his money); 63 (D.L. to Diogenes, pleasure as a honey trap).
c) Only in Arabic sources: 56, woman, the most beautiful animal of prey.

It can be concluded that the gnomology or gnomologies used were circulated within the universe of the gnomologies that we know (A, imp., *CP* once), with one exception that is missing in them. But the textual variants, and especially the variation in attributions, makes us think of the differences. Curiously, it is in the Arabic gnomologies (this one and the others) that the attribution to Socrates is most frequent. Perhaps because of the greater familiarity with his renown?

But there is nothing that cannot be explained by the Greek gnomologies that we are studying. There is nothing Christian and there is no essential alteration or important outside source.

VI. The Greco-Arabic gnomologies: Socrates in the *PQ* *(Philosophical Quartet)*, accompanied or not by H (Hunayn, *Buenos Proverbios*) and M (Mubassir, *Bocados de Oro*)

The previous study is, of course, of interest in itself for the reconstruction of lost Greek sapiential literature. But for us it is also the basis for the study of the Greek gnomological tradition in the Greco-Arabic-Castilian works which we are discussing and of phases of this tradition that, though inaccessible to us, can be reconstructed in this way. All of this will be studied in *Buenos Proverbios* and *Bocados de Oro*.

But this takes us, inevitably, to the theme of the remaining Greco-Arabic tradition, the works that were not translated into Castilian. We have already mentioned the gnomology of Ibn Durayd, which contributes little that is new to the Greek gnomologies. But there are other works that were never translated into Castilian: we have spoken repeatedly of the *Philosophical Quartet*, closely related to this tradition, but there are more.

Nevertheless, it is clear that we cannot embark here on a thorough study of the whole Arabic tradition: among other reasons because to a great extent it remains unpublished. Notable therein are works such as "The sayings of Socrates" by al Kindi (d. c. 873), al Sahrastani (precursor of *PQ*), the ms. Istanbul Köprülü 1608, Ibn Hindû and several other texts.

By way of introduction, we should make reference to what Gutas says in his book, pp. 328 ff. concerning the theme of Socrates. We cannot do a complete critique here for lack of data and also because this is not exactly our subject. But it will be useful to draw some interesting conclusions and provide the indispensable criticisms.

1. For Gutas, it is clear that the entire tradition compiled by the Arabs is Greek. And it is not unitary but rather multiple: it can happen that one particular maxim may appear in several variants, sometimes derived from Greek variants, sometimes adding a new one. There are indications, furthermore, of an Arabic translation of the basic Greek sources.
2. This is all quite acceptable, but I do not agree with respect to the proposition that (here and in the case of Pythagoras) we must accept the existence of two Greek gnomologies, an A, containing "non-apophthegmatic material" namely maxims and stories, which would have given rise to translation Y, and a B with "apophthegmatic material", translated by Hunayn. Then there would be a series of contaminations, intermediate states, etc.: the material of both sources would have reached *PQ*, with M (Mubassir) based on Hunayn.

There are several objections to this. In Greek there was never such a division of materials; *gnômai* and *khreîai* always appeared together. And a variant by M, based on Hunayn is not credible, the differences are too great.

In summary, I will not do a *stemma* because of the lack of precision in the Greek and the even greater imprecision in the Arabic data. Various Greek gnomologies could have reached their authors and later been combined in various ways, following the ancient tradition; and this by way of more than one translation, directly or via Syriac. What interests me in this context is to do a study, based on a limited set of texts, *PQ*, M and H, of what is present and what is missing in the Greek collections, and, if possible, also establish the connection of this set of texts with these collections.

For on various occasions, I have pointed out the presence in the Greek sapiential tradition, especially as regards Alexander, of a phase that is "oriental-Byzantine" (or Byzantine but only indirectly accessible). I remind the reader of what was said in Chapter III about the epistolary novel translated into Arabic by Salim Abu 'l 'Alah, about the laments of the philosophers (in Greek by Eutychius of Alexandria, and in Syriac) and about a strongly Christianized phase, above all Syrian and Ethiopian, of the Alexander and Aristotle legend. I add to that what was said in Chapter IV about Neo-Pythagorean and Hermetic texts in Syriac and in Chapter II about the Syriac collections of Greek maxims with a Christian interpretation. This has led me to propose that the Greek texts found by the Arabs in the Orient and translated by them (sometimes into Syriac first, as I have said) come from an "oriental" Byzantine Syrian branch of which we do not have direct knowledge.

It is clear that this hypothesis must be applied as well to the Socratic maxims that we are studying now. In fact, G. Strohmaier, in two articles that I have referred to[7], has put forth several ideas on this subject. For example, that maxims and *khreîai* not transmitted in Greek may nevertheless be Greek: the theme of "Socrates never sad" or of "if the barrel breaks" (see below), in Mubassir.

But at the same time Strohmaier considers that the presentation of the Greek sages as ascetics (we have seen this above in the *Life* of Socrates in *Bocados,* Mubassir) does not appear in the Greek sources but leads us, rather, to a Nestorian, Syriac-Christian or even Muslim setting. He has doubts, for example, about the Greek character of the pessimistic vision of the world in some maxims in *Bocados*, one of them engraved on the mausoleum of Tamerlane's sister in Samarkand: "Man is tormented in this world ..."; and in various other maxims in *Bocados*, for example the one that paraphrases Matthew 6,26 and incites us to pay no heed to the world and be like the birds and the beasts who are not concerned about their food.

Therefore, we are going to make a first inquiry by compiling the maxims in *PQ* and M and H, or in one or two of these collections, whose Greek sources have not been preserved. But the limits are not clear: we almost

7 G. Strohmaier, "Ethical Sentences and Anecdotes of Greek Philosophers in Arabic Tradition", cit., and "Die arabische Sokrateslegende und ihre Ursprünge", cit.

always find remote Greek sources from which the maxims could, at some moment, have been created in lost gnomologies. Let me add that I do not go into the matter of the variants of the maxims in the different collections that reveal various sources or translations; or into the possible attribution to Pl., D., etc. or the duplications, nor do I deal with their presence in other Arabic sources. What interests us here is the agreement, if any, of Arabic sources, and the relation of these sources with the Greek ones, both those preserved and those lost.

Let it be clear that all the maxims omitted here have a Greek source in one of the maxims listed above with the numbers from 1 to 224, but frequently there are variations, distortions and accumulations of maxims. More details will be given below.

We shall begin, then, with the maxims in *PQ*, and H and M where pertinent. I follow the numbering of *PQ*.

3. S. to a rich man who was rebuking him: I could have lived as you do, but you not as I do. *PQ* M. Cynic theme of wealth.
4. Do not search for wealth, which drives wisdom away; disdain death, kill desire, follow justice and you will attain salvation. *PQ* M. Socratic themes followed by a Christian one.
5. We live to die, we die in order to live. *PQ*. A Christian theme.
6. Asked "Why are you never sad?" – Because I never acquire anything whose loss can cause me unhappiness.

6a. And what if the barrel breaks? The space that it occupies will not break. *PQ* M. Reiteration of Cynic themes, the second one derived from D.

7. He lives in a barrel with a little dog and to the question of a student "What are you doing with that dog?" he replies: It treats me better than you do. *PQ*. The Socratic theme of the barrel and the dog. cf. *Vita Aesopi* 45.

9. Why don't you buy land? – Because I do not want to have problems with Him who owns the whole earth. *PQ*. The Cynic theme of fleeing from wealth, Christianized.

10. Accumulation of themes: S. does not visit the king because the king is the slave "of the one whose master I am." The king summons him and S. explains that he is referring to the passions; he rejects the king's gifts, they will be harmful to him in the other world. *PQ*. A Socratic-Cynic synthesis, perhaps from the theme of Archelaus's invitation in

28 and 29 and from the dialogue of Alexander and the Gymnosophists.

11. A buffoon says to S. that the delights of the world have been prohibited: food, clothing, women. – He does not want to be like the swine and the monkeys, make his stomach a cemetery for animals, prefer the corruptible body to the immortal soul. *PQ*. Socratism, anti-Epicurean controversy, Christianity, possibly Pythagoreanism.
12. A man criticized his old clothing and S. said: New clothes and old clothes do not indicate good or bad conduct. *PQ* M. A theme that comes from X. *Mem.* 1.6.2. and later was connected with Aristippus (26).
13. The best sign of a friend is that he can reprove you and allows himself to be reproved.
14. S. says that being fat indicates lack of culture, ἀπαιδευσία. *PQ*. The Cynic criticism of gluttony and laxity. Cf. *Fab. Anon.* 228 H.
15. Who is the meanest of men? – He who allows you to pursue your passion. *PQ*. Derived from the Socratic theme of passion, cf. 5, 30, etc.
16. What is the worst state? – Old age and poverty. *PQ*.
17. Who is the lowest man? – He who does not trust anyone and who is not trusted by anyone. *PQ*.
18. Who is the meanest man? – The one who does not forgive. *PQ*.
24. When they were going to kill him, his disciples asked what they should do with his body. – The smell will make whoever is present deal with it. *PQ* H M. It derives from ancient Cynic themes (D.L. VI 52, Stob. V 55.10 and especially Luc., Dem. 66).
25. A Sophist offers to give testimony in favor of S.; he does not accept because he is an untrustworthy man. *PQ*. Possibly from the anecdote in Elianus, *VH* VII 20 (also in Stob. 3.12.19): King Archidamus does not accept the words of an old man whose white hair is dyed black.
26. A Sophist said to him: How ugly you are! – Your beauty is not yours or my ugliness mine, but the Creator's. *PQ* M. Christianization of the Cynic theme of beauty and ugliness.
27. A young disciple went to him one night because, he said, he was the one who deserved most esteem. – Go away, because if I am what you think I am, I do not have the wisdom that you are hoping for. *PQ*. Development of a theme of Hippocrates in Pl., *Prt.* 320 and of Alcibiades in *Smp.* 218 c ff.
29. What is the nature of God? – It is concealed, not hidden. *PQ*. Christian without doubt.

30. If the person who does not know were to keep silent, discord would cease. *PQ* H M. Related to the Socratic theme of not speaking of what one does not know, cf. 50.
31. The wise man is a physician of religion, possessions are his sickness; if he contracts the sickness, how can he cure others? *PQ* H M. The Socratic theme of the philosopher as physician (since Pl., *Grg.* 464 a ff.) and the Cynic one about wealth, both Christianized.
32. Kill your will and you will live a natural life. *PQ* M. A fusion of the Socratic-Cynic-Stoic themes of "kill your passions" and of "live according to nature" from these philosophies.
35. Cure wrath with silence and desire with wrath (against yourself). *PQ* H M. Two Socratic themes.
36. Do not fear death, for its bitterness consists of being feared. H M. The theme comes from Pl. *Ap.* 28d ff., *Phd.* 63e ff. and is frequent in the Cynic maxims (61, 66, 211).
40. They said to him: "Your lecture was not accepted." – What is important to me is whether I spoke well or badly. *PQ* M. It derives from X., *Mem.* 4.8.4 (= *Ap.* 3–4), cf. also 66 supra.
41. The universals of this world subsist because of justice, only with justice can the particulars subsist. *PQ* M. Possibly Stoic.
42. A group of maxims: the painters who paint beautiful things and do not imitate their virtuous forbears, guard yourselves from the wrath and inebriety that do not allow you to see their ugliness. *PQ* M. Gutas, pp. 321 ff. finds precedents in Plutarch.
44. Debate between S. and one of his students who is contemplating Hipparchia avidly: he should look at her internal wisdom, which will sharpen his gaze, not her external beauty, which will dull it. *PQ* H. The Cynic theme of beauty, with a great anachronism (Hipparchia is the wife of Crates, the Cynic).
45. What man is most virtuous? – The most virtuous, he who aspires to virtue for its own sake; in the second degree, he who aspires to virtue in order to hear someone. *PQ* M. Possibly derived from Hes., *Op.* 292 ff. via Aristotle, *EN* 1095^{b} 10–13.
46. Geometry is the polish of the soul, the animal pleasures are its rust. *PQ*. Cf. the inscription of the Academy in Elias, *in Cat.*: μηδεὶς ἀγεωμέτρητος εἰσίτω "let no one enter unless he knows geometry", as well as the Cynic-Stoic theme of pleasure.

48. A physiognomist told S. that he was dominated by a depraved desire. – Yes, by my nature, but I have controlled myself in order to conquer it. *PQ*. It comes from Pl., *Smp*. 221d ff. by way of a story between S. and Zopyrus (in Cic., *Tusc.* 4.37.80); at other times it is attributed to Hippocrates. The theme of domination of pleasure is added, in maxims since *PHib*. 182.
49. Whom to ask for advice in all matters? – Ask him who is a human being in acts and not in form. *PQ*.
50. Life is defined by two limits, hope and death. *PQ* H. Without doubt created from Pl., *Phd.* 114d–e.
51. Thought must be in control before, during and after the act. *PQ* H M. This seems contrary to 75.
52. When your soul asks you for the price of tomorrow, tell it to bring you today's. *PQ*. Cynic?
53. The person who is naturally good follows the law. *PQ*. Socratic and later overcoming of the opposition nature/law. *PQ* M.
54. In his illness, one of his disciples asked if they should sacrifice a bird for him. – The hearts of those who know the true principles are pulpits for the angels; those that are full of desires are tombs for animals. *PQ*. It comes from Pl., *Phd.* 118a, Cynicized and Christianized. cf. 11 also.
55. Three things are sought in this world: power, wealth and leisure. They are attained by abstaining from pleasure, contenting oneself and not being ambitious. *PQ* M. A Socratic-Cynic theme.
56. Do not force your children to follow your path, they have been created for a different age. *PQ* M.
57. Yesterday, today and tomorrow: grasp today. *PQ*. Cf. 52 supra.

The following are some considerations that can be made:

1. The Arabic texts mentioned, except for ID, had at their disposal as a model one or various lost Greek gnomologies, characterized by the predominance of Socratic-Cynic material, often clearly Christianized, the Epicurean elements having been eliminated. Sometimes old Socratic material was recuperated, at other times various maxims were fused and combined. Note that this is a procedure very different from that of the tradition we have studied beginning with the 3rd century and later in Byzantium: there pagan and Christian authors, who kept their names,

were joined together; here the maxims of the Socratic tradition are Christianized.

2. The presence of this source is highlighted, too, by another fact: the presence in *PQ* of blocks derived from it, namely 3–7, 10–14, 16–19, 24–32, 40–42, 44 to the end.

In short, these collections provide us with something new, as we indicated earlier and as we will have occasion to see in more detail: the existence of Greek gnomologies (joined to *Lives*) which, based on those of the ancient tradition that have reached us in one way or another, introduced amplifications in a Cynic-Christian as well as ascetic sense. This is the same hypothesis as we presented in relation to the Alexander/Aristotle theme. We consider that it is a tradition with a Byzantine base beginning in the 6th century, later developed more deeply, without doubt in Syria in contact with the Christianity of that region. The Neo-Pythagorean and Hermetic elements studied above also merged with this tradition.

We now pass on to the maxims, identical or more or less exact, that appear in the Greek gnomologies that have been preserved. There are 16: the numbering is according to *PQ*, followed by mine if any and, in parenthesis, by the most indispensable data, all this followed by the Arabic documentation that we are studying.

2 = 5 (*GV* 272) *PQ* M.
8 = 12 (*GV* 479 imp.) *PQ*.
16 (*GV* 479 Stratonicus, MC Democritus, AM Chrysostom) *PQ* Socr.
19 = 2 (*GV* 169 and others, Diog., MC and others, Pl.) *PQ* M: Socr.
20 Socrates in the barrel, "don't block the sun", all that he needs goes with him everywhere (imp., Diog.) *PQ* M: Socr.
21 Why don't you write philosophy? – He prefers reason to the hide of dead animals (cf. 32 var., *GV* 499) *PQ* M H.
22 = 49 (imp.) *PQ* M.
23 = 11 (GV 478) *PQ* M H.
28 = 21 (*GV* 488 approx.) *PQ*.
33 = 223 (gnomologies of the type A AM) *PQ*.
34 = 13 var. with regard to the young (cf. *GV* 480) *PQ* H ID.
37 The sick are cured by physicians, malefactors by the laws (cf. Timothy, MC Epictetus, AM anonymous) *PQ* M: Socr.
38 = 4 (*GV* 471 CP Men.) *PQ* M.
39 = 15 var. (cf. *GV* 482) *PQ* M.

43 variant of 49 (cf. FM 206, Isocr.) *PQ* ID: Socr., M: Pythag. 47 variant of 14 (*GV* 481) *PQ* M.

It is necessary to make some important observations here:

1. Only a minor sector of *PQ* (and of the other collections when they coincide) comes directly from the known Greek gnomologies, and this frequently with variants in the text or attribution: our Arabic texts use the name of Socrates more, attributing to him anecdotes about Diogenes especially.
2. ID belongs to this sector only marginally, but he belongs (unlike the case of the previous sector, that of the maxims not in our gnomologies). It remains to be seen to what extent H and M belong to this other sector.
3. As for the ideology, it is clear that these are Socratic maxims, often Cynicized. The Christianization of the previous sector is missing.

It seems clear, in short, that the composers of the Arabic gnomologies had access to Greek gnomologies close to those that have been preserved, although not identical. To these they added, finally, others also derived from the Greek ones, but with different characteristics, as is the case with Christianization. This is the oriental Byzantine or Syriac sector to which we have been alluding.

VII. The Greco-Arabic-Castilian gnomologies: Socrates in Mubassir and *Bocados de Oro*

I return, finally, to *Bocados de Oro*, about which the most essential things have already been said in Chapter 1. We have labeled it M in the preceding pages, for its Arabic translator, Mubassir. It was later translated into Castilian. Now it must be made clear that the Arabic text does not correspond exactly to the Castilian one. In the latter, which is the one being studied here, some maxims are missing, but this is a minor detail.

This study is, of course, a continuation of the study already done in part in the preceding chapter with regard to *PQ*. It must be emphasized that both works, *PQ* and M, have two common roots: one, the works that are the predecessors of the Greek gnomologies preserved; the other, Greek works also, but not preserved except in the traces that they have left in the two works, which are otherwise independent: from the first group of gnomologies there are maxims in *PQ* but not in M, and the same happens in the second. And even when there is coincidence, M frequently presents a reworked text.

And above all, it adds many new things. What we have said about the *Life* that precedes the collection of maxims gives us a clue. We have a very advanced Christianization combined with the use of ancient Greek sources. It gives the impression that starting at the stage that is the foundation of the *PQ*, M has a gone a step further, but always on the basis of Christianized Greek models from the date and place that we have proposed, models that combine maxims, *khreîai*, debates and biographical anecdotes.

I refer back to the two lists above: the one that contains maxims from gnomologies that have been preserved and to which *PQ* and/or M had access, and the list that has "new" maxims culled from our texts. Actually, the material from the preserved gnomologies that exist in M (sometimes in *PQ* as well) is scanty. From the *PQ* we have 16 maxims and from M we must discount those that are only in *PQ* and add those that are in M but not in *PQ*.

I find it quite noteworthy that most of these maxims (whether they are in *PQ* or not) appear consecutively: 59 = my number 10 (on gifts), 122 = 49 (Socrates learns music as an old man), 123 (from Diogenes in the Greek gnomologies, the theme of the olives), 124 = 5 (the king masters his desires), 125 = 81 (what is most pleasing is to learn new things, cf. a variant in 214 = 204), 126 = 204 (the most noble thing, to avoid bad actions), 127 = 4 (the best acquisition, a loyal friend, cf. variant in *GV* 470 = 3). Evidently the author or his source copied a gnomology related to the Greek ones that have been preserved. It was a gnomology included in A (*GV*, etc.), but also with echoes in Stob., MC, etc.

Naturally, there are also other maxims of similar origin scattered throughout the collection, like 67 = 173 (disdain for death), 145 = 23 (what is important is to know how to make use of things, variant in 255 = 23), 232 = 1 (would you prefer that they killed me lawfully?, but Xantippe is not mentioned), 239, variant of 14 (a fool insults Socrates), 262 = 26 (the law is not made in order to wear new clothing, variant of 26, with the mention of Aristippus omitted). At other times there is a more distant derivation from the Greek maxims, as in 22 = 34 (the theme of taming the wild horse), 27, cf. 37 (how can the physician who is ill heal someone else?), 192, cf. 34

(woman is like a palm tree that bears good dates; the reference to Xantippe disappears). In general terms, *Bocados* presents fairly free versions.

After that come the "new" maxims in *PQ* and M: I have already given a list of them. There was, without doubt, a common source that joined the "known" maxims and these other "new" ones. But, once again, the treatment of M and/or *Bocados* is quite free. Such, for example, is the case of 73, cf. *PQ* 13 (the good friend), 148 (be satisfied with little), cf. *PQ* 10; 164 (don't trust time), cf. *PQ* 52, 57; 200, cf. *PQ* 40 (what is important is that the speech was delivered well), 207, it amplifies *PQ* 26 (What an ugly face you have! they say to Socrates); 263, cf. *PQ* (disdain for death).

It seems evident that both the *PQ* and M, the original of *Bocados*, followed the same Greek gnomologies and reworked them, especially M. It sometimes happened that a maxim was repeated by mistake, as in 203 = 205, continue to do good although it be scorned (with translation variants). At other times there are two different renderings of what is, in essence, the same maxim.

M *(Bocados)* offers many maxims missing in the rest of the tradition. Evidently, the sources cited up to now were augmented with others, either already included in a late version of these sources or added by Mubassir from some other source. What interests us here is to point out their Socratic-Cynic-Christian orientation, their remote sources and their Greek character.

At times sources were used that, in the final analysis, come from the classical epoch, just as happened in the *Life*, as we saw above. Thus:

Hesiod 240: matters are settled by justice and unsettled by injustice (cf. Hes., *Op.* 213 ff.). Cf. above on the most virtuous man in *PK* 45 and M, in Hes., *Op.* 292.

Alcaeus 235: wine and wisdom cannot reside one within the other as they are two opposing things (Alcaeus 366 οἶνος καὶ ἀλάθεα "wine and truth").

Pindar 87: you cannot take back what you have said or what you have done, cf. Pi., *O.* 2.16.

Euhemerus? Critias?: And they made them believe that they were their lords so that they should fear them and avoid doing wrong. Cf. Critias 84b.

Plato: In view of the disappearance of all the ancient personages, Plato is introduced, both in dialogue and giving maxims, in 44, 68 and other places. There is, especially, though I will not give citations, a dependence on various passages from Plato, referring or not to Socrates. 2: wisdom is the stairway for the soul; whoever does not have it cannot be close to God (cf. *Smp.* 211c); 27: the wise man is the physician of the law, cf. Pl., *Grg.* 464b; 36: he who cares about the world loses his soul and he who cares about his soul abhors the world; also 198: preach to my soul; 264: wisdom is that man know his soul, what it is good for, cf. Pl., *Ap.* 30a; 63: life without learning is not the life of a man, cf. *Ap.* 38a; 154: will / mind, cf. *R.* 439a ff. ἐπιθυμία / νοῦς, λόγος; 253: the senses of the body / the spiritual senses … spiritual king, cf. *R.* ibid.; 257: at one man's house they honored someone more than they honored Socrates, a probable reference to Pl. *Prt.* 314c ff.

Heraclitus 87: not all men know the truth though all have ears, cf. Heraclit. 1.

Herodotus 106: the greatest wonder in the world is to feel sorry for a wise man, cf. Hdt. 9.16.

The Delphic maxims 69: the best of all things is the median; 72: he who runs fast always stumbles; 223: only accompany him who knows himself (cf. my 216 MC).

Lucretius. 176: and they said to him: what do you gain from your wisdom? And he said: because of it I am like one who is on the seashore and watches how the fools lose their heads in the waves, cf. Lucr. II 1 ff. The only clearly Epicurean passage.

LXX: Passages on oaths, the same as above in MC: 57, 104.

NT 5: I am the sower and the souls are the sown field and study is the water that nourishes them. Whose sown field is not clean and whose water is not abundant cannot benefit from sowing, cf. *Eu.Matt.* 13.24 ff. (also 217: sow goodness and you will reap happiness); 209: Do to others what you would want them to do to you, and do not do what you would not want done to yourself. Cf. *Eu.Matt.* 6.12 (and 199, MC); 250: and he said to his disciples: leave all your matters to God, cf. *Eu.Luc.* 9.57 ff.

As I have already indicated, both these maxims and the *Life* reveal great sacred-profane erudition in the compiler (or his source). Apart from this, I must mention the following points with respect to the "new" maxims not present in other gnomologies:

1. The frequency of the traditional Socratic themes: wisdom or the mind, good and bad, truth, friends, greed, wrath, death. It is not difficult to

imagine the underlying Greek words: σοφία, φρόνησις, ἀγαθόν, κακόν, ἀλήθεια, ἐπιθυμία, ὀργή, θάνατος etc.

2. The frequency, once again, of Cynic themes: wealth and poverty, criticism of women and marriage, unimportance of one's lineage.
3. But especially the Christian themes, in connection or not with those mentioned: the soul vis-à-vis the body and its pleasures, salvation; the mortal world compared with the eternal one, the good death that leads to the latter, sin.
4. The theme of maintaining silence and keeping a secret is partly Socratic partly Hermetic. For some of these maxims, which relate to well-known ideological currents, specific precedents can be found. For example, the woman-trap of 93 and 180 reminds us of ID 63, also in D.L. An infinite number of more or less similar maxims are found in the *Life of Aesop* and in the *khreîai* attributed to Diogenes, cf. for example the woman swept away by the flood in a well-known inscription at Herculaneum[8] ("let the bad be swept away by the bad"). We could likewise find these precedents in the maxims on wisdom, silence, death, etc., and in a few on practical morals: 258, 259.

Now just as I have said that an entire fragment has been taken from a Greek gnomology of the type known, there are also thematic blocks, especially of the Christian type (with precedents in earlier thought), such as the following:

The soul, the good soul, the bad one, salvation: 8–12, 14–17, 19, 22, 34, 122–127.

The world (disdain for the world, love of the world, an obstacle for salvation, etc.): 31, 33–35, 36–37, 39–42, 52–53, 78–80, 92–101, 160–167, 171–173, 252.

Sin (in connection with the world):43, 45, 251.

Keeping silent (in connection with knowledge, necessary for virtue): 128–133.

Women (in connection with badness, sin, the devil): 47,93, 180–196.

The secret: 150–153.

Death (if it is with virtue, it leads to the true life): 107–118.

At other times the themes intertwine, for instance in 258 ff. those of wisdom, the soul, the king: a new theme, incidentally, in 245, 247, 248, which

8 264 Della Corte.

takes us back to the gnomologies studied in Chapter III and to *Poridad.* At the end, in 109 ff. there is a sort of Appendix of various maxims.

In summary, following the tendency of *PQ* but taking things much further, this work has, with great erudition, Christianized Socratic-Platonic-Cynic philosophy. It is evident that it relied on more than one gnomology and, for the Christian theme, on a gnomology organized by topics. It has, to be sure, given it a Byzantine Christian varnish (the king, idols), eliminating the old features and characters, except for Plato, obviously. But it has not introduced Christ or the saints: it is a philosophical and general Christianity, apt for dissemination in vast circles.

I have already said that this literature, which without doubt originates in Constantinople, was developed especially in Syria, where the Greek original of *Bocados* and those of the other works were collected and studied by the Arabs, in the original Greek versions or in Syriac translations.

But let me reiterate, with special emphasis, that the whole collection is Greek. Certain phrases appear to be translated directly from Greek: 89 καταφρονήσατε τὸν θάνατον καὶ σωθήσονται αἱ ψυχαὶ ὑμῶν, 102 ὅστις θέλει χρῆσθαι τῇ ἀληθείᾳ, 187 ἡ ἀνθρωπίνη ἄνοια, 207 σπεῖρε τὸ ἀγαθὸν καὶ θερίσεις χαράν. In a later chapter I will attempt to use this procedure to progress in the study of the sources.

The structure of the maxims and *khreîai* is also traditional. In the first place, there are long series of maxims in the indicative and of others in the imperative. There are also interjectional and interrogative maxims. In others there is a brief anecdote with the participation of some person (he said, they said, he asked) and Socrates' reply (said S.); very infrequently a dialogue ensues.

At other times there is simply a "said S." or "he said", sometimes mentioning the interlocutor (47 to one of his disciples). But there is also "he saw and he said" (ἰδών, θεασάμενος).

Another formula is "it is in the interest of", as in 52 "it is in the interest of the wise person" (πρέπει τῷ φρονίμῳ). A different type, also seen above, is the question with a superlative: 125 what are the most delicious things?, followed by a reply; or the asseverative maxim with a superlative: 124 the best king is the one who masters his desires.

All this is Greek. So we must consider that we have a combination of *Life* + gnomology of Socrates that Mubassir or his predecessor joined to various other collections, of which we have given a list. This is, as we have said repeatedly, a work from the 6th/7th centuries that made use of precedents related to the gnomologies that have come down to us plus other lost ones: a unique witness to a great misfortune.

In these last gnomologies there was clearly a Christian development that in the case of our texts went much further than in the *PQ*. Or several developments, since what has reached us reveals the existence of other gnomologies: things that are not present in *PQ*, various thematic blocks, etc.

The line of chronological evolution, then, is clear as to content and form: in M *(Bocados)* it was embodied in an important work. It is noteworthy, once again, that it should have preserved its validity in our 13th century, and that in this work Socrates and his continuers, including the Christian ones, should have remained alive in Spain. This is clear evidence of cultural continuity, of live Antiquity, a case of an important work recovered through a history of successive translations.

VIII. The Greco-Arabic-Castilian gnomologies: Socrates in *Buenos Proverbios*

Here we have a work whose Arabic translator, Hunayn, describes it, as I said at the beginning of this book, as coming from Greek books on parchment. Actually, he is referring to various books, both of pink parchment with gold and silver decoration and of purple parchment with letters of gold and many figures. He adds that on the cover of the book (of one of them) was the figure of the philosopher, seated and surrounded by his disciples. I believe that with this, reference is made to at least two books, which coincides with what I noted in Chapter II of this work: that to the story of Alexander, with his life, his moral advice and that of Aristotle, and to the mourning for his death have been added gnomologies of various philosophers, mentioned collectively or by their names.

One of these is the gnomology of Socrates, not preceded by a *Life*, that has come down to us in the *Libro de los Buenos Proverbios*, which we are studying here. It is clearly linked to the tradition that we have been studying, and specifically to the work that we have just seen, the work translated into Arabic by Mubassir and then into Castilian with the title of *Bocados de Oro*. Now then, considering the great coincidences (with the *PQ* as well), I believe that in spite of the chronology (Hunayn is from the 9th century, Mubassir from the 11th), *Buenos Proverbios* marks an advance or culminating point in the evolution of this literature in the hands of the Syrian Greeks.

For once again we must begin with a Greek manuscript from the 6th or 7th century, from the cultural background of which we have spoken. Alongside the traditional cargo of the known Greek gnomologies and the additions partially common to *PQ* and M, the text presents a great number of alterations of this material, plus a considerable input of new material, including Christian elements.

This is always in the milieu that we are familiar with: that of a monarchical and Christianized Greece and with some themes that are essentially the same: the soul, asceticism, the world, salvation and the obstacles it encounters, death, God; but not neglecting the old Socratic and cynic themes of wisdom, disdain for wealth, control of wrath and desires, etc. Forgotten, however, are ancient names and dates: it is Socrates, not Diogenes, who is in the barrel and is visited by the king.

Considering what has already been said, we are not going to make a detailed analysis of each and every maxim, but we will highlight what is most important[9]. We must point out, in the first place, the presence of maxims from *PQ* and (at times) M, both of the maxims that we have called "new" (24, 30, 31, 35, 36, 44, 50, 51) and of those that we know from Greek gnomologies (21, 23, 34).

But there is, as I say, independence. For example:

1. In the introduction of ancient and erudite material, much scarcer here. Two Delphic maxims already appear in M, but translated in a different way from the *Bocados* version: 71.1 "the best thing is moderation", 71.7 "he who hurries a lot, stumbles a lot". I believe that 81.14 ("What is the thing that is closest? – The thing that is most appealing") is Sappho 16.4 "I (think that the most beautiful thing is) the thing that one loves". Note that this philosophy fits into the work badly, but the maxim heads a section on the traditional theme "the thing that most …", which does not fit in either. Sappho penetrated the Christian moralist through pure beauty and humanity.
   Hesiod fits in better, Op. 286 ff. in 71.9, the two "professions" of Good and Bad. And, of course, the well-known Biblical citation *ex abundantia cordis os loquitur* in 72.11 "language is the servant of the heart".

9 Since Sturm's book does not use consecutive numbering, we will cite the maxims by page and number on the page.

As can be seen, a measure of erudition was not scorned by the editors of these late Byzantine works, who used it as seasoning for the materials that they inherited from various sources, which undoubtedly were gnomologies.

2. There are maxims in M and H that are not found in *PQ* and maxims only in H and *PQ*; and there are maxims only in H. But let me emphasize the differences vis-à-vis *Bocados* when it is a matter of versions of the same maxims, as we have already seen with the two Delphic maxims.

   For example, *PQ* simply says "if he who does not know were to keep silent, discord would cease", while H 70.2 begins "Socrates said: if he who does not know would keep silent…" and continues with a long dissertation. In contrast, the "words of advice" of Plato in H 70.2 differ greatly from those in M. 99, which are more extensive.

Sometimes the differences can be attributed to the translation: the "world" *[mundo]* in M is "world" *[sieglo]* in H (also *"mundo"*), "fault" *[yerro]* in M is *[peccado]* (also "*yerro*") in H, and "I never saw any sadness in you" in H 66.6 is "why don't we (ever) see you sad?" in M 46. But it is not merely a matter of translation; many of the maxims are rewritten in different ways in each of the three texts, or in two if only two contain them. In H 77.6, the anecdote of the disciple who was looking at a woman lustfully, the name of the woman in *PQ* (Hipparchia) disappears. The anecdote in M 207, when someone says to Socrates "What an ugly face you have!", is followed by a Cynic and spiritual conclusion, while in M 81.4, it is a woman who makes the criticism, and Socrates' reply is banal: the mirror is rusty.

The long dissertation on the topic of idols in M 7 becomes in H a brief question and reply and also in M 77.3. Or compare M 36 ("He who cares about the world loses his soul and he who cares about his soul abhors the world") with H 72.4 ("He who prizes his soul despises the world. Who despises his soul prizes the world and those in it").

It also happens that a maxim is repeated, as in the case of the one about the old woman wearing make-up in 78.5 and 80.3 (greatly amplified). Perhaps the author was following several gnomologies with the same maxims and neglected to select one single version.

Let me emphasize now the appearance in our treatise of new maxims, almost all of them of either Cynic or Christian character (but not all of them, see above on "What is the most ...?"). If, for example, those regarding women, are reviewed, it will be seen that many maxims and *khreîai* coincide with M and, at times, with the familiar Greek tradition; but not always: the comparison of the woman with the flower of the oleander, for example, is only found here (M 191 and H 81.2). But there are new ones, such as 78.1 "*las mugeres son sengunt costella parada que non cae en ella sinon que se engaña*", derived from the Bible. And topics barely touched on in the other collections are presented here more extensively, with new material, such as the topic of time in 79.4 ff.

As for the rest, the fundamental themes are the same and they are organized in series: 71.9 ff. (good and evil), 78.1 ff. and 80.3 ff. (women), 78.9 ff (conceal a secret), 79.5 ff. (time). As can be seen, themes that we know well from M are scattered or missing. And there is a notable presence of series that we could call "formal", sometimes coinciding in content: the one, the best, the best (feminine) (73.9 ff.), the fact … (73.12 ff.), who, who + preterite – preterite (75.1 ff. for example, who tried, gained in knowledge), he said, and he said (75.11 ff.), and he saw (78.3 ff.), what is the most … thing? (81.13 ff.).

So, in summary, we have in *Buenos Proverbios* a third Socratic gnomology, Cynicized and Christianized, that goes back to the same time and place of origin as *PQ* and M and contains some of the same material and some that is different. It is, as I have said, the most highly developed, with less ancient material and more distortions in what it keeps. Once again we have a Socrates who preserves some of his features but adds those of Diogenes and the Christian ascetic. And all this in the monarchical and theological setting that we are familiar with and that fit so well into the court of Alfonso XII.

IX. Appendix on the "Greekness" of these gnomologies

I would like to offer one more fact on the "Greekness" – the type of Greekness – of the gnomologies that are at the base of the Arabic and Arabic-Castilian ones we are concerned with here. I believe that I have established this without a doubt. But there is a way to adduce more information for those maxims and *khreîai* not documented in Antiquity, especially those with a Christian content. I have already said something about this.

Certain maxims, by their structure and phrasing, reveal ancient Greek models. Just as it is clear that much-repeated initial formulas are translations of Greek formulas such as ἐρωτηθεὶς ... εἶπε "on being asked … he said", καὶ εἶπε τινὶ τῶν μαθητῶν "and he said to one of his disciples", ἰδὼν (θεασάμενος) ἔφη "having seen (contemplated) he said", προσελθόντος αὐτῷ τινος "when someone came up to him", which we find in the Greek gnomologies, we find other phrases in the Castilian ones whose Greek model we can establish. By using the CD-ROM of the *Thesaurus Linguae Graecae*, one can confirm this hypothesis: one can see the literary and philosophical-religious setting in which this material is found. We give some examples taken from *Bocados*.

8: the good soul loves goodness. The phrase ἡ ψυχὴ ἀγαπᾷ "the soul loves" is found, for example, in Iust. Phil., *Ep.Diog.* 498, Mac. Aeg., *Serm.* B 2.7.1.

9: the fruit … is salvation. The phrases καρπὸν σωτηρίας, καρπὸς σωτηρίας "fruit of salvation", etc. are found in Christian authors such as Mac. Aeg., *Serm.* B 16.5.21, Io. D., *Man.* 15.14, Thdt., *Ep. Serm.* 60.16. I believe that this comes from (in the same paragraph) "the fruit … is to repent", because beginning with the New Testament (*Eu.Matt.* 3.8.1, *Eu.Luc.* 3.8.1) the phrase καρπὸν μετανοίας "fruit of repentance" is found frequently in Christian literature: Herm., *Mand.*96.2, Eus., DE 9.5.3, Epiph. Const., *Haer.* 2.374, Ath. Al., M. 27.77, Basil, *Ep.* 22.3, Didym., *in Zacch.* 1.351, Mac. Aeg., *Serm.*, B 12.3, Io. D., *Haer.* 80.85, etc.

13: the person who follows his desires, cf. also 178. Cf. Plu. 2445e ὁ λογισμὸς ὅπου ... ἕπεται ταῖς ἐπιθυμίαις "when reason follows one's desires", the identical theme of the opposition of reason and desire, this one leads to perdition. Similarly, Asp., *in EN* 43.1. It was a common theme. But there is also ἀκολουθοῦσι τῇ ἐπιθυμίᾳ "they follow desire" in, for example, Chrysipp., *Stoic.* 475.49, Gal., *Placit.* 4.6.32, Simp., *in de An.* 295.37; and also in the Christians: Basil. M., 31.937A, Chrys., M 50.813A, etc.

27: the wise man is the physician of the law. This must be compared with the theme of the physician of the soul (ψυχῆς ἰατρός, attributed to the *logos*, to the wise man, etc.). We find it in Plu. 2465d, Ph., *Sac.* 70, Men., *Mon.* 1.622, Origen, *Philoc.* 27.4.2, Chrys., M. 51.279.

32, 99, 171: he who loves the world, the love of this world (in a negative sense, of course). This is clearly an expression that comes from the

Gospel of Saint John 2.15.1, 2 μὴ ἀγαπᾶτε τὸν κόσμον, ὅστις ἀγαπᾷ τὸν κόσμον. They are phrases copied directly or with slight variations by Christian authors such as Origen, *Mart.* 39.16, etc., Chrys., M. 60.713. 64.776, the *Sacra Parallela* of Io. D., M. 95.181, *Barlaam* 168.10, Mac. Aeg., *Serm.* B 68.3.5, etc., *Hom.* 5.167. And, as can be seen, by our Christian gnomologists.

34: goodness of the soul. This translates ἀγαθότης ψυχῆς LXX *Sir.* 45.23.4.

62: it is in the interest of the king. This is a translation of πρέπει τῷ βασιλεῖ, which, with the precedents in Pl., X. and the imperial epoch, is especially frequent in the Ps.-Callisth. (cf., for example, rec. F 28.4.2, Pall., *Geni. Ind.* 2.41, Hippol., *Theoph.* 5.6) and in general in the historians.

65: he who guides his soul …, cf. 64. This is from ψυχὴν ὁδηγεῖν "guide the soul" in Christian authors like Ath. Al., M. 28.837, Mac. Aeg. *Serm.* B 13.2.3, *Hom.* 12.125.

69: the best of all things is the median. This Delphic maxim ran through all of Greek literature – classical, late (Gal. 6.123, etc.) and Christian (Thdt., *HE* 210.16).

108: to the world that perishes. This translates the Neo-Platonic αἰώνιος κόσμος (cf., for example, Plot. 4.1.1.6, Alb., *Intr.* 14.6.6) and Christian (M ac. Aeg. *Serm.* B 27.2.6.).

110: how light death is! This derives from the Neo-Platonic κοῦφον χρῆμα referring to the poet, by Pl., Io. 3254b and imitated by the Christians (Clem. Al, *Strom.* 6.18.168, Thdt. *Affect.* 2.30, etc.).

115: death is good. The phrase ὁ θάνατος ἀγαθός and other similar ones appear above all in the Neo-Platonists (Plot. 1.7.3, commentators of Pl.) and Christians (Origen, *Rom.*, 40.3, Io. D., *Fid.* 45.34, etc.).

123: having spent all his wealth. This could come from *Eu.Luc.* 15.14 δαπανήσαντος δ' αὐτοῦ πάντα "having spent everything" (the prodigal son), but more frequent are phrases like ὑπὲρ τὴν οὐσίαν δαπανῶν "spending more than what was his", for example in Diph. 32.7, also Gr. Nyss., *Hom in Eccl* 304.11, Basil, *Ep.* 272.2, etc.

127: the best thing … the loyal friend. The theme of πιστὸς φίλος or the faithful friend is found in classical literature, cf., for example, E. *Fr.* 277.1, but also in the LXX (*Sir.* 6.14, 16) and later in Christian literature: Gr. Naz., M. 35.832 and other passages, Chrys., M. 62.403, etc., the *Sacra Parallela* 96.405.

130: (and similar). the wise person is known for his silence. In Pi., *N.* 5.18 we already find the σιγᾶν πολλάκις ἐστὶ σοφώτατον "keeping silent is often the wisest", and later it is frequent, in similar contexts, in the Christians, for example, Fr. Naz. 1548.7.

151: it is in man's interest. Cf. πρέπει ἀνθρώπῳ, πρέπει παντὶ ἀνθρώπῳ in Gal. 1.5565, Waltz, *Rh* 4.755.

152: it is nobility of the soul. The expression εὐγένεια ψυχῆς is frequent: Ph., *Mos.* 1.149, Ael., *VH* 12.1.169, Ps.-Callisth., but above all in the Christians, for example Origen, *Pr.* 4.3.6, Gr. Nyss., *Hom.in* 1 *Cor.* 6.18 (GNO 9.213), Basil, M. 30.92.

188: let none of you obey a woman. This is a topic that comes from the laws of Solon (they invalidate the declaration that someone has made "obeying a woman") and runs all through Antiquity. Cf., for example, E., *Fr.* 440.2, D. 46.14, later in popular literature *(Life of Aesop)*, Neo-Platonic literature (Porph., *ad Il.* 9.591) and Christian literature (Epiph. Const., *Haer.* 3.483). This last contaminates the theme with the theme of Eve, cf., Chrys., M. 56.564.

189: demand wisdom. This without doubt has to do with the σοφίαν ἀγαπᾶν "love wisdom" that we see in Plu., *Sol.* 7.1, but especially in the Christians, for example Origen, *Comm. in Eph.* 4.4.

228: believe the truth. This comes from the Christian πιστεύειν τῇ ἀλήθειᾳ, for example in Origen, *Comm. in Mt.* 17.23.

235: οἶνος καὶ ἀλήθεια I have already said comes from Alceus, with an alteration of its meaning. It must be added that it ran through all of Greek literature before reaching *Bocados*: cf., for example, eschewing older citations, Corn., *ND* 59, Origen, *Comm. in Io.* 6.1.5.

243: avoid drunkenness. Cf. Clem. Al. *Paed.* 2.2.34 τὴν μέθην φυλαττώμεθα "let us avoid drinking".

264: let man know his soul. The phrase comes from Pl., *Tht.* 199d and later is in the Neo-Platonists joined to the Delphic expression γνῶναι ἑαυτόν. Cf., for example, Porph. *Sent.* 32.101, Olymp. *in Alc.* 6.3.

It seems clear that a wealth of Greek expressions that in the imperial period were connected preferably with Neo-Platonic philosophy and the Christian philosophy related to it became a part of the gnomologies that in turn entered *Bocados* and, without doubt, the other works that we have studied and that have common sources.

I repeat that I have given only a small sample here. This study is susceptible of enormous amplification.

X. Conclusions

I have studied the descendants of our collections of the Socratic gnomologies in greater detail than I will do for those of the Socratics: Plato, Aristotle, Diogenes and Alexander especially. And this for two reasons: one, because with the preceding study a model is established that can be applied to the rest of the Socratics; the other, because the study of Socrates was more urgent, there was no collection of his *gnômai* and *khreîai*, while there are collections of those of Plato and Diogenes. And for the study of Aristotle and Alexander I have already made contributions in Chapter III. The results are confirmed in this one.

The main result is the one expected: the Arabic gnomologies *PQ*, M and H (the first not translated, the second translated as *Bocados*, the third as *Buenos Proverbios*), do in fact come from Greek gnomologies. But aside from that, they have two components, both complex:

a) The many Greek gnomologies of the Hellenistic and imperial periods that have left traces in gnomologies preserved from these ages and also in the Byzantine gnomologies of the *GV* family and the Arabic ones of the ID type. There are traces in them of various Socratic gnomologies, some coinciding others no, that have left "blocks" in all these gnomologies and that have combined the Socratic tradition proper with another tradition, Cynic and moralistic in general, with scarcely any Christian elements. For when the pagan gnomologies were joined to the Christian ones in the *Corpus Parisinum*, in the tradition of Johannes Damascenus, the procedure followed was juxtaposition: on such-and-such a theme such-and-such an author (pagan or Christian) said …; someone else said … There was no fusion. The old individual gnomologies were organized alphabetically or thematically, the *Lives* practically disappeared. And the different Socratic gnomologies, which coincided only in part, were used in various ways in the gnomologies preserved, which offer coincidences and differences.

b) But the three gnomologies translated into Arabic (and others in the same situation, only touched upon here) have a second component: individual Socratic gnomologies, preceded by a *Life*, which added to the material (or to part of the material) amplified Socratic material that has not reached us directly. These were various Socratic gnomologies, with coincidences and differences, but sharing the common feature of modifications and innovations, especially of a Neo-Platonic and Christian nature. Both these fundamental gnomologies and the derived ones that we have studied here show a concordance not only in orientation but also in date and origin.

As I have said, we must look for this date and this origin in the 6th to 7th centuries and in the setting of a Syrian Christianity whose language was Greek, though it was reflected at other times in Syriac (and later in the translations into Arabic). This Christianity, furthermore, built not only on the Socratic tradition modified throughout the imperial epoch but also on the Christian tradition of the Greek Church fathers and the Christian writers of the early Byzantine period.

I believe that the hypothesis of our Chapter I is now confirmed, and that all that remains is to apply these results to the study of the other gnomologies in *Buenos Proverbios* and *Bocados*, and to augment all of this with a new consideration of *Poridad* and *Donzella Teodor*.

Chapter 6

Socratic and Post-Socratic *Lives* and Gnomologies. II. The Socratic School

I. Plato

1. Analysis of the Dicta Platonica

Plato, together with Aristotle, Alexander and Diogenes, constitutes the group of Socratic philosophers whose maxims (and to a slight extent *Lives*) our Arabic-Castilian works of Greek origin have transmitted to us. We are going to study them in order, although we have already spoken in Chapter III of Aristotle and Alexander, a very special case.

Plato is cited with relative frequency in the gnomologies. Less than Socrates, of course: Our 228 maxims referring to Socrates (a number that can be augmented without doubt) include the 84 that appear in Stanzel's *Dicta Platonica* cited above. And note that this author includes texts that are not true apothegms; at times they are extracts from the dialogues of Plato. Because here there is a difference: we have the complete works of Plato (plus spurious works), and so we can distinguish between what is literally Platonic, what is Platonic in a broad sense and what comes from the moralizing tradition in general. There are frequent changes in attribution: sometimes to Plato, sometimes to Socrates, Aristotle, Diogenes, etc.

On the other hand, it is clear that Stenzel's *Dicta Platonica* should be augmented with certain sayings from Ibn Durayd that obviously come from the same tradition. And, without any doubt, with some from *PQ* and our two treatises *Buenos Proverbios* and *Bocados de Oro* (that is, Hunayn and Mubassir), or at least from some of these sources, which are clearly of the Greek tradition and present the same themes as the maxims and *khreîai* of the *Dicta Platonica.*

In any case, Plato is sufficiently important in the gnomological tradition to have his own chapters in the three works I have just mentioned, chapters in which the strictly Platonic tradition is combined with what is habitual in the Hellenistic, Roman and Byzantine gnomological tradition. Nevertheless, we will point out some differences: the "Platonic" material does not receive a series of Cynic topics frequent in Socrates; doubtless the need to preserve the works of the master prevented straying very far. And his human character as a "divine" philosopher who lived in an elitist circle, and not a popular one, explains the smaller number of *khreîai* attributed to him. Some of them, as I have said, come without any doubt from the material referring to Socrates and Diogenes; at times the attributions change.

What we are interested in emphasizing in this treatment of the Platonic gnomological material, which will be shorter than what we have devoted to Socrates, is that the chapters dedicated to the two philosophers in the Arabic or Arabic-Castilian works are the result of this same tradition.

On the one hand, they incorporate, as I have said, material from various Greek gnomologies that, like a river, finally flowed into Stobaeus and Diogenes Laertius (among other authors), as well as into *GV* and the other Byzantine gnomologies, and also into Ibn Durayd: in no less a case than that of Socrates himself. But on the other hand, they incorporate a long series of maxims, of Greek origin to be sure, but that were submitted to a process of moralization and Christianization in the Byzantine environment, after Justinian and before the Arab invasion.

All this goes to confirm our ideas about the Arabic and Arabic-Castilian works and their sources. If there is anything new, it is, as I have said, the presence of elements that are directly or indirectly Platonic. But these are the exception: in general terms there are hardly any traces of Platonic philosophy, except to the extent that it coincides with the general moralism of the maxims. And there are, as I say, fewer direct traces of other philosophies, Cynic and even Stoic and Epicurean.

Another topic that we must comment on, although briefly, is that fact that no traces of works with the combination *Life* + gnomology have been preserved, as they have for Socrates. What did exist (apart from the autobiographical writings of Plato, especially *Letter VII*) were encomia and biographies beginning with Speusippus. They have been lost, but they are cited repeatedly by Diogenes Laertius, whose *Life* of Plato is a rather jumbled concoction of several of these sources, filled out with a summary of Plato's doctrines and a list of his works.

Fantastic elements, such as Plato's visit to Egypt in the company of Euripides, were added to Diogenes Laertius. And there are very few maxims and *khreîai*: barely three (3.38–39), the one about Plato reproaching the man who was playing dice; the reply to the person who asked him if he would leave any *Apomnemoneumata* (one must acquire a name first); and the one about Xenocrates and Plato himself, who do not want to punish the slave in anger. Cf. also 3.40, "he wanted a memento of himself to remain with his friends or in books".

We have other remnants of *Lives* of Plato, similar in conception but shorter: the remains of the *Academicorum Index Herculanensis* (1st century B.C.); several chapters of Apuleius's work *De Platone et dogmate eius* (2nd century A.D.); the introduction to the *In Platonis Alcibiadem Commentaria* by Olympiodorus; the anonymous *Prolegomena to Platonic Philosophy*; and an article in the *Suda* based on Hesychius of Miletus, these last from the 6th century A.D. To these must be added various Arabic *Lives*, based on late Greek sources[1].

It is noteworthy that we have, in papyri of the imperial period, numerous fragments of Platonic works and a considerable number of testimonies from commentaries, from introductions to the reading of the philosopher and from various incidental allusions. The above-mentioned work *CPF*[2] gives 82 papyri that transmit passages of Platonic works and 60 testimonies, which refer to specific passages or to Plato in general. But they do not refer to the late tradition, if we leave aside T139, a dialogue between Plato and an Egyptian on an astrological subject: this must be understood in relation to Plato's stay in Egypt and to the late association of Platonism, Pythagoreanism and Hermetism. The Platonic maxims that we are studying here are not recorded in the papyri. This sapiential tradition, like that of Socrates and others, seems not to have been very popular.

In any case, not many apothegms and *khreîai* can be garnered: they have been collected in Stanzel's above-mentioned book. And this considering that Riginos's book (note 1) offers 148 anecdotes, true or not, of pure action most of them, or including oral manifestations.

Thus, the combinations of *Life* + maxims in *PQ* and *Bocados* do not reflect the ancient tradition in which both elements were combined, as was the tradition in Socrates (whether or not various gnomologies might have been added). The exiguous introduction of *PQ* is not really a *Life*. It shows

1 For all this see the book by A. Swift Riginos, *Platonica. The anecdotes concerning the life and writings of Plato*, Leiden, Brill, 1976. For the Arabic *Lives* see pp. 216 ff.

2 Vol. II***, Florence, 1999.

a lack of direct knowledge about Plato and confuses his ideas with those of Aristotle: according to Gutas[3] it is the work of Hunayn. On the other hand, in *Buenos Proverbios*, there is only a gnomology, no *Life*. We will go on to study its relation to *Bocados*.

In *Bocados* there is, as I say, a short *Life* that contains ancient material: the young Plato as a poet, then as a disciple of Socrates, a studious life without entering politics so as not to be condemned like Socrates, Aristotle and Cazanocrates (?) and their disciples. There are errors, such as the journey to Egypt (not to Italy or Sicily) and his death at the age of sixty-one. It appears to come from a brief older *Life*, but it is doubtful that it was ever joined to the maxims[4]. Evidently, the Castilian translator summarized.

As for the maxims, if it is the case that at a certain time in the 6th and 7th centuries there was an amplification and a new Christian moralism was introduced, as in the case of Socrates, it seems that we must consider the existence of not one but various collections of Platonic maxims, for there are discrepancies among our treatises. They could have been created out of the thematic or alphabetical gnomologies of which we have spoken, which in turn might have built on monographic collections, in this case on Plato.

H. Chadwick[5] considers the existence of these Platonic florilegia probable. I believe that they surely must have existed in Antiquity, and definitely in the models of the works we are studying. Their origin lies in the fact that if the preservation of the Platonic works in the Greek world is certain, as the papyri prove, no less certain is the difficulty which an extensive readership encountered in gaining access to them. Hence Pseudo-Platonic works like the *Epinomis* and the *Horoi* or *Definitions*, and also introductions, commentaries and glosses that met the needs of the public. As is the case with other philosophers, in the end Plato was known above all through *excerpta* (some collected in the *Dicta Platonica*) and maxims.

What happened in the Arab world, where the Plato of the dialogues was hardly known while, on the contrary, the Plato of the gnomologies was familiar, is simply an accentuation of the same process. So it is not surprising that Platonic gnomologies were gradually created beginning in Hellenistic times, and between these and other collections of maxims and *khreîai* there must surely have been osmosis in both directions. Nor is it surprising

3 *Greek Wisdom Literature*, cit., p. 332.

4 The *Life* is more extensive in Mubassir; see a translation in F. Rosenthal, op. cit., pp. 29 f.

5 *Florilegium*, cit., p. 1142. Riginos disagrees, op. cit., p. 5.

that in the Greek Orient these gnomologies should, in the 6th century, take a tack parallel to the one we studied for Socrates. What seems not to have existed, I repeat, is the combination *Life* + gnomology.

With this we can begin a study, which will be brief, of the maxims contained in the *Dicta Platonica*: for details on the citations, see Stanzel's work. *Excerpta* and maxims predominate, and more rarely they take the form of apothegms, *khreîai* and anecdotes. The nucleus is in the extracts of the dialogues, then come the maxims derived therefrom, which sometimes appeared in various writers, especially the Cynics. Added to these are maxims only secondarily attributed to Plato: they are originally by Socrates or the Cynics or others or they are simply generally known. And there are some *khreîai* and anecdotes. Something has already been said about the contents; we will return to this at the end. And later we will see to what extent this material enters the sapiential treatises we are studying.

a) Citations taken almost directly from the dialogues

1. from *Phd.* 67d (philosophy as the separation of body and soul).
2. from R. 496d (of what use is philosophy).
3. from *Tht.* 173e (the body remains here, the soul flies).
16. from R. 473c (the philosopher-king).
24. from *Lg.* 729b (abandon either decency or gold).
27. from R. 617e (virtue has no owner).
28. from *Lg.* 728a (gold does not have the value of virtue).
30. from *Tim.* 75b (a short good life is preferable to a long bad one).
32. from *Grg*, 512, altered (for the unfortunate person, it is better not to live).
47. from *Lg.* 736e (poverty is not to diminish one's fortune but to increase one's greed).
51. from *Lg.* 729a (have just enough wealth not to be attacked or to suffer privations).
62. from *Lg.* 775b (get drunk only at celebrations).
80. from *Phd.* 250b (he who looks at divinity saves himself from impiety).
81. from *Phd.* 85b (Socrates subject to the same servitude as the swans).
82. from *Phdr.* 85b (books compared to the gardens of Adonis).
83. from *Ep.* 311b (even Zeus had an adviser).
84. from R. 491e (great natures bear great evils and great virtues).

As can be seen, there is a predominance of moral philosophy (themes of the soul, philosophy, knowledge, virtue, wealth) and a preponderance of the Law.

b) Citations derived from the dialogues, sometimes circulated outside of Plato's works

6. the philosopher who contemplates ideas is like a god among men. Possibly from Empedocles, published in Plato *(Phdr., R.).*
7. truth, the most pleasant thing to hear. This begins with Plato, published in X., *Mem.* 2.1.31. Arist., *EN* 1184^{b}28, etc.; it is transmitted to us as criticized by Polemon.
8. take more care of truth than of any other thing. Cf *Phd.* 91b, *R.* 595b, etc.; whence the well-known maxim *amicus Plato, sed magis amica veritas* in Georg., Phlp. and others.
9. only man knows how to count. From Plato without doubt, in Arist. *Pr.* 956^{a}11, *Epin.* 978b, etc.
10. God always does geometry. Not found literally in Plato, but one must agree with Plutarch (2.718c), for whom it is definitely Platonic.
11. beauty as προτέρημα φύσεως, excellence of Nature. This seems to be a derivation of the ideas of the *Phaedro* and finds an echo in Philodemus, *Rh.* 2.85.
13. consider words superior to everything else. Close to *Tim.* 47a
14. a friend is "another I." Attributed to Zeno and Pythagoras, but it is not far from the Platonic world, as in *Alc.*1 and Aristotle's world in his *Ethics.*
17. what is law? – The soul of the city. It is sometimes attributed to Demosthenes, but it is close to Plato's speculations in *Lg.*, *Plt., Ep.* 7.
18. education as the second sun. This seems to come from well-known passages of the *Republic*, but there is an attribution to Heraclitus, perhaps secondary, perhaps original.
19. the Muses live in the souls of cultured men. There are passages of Pl. that relate the Muses to philosophy (*Phd.* 60c, *R.* 499d, 548b–c, *Phlb.* 67b); the schools of philosophers paid homage to them.
20. the educated person needs nature, study, time. Related to *Phdr.* 269d, *Men.* 70a. Similar sayings are also attributed to Democr., Arist., Pyth., Hp.
22. the more you educate impure souls, the more harm you do them. There are precedents in *Phd.* 67d, *R.* 519a, etc. And the saying also appears in Hp., Ps.-Arist., etc.

23. Pl. recommends temperance, silence and decency. There is a departure point in *Chrm.*, 160e, *R.*, 560a, etc.; and false attributions to Plu. and Dem. Phal.
26. the uneducated are like an alabaster vase full of vinegar. This is from the interior/exterior opposition in *Phdr.* 279b, *Smp.* 215a, 222a, etc. There are attributions to Democr., Pyth., Diog., Thphr.
29. the branches of virtue grow with sweat and work. Related to *Prt.* 339e (citation from Pittacus), in turn related to Hes., *Op.* 289 f., Thgn. 1021 f.
31. the good do not need a long life but a brilliant one. Related to 30 cit. and to *Grg.* 512b altered.
33. the need of *phronesis* for a beautiful and just life. There is a clear echo of Platonic doctrines, the same as happened with the Pythagoreans Sext. and Clitarch.
43. How can one do the most harm to the enemy? – By making oneself better. Also attributed to Diog., but related to Pl., *Ap.* 30d.

48 and 49. do not increase wealth but diminish greed. An echo of *Grg.* 493b, among other Platonic passages.

50. the rich and insatiable are like hydropics: though full of water, they are still thirsty. This comes from the previous entry, also in Cynics and others: Diog., Theles, Bion, Plb., Plu., Lucill.
58. it is difficult to find the right pleasure for the corrupt. Related to *Grg.* 491b ff., *Prt.* 351d ff., *Lg.* 732e ff.
59. it has become fashionable in the cities to recognize that one is bad. Probably an authentic testimony of Arist. on Plato.
60. those who are sensible (φρόνιμοι) are aware of the deceptions of the bad.
61. the inebriated are advised to look at themselves in a mirror. Cf. *Lg.* 637 f.; more exact in Anach. and Pyth.
66. diving as a metaphor to try to understand Parmenides. From *Tht.* 183e and S. in D.L. (on Heraclitus, more precise).
67. Thrasymachus was just like the etymology of his name. From Plato's attacks on this Sophist in *R.* and *Phdr.*
68. the measure of the *logos* is in the hearer. From *Prt.* 334c.
75. the life of man is like being imprisoned. From *Phd.* 62b, etc., *Ax.* 365e.
78. leave a memory in your friends or in books. Cf. *Phdr.* 275c ff.

c) Citations of a Cynic-Stoic character

Some of the above citations were widely disseminated in the Cynic-Stoic literature, as we have seen, but we would like to add others that are fundamentally Cynic or Stoic: some ancient, in the form of *khreîai*, others *gnômai*, *apophthegmata* or anecdotes:

35. if you fall into misfortune, give it no importance. Related to an aphorism attributed in D.L. 1.78 to Pittacus, it really has to do with the thesis of the stoics on the ἀδιάφορα or things that cause indifference, cf. Hor., *C.* 3.3.7.
42. some people are offending you. I will see that no one believes them. Also attributed to Chrysip.
46. he dismounted from the horse so as not to acquire a "passion for horses." The theme of the τῦφος is clearly Cynic.
53–55. fear of someone else's errors, and of being the same. Similar maxims in Epict., M. Ant., perhaps Hor., *Sat.* 1.4.136 f.
74. death is more sorrowful for the fortunate. Attributed to Anach., Aesop, Antisth., Diog.

d) Citations of general diffusion

In these the whole Greek moralist tradition comes together, from the poets to very diverse writers, including the Socratics; at times going back to Socrates:

4. a negative response to the question of whether the philosopher should marry. Parallel to the positions of Epicurus and the Cynics, cf. also Socr. 55, 166, 222. There is an affirmative reply in the Stoics and debate among the Peripatetics.
5. if you look for an opportune moment to dedicate yourself to philosophy, you will not find it. Part of the maxim on the καιρός, the opportune moment, in the Seven Wise Men; it is (like 4) a general concern of all the philosophical schools.
12. Hopes are the dreams of those who are awake. A much circulated maxim attributed to Pi., Anacr. and present as anonymous in Quint., Gr. Naz.
15. more benefits are received from one's enemies than from one's friends. Already in Ar. *Au.*, X. *Oec*, later in Antisth., Luc. *Demon.*, Ou.

21. he who is educating himself should avoid the friendship of bad men and the enmity of good ones. Also attributed to Pyth., Hyp., Epict.
25. the educated person should not speak with uneducated ones or the sober person with inebriates. This comes from Thgn., later it is attributed to Democr. and Crates.
34. virtue is more harmed by conduct than by judgment. A position of willfulness quite distant from Socratic thinking.
36–37. Plato does not beat a slave because he is angry. Also attributed to Socrates, Speusippus, Xenocrates, Charilaos, Aristotle, Teano and Architas; it is in Gr. Naz., etc.
39. the only medicine for wrath is the *logos*. Cf. Democr.
52. why, being old, are you a miser? – Because it is better to leave your money to your enemies than to ask your friends for it. This is found in a maxim of the Seven Wise Men and in another one by Aesop. It probably has to do with speculations in the 4th century on the supposed avarice of Sim. and Plato.
57. on the extravagances of the Acragantines: they build as if they were going to live forever and dine as if there were going to die tomorrow. This doubtless comes from Empedocles; in Stratonicus and Theocritus it refers to the Rhodians. There are allusions in Arist. and Luc.
63. to the youth who behaved insolently toward his father: Do you scorn the man whom your pride comes from? This is from Hes., it is in Demetr. Phal., cf. also Pl., *Lg.* 717b ff and Socr. 168, 169.
64. against playing dice. Attributed to Sol.; there are similar things in Arist. and Thphr.
65. carry your mind in your tongue. Reworking of a proverb (from A. A. 36).
73. sleep is like a brief death. Based on passages from Hom. and Hes. (Sleep and Death as brothers), the maxim is attributed to Sol., Pyth., Socr. and Zeno, cf also Pl., *Ap.* 40c ff.
76. life is but an instant. Cf. Hp. and Pl., *Epin.* 974a, later Plu. and others.
77. the shirt of vainglory is the last one we take off before dying. In a Dioscorides and in Tac., Procl., Iul., Simpl., Plot.

e) Citations most frequently attributed to Socrates

It is possible that they were attributed secondarily to Plato. I give a short list of them, but see others above:

40. in the face of threats, conciliation. Zeno, Gr. Naz. Cf. Socr. 170.

41. to the person who is always insulting: speak badly since you do not know how to speak well. Diog., Plu. (in the *Apophthegmata Lacedaemonia*). Cf. Socr. 14, 35.
44. Pl. poured out the water that he was drawing from the well in order to repress his desire. Also in Pyth. Cf. Socr. 129, 148 on ἐγκράτεια.
45. eat in order to live. Diog., Zeno, anonymous in Quint. (= Socr. 12).

f) khreîai and anecdotes

Their authenticity is doubtful. They criticize the Socratic philosophers.

69. Diogenes mad like Socrates.
70. what is not artificious in Diogenes is pure artifice.
71. Plato called Aristotle πῶλος, the animal that kicks its mother after suckling.
72. Speusippus reproached for his life of pleasure.
79. will you leave μνημονεύματα, memories? – First one must acquire a name.

If we review the maxims attributed to Plato, we can see that, just as in the case of Socrates, moralism predominates: virtue, *phronesis*, law, truth, education, continence, avoiding wrath. The epistemological and dialectical part of Platonic philosophy is more neglected. Frequently there is indistinction in attributions to Plato and Socrates, also to poets such as Theognis or Simonides and to later philosophers, especially Stoics and Cynics. But there is seldom philosophy that is strictly Stoic or Cynic: wealth, beauty and matrimony are touched on briefly in derogatory terms, and avoiding vanity or τῦφος is also mentioned.

2. Analysis of Ibn Durayd

In Ibn Durayd's collection there are maxims attributed to Plato: in some cases these maxims are in the Greek gnomologies and in others they are not; some are found in Hunayn, some in Mubassir (but can be missing in the Castilian translation), and some in neither of the two. Furthermore, some of them are attributed to Socrates. A list follows:

5. Pl. cannot tell if someone is rich before knowing how he administers his money. Attributed to Diog., but by Ibn Hindû to Pl., by M. to Socr. Also in the Greeks.
13. how did you acquire so much knowledge? – By burning more oil than the wine that you drank. Not in Greek but present in M.
48. the person who reprehends young men should allow them some possibility of excuse. Not in Greek, present in M.
49. he who looks for causes loves nobility. Not in Greek, present in M. (but not in *Bocados*).
50. what is love? – The irrational movement of an idle soul. Also attributed to Arist. and Diog., this last attribution also in M. and D.L.
51. an educated man should not speak to an uneducated one, just as a sober man should not speak to an inebriated person. Also in the Greeks and in M.
52. how can a man annoy an enemy? – By improving himself. Also in H. *(Buenos Proverbios)* and in the Greeks, here sometimes attributed to Pl., sometimes to Diog.
58. how does education benefit youth? – By keeping them away from evil. In Stob. and Ibn Hindû it refers to Socr., in Stob. to Antisthenes.
59. an old man wanted to study philosophy and was ashamed. – Pl. told him it was preferable to be better at the end of one's life. In the Greeks, as well as in M. (attributed at times to S., at times to Pl.).

As can be seen, these are in part the same maxims, in part others that have not reached us in Greek. There is a certain fluctuation in attributions: sometimes to Socrates, sometimes to Plato. And Cynic material is introduced.

In any case, it is clear that, just as with Socrates, here we are dealing with a series of gnomologies that is quite homogeneous and also free from the new Christianized material of the sapiential books we are studying. There is a purely Platonic part, and the Cynic material is not so relevant as it is for Socrates: there is little against women, wealth and beauty, science, nobility and power; maxims on cosmopolitanism or friendship outside the family are missing. Moralistic maxims widely circulated from ancient times or beginning with Plato predominate.

3. *Platonic maxims in the Philosophical Quartet that are also in Hunayn and/or Mubassir (preserved or not in Buenos Proverbios and Bocados)*

We will review those maxims of the *Philosophical Quartet* that are also found in Hunayn and/or Mubassir (abbreviated H. and M). If any of them have been eliminated in their Castilian translations, *Buenos Proverbios* and *Bocados* respectively (abbreviated *BP* and *BO*), we will point this out. We will also add whether or not we know the Greek source; if we do and these are the same maxims studied above, we will indicate the correspondence; if these are other maxims, we will say so. At the end we will summarize the conclusions.

The numbering is that given by Gutas for *PQ*: the gaps indicate that these are maxims missing from H. and/or M. We take our data from this book, supplemented when necessary, but ignoring the occasional appearance of the maxims in other Arabic sources and the differences between the two manuscripts of H. Of course all of them are in *PQ*, and their absence in H. or M. can be deduced from there being no mention of them. "Not in Greek" means not present in the Greek sources preserved.

2, H. Plato walked around to teach. From the Platonic "Introduction to Philosophy".

6, H. (anonymous, missing in *BP*), M. (anonymous, missing in *BO*): We must be satisfied with our situation, whatever our fate may be. Not in Greek.

10, H. (Solon, missing in *BP*), M.: A man should look at himself in the mirror every day; if he is ugly, let him not add ugly acts, if he is handsome, let him not spoil it with ugly acts. In Greek, cf. above Plato 61 (approximate correspondence).

11. (Solon, missing in *BP*), M. (Solon): the virtuous soul feels happy and does not suffer on contemplating the two aspects of everything. Not in Greek.

12, H. (missing in *BP*): He who is sad should listen to the melodies of the sublime soul. Not in Greek.

18, H., M. What vengeance can be wreaked on the enemy? – make oneself better every day. In Greek, cf. above Plato 52.

19, M. (missing in *BO*): Despise the errors of men. Not in Greek.

20, M. Good men work to benefit the people, not to harm them. Not in Greek.

21, M. (missing in *BO*): The educated man should treat the ignorant person well; in this way he will have the benefit of both superiority and love. Not in Greek.

23, M. A series of exhortations: do not tolerate the power of the people, do not allow two leaders to fight over their supremacy, do not rejoice in the misfortune of others, do not boast in victory, do not ridicule the mistakes of others, accept errors, do not plant a palm tree in your house, put reason at your right hand and truth at your left. Gutas believes that all this comes from a commentary on the Pythagorean *Symbola*; there are partial coincidences in Greek texts transmitted to us: Gutas gives citations from Plu., Porph., Iambl., Hippol. Sometimes it is possible to go further back, for example to *Il.* II 204 and Arch. 209.

26, M. (Pyth., more general): Do not store up gold or silver, which the future husbands of your widows will inherit. Not in Greek.

31, M. (missing in *BO*): Do not associate yourself with a bad person, as your character will be influenced by his. Not in Greek.

33, M. (missing in *BO*): What is extraordinary is not that the person whose desires have been extinguished should become virtuous, but that he should become virtuous who is at war with his desires. Not in Greek.

35, H. (twice, missing once in *BO*), M. (with various attributions, also to Socr.; in two to Pl. missing in *BO*): if it were not because my maxim "I do not know" establishes that I know, I would say that I do not know. This reformulation of the Socratic saying is not in Greek.

36, H. (Arist.), M. (Arist.): The wise man recognizes the ignorant one because he once was ignorant, the ignorant man does not recognize the wise one because he was never wise. Not in Greek.

41, M. (not in *BO*). Let the fear of the measures that you take against the enemy be greater than the fear produced by the measures that he takes. Not in Greek.

43, M. (various maxims, some missing in *BO*): Do not make things that may be left to you possessions of your own; the wise man neither rejoices nor suffers; etc. Gutas establishes that they come from an Arabic collection based on Pythagorean maxims and on the "Golden Verses"; reference can also be made, for example for the first, to sayings of the Gymnosophists in the Pseudo-Callisthenes.

44, M. Do not associate with bad people, as the only favor they can do you is to dissociate you from their company. Not in Greek.

45, H., M. When the affairs of state go well, desire submits to reason, when they go badly, reason submits to desire. Not in Greek.

48, H., M. Evil men attempt to discover a person's bad qualities, like flies that look for what is rotten. Preserved in Greek in MC as anonymous.

49, H. Please a wise man even though you bother those who are with him; you can annoy an unlearned person to amuse his companions. Not in Greek.

50, H. (missing in *BP*): Pardon corrupts the base while it reforms the noble. Not in Greek.

51, H. (missing in *BP*), M. (the attribution to Pl. is missing in *BO*, but the attribution of Lokman is present): In difficult times virtues, being useless, are not valued but vices, which are useful, are; and the rich suffer more than the poor. Not in Greek.

52, H. (missing in *BP*), M. (Solon and Pl., this attribution is missing in *BO*): The king should reform himself before reforming his subjects. Not in Greek.

53, M. (attrib. a Pl. and Alex.): Enemies are more useful than friends. In Greek, Pl. 15.

54, M. Many virtues are bitter at the beginning, sweet at the end; and vices just the opposite. Not in Greek (but it comes from Hes. *Op*. 286 ff. and a long list of descendants).

55, M. (twice). Goodness is reflected in a sense of decency, which comes from the intellect. In Greek it is attributed by one gnomology to Arist.

57, M. The king should not become inebriated because he is the guardian of the state. Not in Greek.

58, M. Do not buy a slave who has great desires or who is irascible, because he has a master stronger than you. Not in Greek.

59, M. Do not inflict privations or unjust treatment on someone who comes to you in need. Not in Greek.

60, M. If someone offends you, do not treat him in the same hostile manner, try to increase the virtue that he envies in you. Cf. 18 above.

62, M. (missing in *BO*): To the vanity of a man in prosperity corresponds his humility in misfortune. Not in Greek.

63, M. (missing in *BO*): He who listens to what someone says is his associate. Not in Greek.

64, M. (missing in *BO*): Do not become the enemy of states that are progressing in order not to suffer harm. Not in Greek.

66, M. (missing in *BO*): When a state tolerates lies from judges and physicians, it is in decline. Not in Greek.

67, M. (missing in *BO*): States that obey God and those who are in authority grow. Not in Greek.

68, M. (missing in *BO*): Justice and fear are in the origin of states, ambition and favoritism at their end. Not in Greek.

69, M. States decline because they abandon the essential: there is abandonment of work, violation of treaties. Not in Greek.

71, M. (missing in *BO*): A king should not do favors without first seeing whether he can cause harm and that the person favored deserves it. Not in Greek.

72, M. The difference between keeping silent of one's own will and not speaking because of not knowing what to say. Not in Greek.

73, M. The noble person should have the patience to improve the inferior one instead of pleasing the superior one. Not in Greek.

74, M. (missing in *BO*): Liberality is your weakness, do not do favors except to him who deserves them. Not in Greek.

75, M. Serve a foolish leader by satisfying his pleasures and an intelligent one by giving him arguments in favor and against. Not in Greek.

76, M. When you speak with someone who knows more than you, speak simply: when speaking with someone who knows less, at length, so that he will understand. Not in Greek.

77, M. (twice, missing in *BO*): True magnanimity only exists when one can also be violent. Not in Greek.

78, M. A king is loved when it is believed that his weakness depends on his desire and his strength on his judgment. Not in Greek.

79, M. The judge should treat wrongdoers with kindness, as he owes them his position. Not in Greek.

80, M. Against those who steal knowledge and wealth and those who obtain them through deceit. Not in Greek.

83, M. The educated man considers the uneducated one as a child who deserves compassion. Not in Greek.

84, M. The vizier (the steward in *Bocados*) should be patient in his dealings with the people, and the king also. Not in Greek.

85, M. The king is not a person who governs slaves but one who governs free men. In Greek, similarly, in several places (Arist., E., etc., see Gutas).

86, H. (missing in *BP*), M. (Arist., missing in *BO*) How the forces of evil and of good operate, now engendering anxiety and grief, now happiness. Not in Greek.

Here we can make a brief commentary. First on *PQ*. Gutas[6] obtains interesting conclusions about the Arabic sources that reorganized the traditional Greek material. He distinguishes the series of maxims 1–43, which he believes come fundamentally from the translation of a Greek gnomology by Hunayn, but with the addition of Neo-Pythagorean sources (23 and 43). Then a second series attributed to Plato and entitled "The Correct Politics of Kings": this is preserved independently in some manuscripts, and it is easy to see its thematic unity. The reader of our Chapter 3, on Aristotle and Alexander, will see that this is a source related to the one used there, a source stemming from the "mirrors for princes" and that culminated in Antiquity with the work of Agapetus. What was attributed to Aristotle or Alexander there here is attributed to Plato.

We are once again, I repeat, faced with derivatives of various Greek works, various gnomologies. For the rest, as can be seen, in relation to the Greek *gnômai* preserved and that are given in the previous section, there is no lack of problems. Only numbers 10, 18, 47, 48, 53, 55, 60 and 85 coincide with sayings given above from the *Dicta Platonica*; and in some cases there is a different attribution or varying attributions.

Only some of the *PQ* maxims, those given above, are in H. and/or M., at times, also, with variants of the text or of the author to whom the maxim is attributed. Add to that the fact that many are missing in the translations of *BP* and *BO*, which evidently were done from manuscripts that were not precisely the ones that we know. Specifically, in H. we have 2, 6, 10, 11, 12, 18, 35, 36, 45, 47, 48, 49, 50, 51, 52 and 86; in M, 6, 10, 18, 19, 20, 23, 26, 31, 33, 41, 43, 44, 45, 47, 48, 53, 54, 55, 57–60, 62–64, 66–69, 71–80 and 83–85. In the final part, especially, the collection of political maxims was

6 Op. cit., pp. 376 ff.

used most. But it is clear that the same Arabic sources were available to all these authors, sources derived in turn from the Greek ones we are familiar with.

I should emphasize here that the long series of maxims missing from the *Dicta Platonica*, included or not in H. / M. (those that are not present are not given here), are Greek. We infer the derivation from Greek maxims or themes. A clear example is found in 35, based on the famous "I only know that I know nothing." Or in 54 on virtue and vice, derived from Hesiod.

But even without going so far, we have the well-known Greek moralistic themes of benevolence toward men (19, 50, 59, 60, 69), virtue, good and evil (11, 12, 20, 44, 48, 86), the educated man and the wise man (21, 49, 76, 83), desires (33, 58), vanity (62), silence (72), abomination of wealth (26, 43), fortune (6). And also the themes relating to the prudence and benevolence of the king toward his subjects. As in the case of the *Dicta Platonica* and unlike that of Socrates, strictly Cynic themes are rare, as are the strictly Platonic themes that we saw above; evidently they were of less interest. But what is striking is the enormous number of Greek maxims that were lost from the Greek tradition and that only survive here. In *PQ*, in the cases where there is no equivalent in H. or M., the situation is similar.

4. *Other maxims in* Buenos Proverbios *and* Bocados de Oro

A review of Plato's gnomology in *Buenos Proverbios* leads us to other maxims, apart from the ones in common with *PQ* cited above. This is not surprising: we have already seen that our three Arabic sources avail themselves of the Greek sources independently. Because the sources are Greek. In *Buenos Proverbios* we can identify two sectors: one, that of maxims of the main tradition, which is reflected in the ones from *PQ* and/or H. and M. given above (independently of whether or not the Greek source has been preserved), but that produce other maxims that are only found here; the other, the sector of the maxims of a Christian nature. We will comment on both:

a) Maxims on the heart or the "intellect" as illumination (pp. 83, 84), on this same "intellect" joined to wisdom and goodness (p. 86), opposed to "taste" or desire (p. 89), or else as the "stairway of the wise man" (p.90), on silence (pp. 84, 91), on education and the opposition wealth/poverty (p. 90), on the soul as beauty (p. 89), on why to strive for *"aver"* (property, wealth) if one is old (better to leave it to one's enemies than to beg from friends) take us, along with an occasional realistic touch as in the last maxim, to themes that we know well and that go from Socrates to Plato and the Cynics. Strictly Cynic is the misogynous tirade on p. 92: "do not believe the deceit of a woman …" But the more radical Cynicism, save a few exceptions, continues to be absent.

b) Furthermore, as in the case of Socrates, there are Christian maxims from that last evolutional phase of the Greek gnomologies in the Syria of the 6th and 7th centuries, a phase that was later than that of the maxims of the central Greek tradition, and with which the *PQ* was, apparently, not familiar.

   To give a few examples, it speaks of "hope in God" (p. 84), "pray to God" in sickness (p. 91), of the six things "that God abhors" (p. 92: pride, lies, bloodshed, evil thoughts, searching for false witnesses, discord among siblings). It also says that death is not the worst misfortune and should not inspire fear (pp. 84, 91), and speaks of disdain for the world or the *"sieglo"* (pp. 84 91) and of pardon (p. 87). A maxim like "the tongue of man is the scribe of the heart" recalls the saying from the Gospels *ex abundantia cordis os loquitur* (*Eu.Mt.* 12.34, Vulgate translation).

Thus the conclusions reached in the previous chapters are confirmed. And they are reaffirmed in the study of *Bocados de Oro*. Disregarding the numerous maxims already mentioned by virtue of their presence in the other treatises, the study of the "new" ones, those that we only know from this work, leads to the same conclusions. Note that the Platonic maxims in *Bocados* are very numerous: 80 in the section entitled "These are his sayings and his predications" (which follows the "acts," already mentioned), and 186 in the section "Counsels of Plato to Aristotle." We cite them, respectively, as D. and C., plus the number. It seems, then, that two different, but similar, traditions have merged. We will establish the same two groups:

a) Maxims from the central tradition of the Greek gnomologies. To this group we should assign numerous maxims, apart from those already mentioned. Some are the maxims attributed in other places to Socrates: apart from the examples given, see how D. 28 (What person is good to govern? – The one who governs himself well, cf. D. 74), is practically the same as Socr. 5 and 124; or see maxims the same as other Socratic ones in C. 171 ("pay no attention to the insults of a fool", cf. Socr. 14, etc.) or C 179 ("do not be ashamed to learn, although you may be old", cf. Socr. 49). Others coincide with Aristotelian themes that we are familiar with, such as the anecdote about what Plato said when he saw Aristotle enter (c. 145: "now the people have arrived").

Wisdom versus stupidity, good people against bad, suffering wrath (C. 185: The most complete goodness? – He who represses his wrath and battles with his will), keeping silent, lineage versus nobility of the soul (C. 4), these repeated themes are well known to us. And especially the political theme and counsels for the king. There is no rampant Cynicism against women, beauty, power, etc. We are, then, on the same course.

That the sources of *Bocados* were especially extensive is proved not only by the *Life* that we have spoken of, but by the presence of maxims that come from ancient wisdom and do not seem to be found in other gnomologies. Thus D. 31 (the most foolish person is the one who obeys only himself) seems to derive from Hes., *Op.* 293 ff.; C. 60 (do not judge ... until you have heard both), from Hes., *Fr.* 338 (in Plu. 2.1034d); C. 70 (he suffers misfortune for doing good) is based without doubt on the famous passage of the Platonic *Gorgias* in which Socrates says that it is better to suffer injustice than to inflict it (*Grg.* 509 c).

b) Christian maxims. To begin with, the Christian orientation of the two prologues is clear: the prologue to D. (gratitude to God, God is wisdom, etc.), and the one to C. (the themes of knowledge of God and of the good death, of prayer and sacrifice, of obedience to the lord, etc.). And then there is the constant theme of God: for example, D. 11 the maker, D. 33 the fear of God, D. 68 God raises up the wise man over the fool, C. 53 God punishes the unjust. Not only this: there are the themes of salvation and of "losing one's soul" (C. 9), of the "bad soul" (C. 77); also on the soul cf. D. 52, 53, 79, 80, C. 156. We find, as well, the themes of disdain for the world (D. 45), of wicked wealth as a danger for its possessor (C 66), sin (C. 154), mutual love (C. 116). C. 29 elaborates on the Gospel parable of the sower.

We can, therefore, confirm the earlier proposition. The Greek gnomologies (several without any doubt), models for our Arabic texts and, later, our Castilian ones, contained part of the same materials preserved in Greek plus other materials lost there. Not always the same materials: some are common to *PQ* and our two treatises, but in the latter, things from *PQ* are missing and vice versa. Those models belong to the Socratic tradition, not greatly modified by strictly Platonic or Cynic features. There is a real common ground, although with some Platonic aspects, to be sure; the purely

Socratic *khreîai* and anecdotes and the more radical Cynic elements are fewer.

But, I repeat, our treatises testify to the existence of a new, Christianized phase of the gnomologies, later than the sources of *PQ* and, of course, than those of the rest of the Greek tradition discussed above. This phase is reflected in the prologues and in individual maxims, some with earlier themes that have been Christianized, others that are purely Christian (but always avoiding details of dogma and of the Gospel narratives).

The works were, no doubt, intended for a wide public, not a strictly Christian one. They were works that established the Greek bases of Christianity and blended both elements, works of proselytism, I believe.

At the same time, these works added elements of a political type: the good king and good governance, clearly Christianized elements. We saw their origin and later development in Byzantium. The maxims are frequently presented consecutively, which points to their origin in specific gnomologies, related to those used in the Alexander and Aristotle theme and to the "mirrors for princes". They deserve a more detailed study.

II. Diogenes of Synope, the Cynic

1. *General considerations*

In our treatises Diogenes closes the school that we have called Socratic, except insofar as he is reflected in different authors also cited, from Homer to Gregory, about whom we will speak in the next chapter. No direct imprint was left on our treatises by Antisthenes or by disciples of Aristotle such as Demetrius Phalereus or other Cynics like Bion and Crates, or authors like Xenophon or Isocrates. And Diogenes himself is present to a much lesser extent than the authors that form the nucleus of the school: Socrates, Plato, Aristotle and, curiously, Alexander. Furthermore, the Digenis orthography points to a popular language and a late date.

The maxims of Diogenes are far fewer than those of the philosophers we have studied, especially in *Buenos Proverbios*; they are somewhat more numerous in *Bocados de Oro*[7]; this contrasts with the frequency of Diogenes' maxims in the Greek gnomologies preserved, although often there are varying attributions. On the other hand, our two treatises do not provide a *Life*, as was the case for other important authors (only a brief introduction in *BO*).

This leads us to formulate some prior considerations on the Diogenian tradition. In the first place, it is doubtful that there was a *Life* of Diogenes followed by maxims as in the case of other authors; in the second place, there was an influence of the Cynic tradition on all the gnomological literature and a penetration, in turn, into the maxims of Diogenes, of others by Socrates, Plato and the rest. Maxims by other Cynics doubtless entered as well (although we know that there were collections of the *khreîai* of Metrocles, Bion, Crates and Diogenes himself that have not reached us). In short, although we possess an extensive list of works by Diogenes, transmitted by Diogenes Laertius VI 80, we cannot say with certainty that what has been transmitted under his name comes from him, while this is the case, at times, for Plato, and for Socrates we at least have near testimonies. Diogenes became a kind of deposit where Cynic and "Socratic" maxims in general ended up.

Some of the maxims center on a biographical or pseudo-biographical scheme: his exile from Synope for "counterfeiting money"; his life in the barrel in Corinth and in the agora of Athens, where he ate and "searched for a man" with a lamp in broad daylight; his anecdotes and dialogues with Alexander and also with Philip, Perdiccas and other powerful men and with philosophers like Aristippus and Antisthenes; the theme of his being sold as a slave and that of his death.

It is difficult to separate anecdotes from biography: his anecdotes are biographical and his biography is a concatenation of anecdotes. Then there are maxims of the Cynic type in general and others simply moralistic, attributed sometimes to him, sometimes to other philosophers. As Packmohr says[8], to separate the true from the false is impossible.

But it is important that we have known various of these maxims and *khreîai* since shortly after his death, from a papyrus that we have already cited together with other later ones: the *PVindob G* 29946. Throughout a

7 In *BP* they occupy four pages of Sturm's edition, from pp. 138 to 141; I will cite them by page as there is no numbering. There is numbering in *BO*, where from pp. 39 to 44, after an introduction, there are 60 maxims of Diogenes.

8 See A. Packmohr, *De Diogenis Sinopensis apophthegmatis quaestiones selectae*, Münster, 1918, p. 7.

series of loosely joined pericopae it offers no less than eleven *khreîai* by Diogenes, anecdotes related to his life in Athens (which he prefers to living with Craterus, although it be in destitution), to his sobriquet of "dog", to the matter of why the Athenians who have already acquired an education come to him, to the satire about the learned men gathered in a barber's, and also the one about the tyrant Dionisius. There is also the theme of why Diogenes did not bathe (what the philosopher must do is make a good man of himself) and the criticism of Menander, the rich poet.

It has been suggested that here there might be the remains of a *Life*, written by Diogenes, Metrocles, Bion or someone else, but this is very doubtful[9]. From the first citation of Diogenes by Theophrastus in the *Megarikos* (fr. 177 Giannantoni), it has always been a matter of anecdotes and *khreîai*. To be sure, an attempt has been made to reconstruct, in the *Life* of Diogenes in Diogenes Laertius, an element of a *Life*, which might have come from Satyros or Hermippus. The biographical element would be composed of paragraphs 20–23 and 74–79 while the intermediate ones contain the *khreîai* and doxography (then come the sections on the writings of Diogenes and on homonyms).[10]

But all this is full of repetitions and contradictions, the two parts are really mixed together. It is more probable that the *Lives* of Diogenes arose secondarily from the material of anecdotes, *khreîai* and maxims. That would explain the fact that there are practically no real *Lives* of Diogenes, at most short introductions to the collections of maxims, as in Diogenes Laertius and our *Bocados de Oro*.

As for the collections of maxims themselves, it must be said that the multiple repetitions, contradictions and variants prove that there were many of them, not just one. And studying the old, but still very useful work by Packmohr suffices to show us the enormous tangle of maxims attributed to Diogenes, but at times also to other authors; some of these have passed into Diogenes and vice versa. Apart from this are the errors that were made when the maxims in certain collections began with "the same person" or

9 On this theme see G. Giannantoni, *Socraticorum Reliquiae* III, Rome, 1983 , pp. 376 ff. and the *Corpus dei Papiri Filosofici Greci e Romani (CPF)* I 1**, cit., pp. 99 ff.

10 On all this see F. Leo, *Die griechisch-römische Biographie nach ihrer literarischen Form*, Leipzig, Teubner, 1901 (Hildesheim, Olms, 1965), pp. 49 ff.; K. von Fritz, *Quellenuntersuchungen zu Leben und Philosophie des Diogenes von Sinope*, *Philologus* Suppl. Bd. 18.2, Leipzig, Dietrich, 1926; I. Gallo, cit., pp. 240 ff.; and Giannantoni, cit., pp. 371 ff.

originated in the confusion between Diogenes, Demeas, Demetrius, Demosthenes or Democritus.

Packmohr's study, speaks, for example, of the confusion between Diogenes and Socrates (pp. 13 ff., 43 ff.); of the identity, at times, with the *Monostichi* (p. 32 ff.), of the attributions to Plato (pp. 44, 55), the maxims that come from the theater (pp. 45 ff.) or that coincide with epigrams from the *Anthologia* or with Cynicizing passages from authors like Horace or Ovid; of the elements derived from Euripides (pp. 57 ff.) or from Homer (pp. 63 ff.). A complicated panorama, to be sure.

In short, in *Giannantoni's Socraticorum Reliquiae*, vol. II, we find all of the maxims and anecdotes that have come down to us from Greco-Latin Antiquity, which excuses us from having to do a compilation ourselves, as we had to do in the case of Socrates (but not in the case of Plato, for whom there is Stenzel's book). There are no fewer than 530 numbers (plus the pseudo-Diogenian epistles, as well as several works by Dion Chrysostom and Lucian). But these are sometimes *khreîai* and maxims, sometimes passages on the philosophy of Diogenes (once again it is difficult to separate one from the other).

This is the material with which we must work to see to what extent it reached our Arabic-Castilian works and to what extent the latter provide new material, either presumably from the same ancient tradition, or from a different later Byzantine-Christian tradition, as happened in the case of the other philosophers. But Diogenes was considered, as I have said, a minor philosopher; furthermore, his works were soon lost to the benefit of the gnomologies. Thus, he was not included in the *Philosophical Quartet*, which has been so useful in analyzing the references to Pythagoras, Socrates, Plato and Aristotle in our Arabic-Castilian works.

We do, however, have some maxims from Diogenes in Ibn Durayd, several of them likewise recorded in other Arabic sources. As in cases studied above, they belong fundamentally to the ancient tradition.

It is not surprising that this tradition should be contaminated with the Socratic tradition in general, for Diogenes, no matter how many differences may be pointed out, is a strict Socratic who continues many of the Socratic themes. Plato once said, in the well-known anecdote, that Diogenes was a mad Socrates. Socrates was ahead of him in his free personal life, in shunning politics, in his asceticism and moralism. And of course, he still felt committed to the ideologies of the city and of the "health of the soul" and to a certain spiritualized religion. But apart from this, the traits in common are many.

We have the themes of goodness, suffering, disregard for wealth, beauty, lineage. Diogenes added themes such as πόνος, effort, and those of nature, and the confrontation with women, physicians, athletes and scientists, as well as the theme of disdain for death. We have already seen how among other Socratic themes the Cynics introduced, for example, the topic of Xantippe, the non-philosophical woman. And even the tale of the barrel in which, according to a late tradition, Socrates lived, in the style of Diogenes.

In summary, to a few traditional anecdotes about Diogenes that exaggerated the Socratic features of asceticism and of distancing oneself from power and desire, others were added in which the Indian Gymnosophists became the replicas of the Cynic confronting the powerful Alexander, as well as others relating to the powerful and to philosophers who were contemporaries of his and still others that were already timeless.

Thus, when these themes appear referring to Diogenes, it is possible that they are from the Cynic school, which exaggerated initial Socratic themes, or that they are additions with Socratic roots. At times it is difficult to decide, and it is difficult, too, to establish the dates when this new material entered the Diogenes gnomologies. It is, in any case, only a small part of what is preserved in Greek.

2. *Diogenes in Ibn Durayd and other Arabic sources*

I go on to indicate the proverbs referring to Diogenes in Ibn Durayd, adding the extent to which we can document them in Greek sources and also, to what extent they appear in other Arabic sources, including H. and M. and their derivatives (*BP* and *BO*): both works, or one of them, sometimes neither because they come from partially different manuscripts. The list of proverbs follows:

2. To a young man who had squandered all of his inheritance and was eating olives, D. said: if you had not squandered your inheritance, you would not have to eat this for the rest of your life. This is from D. according to D.L. 6.50 and *GV* 169; from S. or Pl. according to other sources, among them M (= *BO* 123).

3. To a handsome young man who did not know how to write well Diogenes said: What a house, if only it were inhabited! Among other Arabic sources it is found in H. (= *BP* p. 138) and M. (= *BO* 21). Not in Greek.
4. On seeing a clump of grass floating down the river carrying a serpent with it, Diogenes said: What a likeness between the sailor and the ship! In Greek in the fable H. 98; H. is close (= *BP*, p. 139) and M (= *BO* 21), now it is about a woman.
5. They said to Diogenes that such-and-such a person was rich. He replied: I cannot tell until I know how he manages his money. Attributed by various authors to Metrocles and Pl., by M. to S.
6. Diogenes said to a customs official that he was only carrying what was in his breast. Not in Greek (but the theme is, for example in Phaedrus IV 26). It is in Arabic sources, among them M, (= *BO* 59).
7. Seeing a handsome young man who was studying philosophy, D. said: You are adding to your love of your body's beauty the love of the beauty of your soul." This is in Greek sources (D.L., *GV*, MC, etc.), also in H.M (= *BO* 60).
8. Alexander said: "I am the great king" D. replied: "And I Diogenes the Cynic." In Greek sources (D.L.); the variant of why they call him "dog" is in *CPF* 4, *SR* 34 and in M (prologue).
9. Diogenes asks a spendthrift for a silver mine and justifies this saying that it is his only opportunity. This is in Greek sources (D.L., Stob., MC) and in Ibn Hindû, not in H. M.
10. Alexander asked Diogenes if he did not fear him; D. asked if he was good, and A. said he was. Diogenes replied: "I do not fear a good man, I love him." In D.L., not in H.M.
11. On seeing an uneducated man wearing a gold ring, Diogenes exclaimed: "An ass with a gold halter!". Not in Greek, but present in Ibn Hindû and M. (*BO* 28).
12. On seeing a man sitting on a stone, Diogenes said: "One stone on top of another!" In D.L. 2.72 it is attributed to Aristippus, in M. (= *BO* 22) to Diogenes.
50. On being asked about love, Diogenes said: "It is the senseless movement of an uneducated soul." D.L. attributes it to Diogenes; there are other attributions (Pl, Aristotle, Theophrastus, Teano, Plutarch); Ibn Hindû to Diogenes, M also (= *BO* 25).

52. Asked how to annoy an enemy, he replied: "By making oneself better." In Greek it is attributed sometimes to Diogenes (*GV*, Plu., etc.) sometimes to Pl. *(GV)*. In Arabic both attributions are found: H. attributes it to Pl., M. in one place to Pl, in another to D. (*BO* 48).

All these anecdotes, *khreîai* and maxims belong to the old fund on Diogenes, including, I believe, those that have not been preserved in Greek (3, 6, 11). Note that there are only two that refer to the topic of Diogenes and Alexander (8, 10). The themes are: goodness and badness (4, 10, 52), culture and lack of culture (3, 7, 11, 12), criticism of love (50), of wealth and bad management of money (2, 5, 6, 9). Now of all these, the themes of goodness and of culture are the most strictly Socratic, having entered the Diogenian material early on.

Note, too, that the more recent material, including the Christian material, did not find its way into Ibn Durayd, as was also the case for the philosophers studied above. But he had access to Greek gnomologies that are lost to us.

3. Buenos Proverbios

In the previous section we saw the coincidences between *Buenos Proverbios* and Ibn Durayd: in 2 and 4 (also in 52, but he attributes it to Pl.), notably fewer than in *Bocados de Oro*, no doubt because the chapter dedicated to Diogenes is shorter. On the other hand, unlike the other work, the part on Diogenes in *BP* completely lacks a biographical introduction.

Reviewing now the gnomological literature of Diogenes preserved in Greek, we find the following correspondences:

P. 138. "What a grand palace, but with no foundation" (Diogenes to a handsome youth who lacked knowledge). We have seen this in ID 3; it is *SR* 204 (*PSorbonne*, etc.), also in *BO* 21.

P. 138. He saw a woman hanging from a tree and said: "Would that all trees bore such fruit" (*SR* 202, from D.L.).

P. 139. He saw a woman being swept away by a torrent and said: "Badness with badness dies." This is *SR* 206 (an inscription from Herculaneum), also *BO* 21; and it is close to ID 4.

P. 139. He saw a beautiful woman and said: "Little good and much that is bad." This is *SR* 201 (*GV*, etc.) Also in *BO* 12.

P. 139. This criticizes the fact that he makes some his favorites while others lose their privilege. Also in *BO* 57.

P. 141. They asked him about mealtime and he said it was when he felt hungry. This is *SR* 183 (D.L.).

Add to this the maxim on p. 140 that is attributed to S. in *PQ* 3 and M. (= *BO* 37): He could live their lives but they could not live his.

These are Cynic themes that we are familiar with. In the maxims that are not present in our Greek texts, we find the same themes once again:

Goodness and badness: do not do good just to be thanked for it (p. 138); he who does what is wrong is not good (p. 139).

Hypocrisy: the old man who dyed his beard (= *BO* 27).

Friendship and the family: the rich man and the poor man as friends (p. 139), the youth who was like his father (p. 139).

Wisdom: the understanding of the mind is peace (p. 139), there is no better possession than the mind (p. 140).

Suffering with patience: the good person is one who suffers insults (p. 138), suffering is the best thing man can apply to his sorrows (p. 139).

Wealth: Why don't rich men come to the home of the wise while the latter go to the home of the rich? – Because the wise know the advantages of wealth but the rich don't know the advantages of knowledge (pp. 139–140).

Keeping silent: Don't speak in the presence of any man until you have heard him and compared his wisdom with yours (p. 138).

The king: I am richer than the king of the Franks and without his worries (p.140); D. is free from worries and the king has many (p. 140).

The body and the soul: Illness is the prison of the body, the heart is a tender thing guarded by the body, life is the joy of the heart (all on p. 140).

All this philosophy is partly Cynic, partly Socratic and partly moralist, of an indefinite age. A Christian maxim is added on p. 140: If you desire of this world more than it can give you, it will not give it to you. This is, as it was for the authors studied so far, the indication of a new cultural phase in which, at the end of Antiquity, moralism was allied with Christianity. The themes of suffering, wisdom and not asking for gratitude can be understood both as Socratic and as Christian.

4. Bocados de Oro

In this work, too, we are going to study the continuity of the Greek tradition regarding Diogenes insofar as it has been preserved. In the first place, *BO* offers a brief preface on Diogenes as an "abhorrer of the world," just as is said of Socrates (cf. Crombach's edition, p. 45), which introduces an ascetic and Christian atmosphere. He slept just anywhere, ate when he was hungry, also just anywhere, (an allusion to the *khreía* that we have seen and to another that we will see below), and dressed shabbily.

There follow three *khreîai* relating to the Diogenes/Alexander theme: Diogenes replies to the question, "Why did they call you 'dog'?" (Because he barks at fools and compliments the wise), Alexander is "the slave of the slave" (that is, of the greed that Diogenes has mastered), Diogenes does not want any of what Alexander offers him because he is richer.

The first of these themes is well known in the Greek tradition regarding Diogenes: cf. *CPF* 8 (the *PVindob. G* cited), *SR* 34 (Stob.), 143, 147 (D.L.). The other two themes remind us of the confrontation of Alexander with the Indian Gymnosophists in the Pseudo-Callisthenes, and the third one also recalls the familiar anecdote of Diogenes, in reply to Alexander's offer, asking him not to stand in the way of the sun (*SR* 31 ff., with citations of Plu., D.L., Cic., etc.). The *khreía* that follows (Who will bury you? – Whoever wants to dispose of a stinking body) is close to *SR* 100, 101 (Ael., D.L.).

Evidently this is an introduction of the traditional type, more or less like that of the *Life* in Diogenes Laertius.

Other *khreîai* or proverbs from the ancient tradition follow and are listed below:

2. The theme of dinnertime. Cf. *SR* 183 (D.L.).
4. What are friends? – A soul in two bodies (Stob.).
12. About a beautiful woman: Much that is bad and little good. Cf. *SR* 201 (*GV*, etc.). Also in *BP*, p. 139.
16. Diogenes eats in the street because he is hungry. Cf. *SR* 147, 186, 187 (*GV*, D.L., Stob., etc.).
25. What is being in love? – A sickness. This is an old Greek tradition, from the time of Euripides, *Hipp.* and even earlier. Cf. ID 50.
39. They tell him someone insulted him. – Even though it might hurt me, if I was not present, it would not matter to me. Cf. *SR* 432 (Cod. Ottobon. Gr.) The *GV* attributes it to Demosthenes.

53. Not living to eat but eating to live a good intellectual life. Cf. *SR* 182 (Stob.), at other times attributed to Socrates.
54. One knows who one's friends are in difficult times. Cf. Ennius in Cic. *Lael.* 17: *amicus certus in re incerta cernitur.*
59. The theme of the customs official, cf. ID 6 and the theme in Phaedrus.
60. To a boy who was learning wisdom: you are doing what is right, you are trying to unite the beauty of the soul with that of your face. Cf. *SR* 397 (D.L.).

All this comes from the ancient Cynic tradition, as do maxims not attested to in Greek but present in ID and/or *BP*:

27 (= *BP*, p. 139), the old man who dyed his beard; 28 (= ID 11), the mad man with the gold ring; 33 (= *BP*, p. 138), not doing good in order to be praised; 38 (= *BP*, p. 140, Socrates in *PQ* 3), I could live the life of fools, they could not live mine; 43 (= *BP*, p. 140), illness is the prison of the body; 33 and 52 (cf. *BO*, p. 138), do good for its own sake.

As can be observed, sometimes there are various attributions. The contamination with the Socratic tradition is seen in maxims that go back to Socrates and also to the *gnômai* attributed to the Socratic school, as we saw in Plato. This is illustrated in the following:

23. "I did not call you, I called men." Attributed to Pl. in *PQ* 3 and in *BO*, PL. 145. Of Cynic origin without doubt, it recalls the anecdote about Diogenes (and Aesop) with a lantern, searching for a man.
29. The theme of the "physician of the soul," from the time of Pl. *Grg.*
31. What can a person do in order not to get angry? Cf. S. 35.
32. The versifier as an inventor of lies. Cf. the well-known passages of Pl., *R.*
46. The person who kills me will harm himself more. A theme from Pl., *Grg.*

Finally, we can point out various Socratic-Cynic themes for which we have not found an exact correspondence in ancient sources:

Good and bad, hypocrisy, mendacity, nobility: he is good who does good (1); the virtues of the soul bestow beauty on the face of an ugly boy (2); abhor bad men for their vile lives and good men because they have dealings with the bad (7); the public thief who punishes the concealed one (10); to Alexander: he should pride himself on goodness and frankness (13); the person who considers wrong what he sees in someone else (14); to praise what is not praiseworthy is an insult (19); when punishing someone, do not act as if you were taking revenge (30); the nobility of Diogenes began in him, that of the person who insults him ends in him (44); one troubles his enemy by being good (48); in order that your good deeds be great in the eyes of others, let them be great in your own (49).

Wisdom and foolishness: let the man who asked God for wisdom strive to learn (17); the fool is stone on stone (22); he recommends love, good advice, obedience (35); there is no asset better than the mind (42).

Keeping silent, bearing insults: of all men's virtues, the one that is not good is speech (18); to someone who insults him: every vessel pours out what is in it (38); don't speak until you have heard (34); the strength of the good person is in his ears, that of the bad person in his tongue (45); D. does not reply to the person who insults him (47, 55); a man has two ears and one mouth (56).

Wealth, greed, asceticism: he is idle because he has no home (11); he who is not defeated by greed is most master of his soul (36); what is wealth? – freeing oneself of desires (24).

Wrath: mistakes seem great to a man who is angry (9).

Friendship: avoid the envy of friends and the deceit of enemies (6); don't take in a dog that has left its master and follows you (15); if you let your enemy put his foot on yours, soon he will put it on your neck (50).

Misogyny: on seeing a man who was getting married, he said: a little pleasure brings a lot of sorrow (5); he saw a man who was burying his daughter and said: you have procured a good son-in-law (8); they accustom their women to luxury, not to loving their men (40); a woman is a wrong that cannot be excused (51).

Physicians: the physician's mistake lies hidden underground (20); before going to the doctor, have the doctor come to you while you are healthy (29).

Royalty: let the king take pride in his goodness and frankness (13); the king can earn a reward from God in a day, the people cannot (58).

Once again we must assume that here and in *BP* we are dealing with ancient gnomological material, at times strictly Cynic, at times moralistic and even Christian, that has not come down to us directly but that did, nevertheless, reach the Arabs and through them, our Castilian texts. This material is of variable antiquity, difficult to determine exactly, but which received its final touches in the ambience of the first Byzantine period, described above.

And once again we find the classic Cynic themes, plus others more Socratic or in common with Socratic ones. And also included are themes of the kingdom (the king as a follower of the path of virtue) and the Christians, the latter in relation to the king, in the last maxim cited and in 26: his friends visited him when he was ill and told him not to fear, that it was in God's hands. "That is what I fear most," replied Diogenes.

But there is no great insistence on Christian themes; there is rather a layman's tone in 17, addressed to a man who asked God for wisdom: "Strive to learn," Diogenes tells him, which recalls the Greek, and also Cynic proverb: "with the help of Athena move your hand," in Aesop's fable H. 30.

Chapter 7

New Research on *Buenos Proverbios* and *Bocados de Oro*

I. Plan of the study

Everything essential has already been said in the preceding chapters about the four Arabic-Castilian treatises that we are concerned with in this book. And we have considered in more detail the central nuclei of *Buenos Proverbios* (the novel of Alexander and Aristotle) and *Bocados de Oro* (the Hermetic-Pythagorean gnomologies as well as the gnomologies of Diogenes, Plato and Aristotle, and also those in *Buenos Proverbios*, which we have studied in historical order).

But still to be studied are the marginal elements of *Buenos Proverbios* and *Bocados de Oro*. All this to return later, in the Conclusion, to the general historical line, which takes us from the oriental literatures, classical Greek literature and the late Greek works plus their Arabic alterations or syncretisms, to our Castilian works. And to the school that these four works, and other parallel works that are not under consideration here, created in our literature and our thought.

We will go into this in more detail. And we will do so as well in the context of the two works that we still must study in detail, *Poridad de Poridades* and *Historia de la Donzella Teodor*.

In this chapter we are going to begin with the study of the above-mentioned marginal elements (*Lives* and gnomologies of various philosophers) in *BP* and *BO*, to go on afterward to the other two works.

These marginal elements will be divided into various sections in order to study them:

1. Buenos Proverbios

1. External prologue by Joaniçio (the discovery of the manuscript). 2. His internal prologue: how they killed the prophet Anchos and the cranes revealed the crime (ch. I). 3. Joaniçio's connecting comments; nothing can be concealed from God, a note about the seals and the "examples" of the philosophers (ch. II). 4. Proverbs on the seals of the philosophers (ch. III). 5. Various assemblies of the philosophers (chs. IV–XI). 6. After the teachings of Socrates and Plato (chs. XII–XIII), already seen in our Chapters V and VI, there follows a final appendix (chs. XXVII–XXIX), with teachings of Diogenes (seen in our ch. VI); Pythagoras (seen in IV); and Hippocrates (which we will see when *BO* is discussed).

2. Bocados de Oro

1. Well-identified Greek writers and philosophers: Homer, Solon, Hippocrates, Zeno, Galen, Ptolemy, Gregory (Hippocrates also in *BP*). 2. Those not identified (Assaron, Enesius, Medargis, Thesileus). 3. The proverbs of Loginem (Lokman), which are a special case, that of an Arab sage with abundant Greek and Christian wisdom. 4. The proverbs that our treaties do not identify or identify in various ways, specifically those of XXIII (the chapter of the sayings of many sages) and XXIV (the chapter of the sayings *"que no sopieron quien los dixo"* (that no one knew who said them).

There remains, of course, the problem of who added this material to the Greek works: some late Greek compiler, or the translators Hunayn and Mubassir (or the latter's source). Note that with *BP* already translated into Castilian, initial additions were made in some manuscripts (the voyage of King Bonium to India), and many maxims were removed[1]. It is not surprising that the Arab translators should do the same thing. We will return to this.

1 See data in J. T. Walsh, "Versiones peninsulares del *Kitāb ādāb al-falāsifa* de Hunayn ibn Ishaq", *Al-Andalus* 1941, 1976, pp. 359 ff.; and Crombach, op. cit., p. XXI. Also F. Rosenthal, *The Classical Heritage in Islam*, London, Routledge, 1975, pp. 28, 30 and 124 ff.

II. Marginal elements in *Buenos Proverbios*

1. *The external and internal prologues*

As we know from Chapter I, there are in *Buenos Proverbios* an external prologue and an internal one. The former is the account that the translator Joaniçio gives of the original Greek book that he translated into Arabic; the Castilian translator adds the mention of this second translation. There is no doubt that we have a secondary element added to the Greek original.

The same must be said of the internal prologue (also in ch. I): Joaniçio reports that he found the story of the cranes that revealed the death of Anchos at the hands of thieves "in some books of the Greeks." The action takes place in Greece; a king of Greece is mentioned and also a festivity of the Greeks. This is a story that Joaniçio inserted here linking it (ch. II) to the moralistic theme that it was God who did not allow this evil deed to be concealed. Thus we have a Greek theme, but an independent one: it is owing to Joaniçio, that is, to Hunayn, that it was made the leading item of the book that he translated.

It is, in effect, a Greek legend: the death of the poet Ibycus was revealed by some cranes that witnessed it. It is a theme known since the 1st century B.C., cf. Antipater of Sidon, *AP* 7.745, Statius, *Silu.* 5.3.152, Plutarch, *Moralia* 509f, the Suda. Also it is found in Arabic as an independent theme[2]. It is without any doubt a recurrent theme of folklore, as has been said, but in Greece it had been fixed in the legend of the death of Ibycus since the 1st century B.C., as I say above. The version of Hunayn is essentially faithful, although he adds the Greco-Christian atmosphere of the literature that we are studying. All Hunayn did was to take the theme and use it as a prologue to the work he was translating.

It is perfectly clear, therefore, that Hunayn had a hand in completing this work, with Greek material, to be sure. Let us see if other additions to the central work can be discerned, since this is, as we have said, the novel of the life and death of Alexander, already studied in our Chapter III. They

2 See in F. Rosenthal, *The Classical Heritage in Islam*, London, Routledge, 1975, pp. 258 f. the English version of the Arabic one by Abu Hayyam at-Taubidi. For the success of the theme in the Middle Ages, see Mª Jesús Lacarra, *Cuento y Novela corta en España. I. Edad Media*. Barcelona, Ariel, 1999, p. 51.

exist, of course; we have already made that clear. And the fact that Hunayn was, without any doubt, the author of some of the additions opens the possibility that he may have been the author of others as well.

2. *A general idea of the other marginal elements*

Before the central nucleus, the legend of Alexander, there are the teachings of Socrates and Plato, followed by those of Diogenes, Pythagoras and Hippocrates, all of which we have already studied or will study (the teachings of Hippocrates). But in between the two prologues, external and internal, and the teachings of Socrates there is a second short internal prologue, also by Joaniçio (ch. II: *"de como onbre deve estar en todos sus fechos bien con Dios faziendo buenas obras"* [on how a man should be at peace with God in all his acts, doing good works]); a chapter that records the proverbs of various Greek philosophers, many unidentifiable (ch. III "on the proverbs that were written on the seals of the philosophers"); and various others (from V to XI) that again contain *"ayuntamientos"* (assemblies) and meetings of various philosophers (only VII refers to just one single philosopher).

The second internal prologue (ch. II) is interesting because its two paragraphs commence with "Joaniçio said." His words link the theme of the cranes to that of the punishment of the evil person at the beginning, and to the theme of the philosophers or "sagacious wise men" at the end. In other words, Hunayn links the theme of the cranes to that of the seals of the philosophers. Consequently, both themes appear to have been introduced by him. He wanted to prepare the ascetic treatise on Alexander with a series of similarly ascetic maxims. This treatise is a Greek work that Hunayn has connected to the theme of the cranes and that he has continued with various dialogues between philosophers.

These dialogues belong to the Greco-Christian background that we are familiar with, they were not invented by Hunayn: he simply thought that they fit well here as preparation for what followed. I believe this is the case, especially because in ch. VI ("The Chapter of the Assemblies of the Philosophers") Hunayn speaks again (Joaniçio said): and in his words he mentions the synagogues of the Jews, the churches of the Christians and the mosques of the Muslims, which reveals the age in which he wrote.

But Hunayn goes further when he narrates a theme that is traditional without any doubt: how Aristotle was received as a disciple of Plato instead of the king's useless son, Nitaforius (see what is said on this episode in Chapter I above). Evidently Hunayn wants to prepare for the story of Alexander by using the story of Aristotle: his novelistic adoption by Plato as a philosopher and his maxims. Thus, the figure of the wise Aristotle of the letters to Alexander finds its preparation here. The Plato-Aristotle line is established, based on Greco-Christian material that circulated in Syria. I cannot but think that this organization is Hunayn's work. In Chapter VII he returns to the theme of Plato, Nitaforius and Aristotle. Later, in Chapters VIII to XI, he comes back to the assemblies of philosophers and sapiential material: notably in Chapter X, laments for the dead kings, which are preparation for the lamentations for the dead Alexander. And in XII, the teachings of Socrates are added: clearly he wants to join Platonic-Aristotelian philosophy to its roots in Socrates. In Chapter XIII he recuperates chronological order and takes up the teachings of Plato again.

With this chapter we come to the work about Aristotle and Alexander: the legend of Alexander. For me there is no doubt that Hunayn prepared his work using various materials that pre-dated it, and that considering it lacking or incomplete at the end, and not only at the beginning, he added the final Chapters (XXVII to XXIX) on Diogenes, Pythagoras and Hippocrates. Thus he achieved the insertion of the central work into the body of Greek moral philosophy. He created something close to an anthology, as Mubassir would do afterwards.

So far we have concerned ourselves with the central theme and the collections of maxims of Socrates, Plato, Aristotle, Diogenes and Pythagoras; we will discuss the maxims of Hippocrates below. Here, as I said before, I will analyze the remaining marginal themes. It must be understood that in these Hunayn is only the translator. But he is responsible for the total composition. That is my opinion.

3. *Analysis of the marginal elements*

As we have seen, a series of "signed" proverbs are put in first place and are followed by various series of anonymous proverbs. The first group were written, we are told, on the "seals" of the philosophers, and at other times on the walls of their houses or on their *"cintas"* (sashes); the allusion is to seals on documents and to emblems, and also to simple inscriptions. The anonymous proverbs, in turn, are on the occasion of the *"ayuntamientos"* (assemblies) or *"juntas"* (meetings) of the philosophers: sometimes these meetings are presented with no introduction, sometimes it says they took place "to speak of wisdom," and at other times that the kings convoked them at festivities or in their palace. I have already said that synagogues, churches and mosques are mentioned: all of this comes, without doubt, from the Ommiad period.

In any event, this is traditional material, evidently late Greek, but with traces of earlier Greek wisdom. It is an aggregation, like the proverbs of Socrates and Plato before the central nucleus, which is the life and death of Alexander, and those of Diogenes, Pythagoras and Hippocrates that come after it, a secondary aggregation, I suggest, but, as I say, with strictly Greek material. And it is very close to what is equally marginal in *Bocados de Oro* (the same as the maxims of the philosophers that we have studied).

Likewise, Hunayn must have taken the device of the "seals" from earlier sources. This is a long list of the philosophers' proverbs comparable to the penultimate chapter of *Bocados.* As is true of this latter case, there is little relation between the doctrine of the philosophers, to the extent that we know it, and the proverbs that are attributed to them here. The list of these philosophers goes from Pythagoras to Hippocrates, Plato, Aristotle, Alexander, Diogenes, Ptolemy, Locanem (Lokman), Galen and Gregory; there are also many, as I have said, that are not identifiable.

But, again as in the chapter from *Bocados*, there are some exceptions. Not unrelated to Socrates is the maxim that says that the man whose *"sabor"* (desire) overcomes his *"seso"* (intellect) is disgraced. Medical matters are attributed to the physicians: there can be more hope for the sick person who desires something (Hippocrates, cf. *Aphorisms* 32 and 33, as well as the comments of Galen 17(1).528); the person who conceals his illness is hard to cure (I do not find this in Galen, but cf. Hippocrates, *Diseases of Women* 1.62). These are exceptions. For example, the maxim *"non pongas culpa a Dios en yerro que tu fagas"* (don't blame God for the mistakes that you make) (this recalls *Od.* I 32 ff.) has nothing to do with Diogenes; nor with Aristotle the Socratic maxim that says that he is wiser *"el que negava lo que sabíe ... que el que manifestava lo que non sabíe"* (he who denied what he knew ... was wiser than he who showed what he did not know); Ptolemy's maxim *"el pesar faze al omne ser aborrido"* (sorrow makes a man be shunned) recalls Theognis 359 μηδὲ λίην ἐπίφαινε "Don't allow too much to be seen."

In short, these are, as on other occasions, arbitrary attributions to various philosophers of maxims of the moralistic philosophy that we have seen.

It must be said that, in spite of what has been discussed above, there are maxims on Christian themes on the "seals": fear God, do not attribute your own mistakes to him, do good if you want good to be done to you. But not only that. Some refer to philosophical investigation: suspicion and persistence are the two "paths" to discovering what is concealed. And they also refer to themes well known to us: the reason of the mind as opposed to stupidity or wrath, denying what one knows, the person who loves out of self-interest (there are three maxims in a row on the man who has *"mester"* (need) of someone and then abandons him), the theme of language, that of concealing *"la Poridad"* (the secret) or what one "saw". That is, we have the usual mixture of moralistic and Christian themes.

And the same occurs in IV, "The assembly of four philosophers": the Hermetic theme of the *"Poridades"* (secrets), the Platonic theme of the "clarity" and the "light" of knowledge, the Christian theme of everlasting life.

V ("The assembly of five philosophers") is monographic on the theme of wisdom. Wisdom as the mind and language of truth, light and clarity of men's hearts, the "garden of thoughts" in relation to this world and the other one. The name of the wise man does not die.

VI ("The chapter of the meetings of the philosophers") speaks once more of wisdom and philosophy and narrates the episode that we have already discussed in which Aristotle proved better in wisdom than Nitaforius, the son of the king. The narration relates this wisdom, which he learned from Plato, to *"Dios que vos fizo"*, *"es cabeça de todos los sabers e los enseñamientos buenos"* (God who created you is the head of all knowledge and good teachings). Once again Socratic-Platonic wisdom and Christian wisdom are combined. And this, as I have said, as a prologue to the Aristotle-Alexander theme. In Chapter III above, I have already mentioned that the theme of Nitaforius is the equivalent of a novelized *Life* of Aristotle, placed before his maxims, of which I gave a selection.

In general terms, it must be said that there is hardly any Cynic material that is not Socratic as well: we can cite *"qui mucho se trabaja en mugeres par es de loco"* (he who is too fond of women is like a madman). And there is little explicitly Christian material, save the union of knowledge and fear of God ("fear of God is the garment of wise men" and the mention of "this century/this world", of risking one's soul and of chastity). Almost all of it is Socratic or moralistic in general: there is the theme of "I do not know," and that of knowing oneself. And certain maxims from an earlier date: *"los dias fazen al omne maestro de todas las cosas"* (time makes man the master of all things) (cf. Solon 22.7), "custom is the king of all things" (Pindar, *Fr.* 169.1), the proverb of the Seven Wise Men "who hastens more than he should deceives himself"). Linked to all the traditional philosophy of the fable is the theme of nature: "everything in the world can be changed except nature."

The Socratic themes are the ones that are repeated over and over: knowledge, truth and maintaining silence; justice; humility, effort, suffering, meekness; greed and cruelty as opposed to doing good.

VII ("The skill that a philosopher used with his disciple") continues the recurrent theme of Plato, Aristotle and Nitaforius.

In VIII we have the brief "gathering of seven philosophers." Again the theme of knowledge and of knowing oneself, joined to that of "knowledge of God" and of leaving this world.

IX is about ten philosophers with their disciples: they begin with prayer and a sacrifice. The dominant themes are, again, wisdom, maintaining silence and suffering, the "language of stupidity", poverty; and alongside these, the Christian themes of fearing God, of the "other world", to which the "good intellect" belongs; and the theme of the true God. Curiously, Hesiod's maxim about the two paths and Galen's on the sick person who conceals his illness are repeated. The pull of tradition is strong.

In X there are thirteen philosophers. What is notable here is that the philosophers are seated facing the dead kings, which reminds us of the theme of Alexander's burial. If this passage has been placed precisely here, it is in anticipation of Alexander's burial and the mourning for him. There are the maxims about how the passing from this world to the next is an example for those who are to go; there is the one that says "he has not died who left a good name" or the one about the inevitability of death. But in general terms, the emphasis continues to be on wisdom, silence, temperance and meekness.

Finally, XI presents a meeting of four philosophers. Here there appears a well-known formula, that of what is the best or the wisest: to keep silent, *"el saber omne quamaño es su estado"* (that a man know the greatness of his condition), not to trust this world, to be a firm believer. In other words, there is a variation; another well-known structural form is introduced.

There follow the parts relating to Socrates and Plato of which I have already spoken. The chapters that we have just seen are, as I have said, preparation for these others which, in turn prepare the central theme of Alexander/Aristotle. The story of Aristotle and Nitaforius is a forerunner of what is to come; and also the sayings of the philosophers before the dead kings. So the additions are merged, to a certain extent, with the themes that follow, for which they serve as preparation.

At the same time, they continue the Christianized theme of Ibycus' cranes. As I indicated in Chapter I and explained in detail above, it gives the impression that this is something added, that Hunayn transformed a life (and death) of Alexander into a larger work, a gnomological anthology, in part under the name of Greek philosophers, in part anonymous. This is the part to which I have just referred, the part following the theme of Ibycus' cranes. It has a moralistic, Christian character with an almost complete absence of Cynic themes.

I must stress the conclusion here that Hunayn was probably the architect of this addition, certainly constructed with Greek materials, materials of the moralistic Christian type to which we have referred repeatedly.

To confirm our hypotheses, and in consonance with what we have done in our Chapters IV and V, we are going to point out some correspondences in the in Greco-Christian literature with the maxims on the "seals" and in the *"ayuntamientos"* that follow[3]:

P. 48. *tod omne que el su sabor vençe al su seso* (every man whose pleasure defeats his intelligence): cf.: οὐδὲν οὕτω τυφλοῖ νοῦν ὡς θυμός (Origen M. 12.1176).
O tu omne, si temieres a Dios tu señor (O man, if you would fear God your lord): cf. εἰ φοβῇ κύριον τὸν θεόν σου (*Hom. Clem.* 16.13.4) and a frequent οὐ φοβῇ θεόν (or τὸν θεόν); (Gr. Naz., *Chr. Pat.* 191, Basil *Ep.* 8.8, Chrys. M. 49.412, etc.).
Non pongas culpa a Dios en yerro que tu ffagas (Don't blame God for your mistakes): cf. ὃς ἂν τῶν ἁμαρτημάτων μὴ ἑαυτὸν, ἀλλὰ θεὸν αἰτιᾶται "he who attributes his faults not to himself but to God" (Ph. *Fug.* 80), ἵνα τῶν οἰκείων ἁμαρτημάτων τὴν αἰτίαν ἐπὶ τὸν Θεὸν ἀγάγωσιν (Chrys. M. 47.435); etc.

P. 49. the sick man who covets something: cf. τίς δὲ νοσῶν οὐκ ἐπιθυμεῖ ὑγείας; "who, being ill, does not desire health?" (Simp., in *Epict.* 8.43, cf. Olymp., in *Grg.* 33.3).

P. 51. to the spiritual intellect: cf. πνευματικὸς νοῦς (frequent, for example Origen M. 12.1492, Mac. Aeg. *passim*).

3 As in the previous case, the search was performed by Juan Rodríguez Somolinos. I follow the abbreviations of the *Diccionario Griego-Español*, Madrid, CSIC, 1980 ff.

Everlasting lives: cf. βίος αἰώνιος (frequent, cf., for example, Eus., *PE* 4.19.2, Origen, *Cels. 430*, Chrys. M. 60.748, Dam., In *Prm.* 33.3).

P.53. wisdom is the life of the soul: cf. μία ζωή τῆς ψυχῆς ἐστί … "it is the only life of the soul" (Chrysipp. *Stoic.* 826) cf. Nemes., *Nat. Hom.* 2.364, Gr. Nyss., *Infant.* 80, Eus., *LC* 6.19, Iambl., *Myst* . 4.4.10, 8.4.18, Mac. Aeg. *passim*).

The understanding of this world and of the other: cf. οὔκ εἰσι τοῦ κόσμου τούτου, ἄλλου κόσμου εἰσί "they are not of this world but of the other" (Mac. Aeg., *Serm.* B 64.26.1 and *passim*).

La sapiençia … es siella del sesso (wisdom is the seat of the intellect): cf. ὁ θρόνος τοῦ νοῦ ἡ θεότης ἐστὶ "the throne of the spirit is divinity" (Mac. Aeg., *Hom.* 50.6.73, cf. also *Serm.* B 64.4.16).

The wise man's name does not die: cf. τὸ ἀνώνυμον ἀποθανεῖν "to die without a name" (Chrys. M. 55.88).

P. 58. *la sapiençia es dono de aquel que da y tuelle* (wisdom is the gift of the person who gives and takes away): cf. θεόθεν τῆς σοφίας τὸ δῶρον δεξάμενος "receiving from God the gift of wisdom." (Thdt. M. 80.676. cf. 700).

Philosophy … is the fruit of understanding, cf. ἀπὸ γὰρ καρποῦ διανοίας ἀγαθῆς, λόγος ἀγαθός "from the fruit of good thought, good discourse" (Chrys. M. 64.693, cf. also Amph. *Or.* 7.115, Io. D. *Dial.* proem. 41).

Con el fablar en su logar y con rrazon crece el prez (with speech in its place and with reason value grows), cf. σὺν λόγῳ καὶ καιρῷ χρώμενον (Gr. Naz., Or. 43.64).

P. 59. *Los días fazen al omne maestro de las cosas* (time makes men the instructors of things), τοὺς λόγους ... διδασκάλους τῶν πραγμάτων γίγνεσθαι "words are the masters of things" (Th. 3. 42.2, cf. Origen, Cels. 7.42, Lib., Ep. 99.4, Proc., in R. 2.103, Thdt., M. 81.1089).

Extensive use sharpens the understanding: cf. τὸν νοῦν ἀκραιφνῶς ὀξύναντες (Thd. Stud., Iamb. 8.8).

P. 60. use reigns over all things (much cited from Pindar on, Fr. 169.1, cf. the book by M. Gigante, *Nomos Basileus*, Naples 1956.

P. 61. who found the end of truth …: cf. ὃ κινεῖ πρὸς τέλος ἕτερον τῆς ἀληθείας "what moves at the other end of truth" (Eustr., in EN 284.36).

P. 67. he who left a good name did not die: cf. τὸ καλὸν ὄνομα τὸ ἐπικληθέν ἐφ' ὑμᾶς "the good name that he gave you" (Ep. Iac. 2.7).

P. 68. *la rrayz de las cosas es el sesso* (the root of everything is the intellect), cf. ἡ γὰρ φιλαλήθης ψυχὴ τὴν ῥίζαν αὐτὴν τῶν πραγμάτων ἐρευνᾷ "the soul that loves truth investigates the very root of everything" (Mac. Aeg. Serm. B 64.52.1), τὴν ῥίζαν ... τῆς τῶν ὄντων φύσεως οὐχ ὁρῶν (Eus. *PE* 14.27.4).

P. 69. the greatest wisdom of good men is to remain silent: cf. σοφίαν δὲ μεγίστην (Democr., Fr. 118.6), μεγίστη σοφία τὸ θεοσεβεῖν (Chrys. M. 64.628), cf. Olymp., in Grg. 27.3

The presence in *Buenos Proverbios* of maxims from ancient Greek wisdom is perfectly clear, some of them coming from Antiquity but taken without doubt from later works. Others are taken, in turn, from these later works: Neo-Platonists and Neo-Pythagoreans, Christian writers from the New Testament, pagans from the Stoics and the Pseudo-Democritus to the rhetors, the commentators of Plato and Aristotle, etc. As can be seen, the compilation of maxims of the Pseudo-Macarius occupies a pre-eminent position.

Note that this is only a sample; a full investigation is necessary. And also that not included in the above is the great number of maxims known through the ancient tradition of Socrates, Diogenes, etc., which we have already seen. Here we have restricted our study to the maxims most difficult to locate and especially to the Christian ones.

4. *The end of* Buenos Proverbios

The end of *Buenos Proverbios*, namely the gnomologies of Diogenes, Pythagoras and Hippocrates, is manifestly an addition. They are closely related, as we have seen, to the gnomologies of these same authors in *Bocados de Oro*: they come from widely circulated gnomologies related to other earlier Greek ones and also from the gnomology of Pythagoras in the *Philosophical Quartet*.

It was probably Hunayn himself who added them at the end of his translation; he doubtless thought that the image of Greek wisdom, even with the initial additions of Socrates, Plato, Aristotle and other philosophers, many of them anonymous, was, nevertheless, incomplete. The three authors added at the end were essential to the concept that was held at the end of Antiquity and that the Arabs inherited from Greek thought and science.

And so, in short, Hunayn converted the book about the legend of Alexander into the center of a gnomology of Greek thought, with an orientation between moral and ascetic, of the utmost importance for the Arabs. To do this, he joined diverse works, always of the Greco-Christian tradition. In this Mubassir imitated him, but he also amplified that anthology with various other authors.

III. Marginal elements in *Bocados de Oro*

With this I refer to everything that is added to the maxims already studied, i.e. to the Hermetic and Pythagorean maxims and those of Socrates, Plato, Aristotle, Alexander and Diogenes.

1. *The lives and maxims of well-identified Greek writers and philosophers*

a) Homer

Without doubt the Arab compiler wanted to extend his initial collection of Lives and gnomologies, which centered on the Hermetic-Pythagorean and Socratic ones, with others connected to the great names of the Greek past: the earliest of that literature, namely Homer and Solon; the great sages that Hippocrates, Galen and Ptolemy represent for them and that had already been translated in Bagdad (the interest in Ptolemy is manifest in the fact that the chapter dedicated to him was translated into Latin before the complete work was translated into Castilian); and Gregory, who, as I have said, penetrated the Greek gnomologies with Basil starting just at the end of Antiquity.

It is a fact that Greek poetry did not interest the Arabs, although the great name of Homer was, naturally, known[4]. Mubassir, who follows an approximately chronological order, puts him after the Hermetic sages (it is not by chance that Hermes Trismegistus is called Homer the Greater in *Poridad*) and states that he lived five hundred years after Moses and that all later versifiers (poets) drank at his fountain.

But he knows very little, or rather, nothing of Homer. The minimal biography that precedes his "counsels" preserves nothing of the *Lives* of Homer that we know in Greek. It only contains, before a (typically Byzantine) physical description, some anecdotes of a Cynic stamp.

Homer was captured and sold (just like Diogenes and Aesop). In his dialogue with the buyer Cynic themes appear, such as his cosmopolitism ("Where are you from? – And he said to him: from my father and my mother"), cf. *Vit. Aesop.* G 25, and his freedom. To the buyer's question "So you want me to buy you?", he replies: "You want to be my companion in slavery." Then to another question Homer replies that it is good "to be free." Diogenes, according to the multiple testimonies of *SR* 70 ff., says that what he knows is "how to command men" (Aesop that he knows "nothing at all").

We are left with the doubt of whether this minibiography is Byzantine (by a writer who is quite ignorant, to be sure, but he is not the only one) or Arabic, with Cynic themes in any event. Greek, very Greek is the collection of 29 maxims that then follows, although not a single one of them has the slightest relation to Homer. They belong to the Socratic-Cynic level that we are familiar with: the themes of knowledge (the intellect, the wise man, the fool, keeping silent, repressing greed, the good and the bad, mendacity, meekness). We reencounter some of the maxims almost literally in other places: for example 1 ("the sagacious person is he who holds his tongue" is the same as Socrates 130 in our collection, "the sagacious person is known for often maintaining silence"). This theme of "keeping silent" is, as we know, Hermetic-Pythagorean. The maxim on greed (19 "suppress your covetousness") finds an echo, for example, in Plato 48–50 (Stanzel) and in those of Aristotle's that we have seen.

The maxims of the absolutely Cynic type are notable: 18, the fable of the two knapsacks (H. 229); and especially 17, which tells of a wise man who, having been shipwrecked on an island and lost all his belongings, is

4 See Vernet, op. cit., pp. 82 f.

praised by the king because he still has "the true knowledge and good works." I have already mentioned the fable about Simonides being saved from a shipwreck in Phaedrus IV 23 and to a replication of it in Diogenes, cf. *BO* 59; cf. also Aristotle in *BO* 58 ("What are the things that it behooves the wise man to obtain?" – "The things that, when his ship is wrecked in the sea, will float with him").

But equally notable are the maxims of the Christian type: 14, "he is a marvel who can resemble God (in his acts) and struggles to resemble the beasts" and 24, 28, the theme of the world, which we are familiar with and that is not only Christian but also Cynic (Diogenes as an "abhorrer of the world" in *BO*, maxims of Aristotle in *BP*, etc.). And one related to the appearance or the physiognomies (11).

All of this takes us back, once again, to late Antiquity. There not being maxims that were strictly from Homer, use was made of the Socratic-Cynic-Christian ones that we already know[5] .

b) Solon

What is said of him is minimal: that he wrote many books of good sermons, that Athens was "the city of the sages" and that he wrote verses *"por que ganan los omnes voluntad de usar lides e matarse con sus enemigos"* (so that men would be willing to engage in combat and battle to the death with their enemies) (it seems that he is thinking of warlike verses in the manner of Tyrtaeus).

The maxims are of the same type as those we are familiar with. This is notable in 3, where the Delphic precept of knowing oneself, which we have seen in other places, is joined to the *"non fablar en lo que non ha de fablar"* (don't speak about what should not be spoken of) and not complaining about not getting what one wants. In 4 this reprehension of greed and desire acquires a strictly Socratic tone: he cannot command others who cannot command himself, see our Socrates 5. Other Socratic themes (at least from the Socrates of the gnomologies) are suffering (12 "suffering is a sturdy castle"), excusing a friend's mistake (10), truth (11, 12), goodness (6).

But there are other, strictly Cynic maxims: being frank (7, 12, parrhesia), the tongue of the bad man as the worst thing of all (8, cf. *Vit. Aesop.* G 51

5 I do not believe, as J. Krämer says, "Arabische Homerverse", *ZDMG* 106, 1956, pp. 486–506, that the source is Menander's monostichs, although, of course, there can be coincidences.

ff., also in the *Altercatio Hadriani et Epicteti* 19), the true *"aver"* (possession), *"aquel que non lo puede omne del mundo aver sin mi voluntad"* (that which no man in the world can have unless I wish it) (9). We can add the theme of consolation (in *BP* in relation to Alexander's death), the concealed thief and the public one (cf. *BO* Diogenes 10) and above all, the theme of the king, which presents strict coincidences with what we have seen in our Chapter III. This is a real series, 18–22, without doubt taken in a block from a "mirror for princes". The king should act with right and justice, he must "set himself to rights", etc. This already has a certain Christian tint and more so in regard to (14) "the good soul" that sees what is good in things and not what is bad.

The conclusion is the same: we have a small early Byzantine collection of the Socratic-Cynic-Christian character that we have seen above.

c) Hippocrates

He was well known to the Arabs, and through them to the Christians. It is no wonder that this section is preceded by a long and fantastic *Life* that connects him with Escalibus (that is, Asclepius the Hermetic) and Plato. There is without doubt a Hermetic source. But some truth is preserved: the mention of the island of Cau (Kos) and of the practice of medicine (which Hippocrates did not want to take to the Persians because they are "enemies of the Greeks"). Of course in Cau there is a king, like the king of Greece who is mentioned in other places. But our author is acquainted with the thirty books of Hippocrates, which must be studied after Galen's sixteen. It is probable that a Byzantine original (which adds a physiognomy at the end) was reworked by the Arab translator.

As for the maxims (in *BO*, we will add something later on the less numerous ones in *BP*), the first thing we look for is to see whether, here at least, there is anything of the true Hippocrates, who had been translated into Arabic, as is known, since Hunayn. Nevertheless, the result of this investigation is quite frustrating[6]. The greatest yield is 2 (*la vida es corta e el arte es luenga e la prueva es peligrosa e el juizio es grave* [life is short, art is long, the test is dangerous and the judgment is serious]), the well-known aphorism 1.1. 3, in turn, (*la salud dura, por no haber pereza de lazrar, e por no se fenchir de comer e de bever* [health lasts by not being unwilling to suffer hardship and by

6 In this I had the help of Dolores Lara, a well-known expert in this author.

not eating and drinking in excess]) may be derived from *Epid.* 6.4.18 (against the abuse of food) and 4 (*menguar de lo que nuze es mejor, que non amuchiguar de lo que aprovecha* [restricting what is harmful is better than overindulging in what is beneficial]) can be related to *Epid.* 1.11 ("help or at least don't harm"). In the end very little and passages that are well known. This in *BO*; *BP* adds nothing.

We would be mistaken if we tried to attribute to Hippocrates the following maxim, which begins: *"El coraçón ha dos maldades: tristeza e cuidado"* (the heart has two evils, sorrow and care). It does not seem to be found in Hippocrates, but something similar appears, attributed to Diogenes in *BP*, p. 140, on the sorrow and joy of the heart. And the same treatise, p. 100, speaks of the sorrow that destroys the heart, words of Aristotle to Alexander that the latter tried to put to the test by performing an autopsy on an animal. It seems that this was a common theme of unknown origin.

What we do find in Hippocrates are the habitual Socratic, Cynic and Christian maxims, sometimes attributed to other philosophers, fairly close in form, sometimes with a similar meaning. We find, for example, the famous maxim (10) "The best thing I acquired through learning is that I know that I do not know"; there are others on knowledge; 9, 18, 19, 20 run in a series as if they came from a thematic gnomology. Also on greed: for example 12: "he who wants to be free should not covet what he cannot have", 14 "covet what you can have", cf. in Diogenes the theme of Alexander "slave of the slave", that is, of greed (p. 39 Crombach); on friendship, characteristic of the wise man (9); on moderation in eating: leave this world as you would a banquet, accept the glass that is offered to you, do not ask for it (13, cf. Aristotle *GB* 61 = MC 957 (leave life as you would a banquet, neither thirsty nor inebriated), plus the familiar anecdotes of Diogenes.

And then there are the Christian themes, well known to us: the life of the soul, which must be "tempered" (8); being near to God, avoiding sin (11); the world that perishes (16), cf. for example Aristotle *BP* 4, 6, 30, 35, 36).

The Hippocratic maxims in *BP* are approximately the same, although fewer, but, nevertheless, there is the addition of a long explication on love, greed and mendacity. Both collections must be derived from a common source.

d) Galen

Altering the order in *BO*, I refer to Galen because for the Arabs and later for the West he forms a block with Hippocrates. He was the physician most translated into Arabic and then into the other languages, as is known.

This chapter is notable because it provides a starting point for Hermetism, placing Galen, in the line that begins with Escalibus, as occurred with Hippocrates, with certain data on his birth in Pergamon, his father, a geometrist, his stay in Egypt, his arrival in Rome in times of Antoninus, his many books. There are, to be sure, fantastic elements and a physical description no less fantastic. And there is the early Byzantine theme, now familiar to us, of "the kings of the Greeks", who worked harder in governing their kingdoms than in the pleasures of the body and who appreciated the Sciences and Medicine.

It is interesting that some of the maxims have to do with Medicine: 4 on the sick man "who has the desire to eat", 7 a lamentation on the submission of the physicians to their powerful patients. 14 develops the Platonic theme of the health of the soul compared to that of the body; in 8, the theme of the excessive imbibing of wine compared to the old banquets in which they drank moderately and sang.

And there are old traditional themes: the Delphic ones of knowing oneself (2) and of moderation (9). And the habitual ones on wisdom (1, 6, 12, 15), justice (13), goodness (16) greed (9), the good soul (5, 14, 16). Sometimes, as can be seen, two or more themes appear in the same maxim. But we do not find any that are strictly Cynic or strictly Christian. Nor does the political theme of the good king appear. There is, therefore, a special tint to these maxims; but nothing really of Galen's own, save generic allusions to medical themes.

e) Zeno (Rabion)

In an initial *Life*, followed by a physical description, Rabion appears as a knight who defends his friends from the king and for this is taken prisoner. The king threatens him if he does not reveal the whereabouts of his friends; he refuses to do "anything so vile", and as a result, he is tortured. Rabion cuts out his tongue to avoid speaking and he dies. This story is somewhere between chivalry and Stoic or Christian martyrdom; strictly speaking, it has nothing to do with the founder of Stoicism.

As for "his words", they are addressed to his disciples or to "a youth". They correspond to an environment partly Socratic-Cynic and partly Christian, not really related to the *Life*.

We have, in effect, the theme of friends (2, they are "a cure for the soul"), the misogynist (3, the theme of not marrying a beautiful woman, because many will become enamored of her, cf. Bion, *GV* 2, also attributed to Antisthenes and others), the rejection of desire and greed (4, "everything bad comes from love of possessing"), consolation for the death of one's child (5, "how well I knew that my child was mortal", cf. *BP* XX, XXIII, etc.), the theme of the death of the soul (6, 7). In 8 we have a youth on the seashore who was sighing because of the cares of the world; Rabion, in a dialogue, consoles him, describing a rich man or a king surrounded by grave dangers that the youth does not have to face.

This theme *de consolatione* closes this brief, basically Cynic gnomology, which, as I say, has little relation to the *Life*.

f) Ptolemy

BO knows that Ptolemy was an outstanding figure in the science of astrology, that he wrote the Almagest, and that he lived in Alexandria in the time of Hadrian; it says little more about his life, except that it warns against confusing him with Ptolemy the king. But the maxims have nothing to do with the sciences that Ptolemy cultivated: they belong to the same moralistic vein that we have been studying.

There are, perhaps, two exceptions, which sound like profound reflections of the sage: as in Galen, the maxim on the power of the patient over the physician; and maxim 9, which says that "wise men stand out like aliens because there are many fools around them", sounds like Plato, in a well-known passage from the *Republic* (517 a): no doubt a wise man like Ptolemy agreed with this idea. Here I add 29: men never attempted to discover something hidden that they did not discover. A fine expression of faith from a wise man.

Apart from this we find the usual Socratic-Cynic-Christian philosophy. Here are the main themes:

Not speaking: 2 "the intelligent person is the one who restrains his tongue from speaking", cf. Homer 1.

Wisdom: besides 2, we can include 1 (the intelligent person should be in awe of God), 6 (wisdom is never found in the heart of a madman), 7 (teaching and intellect), 8 (he who has knowledge does not die), 9 already cited, 10 (wisdom is born in the heart and bears fruit on the tongue), 11 (wise men are humble), 12 (the vices of fools), 21 (the person who conceals his knowledge), 34 (the difference between knowledge and intellect), 42 (the wise man should not look at fools but at wise men), 44 (a foolish soul as the worst enemy). Some have a Cynic-Christian or Christian tone (8, 44).

The body, prison of the soul: 47, the same as Diogenes, *BP* p. 140.

Goodness, benevolence: 4 (the good that God does), 18 (the hearts of the good are castles of secrets), 41 (God rewards those who repay iniquity with goodness), 46 (avoid harmful suspicion). Sometimes there is a Christian tone here as well.

Joy, hope, suffering: 14 (have a patient heart), 16 (rejoice in being able to speak justly), 26 (hope, a comforting companion), 43 (the soul must never lose hope).

Greed, wrath, presumptuousness: 3, (the person who considers himself highly is humbled by God), 13 (do not quarrel), 17 (do not let your anger last long and pardon), 31 (the person who finds something and wants nothing more and the one who asks for something and does not find it, cf. Hippocrates 12, 141), 35 (the slave of greed, recalls Diogenes' "the slave of the slave"), 36 (the prouder a man is of his power, the more he suffers when he loses it).

Austerity, detachment from power: 24 (he does not want to eat with a king who invites him), 30 (the most esteemed man in the world is the one who takes no interest in the man who has the world in his power).

Once again we have returned to the Socratic-Cynic-Christian environment, although there are certain Christian themes that are missing, such as that of the uncertainty of the world.

g) Gregory

A small collection of 16 maxims: the themes of envy, knowledge ("a light for all of life"), poverty instead of wealth, suffering insults, accepting the small things. And then strictly Christian themes: put the beginning and the end in God, chain your body, do not rejoice in the fall of another, accept everything that comes from God and the fact that we are mortal.

2. *The lives and maxims of unidentified writers and philosophers*

These are brief collections, basically monographic, but always within the sphere that we are studying.

a) Assaron

The counsels of Assaron refer quite specifically to what the comportment of the king should be. They coincide, though only partially, with the most extensive treatise on royalty in *Poridad*, of which we spoke in our Chapter III: we said there that this is something that came from the idealized figure of Alexander, having passed through the Roman panegyrists and through Agapetus' treatise addressed to Justinian, and had an enormous influence on the concept of royalty in our Middle Ages and on the monarchies of the ancient regime. See Chapter VIII below.

We are looking, then, at a kind of abbreviated treatise. At times the coincidence with *Poridad* is considerable, as when the king is put on his guard against women, wine and hunting (1, cf. the second treatise) or the king is told to follow the course of justice (17, cf. the third treatise); and this is also seen in the insistence on the "intellect" (19, 12, 18, cf. the fourth treatise). Another notable coincidence is the expression "it is in the interest of the king" (3, 4, 12, 14, 16, 17), whose Greek origin we have established. The king must obey God (18) and know that the love of bad men is not lasting (19).

Actually, the maxims of Assaron (which have no preceding *Life*) seem to be a fragment of a "mirror for princes" referring to the theme of the adviser to the king: he should disabuse the king of his errors (4, 6, 7, 8, 21, etc.); the king, in turn, should take counsel (12, 13) and, above all, follow his mind and obey God, as has already been said.

We have here, then, a fragment of the familiar, more or less Christianized Hellenistic-Byzantine literature of counsels for kings.

b) Enesius

There is no Life, only a brief gnomology of 10 maxims. The theme of kings, the powerful and the rich predominates.

One cannot command many if one cannot command his own soul well (8, a theme of Socrates 5); and the king should act with law and justice in order to win the hearts of this subjects (10, common in this literature). The death of the nobles is preferable to the lordliness of the dishonorable (2, justification of the uprisings of the people). In bad times it is the rich man who fears most (1), it is preferable to have little and spend it with moderation (3), a Cynic theme.

We also have the Socratic theme of not treating the person in difficult straits fairly (5), of repentance (6), of goodness (7), and of friends (4, 9).

c) Medargis

First there is a physical description: he was a person who carried a staff, on top of which there was "a figure of the moon". Perhaps it came from the Hermetic sphere7.

The theme is that of the king, who attempts to "set his people to rights" (10) and the lords and nobility of lineage (8), which, to be sure, requires good training and wisdom. He conquers his enemies who only asks for what by rights he can demand (19).

Apart from this, the moralistic theme predominates: a man in this world must be able to set his soul and his life to rights (1) and pacify his enemies no matter how powerful he is (13). There is the constant theme of the *"seso"* (intellect) (6, it conquers wrath; 7, it points out the right path and leads away from the wrong one, 12 it puts the soul to rights; 14, trying to put a fool on the right path is a "misery for the intellect"; 17, triumph of the will, a Socratic theme).

We also have the themes of the nobility of the soul (4, it is the true wealth), of keeping oneself from meanness (5), of doing good before you are asked (11), of wrong suspicions that ruin a good life (15), of the bad person who is ungrateful (18).

On the other hand the most typical and extreme Cynic themes are missing and the Christian ones are merely suggested.

7 K. Merkle, *Die Sittensprüche der Philosophen, Kitāb ādāb al falāsifa,* Leipzig, O. Harrassowitz, 1921, p. 10, suggests that with this name Hunayn is referring to himself.

d) Thesileus (Basil?)

This is a series of 12 maxims of a fundamentally Christian type: they center on the opposition between what is ugly or unacceptable ("e fea cosa es", "es feo", "fazer cosas feas" ["and it is an ugly thing", "it is ugly", "to do objectionable things"]) and what is beautiful (but "beautiful words" [1] can deceive in human actions), and on the body and soul. Through a series of comparisons the perfection of the soul is sought.

For example, the maxims speak of "the food of the soul", which must not be "false or harmful" (2), of "letting go of our soul" in any situation, whereas the seaman does not do this with his ship (3), etc., etc. The body is like the instrument of the soul (4), the fat man raises the walls of his prison (11, the theme of the prison for the soul that we are familiar with). A dirty body is ugly as is a dirty soul (7), it is unacceptable for a rider to allow himself to be guided by the horse and for the soul to be guided by the body. The maxims speak of the intellect, which is the most important part of the soul (8), of the senses of the soul (9).

At the bottom of all this is the Platonic theme of the physician or doctor of the soul, which is reflected here (12). Based on the old opposition between body and soul, especially from Plato on, we arrive at these maxims with a Christian cast: one should not become angry, for fear of the heavenly king (9). One must tolerate the mistake of another, "God sees it" (1). The best-known and most radical of the Cynic themes are missing.

In short, in this case as in those of the unidentifiable aphorists discussed above, we are dealing with short, specialized gnomologies as regards orientation and themes, always within the sapiential sphere that we have seen. At times the Socratic, at other times the Cynic, and at still other times the Christian influence predominates; now the themes of the king are predominant, now various other themes. Mubassir, or whoever was responsible for the additions to *Bocados*, wanted to complete the sayings of the famous great philosophers and of a few more that were added in abbreviated form (Homer, Solon, Hippocrates, Galen, Ptolemy) with these others that represent brief supplements.

3. The maxims of Loginem (Lokman)

In a sense, Chapter XVII, relating to the counsels of Loginem, the philosopher, stands apart from the rest of the book. For this chapter, whose doctrine is, in general, similar to what we have been seeing, that is, Socratic and Christian moralism, refers to an Arab sage, Lokman, already mentioned in the Koran. To him was attributed, in the Arab world and from the time of the Koran itself, great wisdom of the Aesopian type: maxims and fables. In spite of this assimilation to Aesop, which I will discuss later, this in its origin is a matter of an Arab sage; we are told (40) that his "fuesa" (tomb) is "between the mosque and the sand bank". It seems clear that his *Life* and "counsels", however Greek they may be, represent a synthesis, and that, in consequence, they were added only secondarily to the other *Lives* and gnomologies of *BO*.

For Lokman I refer the reader to the corresponding article in the Encyclopaedia of Islam[8]. Many of his sayings and his figure itself find a correspondence in the Assyrian Ahikar. He is, in the Arab tradition, a wise man inspired by God, who gives counsels of wisdom; many of them are addressed specifically to his son ("Oh my son" they begin). These are none other than the counsels of Ahikar: those of the Arab tradition, not those of our work, are at times identical. This is without doubt wisdom of the Middle East.

But when the Arabs occupied the Greek Orient, they found coincidences with the Aesop of the *Life* (and the fables), which furthermore offered parallels with Ahikar. Lokman received this influence to a great extent; it is reflected in the fables that are attributed to him, which we do not discuss here, but also in his *Life*.

The synthesis Lokman-Aesop was, without doubt, created in the Ommiad period, in the Syria occupied by the Arabs. One of its variants, the one we are dealing with here, is clearly Christian: it probably arose in the

8 Art. by B. Heller and N.A. Stillman, "Lukman", in *Encyclopaedia of Islam*. For Ahikar see my "The Life of Aesop and the Origins of Greek Novel in Antiquity, *QUCC* N.S. 1, 1979, pp. 93–112, as well as my *Historia de la Fábula Greco-Latina*, I, Madrid 1979, pp. 313 ff. and 661 ff. (= 299 ff. and 647 ff. of the English translation, Leiden, 1999). We must recall here not only the influence of the legend of Ahikar in the origin of the Aesop legend, but also the translation of *Ahikar* into Greek in the 5th century and the insertion of a part of his *Life* into the *Life* of Aesop that has been preserved. On all of this see my works cited.

environment of the Syrian Christians, who received a double influence, Greek and Arab.

This Aesopized and Christianized version of Lokman (but the mention of the mosque should not be forgotten) appears in the chapter of *BO* that I am discussing, It consists of three parts: the *Life*, his maxims, his death. We will analyze them in order.

1. The Life

Lokman is a black man born in Ethiopia; he was one of the first slaves of the Arabs in the land of Sen; later he lived in Palestine, all of this in the time of David.

It is told of him that he was sold as a slave, the same as Aesop (to a Jew, it is said); and we have the narration of the way in which he got his master out of a difficult situation with an anecdote similar to Aesop's, when he told his master, who had gambled and on losing his bet had to "drink up the sea", that he should ask them to separate the water of the rivers from the sea and then he would drink it. Lokman's master had also lost at dice and had to drink up the stream that passed in front of his door; Lockman told him to ask whether he should drink the water that ran down the street from above or the water that was at his door; and on receiving the latter reply, told him to ask someone to cut off the water coming down and he would drink the water before his door.

There is a clear derivation from the Aesopian theme (not only in the *Life*, also in Plutarch's *Banquet of the Seven Wise Men* 151a–c).

Another equally Aesopian theme is that of the heart, a man's best and worst "bet" (in the *Life* of Aesop, and again in the *Banquet* 146f the tongue is discussed).

Now, together with these elements of popular wisdom connected with the name of Aesop, there are other, ascetic ones, for example, when Lokman declines to be lord of this earth and to be king; he preferred being despised to exchanging this world for another one. We are also told of his silence, his almsgiving, his lending without interest, his distancing himself from the world "between the sand bank and the temple" until he died. We now have a Lokman who has become a Christian anchorite.

2. *The maxims*

The chapter adds that he preached to his son: the maxims are addressed to his son, on the model of the Ahikar. They are sapiential and Christian maxims, like the ones we already know: on wisdom, the good intellect, maintaining silence, doing good and being long-suffering, justice and humility, piety, friendship, the commandments, avoiding bad persons, greed and the "bad woman", "not doing what your will demands". Well-known themes, some in almost literal form. But above all, there is the Christian theme: abhorrence of the world and the search for the other one, sin, prayer, obedience to God, fear of God, service to God. All of it moralistic and Christian.

3. *His death*

The same thing may be said of death (74): when he is going to die, he weeps because *"he de andar grant camino e pasar fuerte puerto e llevo mucho conducho e grant carga"* (I must walk a long road and pass through a difficult defile and I am carrying many provisions and a heavy burden).

The Arab sage, with traces of the Assyrian Ahikar and blended with the Greek Aesop, is turned into a Christian ascetic buried beside a mosque. This is one of the Greco-Christian elements that Mubassir combined in his anthology, and it is, quite clearly, one of the last, from the time in which the Greek-speaking Christianized Syrians lived side by side with the Muslims. Remember that these Syrians knew the Assyrian Ahikar; I have studied this elsewhere[9]. The different cultures blended with each other.

4. *The maxims of various philosophers or of anonymous ones*

a) *The Chapter of the sayings of many sages in* BO

The complete title is "The chapter of the sayings of many sages and none of them was found to have enough sayings for them to be put in separate chapters". This is, then, a second anthological supplement to the Socratic philosophers, justified by the small number of maxims of each philosopher.

9 *Historia de la Fábula Greco-Latina*, II. Madrid, 1985, p. 389 (p. 421 of the English translation, Leiden, 2000).

There will follow another supplement, the next chapter, which is the final chapter of *BO*: maxims with no precise attribution.

In other words, *Bocados de Oro* adds various supplements to the central philosophers. It is, therefore, an anthology of anthologies, either Byzantine or more probably Arab, by Mubassir or some predecessor. But the whole thing made use of Greek material.

Let us examine the characteristics of the chapter that we are studying now. It contains maxims under personal names, most of them attributed to Greek philosophers and writers, plus others with the names of other philosophers, no doubt Greek, but not identifiable. These begin with "he said" or "and they said to", "and they asked", "and he saw", well-known Greek phrases. They give a maxim or a question and reply. Maxims are added that begin with "and he said" (=ὁ αὐτός), or else "and they said to", referring to the preceding philosopher, just as when it says "and they said to him". At other times it says "and someone else said", which can be understood as a debate with the preceding philosopher, but sometimes introduces another one. The anonymity is complete when we have the introduction, for example, (19) of a king and three wise men: the traditional theme of the wise men who reply to the questions of the king.

None of this differs from Greek gnomologies that we know. We find, in effect, small anthologies: for example in 83 ff (Bracalitos, Heraclitus), 87 ff. (Tenparastis, Theophrastus), 104 ff (Arsides?), 107 ff. (Pythagoras, ordered by themes: friends, wrath). The author has taken this material either from complex gnomologies ordered by authors (sometimes within these, by themes), or from gnomologies of individual authors. Some are unidentifiable: Lidanes, Dicemus, Grenes, Quedaris (or Quedaras), Anicus, Crianus, Quenis, Ocason, Tisenus, Armesis, Arianus, Ascidus, Arsides, and others are of dubious identification. But more usually they are identifiable. And on rare occasions we can even identify the authors of anonymous maxims from their content; or else it happens that where *Bocados* gives the maxim as anonymous, it bears the name of the philosopher in the Arabic original of Mubassir[10]. See our Chapter I, note 29 for more data.

All of this is Greek, in any case. When in 59 Phaedrus (!!) says that *"el bárbaro no puede entender lo que dize el arávigo"* (the barbarian cannot understand what the Arab says), it is quite clear that the Arab translator has written

10 F. Rosenthal, op. cit., pp. 121 ff. has made a great effort to augment the number of these identifications.

"arávigo" for "Greek". And it is a late Greek scene, with "kings", and bath houses in which there are beautiful paintings (81). On the admiration for old books, Greek books without doubt, cf. 40, 51.

To all appearances, the anthologist avoided the authors already included, Socratic and otherwise: it was a matter of completing. Plato, for example, is not included but the characters of his dialogues are (Timaeus, Ecliton = Crito, Polo). Also included are the ancient Hermetics (Escalibus), poets (Aseres = Hesiod), Philosophers (Bracalitos = Heraclitus, Dimigratis, Domiciatis = Democritus), Pythagoras, the Seven Wise Men (Talis = Thales, Vastacos = Pittacos, Solon), the Socratic philosophers or persons connected with them (Engenius = Xenophon, Nichomatus = Nichomacus, Tenparastis = Theophrastus), the playwrights (Aristophanes, Eclimon = Philemon), the Hellenistic writers and men of science (Plimes = Polemon, Calides = Euclid, Abrachis = Hipparchus), the writers of the Roman epoch (Ajasogonis, Asigranis = Archigenes, Proteus, Polutucus = Plutarch, Plinit, Aplino = Apollonius of Tyana, Anicus = Epictetus, Aristides = Aelius Aristides?, Philip "the disciple of Pythagoras", Ammonius), others from the world 8of the novel and the fable (Aseus = Aesop, Loginem = Lokman, Pirgonos = Phaedrus). And the Christians, who, as we know, entered the lists of the gnomologies in the 4th century (Silus = Basil, if not Zosimus, Gregory of Nyssa). Sometimes when the name is not given in *Bocados*, it does appear in Mubassir: 13 is Anaxarchus, 35 is Pindar. For others there are inexplicable correspondences: 30 Grenes = Telemachus (?), 52 Ocason = Xenophon (?).

Note that these are basically marginal characters; the great Socratics like Antisthenes, the great Cynics like Bion or Crates, important later personages like Porphyry do not appear.

The first thing to be said is that the correspondence between the name and the doctrine is rare. 22 Aseres (Hesiod in Mubassir) says: *"dizen por el ome que es bueno en el primero grado, quando él por sí asaca las fermosas cosas, e dizen que es bueno en el segundo grado, quando las sabe por otro"* (they say of a man that he is good in the first degree when he comes to understand beautiful things on his own, and they say he is good in the second degree when he knows of them from another). This corresponds exactly with Hes., *TD* 293 ff., just as 65, attributed to Eckriton (= Crito) *"non ha cosa que tuelga al ome el cuidado de la muerte, si no el conplimiento del saber"* (there is nothing that takes away man's fear of death like the fulfillment of knowledge) is close to Pl., *Cri.* 48d.

And with no name in *BO* ("and someone else said") we have in 35 *"lo que es fecho non lo podemos tornar non fecho"* (what is done cannot be undone), which is from Pindar, O. 2. 16 ff. (Mubassir says this). With a name in *BO*: of Aseus (Aesop) things are said that we know well from the *Life of Aesop*: captured and put up for sale, he does not reply about his lineage, but tells them to ask about his intellect and knowledge (7). He says that he is good *"para ser forro"* (that is, free), he converses with the buyer who is hesitating (9).

Aside from these few passages, the Socratic-Cynic philosophy (and Christian too, as we shall see) applies to any one of the authors. To Plutarch is attributed (1) the theme of the old man who dyed his hair, a Cynic theme from *BP*, p. 139, *BO* 27; the "I only know that I know nothing" is attributed to Democritus (4), and later more or less similar phrases to Ajasagonis (Archigenes) 36, 37 and Polutucus (Plutarch) 39. The Socratic theme (S. 32) of the "dominated will" is attributed to Plimes (= Polemon). I believe that the one that says "the tongue can swear falsely but the intellect no", from Arsides (9), comes from Euripides, *Hipp.* 612. On the other hand, maxims are attributed to various philosophers, to Heraclitus or Theophrastus, for example, that have absolutely nothing to do with them. Nor does it seem especially Christian when in 23 Basil (?) refuses a loan to a friend or in 56 when Gregory speaks of interior beauty.

All of these are maxims that belong to the circle that we have been referring to. At times there is a complete or almost complete coincidence with some that we have found in previous chapters; I have already cited the old man who dyed his hair. Here are other examples:

16, the question put to Loginem on what he earned with his wisdom is parallel to the one put to Diogenes in *SR* 360, 361, 365. 21, the best king is the one who is not a slave of his will, is S. 5. 27, the theme of the rich man with restraint, cf. S. 9. 33, against the king who drinks, listens to songs and loves women; cf. Assaron 1, also *PQ* 57 and *BO* 113, among others. 42, Domiciatis (Democritus), suffering is a strong castle: cf. Solon 12. 52, Ocason (?), as in a glass, the heart has room for only a certain amount of wisdom, cf. *BO* 38. 55, Tisenus (?): do not try to get what you want to have but rather what you can have, cf. Hippocrates 12, 14. 60, Quedaris, the theme of the stench of the cadaver, cf. S. 24. 64, Engenius = Xenophon, the theme of the "food for the soul", cf. Thesileus 2. 80, Domicatres (Democritus?), the theme of keeping one's friends and turning your enemies into friends, cf. S. 178. I could continue, although the limits with simple common doctrine are blurred.

This community of doctrine is perfectly clear. The examples given are either of a Socratic or a Cynic character. Here are some others:

Wisdom: 6 (knowledge and not lineage is what is important), 13 (abhor stupidity and love knowledge), 28 (the best things are the intellect and time), 30 (one loses when he does not receive wisdom), 31 (do not discuss matters of wisdom before the fool), 48 (the end, avoid stupidity), 51 (the wise men who amassed treasures), 58 (wealth versus wisdom), 59 (the fool does not understand the wise man), 60 (the tongue of the unlearned person stinks), 67 (suffer the "misery" of wisdom), etc.

Keeping silent: 19 (the advantages of keeping silent according to the three sages before the king), 24 (it is an attribute of the wise man), 97 (why did you not learn to keep silent from the person who taught you to speak?), 107 (do not use your tongue except to show what is happening in your soul).

Wealth: 45 (the pride of the rich), 54 (lose your possessions and be afraid), 58 (those who take risks to gain wealth and who do not know to whom they are going to leave it), 73 (the wise take wealth with moderation), 101 (true wealth is the wealth that remains forever); 102 (the greedy person never becomes wealthy).

Wrath: 113 (do not insult, it will fall back upon you), 115 (keeping silent kills wrath).

Shame: 9 (be ashamed of yourself and not of other men), 13 (do not be ashamed to learn, cf. S. 49).

Women: 3 (to lie with a woman is to weaken the body), 117 (women get angry more than men).

Friends: 10 (one guards himself against his enemies, not so well against his friends), 80 (see above, cf. S. 178), the whole series 110 ff.

The king: 21 (the best king, the one who is not the slave of his will, see above), 48 (who keeps the company of the king is the person who was brought up in sin), 59 (if you had me as a king, I would be like a brother), 71 (one person should command and the other obey), 77 (the bad lord is like a drunkard), 78 (the king should not treat his people with injustice, they would all turn against him).

More details could be given, but it is easy to see that the background is basically Socratic and moralistic, Cynic also, to a lesser extent; this, doubtless, because the Christian orientation predominates. For example: 10 (the person who asks God to protect him from his friends), 11 (paradise is for the man with a great heart), 45 (wise men know God, they do not boast before Him), 66 (the soul of the wise man), 70 (the world is not a permanent thing), 83 (the wise man always obeys God), 90 (ten ways to serve God), 101 (true wealth is the wealth that remains for ever, after death), 106 (wise men know that God is everywhere, not only on the altars, and they obey his will).

Other maxims (the opposition soul/body, interior beauty, death, etc.) can be understood both in the Socratic or moralistic sense in general and in the strictly Christian sense. And the same is true of the "commandments" of 90: be grateful, suffer with patience, keep your promises, tell the truth, judge rightly, be temperate, do good without being told, honor your friend, pardon his mistake and that of the enemy, do not want for your friend what you would not want for yourself.

It is perfectly clear that the gnomologies of this moralistic and Christian type were much more abundant in late Antiquity than what might be supposed from the collections preserved in Greek. On the other hand, these Greek collections contain copious material that is missing in our treatises. The "anthology of anthologies", *Bocados de Oro*, helps to reconstruct the gnomologies of late Greek Antiquity, without doubt Byzantine-Syriac, since it was in Syria that Mubassir was born and where he most probably collected his materials.

b) The Chapter "of the sayings that they did not know who said them or their names"

This final chapter presents us with a partially different panorama. This is substantially Christian: God, the soul, disdain for the world, salvation, death are its fundamental themes. It adds the habitual topics of goodness, suffering, knowledge, keeping silent, contempt for wealth and greed, envy and wrath.

Now, my investigations into Christian gnomological literature (maxims included in Maximus Confessor, Antonius Melissa, anthologies of Basil and the two Gregorys, Macarius, Evagrius, etc.) bore no fruit when I tried to find a model. There are, of course, themes that coincide, but the details vary. If we look back now, we can see that the Christian message connects with that of the Greek moralistic tradition. Here are just a few examples:

8: behave with men as you do with fire, do not get too close or too far. Cf. Diogenes 357 *SR*.
18: death is the same, in a foreign land or at home. A Cynic theme.
20: what is the tastiest thing? – what a man covets. Cf. Socrates in *BP*, p. 81. 14, from Sappho, I think.
22: the root of love is being like your friends. Cf. Pl. 14, D. 4 in *BO* = 416 *SR*.
40: love is the sickness of the soul. A well-known theme.
41: the theme of the king and the wise man. We have followed this from the Orient to the Middle Ages.
45: woman like a deaf viper. This recalls similar Cynic themes.
56: the bad food taken to the other world. Cf. above Engenius 64 and Thesileus 2, also Loginem 74.
86, 87: the Socratic "I do not know".
94: let your intellect defeat your will. Cf. S. 32 *PQ*.
98: what does the wise man obtain? Cf. Diogenes 362, 363 SR, but Christianized.
156: know yourself. A Delphic and Socratic theme.

There are also maxims that we could call of a "practical" type, such as 30 (the "fine friend" who has "sweet words and bitter acts"), 46 (do not reveal your enmity to your enemy). But the Christian theme predominates within a loose organization, having recurrent and sometimes mixed units of structure and content.

The structural units we have already seen. The affirmative maxim is most frequent, mixed with the exclamatory and imperative maxim (9 "be with the sages", 104 "do not fight to win …"). Both types can generate series of "commandments", as in 58 "five things are good to have" and 22 "do not speak unless…". And there is the question or the order addressed to another person and his reply, for example 14 and following, 69 and following: "and they said to another" … "and he said". There is also the type "what is the most … thing?" (20). There is a series of comparisons "like …" and "just as …" in 109 ff.

As for the units of content, I have already mentioned their changeable, mixed character. Even so, some themes are especially clear, such as the themes of wisdom, sages and wise men, and fools, combined with a Christian vision, which is the essential theme, for example in 31–38, 78–88, 116 ff. (going on to the themes of greed and of God). In 105 ff. the theme of God and the fear of God predominates, but mixed with that of wisdom. In 202 ff. the theme of God and that of disdain for the world are combined. In 168 ff. there is a series on the theme of man. Other series are shorter, sometimes of only two maxims: the theme of the son (16–17), of the bad king and the just king (154–155). But the themes recur and there are brusque changes.

All this Christian philosophy combines an intellectual moralism with the theme of love of God and one's neighbor, cf. for example, 32 "if you cannot be loved, be one who loves". And there is the constant theme of love of God and disdain for the world, as well as the condemnation of vice and the cultivation of generosity and sacrifice. But also recommended are practical behavior and adapting oneself to the world in what is inevitable. The themes of poverty and simplicity in life also appear, but not the most harshly Cynic ones, with exceptions.

This is the culmination of the synthesis of ancient and Christian philosophy of which we have been speaking. Distant now from any adhesion to the great names and from an excessive rigor, it constitutes a fitting conclusion to *Bocados de Oro*. It is a Christian closing, but not far removed from ancient thought nor, I believe, is it incompatible with the illustrated Muslims, who adopted it, as the Medieval Christians did later.

5. *Conclusion*

It is quite clear that Mubassir, a native of Damascus and physician of the Fatimid caliph Az-Zahir in the 11th century, had at his disposal the richest collections of late Greek gnomological literature. He organized it into approximately chronological form: first the Hermetic sages; then, filling in the gap rather inadequately, Homer, Solon, Zeno and Hippocrates; the central element follows (Pythagoras, Socrates, Plato, Aristotle, Alexander), an element which likewise forms the center of Buenos Proverbios; various supplementary sages are added, among them Ptolemy and Gregory, and the presence of Loginem or Lokman is especially noteworthy; then after Galen, two anthologies close the text: one of the sayings of many wise men whose names we are given, the other anonymous and principally Christian.

We have, therefore, a sort of late Greek gnomological *corpus*, although it cannot be denied that some authors that we know directly in Greek are missing. It is an important *corpus*, which adds greatly to our knowledge of this literature.

The sources that Mubassir used in the case of the most important ones (those of the Socratics and also Hippocrates) are related to those used by Hunayn in *Buenos Proverbios*, but they are not identical, nor are those of *PQ*. This is proof of the wealth of variants of this literature.

It is evident that they were separate, individual works that were gathered and organized either by a Byzantine compiler or by Mubassir himself. The presence of Lokman's work inclines me to this second hypothesis: it is from the Muslim period, but from a Christian background, very probably from Syria. The special interest for the Hermetics, the physicians and Hippocrates points to the same conclusion: they were the favorite authors of the Arabs, and Mubassir chose these instead of so many others whose gnomologies we know, more or less partially, in Greek. At times the various gnomologies permit us a glimpse of the organization of their models by themes or structural types.

Like Hunayn, Mubassir was concerned with giving the most complete account possible of Greek wisdom, and for this reason, not satisfied with the number of philosophers he had collected, he added the two final chapters. The first comes from a gnomology organized by authors, and within these, sometimes by themes; he selected the authors not included in the earlier chapters, with certain exceptions. The final chapter is an anonymous Christian gnomology.

It must be said, though, that the general characteristics of the maxims in his work are not very different from those of the other works; I have already said that the sources are undoubtedly related. Furthermore, this is the case of the confluence of Socratic-Platonic philosophy with Cynic and later Christian philosophy that evolved throughout the Hellenistic and Roman periods and that culminated in the first years of the Byzantine age, the age when in Syria, we believe, the gnomologies later translated by the Arabs obtained their definitive form. This kind of philosophy was often imposed on the gnomologies of all the authors, in a totally anti-historical manner.

Nevertheless, there are differences. There remains more that is authentic in the gnomologies of Socrates, Plato and Diogenes. In others, the Cynic element is more or less important, in still others the Christian element. The Muslim element, as I have said, does not exist, but the Christian element consists of general themes on God, "this world" and moral themes that the Muslims could often accept; there are no dogmatic themes or mentions of Christ, the Virgin or the saints.

After Hunayn, who rather arbitrarily enlarged an earlier, well-organized book, Mubassir merely added gnomological anthologies and gnomologies of gnomologies. He attempted a chronological and rational organization, not very successfully it must be said. But he composed a kind of *corpus* (sometimes making double use of the earlier works, at other times not) of the sapiential philosophy that we have been studying. His work had a much greater impact in the West than did Hunayn's work; only *Poridad* came close in its circulation.

From the general point of view of the relation of the gnomologies collected in these works and the multitude of gnomologies, of quite varied types, that we know or assume existed in the Greco-Roman and Byzantine world, several observations must be made.

First, we now have only a part of the Greek gnomological material, furthermore in a very repetitive form, in spite of the variants. Many philosophers or Greek writers, authors of *gnômai* (collected by themselves or by others), to whom we have referred in Chapters II and IV above all, are not discussed here or are barely mentioned. And Socrates, Plato, Aristotle and Diogenes, who occupy the principal place, are included only partially. And in the case of still other authors, almost the only maxims attributed to them are the moralistic and Christian ones, and nothing or almost nothing of their own.

This is a process of reduction and Christianization that probably began in Syriac Antiquity; we have mentioned various Syriac gnomologies of this type. Later these collections proliferated in the Arab world: those that have reached us are only some of the ones that existed. But all of them (with a few exceptions, such as Ibn Durayd's) are of approximately the same type.

The Greek gnomologies are, then, at the foundation of all this, as are the letters, novels, "mirrors for princes", *Lives*, speeches of consolation. But we have a reduction and an amplification at the same time. The general panorama is very different. The understanding of what is Greek, even in the popular and reduced form that we are discussing, had greatly diminished. Greek wisdom had tended to be reduced to a moralistic and Christian *corpus* (but with only certain Christian themes that proved acceptable to the Arabs).

And the sense of a well-organized structure of the story and the novel had been lost, to say nothing of the ideas. Well-designed narrative schemes like that of the nucleus of *Buenos Proverbios* were smothered with additions. The principle of accumulation prevailed. It was probably already present to a certain extent in late Greek literature as well as in the gnomologies, but the tendency continued to grow.

Nevertheless, late Greek literature was composed of well-organized works, for example the above-mentioned nucleus of *Buenos Proverbios* and, as we shall see, *Poridad de Poridades* and *Donzella Teodor*, works constructed with the elements we are familiar with, such as epistolary novels, "mirrors for princes", novelized histories, etc. To be sure, they gradually admitted additions like those we have pointed out and others in the last works mentioned, additions from the Greek and the Syriac periods. Thus by the time of the Arab period the way was open for the combination and massive addition of elements.

But the total, the basic materials, continue to preserve very important traces of a literary and ideological evolution that originates in the classical Greek age and that only culminates in the early Byzantine period. The Arabs did nothing more than combine these elements with each other, and the Castilian translators did the same, although not very decisively: what they added or changed is very little. In short, what has reached us, through one group or another, is Greek sapiential literature of different orientations, Christianized in the end. In Spain (and in Europe via Spain) it imposed its literary style and its ideology. Its influence was enormous.

Chapter 8

Poridad de las Poridades and *Historia de la Donzella Teodor*

I. *Poridad de las Poridades*

1. Overview

In Chapter I we gave a brief description of this work, translated by Ibn al-Batrik ("son of Patrick") in 9th century Bagdad, commissioned by the caliph, or Miramamolin al-Ma'mun. The translator, a slave liberated by the Miramamolin, was a Nestorian Christian who worked in Bagdad around 800 A.D. And the book was Greek (details are given in the manuscript) found in a temple of Homer the Greater (Hermes Trismegistus). We have already said that it consisted of an external prologue (the discovery of the book, supposedly written by Aristotle), an internal prologue (brief letters between Alexander and Aristotle) and a treatise in eight books on the king and his government: a treatise that takes the form of a letter from Aristotle to Alexander. It must be noted that the eighth book, a *Lapidarium* that only appears in certain manuscripts, is considered an addition.

We have, then, a prologue by the translator in which he introduces himself and recounts his discovery of the Greek book after searching for it at the behest of the Caliph Miramamolin: a well-worn theme, taken without doubt from the *Calila*[1], an internal prologue with a letter from Alexander to

1 There are other parallels in Hermetic literature, but it is not necessary to think of a pagan temple to the Sun in Harran as Manzalaoui does, "The pseudo-Aristotelian Kitāb Sirr al-āsrār", *Oriens* 23–24, 1974, pp. 147–247 (p. 218). This is a literary device. There are not very many Hermetic elements in the work aside from the title; also, it recalls the Socratic theme of "keeping silent". The Hermetic elements, as said, are few, cf. L. Kasten, "Poridat de las poridades. A Spanish Form of the Western Text of the Secretum Secretorum", *Romance Philology* 5, 1951–1952, pp. 180–190, a very interesting article for the origin and formation of the work.

Aristotle on government and Aristotle's reply, and, after its discovery, the great letter from Aristotle, which is really a treatise.

This whole work clearly includes various additions, which will be discussed below; but in itself, it constitutes a literary creation. This creation is basically a treatise on government (a "mirror for princes") in letter form, which has incorporated into the external prologue two short letters, from Alexander to Aristotle and from the latter to the former, that originally were independent: there are data in favor of this idea, as the letters appear separately in other places in Arabic literature[2].

Evidently, al-Batrik took an earlier treatise and, in the manner of Hunayn, added a prologue to it. This prologue shows us an Aristotle, old and ill, almost a saint, as we have seen in certain Byzantine, Syrian and Ethiopian traditions: God told him that he was closer to being called an angel than a man, and according to some, he went to heaven. It is possible that there might be a Hermetic influence in this[3], especially if one thinks of the discovery of the long letter from Aristotle (the treatise) in a Hermetic temple.

In any case, this initial introduction continues with the brief letters (from Alexander asking Aristotle for advice, from Aristotle to Alexander in reply). They were inserted by al-Batrik, or by his source, into the prologue, which culminates with the discovery of the book. Furthermore, they are Greek, for all the letters, the two brief initial ones and the extensive one that constitutes the body of the work, are derived from an epistolary novel translated from Greek into Syriac, which we have already mentioned and whose existence was noted by M. Grignaschi[4]. However, the epistolary form of the central treatise is merely a device, taken from the tradition of pseudo-epigraphic letters, to present a "mirror for princes", a type of literature that I have already discussed.

Moreover, in the letters included in *BP* we already have the theme of the kingdom, in a moralistic environment. Both works (whose coincidences we have already pointed out) are nothing other than derivations of the same literature, contaminated with other literary genres, to be sure. They are, as I have said, true "mirrors for princes", as the epistolary novel really was already. Aside from that, the novelistic frame is different: *BP* treats the theme of Plato-Aristotle-Nitaforius, *Poridad* the conquests of Alexander and his

2 See data in M. Manzalaoui, art. cit., pp. 147–247, especially p. 164.

3 See Manzalaoui, art. cit, p. 190.

4 In "Le roman épistolaire ..." and in "Les Rasa'il Aristatalisa ..." cited.

requests for advice from the old and sick Aristotle (a theme that also appears in *BP*).

It is quite clear that there is as tradition of adding a novelistic setting to a work, as, for example, in the *Life of Secundus*. Sometimes there was added a note on the discovery of the work, as in the *Calila* in its Arabic version and, much earlier (possibly in the 1st century A.D.), in the work of Dictys Cretensis on the Trojan War, which we have in its Latin version of the 4th century A.D., but whose original Greek version has left papyrological traces[5].

And it must be pointed out that the technique of converting a treatise on various themes into a letter sent from Aristotle to Alexander has, apart from what we know from our two works, other precedents: specifically, the *Rhetorica ad Alexandrum* attributed to Anaximenes and dated in the same 4th century B.C. This is a treatise on rhetoric, as *Poridad* is on political advice. And the initial letter is, without doubt, a late, secondary addition, in any case earlier than Atheneus, we are told[6].

These are, then, procedures that have been employed since the imperial Roman period. Making use of them, al-Batrik added the report of the discovery; as for the initial letters, we cannot determine when they were inserted before the central "mirror for princes". They come from the widespread flowering of the tradition of pseudo-epigraphic letters of which we have spoken and which is Hellenistic. In Plezia's edition[7] can be found what has been conserved of this tradition in Greek (save the pseudo-Callisthenes and the others).

But I consider exaggerated Manzalaoui's proposal[8] that what *Poridad* and the works of this type in general attempt to do is join in one treatise doctrines of the Pseudo-Aristotelian literature plus certain notes from Aristotle's *Nicomachean Ethics*. The coincidences cannot be denied, but this is a very general field. Neither Manzalaoui and the Arabists nor the scholars of Spanish literature realize that this general fund is the fund of moralist phi-

5 The theme of the discovery of ancient books, especially in temples, also has roots in the pseudo-Aristotelian and the Hermetic literature. And there is also, quite probably, an echo of the embassy sent to Byzantium by al-Mamun, after a dream in which Aristotle appeared to him, an embassy that precisely al-Batrik formed a part of. Cf. M. Manzalaoui, art. cit., p. 192.

6 See the edition of M. Fuhrmann, Leipzig, 1966, p. XXXIX.

7 M. Plezia, *Aristotelis privatorum scriptorum fragmenta*, Leipzig, Teubner, 1977.

8 Art. cit., p. 202.

losophy of Greek origin and its fusion with Christian philosophy, sometimes in the gnomologies, sometimes in the "mirrors for princes", sometimes in works in which there are both, as there is no strict separation. And we have seen counsels on governing not only in *Buenos Proverbios* but also in the section on Plato in the *PQ* 44–46, in *Bocados* (Assaron, Enesius, Medargis) and other places in the works studied.

The starting point is, therefore, a Greek "mirror for princes" addressed to Alexander, although other elements, also Greek, have been added, some without doubt during the Arab period, just as happened in Hunayn's case, as we have seen. But fundamentally, all of this, even the accretions, is at bottom Greek.

This has sometimes been in doubt. M. Manzalaoui, without much personal conviction, presents certain attempts to date our work in a strictly Arabic period[9], and emphasizes the Indian and Persian elements. But he himself gives considerable attention to the Hellenistic and the Hellenized Persian environments, to the inclusion of Aristotelian and Pseudo-Aristotelian themes, to the influence of the Hellenistic and Byzantine treatises on tactics, and to the relation with Platonic and Aristotelian philosophy and various ancient "mirrors for princes"[10].

I consider the references to Persia and India scant and superficial, apart from the fact that they could easily fit into the Hellenistic-Roman or the Byzantine periods, or could even be additions from the 9th century. To deny al-Batrik's authorship is pure, unfounded speculation.

Of course, this system of additions, as I have said, was usual in late Roman as well as Byzantine, Syrian and Arab times, and also in Christian periods: we have seen this in the other works we have studied and also here, in the initial parts of our work. To begin with, we have already said that the Castilian text and the previous translations, the partial Latin translation by Johannes Hispalensis and al-Harizi's Hebrew translation, belong to a "western" recension which was enlarged (this is the current opinion) in the "eastern" version translated into Latin by Philip of Tripoli, and which is the version that had the greatest influence in Europe. The comparison of the two recensions allows us to see the additions in the oriental version, which come from its Arabic text[11].

9 See p. 193.

10 See art. cit., pp. 203 ff.

11 See L. Kasten, "Poridat de las poridades", cit. p. 185.

But it is not a matter of this alone. The *lapidarium* in Chapter VIII, with a completely different theme and without the exclamation *"Oh Alexandre"*, which is missing, furthermore, in various manuscripts, is without any doubt an addition. And other parts, from different periods, can also be additions that are actually independent[12]: in Chapter VII, the part on *"las fechuras de los omnes"* (of the acts of men) (ed. Kasten, pp. 62 ff.), which is a physiognomy like those that are found in Greek from the time of Polemon and were later continued by the Arabs; the part on el *"ordenamiento bueno en pensar del cuerpo"* (the correct order to consider the body) (ed. Kasten, pp. 66 ff.), which includes meals and a way of life and is of the Hippocratic line. Other parts (ed. Kasten, pp. 41 f.) have a relation to Ptolemy (*Tetr.* I 2–3), a defense of astronomy; and see, also in Kasten, p. 61, an astrological addition from several manuscripts.

It is clear that this is not the appropriate place to deal with the possible dates of the various interpolations, but I cannot avoid mentioning some of them. Noteworthy are the coincidences that have been pointed out between passages like Kasten p. 44 (the first thing that God made: the intellect, and from that the soul, etc.) and 49 (the nature of man compared with that of the various animals): all this coincides with passages from *Rasail* by Ihwan al-safa (10th century), a work that figures much more frequently in the oriental version. The first passage, clearly Neo-Platonic, has been attributed to the brotherhood of the "brothers of purity". All of this is, for the moment, uncertain; in any case it is of Greek origin; the problem is the date of insertion.

We have the same problem with the brief passages offered by the *"enxiemplos"* (apologues), the short novels and the like: the woman-viper sent by the king of India (p. 41), the simile of the world as a garden, seen above (p. 43), the two *"enxiemplos"* on the immutability of nature (p. 45), the curious advice to mistrust blond men (p. 49: because of the Gothic mercenaries in Byzantium?), the various allusions to India and Persia (for example, p. 57).

It is difficult to determine the route of entry and the date of the additions of the doctrines that find more or less close parallels in Antiquity and that, as we know, can come from the original sources or, more frequently, from the gnomological tradition. Manzaloui speaks of the theory of justice in Plato's *Republic*, and the first books of Aristotle, *EN*, as well as of diverse

12 See M. Manzalaoui, art. cit. pp. 221 ff.

Pseudo-Aristotelian works, of the doctrines of the Greek, Roman and Byzantine tacticians, and of the Hermetic elements (rare). All this had already coalesced in *Buenos Proverbios* and earlier, as we have said, and this takes us to the early Byzantine and Syriac period that we are now familiar with.

A central nucleus that comes from the Byzantine gnomologies appears as the theme of the advice given to the prince or the king, as in *Buenos Proverbios* and in its precedents. To this has been added everything that in one way or another has a relation to the theme of the kingdom, and also those other more marginal additions, whose date of entry is uncertain but which, in any case, had already been translated by al-Batrik.

Manzalaoui[13] tells us little about these gnomologies, the Greek and the Christian ones, in spite of the fact that they are clearly dominant, and even at first sight *Poridad* is within the tradition familiar to us. In summary, the body of the work is not unworthy of the literary and philosophical environment that we recognize as the base of *BP* and *BO*. There can be no grounds for taking this work out of the of late Greco-Christian Antiquity. The date of insertion of some parts that count as additions can be uncertain, but not the homogeneous character of the whole.

Poridad is defined by al-Batrik as *"el libro de manera de hordenar el regno"* (the book on the way to organize the kingdom). It is a book on government, a "mirror for princes", then, within a familiar tradition. We have indicated the points in common with *Buenos Proverbios*, but this work is fundamentally an ascetic book, dealing with the themes of the fall of the great and of death. In spite of having different purposes, the two have common roots and elements.

And *Poridad* includes, to a greater extent than *Buenos Proverbios*, the element of advice to the king in matters of government that we could call practical. We will return to these, but first we will look at the maxims, which always fall within the Greco-Christian (and Syriac) spirituality of the early Byzantine period, the culmination, in its ideas and in its combination of genres, of the oldest Greek spirituality. There is a new organization of old materials, later reworked in Syrian or Muslim times, with the addition of other materials of the same origin.

13 On p. 190 he speaks of Hellenistic gnomological elements that were included.

2. Poridad *and the Greco-Christian gnomologies*

The theme of the dependence of *Poridad* on these gnomologies is, as I say, barely recorded, and nevertheless, it is essential. All of the gnomological wisdom that we know is set forth in this work, sometimes in general terms, sometimes as maxims addressed to the king: to Alexander, naturally, but through him, to kings in general. Note that the exclamation *"Oh Alexandre"* comes, of course, from the epistolographic literature that we know but, through it, in the final analysis, from the style of the ancient maxims addressed by the sage or philosopher to the king or the person being instructed. We have already discussed this theme, which comes from the ancient Orient, from *Ahikar*, from *Ptah-Hotep* and from some of the treatises we have referred to; and in Greece from Hesiod, Theognis, Isocrates and the others.

The doctrine, naturally, is characteristic of the times, though it does preserve, as usual, traces of earlier stages. Something must be said about this doctrine, comparing it with that of *BP*, *BO* and *PQ*, and also with the gnomologies and "mirrors for princes" that we have seen.

This is, however, a difficult task, as we do not have a data base that includes the maxims that have been preserved in Greek and those that have reached us by way of translations; if we had one, we could surely advance greatly in the search for precise models. Neither does there exist a systematic study of the "mirrors for princes"[14].

Still, anyone who has read the preceding chapters of this book and has a look at *Poridad*, however brief, will find very great coincidences in the theme of the king. In Chapter III we point out some notable coincidences with *BP* and/or *BO*: the necessary renown of the king, giving in proportion to merits, the world as a garden, the maxims against wine and fornication, not reigning over slaves, etc. But all this can be seen better if we simply give a general idea of the maxims in *Poridad.*

14 A good orientation can be found in the cited article by P. Hadot, "Fürstenspiegel", in the *Reallexikon für Antike und Christentum*, vol. VIII, Stuttgart, 1972, cols. 555–632. But it is unfortunate that the tradition should be so fragmentary and that there should have been lost so many texts Περὶ βασιλείας or of similar theme: from Aristotle, Antisthenes, Zeno, Sphaerus, Perseus, etc.; or that only extracts should be preserved, as in the case of Diotogenes, Ecphantus, etc. To be sure, we have abundant documentation, but no one has systematized the content of these works.

From the very beginning we have the themes of fear of God, of the love of justice and truth, of clemency. Other virtues of the king are frankness and moderation, giving to who has need, the intellect that entails setting the soul to rights and the disdain for sorrow, reigning according to the law, avoiding greed, making the kingdom obey the law and taking away "wrath", being master of his own will, maintaining silence. Moreover, the king must want only the wealth that cannot be lost, and must avoid vice and fornication. He must be calm and modest, and must obtain the obedience of his subjects with the aid of the law, affection, hope and also fear. Thus he will earn the love of men and their obedience and will please God. He must guard his soul, which is noble and heavenly, and search for the kingdom that must never be lost.

Other maxims refer to the attention that the king must devote to his favorites and agents, to asking their advice, and also to the way he dresses. We will return to this.

It is not necessary to point out that all of this is, in essence, Socratic, moralistic and Christian. Also Cynic, but, as occurs in the gnomologies that we have seen, what is fundamentally Cynic has been expurgated: its concept of power has evolved since Diogenes[15]. The Christian aspect is always within the limits that we have indicated.

There are, of course, additions to which I have alluded, plus others such as those relating to military tactics, which we will come back to, plus the definition of man (ed. Kasten, p. 49), who is *"de la mas alta natura que todas las cosas biuas del mundo, et que no a manera propia en ninguna creatura de quantas Dios fizo"* (of the highest nature of all living things in the world, and there is no similar manner in any creature of all those that God made): comparison with the deer, the leopard, the cock, etc., etc.

In any case, it would be useful for the reader to review what we have said about the themes of the king with regard to various passages of *Buenos Proverbios* and *Bocados de Oro*: themes that either coincide with or are close to those of *Poridad*.

For example, in *BP* the theme of the king appears over and over in the initial letters from Aristotle to Alexander (ed. Sturm, pp. 93 ff.): he should rule over his peoples treating them well and favoring them and so he will obtain their love; he should eliminate their wrath, grant them pardon and

15 See my *Filosofía cínica en las fábulas esópicas*, Buenos Aires, Centro de Estudios Filosóficos, 1986.

mercy, and earn renown with his good actions. And the same is true in the maxims that he addresses to Alexander (pp. 58 ff.): keeping silent, justice, meekness, moderation, fear of God, wisdom, having good sense are all required of him. In Plato's maxims the theme of the king appears once again (p. 85): in bad times do not allow the power of the children to grow, he should improve the kingdom of the father and have intelligence, a soul, education, hope; he must pardon cowards and mistrust this world.

In the section of *PQ* on counsels to the king referred to above, we have the same ideas: virtue, goodness, education, wisdom, control of his desires, benevolence toward his subjects. And there is the same situation in different passages of *Bocados*. For example, in the maxims of Diogenes (ed. Crombach, pp. 39 ff.): the themes of frankness, good, that the king can earn God's reward. And in the passage of Alexander's maxims (ibid., pp. 133 ff.): the king must think night and day about the good of his subjects, not consider as a day of his reign the day on which he has done nothing, not be a king of slaves, earn the love of men by doing good, make friends and do good to his enemies, pardon mistakes and rule with justice.

And there are those of Assaron, Enesius and Medargis (pp. 143 ff.), real gnomologies on royalty, whose main precepts I have pointed out (justice, avoiding wine and women, receiving counsel, goodness, intelligence, setting the people and his soul to rights, not being a slave of his own will). In the maxims of Loginem (pp. 146 ff.) too we have seen a similar passage on royalty.

This, and none other, is the central line of *Poridad*, although there can be allusions to Hermes or to the Persians or the Indians or astrology or a physiognomy, or passages related to the tacticians; I mentioned these before and will return to them. And it must be said that along general lines, there is a correspondence with the doctrine of the "mirrors for princes" that we have seen from Plato and Isocrates (and earlier) on.

3. Poridad *and the "mirrors for princes"*

To make a few brief comments, Alexander was the model on which from the time of the Pseudo-Callisthenes and later in Plutarch and other bibliography[16] the image of the good king centered; later, in Trajan (see Pliny's panegyric and Dion Chrysostom's orations περὶ βασιλείας "On Royalty") and in other "Princes". The Christian writers that we have mentioned sometimes give the general figure of the Christian prince, sometimes they apply it to a specific person: Synesius to Arcadius, Agapetus to Justinian. This theme of the good king, of the Christian prince gave rise to an enormous bibliography in the Middle Ages of the Orient and the West (in Spain from the time of Martin of Braga and Isidore of Seville); in the epoch of Humanism Saavedra Fajardo and Quevedo are the best-known representatives. And equally representative is the counter-image created by Machiavelli in *The Prince.*

From the time of the pharaohs and Homer to Alexander there is an idea that joins royalty to divinity and justice, and this line, passing through Stoics, Cynics, and Hermetics, by that time Christianized, reaches the conception of monarchy held by the *ancien regime.* There is no question of looking into this here, but we must give certain information on the coincidence of the "mirrors" that we know of with some of the most outstanding points of the ideology of our treatises: *Buenos Proverbios* and *Poridad*, but also *Bocados de Oro* and *Philosophical Quartet.*

I describe the general lines; it is impossible to give an erudite treatment, which would really be that study of the "mirrors for princes" that we are lacking. As early as Isocrates the virtues of the king are love of men and love of the city; for Plato, the ascendancy of the *logos* in his soul, which leads to the supreme wisdom and knowledge of God, when he sacrifices himself for the common good and the happiness of his subjects, renouncing the life of pure knowledge. And Xenophon's Cyrus is characterized by his αἰδώς or respect, his humanity, his capacity for helping, his liberality, his moderation: virtues more practical than Plato's intellectual ones. I will not mention the ideal image of Alexander as I have already discussed it above.

What we know from the treatises of Zeno and other Stoics about the virtues of the ideal king concerns his piety before the deity, his justice, his respect for the law, his benevolence and mercy: here too can be noted a

16 For a general idea see my work "Las imágenes de Alejandro", in J. Álvarez and S. M. Blázquez (eds.), *Alejandro Magno. Hombre y Mito*, Madrid, Editorial Actas, 2000, pp. 15–31. And remember what was said in Chapter III.

lesser insistence on the intellectual virtues, which in our gnomologies we have shown to derive, fundamentally, from Socrates and Plato.

Then, in the *Letter of Aristeas*, which comes from the Judeo-Christian environment of Hellenistic Alexandria, there appears, together with the themes of justice, piety, truth, moderation, etc., the theme of fear of God, which the Christians will adopt. And the Pythagoreans (we have fragments from Diotogenes, Sthenidas and Ecphantus in Stobaeus) will advocate a close relation between the king and divinity.

For Diotogenes the king's grace and his virtues come from God. "Of the things that exist in nature, the most excellent is God and of the things of the earth and men, the king." For this reason, he is not dependent on his subjects, he is a "living law", he possesses wisdom. He controls his passions, he is just, obedient to the law, understanding, wise. We seem to be hearing the doctrine of the divine origin of the power of kings and of their virtues. Later this will be heard clearly in Agapetus; our gnomologies do not go so far as that.

But the idea of the king in Seneca, *De clementia*, is not far off: chosen by the gods, the king is the soul of the state and should behave toward his subjects as he would want God to behave toward him. Musonius, on the contrary, centers on comparing the king with the philosopher, as Plato did earlier: only the king knows how to control himself, not fear death or pain, represent the law (common themes in our gnomologies, which add, as I say, a more intellectual element).

The themes of the relation with God are important, again, in Dion Chrysostom's four orations addressed to Trajan. This is a new Cynicism, different in part from that of Diogenes. But there is coincidence in the general themes: the king must be temperate, valiant, just, humane, obedient to the law, unlike the tyrant. All of this linked at times to passages from Homer, at times to the idealized image of Philip and Alexander.

The theme of the fear of God is relevant in Marcus Aurelius and in the rhetor Menander. And in Themistius: the king is a divine force, he must imitate the love of men characteristic of divinity. We could continue with Procopius and the Greek and Latin panegyrists, the most famous being Pliny the Younger; Pliny describes the virtues of Trajan, who respects the laws and loves his subjects.

If we go on to the Christians, in Synesius we find the themes of piety, temperance, *phronesis*, the bravery of the warrior, a peace-loving nature. In the king the rational part of the soul prevails, platonically, over the hydra of the passions. He is not God, but appears as a sacred vision "in the sea with no waves of mercy". In Socratic terms, he is king of himself. The "strength of his soul", the cult of his friends are emphasized. He is, in short, "a common good" who restores the ancient virtues. He must attempt to return his kingdom to the golden age.

In the Christian writers the Gospels have already exerted an influence, with their idea of the kingdom of God or of the heavens, which sometimes finds an echo in our treatises. In Eusebius, the emperor, who carries within himself the image of God, imitates him in the administration of human matters.

And in Agapetus, whom we mentioned earlier, all this reaches its culmination: his was a collection of maxims that had an extraordinary diffusion. The king receives the ray of divine inspiration and so learns to make judgments on everything. In his physical faculties he is just like any other man, but because of his dignity, he is similar to God. This is a development of the Platonic ὁμοίωσις θεῷ (being similar to God), as there is an echo of the Platonic king-philosopher and of the Socratic "know thyself". His *nous* or spirit is "of many eyes", it is all-seeing. He possesses all virtues: a φρόνημα ἴσον "balanced mind", εὐσεβὴς λογισμός "pious thoughts", control of his passions, beneficence, love of his people, ruling "over those who consent to be ruled", giving, compassion or ἔλεος. And he is the "slave of God", he disdains the things of this world and yearns for those that last forever and ever. But above all: it is God who "has entrusted him with reigning over the whole world", "from God he has received his scepter and his royalty".

At the end of the maxims he is exhorted, in the Platonic manner, to climb the stairway of beauty, "to enjoy the heavenly kingdom". May Christ grant this to him and to his wife.

I believe that this abbreviated history of the ideal image of the king up to the Byzantine 6th century is of interest. We already know the points of contact with what appears in our treatises, the importance of reason and wisdom, and also the differences. This leads us to the religious motifs and to those regarding the king's relation to his subjects, partly a matter of affection, partly of expediency. But there is much less emphasis on the quasi-divine nature of the king, a characteristic of the Jewish, the Stoics, the Hermetics and the Christians. What is highlighted of Christian doctrine is, rather, the remembrance of death, the fear of God, the hope of another life. This is what I have called the Socratic-Cynic line with a certain Christian ingredient.

4. Poridad *and the practical needs of the kingdom*

Not everything in *Poridad* or in the other treatises is moral and religious idealization with regard to the king. That same ideal conduct in certain passages is considered a necessity to avoid rebellions and discontent, not to mention a situation of intolerable poverty. Furthermore, the king must rely on aspects that we might call external. He must have "renown". He must be distinguishable by his dress. He must maintain special relations with his ministers and functionaries: invite them to dinner, ask for their advice. And he must know how to wage war when it is necessary.

This is not a matter, then, of an ideal king in the manner of the Stoic or Cynic sage or the philosopher or the Christian saint. Actually, in the image of the king there are elements taken from all of these backgrounds and others taken from the reality of the circumstances. Therefore, certain extremisms are denied to him, as we have seen. The counsels given to the king are not exactly the same as those given to the private person who is simply searching for perfection. In spite of all this, in the king we still find much of the Hellenistic, Roman or Byzantine monarch.

All this goes back to the fact that the starting point is, precisely, Alexander. In certain literature he became a philosopher and even a saint, but it was not possible to erase his human character completely. In *Buenos Proverbios* the triumphs and military aptitudes of Alexander were only the beginning; they were summarily dealt with, taken for granted, much more than in the Pseudo-Callisthenes. In this way the "mirror for princes" developed, a genre whose mixed character, we might say, is between the king who must reign in the real world and the ideal king. For example, Synesius adds to his theory of royalty matters relating to the embassies, the soldiers, not overwhelming the people with taxes, the functionaries sent abroad. This mixed character is maintained in *Buenos Proverbios* and *Poridad*, as we have seen in our analyses. In the other texts that we have discussed this is sometimes the case and sometimes not. And, really, we need a more precise study of the relation of *Poridad* to this part of the message of *Buenos Proverbios*.

It was, then, necessary to take information from sources outside the purely moralistic tradition: from reality, from the historians and from diverse bibliographic funds, the physiognomies, for example. Even a *lapidarium* was included! And other themes that we have pointed out were added. The oriental recension went much farther with these additions.

But let us begin by giving an idea of this other type of material in *Poridad*. When, after the prologue and the initial letters the "mirror for princes", strictly speaking, begins, it is basically the treatises or beginning chapters, I to III, that set forth all of the gnomological wisdom that we have been discussing. But they present it mixed with themes referring to the practical administration of the kingdom, at times combined with moral themes: this is the same as occurs in *Buenos Proverbios* and in the maxims on government inserted in *Bocados de Oro*, especially the chapters on Aristotle and Alexander. Sometimes there is complete concordance in the doctrine imparted.

In the first chapter, for example, after referring to moderation and freedom of speech, which are recommended to the king, there comes the familiar theme of the king's obligation to give "to who has need of it" and the whole theme of "giving", followed by the philosophical theme of the "intellect" and the Christian theme of the fear of God and God's justice.

The second chapter commences with the theme of the law and of cruelty, but it quickly goes on to that of the king's dressing very well, of his appearance at celebrations, that he should not charge toll and thus "his revenues will increase". But we immediately return to the Christian theme of seeking the wealth that never ends and the kingdom that can never be lost, and the theme of avoiding fornication. And then to return to the practical theme of recommending to the king that once a year or more his favorites and the rich men eat with him! It goes on with the sedateness that the king should have and with the obedience of all men. And back to the practical: the king should give without being asked; this will make his reign last and will make men love him. Moral and practical at the same time is the following: the king should not take oaths, he should keep his word.

The third chapter is on justice and on the world as a garden. Then, in the fourth chapter come the themes that we have encountered among the "additions": the order of the things that God made, the *"enxiemplos"*, the election of the *"alguaciles"* (governors), the qualities that they should have, man compared to the animals, the scribes, the revenue collectors. It seems that, after a philosophical interval on wisdom, the soul and nature, we arrive at the practical theme of the election of the components of the court (but moral ingredients are not lacking). Then follow the fifth chapter (the envoys), the sixth (the good knights), the seventh (battles and armies, the knights who go to battle, the "deeds of the men", the "think of your body"). After a royal court and military component there is a return to various additions of a more or less philosophical type.

Although this would require a more detailed study, a study in its own right, the impression given is that the chapters that are traditional, between moralistic and "mirrors for princes", are followed by others that are concerned strictly with the regime of the court and the kingdom, with the intercalation in the gaps of others that depend, when all is said, on the ancient Neo-Platonic, physiognomic and Hippocratic philosophy.

No study has been made of all this, but let us at least give our attention for a moment to a source that should be taken into account: that of the writers (Greeks of various periods and Romans) on military tactics. M. Manzalaoui, in his repeatedly cited article[17], has touched on this theme. He suggests that Onasandrus (1st century A.D.) is the first of the Greek tacticians to have points in common with our works[18].

And in effect, looking through Onasander, we find as the first theme the election of the generals and their characteristics[19]. There is a clear point of contact with *Poridad*, ed. Kasten p. 47, where the election of the *"alguaciles"* or governors is discussed. In passages like these physical and practical considerations (being well built, wearing clothing of quality) are joined to moral matters: loving the king and obeying him, possessing understanding, "knowing how to speak", not being a *"beuedor ni fornaguero"* (a drunkard or a fornicator), loving justice, etc. There is evident coincidence.

There can also be coincidence, more or less precise, in the practical counsels on war: knowing astrology, frightening the enemy with the trumpeting of the elephants (*Poridad* recommends the camels of Bactria). In short, the Greek, Latin and Byzantine military treatises should be studied to find exact parallels, if possible.

To summarize, a "mirror for princes" became a letter from Aristotle to Alexander, it acquired a prologue amplified by two short letters and later added elements characteristic of a treatise on military tactics (and other elements on the conduct of the kings in their court), as well as elements

17 Pp. 203 ff.

18 Edited together with Aeneas Tacticus and Asclepiodotus by W. A. Oldfather, Cambridge, Mass., Harvard University Press, 1923.

19 Ed. cit., pp. 375 ff, 386 ff.

dealing with various philosophies and sciences, thus producing a mixed composition.

Perhaps al-Batrik added other supplements taken from Arabic sources (which in turn came from Greek sources); certainly the oriental version of *Poridad* acquired some. Others entered the Castilian translation of the western version or some of its manuscripts. A detailed study of this tradition and its relation to the translations of Johannes Hispalensis and al-Harizi needs to be done.

But we are still in the same environment of late Greek literature, derived from earlier Greek literature and later translated into Syriac, Arabic and Castilian; in short, a derivation of Greek sapiential literature: gnomologies, "mirrors for princes", diverse treatises synthesized in successive phases not always easy to identify. This is a sapiential literature whose fundamental phases, Greek and Christian moralistic, we know. At times these sources were the same as for *Buenos Proverbios*, at times they were simply related sources.

II. *Historia de la Donzella Teodor*

1. *Overview*

In Chapter I we gave a general idea of the work and of its organization and contents. Here we will simply add certain things. We must remember that there is only one indication of the existence of a Greek original: the version in the *Fihrist*. But as the theme in general is ancient oriental and was developed especially in Greek, there seems to be no doubt that the translation into Arabic comes from Greek (there are no traces of a Persian original, which would be the alternative). More exactly, it comes from our now familiar Greco-Christian tradition.

But the theme has been transposed to the Arab world: it was placed in the time of Harum al-Rashid and was reworked in the period of the Egyptian Fatimids, when it was incorporated into *The Thousand and One Nights* and into a later work. *La Donzella Teodor* acquired many Muslim elements, more than did the other works we have studied; and it acquired new Christian elements in the Castilian versions: again many more than the other works studied here. It mentions (and this is new) the Virgin Mary and Jesus Christ.

The Muslim and Christian elements have been studied on many occasions, either in relation to the Castilian versions or to the version in *The Thousand and One Nights*. About the early Greek origins little has been said, although the parallels with the *Life of Secundus* and the *Altercatio Hadriani et Epicteti* have been noted[20].

We have already pointed out the setting within a short novel of the questions put to Teodor by the sages and her replies, which give her the victory. This story of the woman who defeats the wise men offers a number of comparisons:

1. In general terms it derives from the person of lower status or age who triumphs over the powerful: Ahikar over the kings, Solon over Croesus, the Cynics over Alexander, Antigonus, etc., the Gymnosophists over Alexander, Aesop over the philosophers who are friends of his master, Secundus, Epictetus and the Hebrew sages over Hadrian, the wise men over Amasis, the sage Nagasena over King Milinda, Albinus over Pippin, cf. the *Enfant Sage* of the Provençal tale, etc.[21] It is the setting for a dialogue of questions and replies.

20 Among others see: M. Menéndez y Pelayo, "La *Donzella Teodor* (un cuento de *Las Mil y Una Noches*, un libro de cordel y una comedia de Lope de Vega", in *Homenaje a D. Francisco Codera en su jubilación del profesorado*, Zaragoza, Mariano Escar, Zaragoza, 1904, pp. 483–511; C. Gerresch, "Un récit des Mille et Une Nuits: Twadduh, Petite Encyclopédie de l'Islam medieval", *Bulletin de l'Institut Français de l'Afrique Noire* 25, series B, 1, 1973, pp. 57–175; A. Miquel, "Twadduh la servante", *Sept contes des Mille et une Nuits ou Il n'y a pas de contes innocents*, Paris, Sindbad, 1981, pp. 13–49; B. Darbord, "La tradición del saber en la *Donzella Teodor*" in *Actas del V Congreso de la Asociación Hispánica de Literatura Medieval*, Granada, Universidad, 1995, pp. 13–30. The relation and contamination of the two ancient works mentioned had already been intuited by the first editor of these treatises, H. Knust, *Mitteilungen aus dem Eskurial*, Tübingen, 1879, pp. 602–630. The secondary inclusion of maxims from the *Altercatio Hadriani Augusti et Epicteti Philosophi* in the Toledo edition is accepted as are others from the Zaragoza edition of *Secundus* (see Darbord, p. 28); and of maxims from the "enfant sage" tradition, see W. Suchier, *L'enfant sage*, Dresden, 1910, but the *Altercatio* of Hadrian and the child Epitus is derived from the *Altercatio* of Hadrian and Epictetus. But never, to the best of my knowledge, has a Greek origin been proposed for our work, which is related through its literary genre to others of this type.

21 See more details in my works cited above "The Life of Aesop …", "Documentación suplementaria …" and "Generos helenísticos …". For medieval data see L. W. Daly and W. Suchier's edition of the *Altercatio Hadriani Augusti et Epicteti Philosophi* (Urbana,

2. The secondary character can be a slave: Diogenes, Aesop, and remember Homer in *Bocados*.
3. Or it can be a woman: the queen of Sheba before Solomon, Scheherazade in *The Thousand and One Nights*, Saint Catherine before the doctors, Tarsiana in the *Vita Apollonii*. Teodor is a slave and a woman[22].

We find here a fusion of several of these themes in the service of a dialogue consisting of questions and replies. This is a novelization not unlike, for example, that of the *Life of Secundus*, within a genre to which also belong the *Life of Aesop*, the dialogue of Alexander and the Gymnosophists, the *Altercatio* and other texts that we have mentioned. It was a genre created *ad hoc*, not found previously: it was created as a setting for the dialogue.

Moreover, I must emphasize that it is a Greek novelization of Greek origin; it must be compared with various others that also produced novels in *The Thousand and One Nights*[23]. And in the final analysis it depends on the "framed narratives" that we know of from Mesopotamian times, narratives that passed to India and to Greek and Jewish literature, and finally, by one channel or another, reached our medieval literature, where it proliferated. I have dealt with them in various places.

1939). On the contact between Byzantine and Arabic literature via Syria, my "Siria, cruce de caminos de la narrative bizantina y oriental", *Aula Orientalis* 3, 1981, pp. 17–29. The echo of all this in ancient Jewish literature can be found in my "Literatura sapiencial antigua en la Haggadah y en Pedro Alfonso", *Illinois Classical Studies* 18, 1993, pp. 229–236. See also, among others, the article "Fable" in the *Encyclopaedia Judaica*, vol. 6; F. Manns, "Une source de l'Aggadah juive: la literature grecque", *Liber Annuus* 29, 1979, pp. 111–144; Sh. Bat Moshe, "Fuentes judias. Leyendas del Talmud y del Midrash", Jerusalem, Organización Sionista Mundial. Departamento de Educación y Cultura Religiosas para la Diáspora, 1980, pp. 132–151. There is this same influence in medieval Spanish literature (Petrus Alphonsus , *Sendebar, Conde Lucanor*, etc.).

22 On other wise women in the Muslim and Christian tradition see B. Darbord's cited article, pp. 18–19. The author points out that in Arabic literature they are always foreigners, almost always Christians (like Teodor in our texts). As for the choice between the Arabic name Twadduh "delight" and the Greek name Teodor "gift of God", the authors I have mentioned prefer the first. It would not be strange that there might have been, inversely, a first Christianization of the theme, with the name Teodor, and then an Arabization, with Twadduh, a popular etymology.

23 See G. E. Von Grunebaum, *Medieval Islam*, Chicago, University of Chicago Press, 1947, chapter "Creative Borrowing: Greece in the Arabian Nights", pp. 294–319, where he develops the thesis of the Greek origin of many novelistic motifs in *The Thousand and One Nights* and other places. I believe that this thesis should be applied to the development of the short initial novels in our treatises.

The work was written, so to speak, at one sitting. It is well composed, with a growing interest: the tension increases gradually as the three sages come onto the scene, concluding with the final wager of leaving the third wise man naked if he is defeated, a situation solved with the contribution of ten thousand *"doblas"* (doubloons) of gold. And there are exciting moments when Teodor hesitates, out of modesty, to reply to the erotic questions, and especially, at the end, when she reacts to the arrogance of the last sage, Abraham the troubadour, a Jew, who proposes a wager: whoever loses should undress completely. And when, after the entreaties of the wise man, she consents to pardon him, again in exchange for ten thousand *"doblas"* of gold.

Independently of the ancient materials that it may contain, later mixed with others, which I will mention, it is clear that the work has a specific author, although, as usual, there remains the doubt about the date in which the various added elements were introduced. As for the rest, it is quite evident that it contains ancient elements: Socratic and Hippocratic elements, coincidences with Secundus, etc. I cite here one of them, the reply at the end of Title Seven on the condition of man, a reply that definitively defeats the third wise man: man is brave as a lion, frank as a cock, etc., which coincides almost exactly with the same theme in *Poridad*, as we have seen.

We are dealing, then, with a dialogue of wisdom set in a very traditional novelistic configuration, a work that is closed and complete, traditional as well, and Greek without any doubt. It can be compared with the nuclei of *Buenos Proverbios* and of *Poridad*, except that here we do not find any secondary added elements, as far as we know.

But we must return to the theme of the great differences existing between the versions that have reached us: in Chapter I we have indicated the main ones found between *The Thousand and One Nights* and the Madrid manuscript (the Gayangos manuscript in the Academy of History), closer to the Castilian versions. These, in turn, present differences: it is assumed that they come from a first version, from the end of the 13th century[24].

In the first place, there is the problem of the differences between *The Thousand and One Nights*, the Madrid Gayangos manuscript and the set of Castilian versions. In principle, the elements present in *The Thousand and One Nights* and missing in the later versions have been lost. Besides that, elements have been added (only in the Castilian versions or in these and in

24 See F. Gómez Redondo, op. cit., p. 484.

the cited manuscript), elements that seem to be recent, although the matter is not always so clear.

And if these "extra" elements are in the printed versions or in any one of them and not in the Castilian manuscripts, then it is certain that they are additions: in the Toledo manuscript edited by Mettmann there is a calendar from a *Repertorio de los tiempos*, by Andrés de Li (Zaragoza, 1492) and a long series of maxims taken from the *Altercatio*. Other cases are more doubtful.

There are five manuscripts from the 15th century that are quite defective. Mettmann first edits the printed version, which is more extensive, and which he calls B (Toledo, c. 1498), which derives from ms. *a*, from the Madrid National Library, the same as other later impressions. In two Appendices, 1 and 2, he offers the variants of these impressions. In Appendix 3 he edits the other four manuscripts, *m* (from the University of Salamanca), *h* (from El Escorial) and *g*, *p* (from the Madrid National Library) and in Appendix 4 he edits the abovementioned manuscript *a*[25].

It is clear that the strict relation between the materials that appear in one or another of these manuscripts and editions has never been established exactly, nor has the age of all of them been studied in depth. I have said something about this above and a great deal can be obtained from the valuable Notes in Mettmann's book, pp. 160 ff. But there are still many problematic questions. Here I will make some contributions to the theme, but a detailed study must be left to future researchers.

I will start with the Toledo impression, the one followed by Mettmann, which is the most extensive text and which, as I said, in certain points has clearly been amplified. Apart from what has already been discussed, the sciences that the maiden claims to know on p. 109 are many more than those mentioned in *The Thousand and One Nights.*

It must be understood that what Mettmann edits is the printed text, based on the impression that he calls B (Toledo, c. 1498); apart from that, as appendices, he gives the texts of later impressions and of the much shorter manuscripts *m* and *a*. Comparing them with the *The Thousand and One Nights*, we can propose conclusions on the age of the passages that are missing in the manuscripts. But this is neither easy nor reliable. We will discuss this matter.

To summarize, the scheme is old, but variations on the wise men and the questions were introduced, to say nothing of those found in the enor-

25 See Mettmann, pp. 80 ff. for details of the edition.

mous number of editions that proliferated in Spain and that Mettmann includes. Our study is grounded on his edition, which is based principally, as I said, on the impression that he calls B, but separating, for the purposes of its study, what does not appear in the manuscripts.

2. *The sapiential elements in Donzella Teodor*

To begin with, the list of sciences that the maiden claims to know (p.109) is much more extensive, as I said, than the list in the *The Thousand and One Nights* and in mss. *m*, *g*, *p*, *h*: it must include additions. The passage on astronomy that follows, in the examination by the first sage, may contain old items, to judge from *The Thousand and One Nights*; and then there is a brief sapiential passage on prayer and alms that can also be old, but that has acquired Muslim and Christian alterations. Following that is a catalogue of the months, manifestly modern. But in it can be found old features: through whatever stages it might have gone, in the final analysis the affirmation that "in this month (August) the company of women is dangerous" comes from Alcaeus 347: it is the season in which men are weakest, women most lascivious.

The examination of the second wise man, the physician or doctor, does not hold great interest for us, but there are old themes in this passage. The theory of humors, also in *The Thousand and One Nights*, is obviously ancient, although it continued to be valid throughout the Middle Ages and even later. Then comes a passage where the question "what is the most …?" or ("what is …?") is posed, questions clearly characteristic of the ancient gnomologies. The themes are: "what is the healthiest fruit?", "what can you say about leeches?", "what is it that most makes a man grow old?", "what can you say about the bath?", questions on various meats and whether it is or is not better to sleep with a woman often. That is, questions on daily life, within the well-known line, and with replies that we sometimes know from other sources.

The healthiest fruits are pomegranates and quinces (pomegranates and lemons in *The Thousand and One Nights*); leeches and blood-letting represent a medical tradition that comes from Antiquity; what most causes one to grow old is "sleeping with women too much" (*"yacer con mugger vieja"* [lying with old women] in the mss.), according to Aristotle; Mettmann considers that it can come from *Historia Animalium* 581 b (but note that it appears also in *Bocados* as a reply by Aristotle himself). In any case, this is a theme from ancient medicine[26]; the praise of the bath and of beef is in *The Thousand and One Nights* and can be Muslim elements (pork is not mentioned, of course).

In short, we find ancient Greek elements and others that we cannot certify as being earlier than the Arab epoch.

There follows the erotic passage in which the maiden (after having refused to discuss the theme because she is a virgin, a stylistic effect sought by the author) speaks of the theme of when it is best "to sleep with a woman". She cites Aristotle (the citation cannot be found), who says, supposedly, that it is best to lie with a woman "garça" (with blue eyes) who has given birth or is nursing or is pregnant. All of this has to do with ancient theories (and from the Bible) on the maleficent effects of menstruation[27]. Our author once again takes up ancient medicine and follows this in turn with medieval medicine.

He then describes the way to excite women sexually. This does not appear to be old; it is found beginning with Avicenna and Bernard Gordonius and is greatly amplified in the Toledo impression. It does not seem that there are ancient sources here, especially because the theme is barely outlined in *The Thousand and One Nights*. Medieval medicine, derived, to be sure, from ancient medicine, seems to be the source.

Next come the two passages on the age of women and on the features that women must have to be beautiful. The first theme (qualities of women in the various ages) is missing in *The Thousand and One Nights* and in the Gayangos ms. The second is present, though not identical, in this ms. and in the Castilian ones; it probably comes from Antiquity, as it appears in more or less similar form in the *Altercatio*[28].

Add to this the questions of the mss.: in *m*, *h*, *g*, *p* on the commandments of God, a theme close to *The Thousand and One Nights*, cf. p. 79 (which adds the signs of the zodiac and the composition the human body).

26 This is in Rufus of Ephesus, Oribasius and Galen; later it is a common theme in Greek and Christian medicine. See M. Haro, "Erotismo y arte amatoria en el discurso médico de la *Historia de la Donzella Teodor*", *RLM* 5, 1993, pp. 113–125 (the theme that interests us here, pp. 117 ff.).

27 See M. Haro, art. cit., pp. 120 ff.

28 The theme circulated widely in medieval and later literature, see Mettmann, p. 164; also our Arcipreste, *Libro de Buen Amor*, 1606 ff.

In *a* (p. 156) there is emphasis on the theme of man's constitution, related to that of the four elements. This is without doubt of ancient origin.

In any case, the medical, dietetic, erotic and feminine themes of the first two parts of our work were marginal in sapiential literature. There is more interest from the point of view of this literature in Teodor's debate with the pretentious third wise man and the wager that the one who loses must take off all his clothing, leading to the burlesque denouement in which Teodor triumphs and, incidentally, wins a considerable amount of money.

Now here there is no lack of problems either. The following can be pointed out, using the order of the Toledo impression:

a) Questions from 1 to 14: 1–10 "what thing is the most ...?", 11–13 "what is the pleasure of ...?" (of a day, a week, a month), 14 the enigma of the grasshopper ("what is a bird that ...?").
b) Questions 15 to 57 ("what is ...?", "what is the thing that...?") come from the *Altercatio*, except 42; there are some duplications.
c) Also in this text, question 58, "what is man's condition?" coincides with *Poridad*, as we have seen; it might have been taken from there.

It is evident that the center of the work refers to questions 1 to 14, which appear, similar to a greater or lesser extent, in all the Arabic and Castilian texts. Mettmann, p. 165, has established the ones that, in his opinion, were the original questions in the Castilian translation, as well as the correspondences, which are quite close, in the Arabic texts. The Castilian ones would be:

1. The thing that is heavier than the mountains is debt.
2. The thing that is sharper than the sword is the tongue.
3. The thing that is faster than an arrow is sight.
4. The thing that is hotter than fire is the heart.
5. The thing that is sweeter than honey is a good son (a good daughter).
6. The thing that is bitterer than gall is a bad daughter.
7. A bad son is the tears of the eye.
8. The sickness that has no medicine is madness.
9. The thing that is harder than steel is truth.
10. The surest thing is the call of God.
11. To lie with a woman is the pleasure of one hour.
12. For sweethearts to lie together is the pleasure of a week.
13. For a man to return from a long journey is the pleasure of a month.

14. The animal to which the riddle refers, compared with various animals, is the grasshopper. This enigma, which, as I said, is also in *Poridad*, apparently comes from the *Apocalypse* of Saint John[29]. It is, therefore, one of the Christian elements in our work, as are certain maxims in the preceding list.

It should be remembered that the questions of the type "what is the most ...?" and "what is ...?", including the enigma, are traditional in the ancient gnomologies; we have encountered them repeatedly. They made possible the addition of maxims from the *Altercatio* that begin with "what is a man?", "what is a woman?", "what is sleep?". Close to one or another of these are certain questions from the *Vita Secundi*, among others. Note that the moralistic theme predominates: things that are heavy, fast, hot, sweet, etc. come into play to define debt, thought, the heart, parent-child relations, madness. Questions 11 to 13 refer to delight or pleasure.

As for the contents, parallels can be found for the themes of language ("the best and the worst"), of the certainty of death, of the sexual pleasure that is short-lived, of madness or foolishness, of sight, truth and the heart, always within the Socratic-Cynic and also Christian spheres. Themes on family relationships were added, Christian in my opinion.

In short, we are dealing with a work in which the sapiential literature is presented as a short novel that is well preserved throughout the whole tradition and that was amplified in successive stages, namely, in the Muslim stage (where it was diversified) and in the Christian one. The latter is more explicit than in the other works ("God our Lord", etc.); without doubt there were added to the Christian themes of Antiquity those of the 13th century. These are sometimes questions on "the most ..." or "what is ...?", relating to the area of health and way of life, at others times to the moralistic sphere. We have the impression that there were great amplifications that took form within a complex tradition; perhaps there were reductions as well.

Throughout this development, the work had gradually gotten farther from its origins. Even so, it seems clear that both the novelesque and the gnomological elements must be situated within the late Greek tradition which we have been discussing. Except that in this case, as I have said, the alterations undergone by the text in the medieval stages seem greater than in the others.

29 See 21 f.

As for the rest, we must not overlook the fact that this is a diversified variant of the sapiential tradition, in the line of the *Lives* and debates which we have mentioned in relation to the *Lives* of Aesop and Secundus, the *Altercatio*, etc. In spite of the fact that there are present in this literature maxims similar or identical to those attributed to the great ancient thinkers, none of these personages is mentioned here. Furthermore, the philosophers' maxims and the anonymous ones appeared in that other branch too, at times intermingled with somewhat unconnected sapiential themes, such as the "mirror for princes" and others that we have mentioned.

In summary, *Donzella Teodor* is quite far from the other three works translated by Alfonso X. It belongs to a separate branch of the sapiential tradition: the *Life* or short novel followed by a debate with questions and replies, a branch related, but not identical, to those that gave rise to the other three works: gnomologies, "mirrors for princes" and epistolary novels. All this is combined in one way or another, all this creates different works. But all of them have unequivocal traces of their Greek origin and their reworking in the early Byzantine epoch.

Conclusion

I.

The four works that we have studied reached Al-Andalus from the Orient without doubt at some time during the 9th, 10th or 11th centuries. There are traces of the presence of some of them there at a date earlier than Alfonso X: the translations of *Poridad* by Johannes Hispalensis (into Latin, and fragmentary) and al-Harizi (into Hebrew), the influence of all this literature in Petrus Alphonsus. The preservation in Spain of Arabic manuscripts of some of these works is evidence of this avenue of entry.

And it is no less certain that Andalusian Arabic texts, like that of the legend of Alexander studied by García Gómez, come from a Latin original (in this case the translation of the Archbishop Leo of Naples). And that, inversely, some of our texts were translated into Latin in the Orient: the *Secretum Secretorum*, an amplified version of the text translated in Castile as *Poridad de las Poridades*, which was translated into Latin by Philip of Tripoli.

But in general, the line is clear: Al-Andalus imported manuscripts that came from the Bagdad translations of the period of Harun al-Rashid, al-Mansur and al-Mahdi; and, at a later date, from the translations of the Fatamid court in Egypt, where al-Mubassir worked and where *The Thousand and One Nights* acquired its definitive form. No one in Cordoba knew Greek; I have already mentioned the anecdote about Abderraman III and the Dioscorides codex sent by Romanos, the Byzantine emperor.

According to the evidence, in Al-Andalus the translators of Toledo found the Arabic manuscripts, not only of the four works studied here, but also of the philosophical and scientific texts translated from Greek and the sapiential texts translated from Pehlvi. For it was not the Isidorian culture whose influence was felt in the Andalusian world, but the culture of Bagdad starting with Abderrrman II (822–852). From then on, and especially in the 11th and 12th centuries, a partially original school of thought was developed, but always based on Greek works (physicians, astrologers, Plato, Aristotle and his commentators, Porphyry and the Neo-Platonics, etc.) or else based on oriental Arabic works of the same inspiration. See Cruz Hernández, op. cit., 2, pp.19 ff. But, I repeat, Greek sapiential literature, with its Arabic and Castilian derivatives, occupied a place scarcely recognized by modern bibliography.

In Seville there were translators too, but it was above all in Toledo, with Archbishop Raimundo in the 12th century and Alfonso X in the 13th, that Jewish sages carried out the all-important mission of transferring this wealth from Arabic to Castilian[1], just as earlier, in Bagdad, the Syrian Christians and the Persian Zoroastrians had transferred it from Greek and Pehlvi to Arabic. As I have said before, for Greek wisdom there is at times a previous Syriac phase.

Thus there arrived in Castile a body of Greek and Christian morality presented as novels and anecdotes, apocryphal for the most part, it must be said. Apocryphal literature had been important since the Hellenistic epoch.

This, summarized once again, is the history. Later will come the creation of a Castilian sapiential literature founded on it.

II.

It should be useful, here at the end of the book, to summarize the great river of Greek sapiential literature of which our four works are simply four late crystallizations of the many that existed and that we know to a considerable extent in Greek (or in Latin translation or imitation) through manuscripts and papyri and also, at times, in Arabic translations that did not pass into Castilian. Just as we know their precedents in the ancient Orient.

Note that this sapiential literature cannot always be separated from literary or philosophical authors: we have continually cited authors such as Seneca, Plutarch, Lucian and Epictetus among many others, not to mention the ancient ones, going back to Homer. To isolate sapiential literature completely is impossible.

1 See, among others, G. Menéndez Pidal. "Cómo trabajaban las escuelas alfonsíes", *Nueva Revista de Filología Hispánica* 5, 1951, pp. 363–380 (but he does not speak of sapiential literature). Also A. Steiger, "Tradición y fuentes islámicas en la obra de Alfonso el Sabio", *RIEI* 3, 1955, pp. 93–109.

We find it in the maxim, the anecdote, the fable, the parody, the diatribe, the apocryphal letters, the novelistic elements of various *Lives*, and, naturally, in the teachings of the philosophers, which it popularizes. Throughout this book we have had many opportunities to see that the maxims and anecdotes in our works, which entered them by various routes, find their antecedents in Homer, Hesiod, Archilochus, Solon, Pindar, and the authors of tragedy and comedy. And, of course, in the philosophers: Socrates, Plato, Aristotle, the idealized Alexander, but also Anaxagoras, Democritus and others, as well as Xenophon and Isocrates, and later Diogenes and the Hellenistic philosophers and playwrights.

To be sure, at times there is a considerable difference between what these authors said or wrote and what the gnomologies, apocryphal letters, *Lives* etc. later attributed to them. Popular literature underwent a constant process of remodeling: Socratism colored the citations of older authors, Cynicism those of Socratic literature, Christianity all of them. And there was a process of selection: from the enormous mass of sapiential literature that we know, only some of the themes and personages remain in our works.

The Socratic-Platonic and Cynic-Stoic moralism, together with elements of satire, irony and the novel, constitute their center. Note that at times they include maxims or letters attributed (rightly or wrongly) to an author or person from Antiquity, at times they are spoken by fictitious characters such as Aesop or Teodor, and at other times no author's name is given. And also that the relation to the names of the supposed authors of the maxims or the protagonists of the anecdotes is highly labile; there are fluctuating attributions and the philosophies are mixed together.

In any case, the predominant vision is the concept that the Cynics and Stoics had of Socrates, Plato, Aristotle, Alexander and other philosophers and persons. But there is no absolute uniformity; for example, at times we see a Cynicism that is brutal and blatant, anarchistic and misogynous, while at other times the rough edges are smoothed and it reflects a more human kind of power and life.

And, as I have said before, this concept is combined with material of different origins, Neo-Platonic, Neo-Pythagorean and Hermetic and, above all, Christian material. For beginning with Saint Paul himself, the Christians began to cite the pagans. A little later the pagan gnomologies began to admit maxims from the Bible and from certain Fathers of the Greek Church, and the Christian gnomologies did the inverse. The central themes of morality were common to both.

Nevertheless, sapiential Greek literature rarely admitted a more profound Christianization, for example theological, evangelical or hagiographic elements. But in the first Byzantine epoch, in Constantinople and especially in Syria, things were more advanced. Socrates and Aristotle were inserted into the Christian sphere as ascetics or saints; Alexander, as the diffuser of monotheism and of the kingdom of God.

It is this last phase, which coexists with the previous ones, that predominates in our four treatises. It adds a conception of ancient Greece as a monarchical state, with its king, its palace and its philosophers, who are like preachers or ecclesiastics. We have encountered this same background in Greek Byzantine texts at times, and also in Syriac, Ethiopian and Arabic texts translated from Greek and lost in their original language.

It was with the Arabs' conquest of Damascus (635) and Cairo (641) that they discovered Greek sapiential literature, both the literature that has reached us through manuscripts and papyri and the literature that we have only through their translations. This is literature that at times coincides exactly with the oldest Greek literature, and at times adds a Cynic, Christian and monarchical quantum. Only later, in the 11th century, did the Arabs reestablish direct relations with Constantinople, with the result that many new manuscripts poured into Bagdad.

It is not even certain that those that interest us reached the libraries of Constantinople. They were known and sometimes translated into Syriac or Arabic in Syria in the Ommiad epoch (up to 750), and later in Bagdad in the Abbassid period, but always by Syrian translators. Of course, apart from our four works, there were other more or less similar ones that never passed into Castilian but remained in Arabic. We have mentioned some of them.

In general terms we can say that our four works were created from Greek genres of which we have direct knowledge:

1. The gnomologies, some anonymous, some attributed to specific authors, some organized by themes and within the themes by authors. These authors go from Homer to those of the 5th century A.D., including some Christian authors.
2. The collections of apocryphal letters, like those included in *Buenos Proverbios* and *Poridad.* Sometimes they proffer advice, sometimes they are letters of consolation.

3. The "mirrors for princes", which, of course, make use of maxims and letters.
4. The sapiential novels, in which a fictional character replies to difficult questions and solves enigmas.

The question is how, from this starting point, our four Greek works were created. I repeat my conclusions here:

Buenos Proverbios is a *Life* (and death) of Alexander, presented as a "mirror for princes" with the help of an epistolary novel. Certain gnomologies were added, but only secondarily, in the Arab epoch (but they are Greek).

Bocados de Oro is a group of Greek gnomologies, possibly collected by the Arab compiler and translator.

Poridad is a "mirror for princes" fashioned with the help of a novelistic beginning and apocryphal letters, without doubt from the Greek epoch.

III.

All these works, plus the material that was later added to them, were without doubt found in the libraries of Damascus and other conquered cities, as I have suggested. We must consider that for a long time the Greco-Christian population, who spoke Greek and Syriac, were in the majority. They were employed in the administration of the caliphate and of the cities. And the conquerors were obliged to turn to them when they wanted translations of the ancient Greek wisdom (which was already partially translated into Syriac). They enjoyed an immense prestige.

The Arabs, as we know, wanted translations of works that were scientific (including astrological), medical, philosophical, etc., but also, to a lesser extent, translations of sapiential texts for moral instruction and for entertainment (this combination being a Cynic inheritance). This is a movement that began in Damascus and that later grew in Bagdad, beginning in the middle of the 8th century, and in Cairo in the 9th, always with the help of the Syrian Christians.

There was no religious problem. The caliphs admired Greek science and philosophy (Al-Mamún saw Aristotle in his dreams). They searched for manuscripts of Aristotle and of the other sages. The great Greek names (even in spurious texts or mistaken doctrines) were thought to represent ancient Greece, which was idealized compared with the Byzantine enemy.

And as regards sapiential literature, it was Greek texts, by then in the Byzantine and Christian phase, that they were translating! But I have already said that the Christianization of these texts did not go beyond what an enlightened pagan or Muslim would accept: monotheism, the government of God, asceticism, mistrust of this world and the search for the true one via virtuous conduct, disdain for death, etc. Strictly Muslim themes were not included save rare exceptions. It was not customary among the translators, who, besides, were Christian. What they did do at times was to create a body or aggregation of Greek elements.

Thus was created, from Greco-Christian sapiential literature, an intellectual space that was common to the Arab intelligentsia as well. And later common to the Christian intelligentsia of Castile and the rest of Europe. What was most specific and conflictive of the two religions traveled through different channels. But sapiential literature, the line that goes from Athens (and earlier from other Greek cities) to Alexandria, Damascus, Bagdad and Toledo was, for many centuries, what marked the center of morality for individuals and nations.

And it did so for kings as well: the thesis of the divine origin of royal power runs through this literature from Alexander to Justinian, to Roman emperors and Muslim caliphs; and later it reaches the medieval kings and those of the *ancien regime*. If we wanted to, we could find antecedents of divine right in Egypt, where Alexander found it; but also in Homer, who spoke of the kings "nurtured by Zeus" and in Hesiod, where the good king sees his kingdom with an abundance of prosperity.

IV

The Castilian and Christian influence, as I have said, was not great once this literature had arrived in our Middle Ages. To be sure, we read of kings and various court officials, and in *Donzella Teodor* there are references to Christ and the Virgin. But nothing beyond that.

What we are interested in emphasizing now is how this literature (and specifically of our four works) was received in Castile (and later in Europe). And in the influence it exerted, or rather, continued to exert on works that were imitations, alongside the literature of Persian, and in the final analysis, Indian origin (*Pañcatantra* and the others), which in these derivations ended up blending with that of Greek origin.

But before going on to this theme, which we will treat briefly, I must repeat that I feel it has been made clear that the influence that reached our Castilian sapiential literature, by the routes we have seen, is of Greek or, if you prefer, Greco-Roman and Greco-Christian origin. The cultural role of the Arabs was essentially that of transmitting part of this ancient culture: an important role, since without it, some elements would have been lost. In another place I have spoken of a re-Hellenization (and re-Romanization) of Spain.

Apart from this, beginning at a certain moment, the enlightened intellectual strata of Muslims became saturated with Greek wisdom and created new developments in science and thought; and, as we have seen, this wisdom also reached Hebrew literature. It is evident that these developments had an influence, as did works of Muslim creation translated into Castilian, such as *La Escala de Mahoma.* And all medieval science depends on Arabic works, which sometimes are not simple translations from Greek but are compilations and amplifications, like those that entered Alfonso X's *Libro del Saber de Astronomía.*

But this influence was secondary compared to the influence exerted by the mere transmission, via translations, of Greek science and literature. Naturally, this is not to say by any means that we deny the existence of Islamic (and Hebrew) science and philosophy in Spain beginning in the 11th century. But it is a fact that the inspiration for these disciplines was in the Greeks: they arrived sometimes via Arab and oriental Hebrew thinkers (Isaac Israelí, al-Farabi, Avicenna), at times directly, though with knowledge of Arabism and oriental Judaism (Ben Masarra, Ibn Hazam, Ibn Gabirol, Ben Ezra, Abu Salt, al-Sid, Avempace, Maimonides, Averroes). Arabism and oriental and occidental Judaism are, really, the same thing: variants of Platonism and Aristotelianism, but in a philosophical and theological version, not in the popular version of the sapiential literature that we are studying here.

And I believe that the much-discussed thesis that in the origins of Spanish culture there is a fusion of the three cultures, the thesis of Americo

Castro, is greatly exaggerated. It converts marginal facts into central ones; it presents as an influence of its own what is more often only a transmission. This is not a matter of slighting anyone but of giving each his due.

What was most intimate in the Hebrew and Muslim cultures did not pass into Spain. What there was in these cultures that did reach the central river of Spanish history is, essentially, a complex of late Greco-Roman (and even Christian) elements. And what is true of sapiential literature is equally true of other kinds of literature and of other cultural manifestations (architecture, sculpture, gardens, baths, irrigation systems, etc.), though this is not the place to go into these matters. But an ineluctable myth was created. When in 1998, at the Seneca centenary in Cordoba, I spoke about the Greek and Roman roots of Andalusia, the newspapers of Cordoba said that I had spoken of the famous synthesis of the three cultures.

Christianity and Islam were very early on infiltrated by Greek culture; without it their cultural role would have been severely limited. Hebrew culture was likewise influenced. To the Greek and Roman influence which had arrived via various routes was joined the influence that came via the Muslims. And medieval Jewish literature, in Hebrew and Castilian, received from Castile and even from the Arabs, the ancient influence that at times had already reached them directly from Antiquity.

And that is all there is to it. To speak, in the case of our four works, of "oriental" or "Arab" influence is the height of absurdity. But this is extremely frequent; I have already said that this idea is common in our histories of literature when they discuss the four works studied here. The same is true at times of Castilian sapiential literature, for example, of *El Conde Lucanor*[2] or the *Libro de Buen Amor*[3] or the *Celestina*[4]. What is called "Arabic" and "oriental" is simply Greek or Pehlvi, which reached these works via Arabic translations, if not Latin ones.

But let us return to the influence of these works in our literature, including things already mentioned and adding others.

To begin with, what the translations of Arabic works, sometimes coming from Greek and from Pehlvi, did was to emphasize translation as an instrument for augmenting Castilian culture and creating Castilian prose,

2 Cf. J.L. Alborg, *Historia de la Literatura española*, Madrid, 1972 (2nd ed.), 1, pp. 288 ff.

3 See below.

4 Cf. my polemic in my "Orígenes del teatro español en Salamanca", in the book *Salamanca y la Literatura. Ciclo de conferencias pronunciadas en Fundación Ramón Areces (Febrero 1996)*, Madrid, Fundación Ramón Areces, 1996, pp. 13–38.

for the oldest translations, of ancient or medieval or Biblical texts, were from Latin. In the 12th century the *Fazienda de Ultramar* was translated and romances were created from Biblical texts (sometimes with the help of Hebrew). At other times Latin texts appear as sources: for example for the *Semejança del mundo*, for the *Historia de España*, and the *Crónica General* of Alfonso X, for Berceo, etc. The *Vida de Secundo*, the *Altercatio*, the *Vida de Apolonio rey de Tiro* etc. were translated from Latin. Medieval Latin works were translated as well; an example is the *Libro del Tesoro*, translated from the Latin of Brunetto Latini. Sometimes things are more complicated: there can be a French intermediate stage, as is the case of the *Libro de Alexandre*.

With the inspiration of these and other sapiential works others were created in Romance, such as the *Disputa de un cristiano y un judío*, etc. All this is obvious, but it is necessary to keep it in mind when we are insisting on the thesis of the origin of Castilian literature as literature in translation (and then literature inspired by Latin translations or texts).

Now, the Greek sapiential texts translated from Arabic, which are what we have been dealing with here, were also the basis for new developments in Castilian literature, or more specifically, in Castilian sapiential literature, sometimes fused with elements from the other branch of sapiential literature: that of Indian origin. In Petrus Alphonsus, in the Archpriest of Hita and in D. Juan Manuel the two currents come together. It seems odd, therefore, that in the histories of medieval Castilian literature like Gómez Redondo's, these derivatives, which I will mention in a moment, are discussed before their sources, which have been studied here. The perspective that we introduce is missing[5].

This confluence of the two branches of sapiential literature can also be seen in the fable. I have studied this in great detail in my *Historia de la fábula greco-latina* and elsewhere[6].

I am going to offer a concise idea of the Castilian sapiential literature that can be considered as derived from Greco-Arabic literature (at times, as I say, from Pehlvi-Arabic). This is not a study but rather a mere indication to obtain a very necessary perspective, because from the time of Don

5 The same is true of J. L. Alborg's *Historia de la Literatura española*, Madrid, Gredos, 1992, pp. 148 ff.

6 See *Historia* ..., II; 1985, pp. 511 ff., (559 ff of the English translation, Leiden, 2000) as well as "The earliest influences of Indian fable on medieval Latin fable", *Classica et Medievalia* 35, 1984, pp. 243–263 and "La fábula en Bizancio, entre Grecia, el Oriente y Occidente", *SIFC* 11, 1993, pp. 196–204.

Ramón Menéndez Pidal the historians of Spanish literature have devoted more study to Islamic sources than to Latin ones and hardly any to the Greek ones.

Far back, in the period of Fernando III, at the beginning of the 13th century, we have the *Libro de los Doze Sabios*[7]. The King, Don Fernando, we are told, convoked twelve wise men to give norms of conduct to the crown prince: the work is, therefore, a "mirror for princes" like those that we have seen and with a similar orientation. This is also true of the *Flores de Filosofía*[8], of the same period. After a brief prologue, it goes on to discuss how a man must love God, the king and the virtues of men. As in the previous case, it is in exactly the same line that we have seen: the themes of being long-suffering, the intellect, wealth and poverty, "watching one's tongue", etc. The derivation from our treatises is obvious. They were, without doubt, well known before being translated in the following period.

And the same is true of works from the middle of the century, the epoch of Alfonso X, for example, the *Libro de los Cien Capítulos*, which commences with a "regimen for princes", centering on the well-known themes of the king, the law and the people. And then, at the end of the century, in the epoch of Sancho IV, we have works that are absolute parallels: the *Lucidario*, which, using the device of a dialogue between teacher and student, speaks of theology, nature, the king; the *Castigos de Sancho IV*, for the instruction of his son, is another "regimen for princes" with the familiar themes of God and the king, of the religious conduct of the king and of his salvation[9]. And we must mention, too, with the same theme and of the same period, the *Libro del Consejo e de los consejeros*, which centers on the theme of God and on the moral virtues that the king's counselors must have. All of this reminds us greatly, even literally, of the sapiential literature we have studied.

7 What has reached us is a text reworked in the epoch of Alfonso X. There is a Madrid edition, 1975, and one can read the article by H. Bizarri, "Consideraciones en torno a la elaboración de *El libro de los doze sabios*", *La Corónica* 18, 1989, pp. 85–89. Also Gómez Redondo, op. cit., pp. 241 ff.

8 One can consult Hermann Knust's edition, with a good introduction, Madrid, 1878, and that of Lee Thomas Fouché, Columbia University, 1979. Also Gómez Redondo, op. cit., pp. 260 ff.

9 See H. Bizarri's important study, "La estructura de *Castigos e Documentos* del rey Don Sancho IV. Apuntes para la historia de la formación de la ciencia política en la Castilla del siglo XIII", *Incipit* 17, 1997, pp. 83–138. He deals with all these works as the basis of later political science.

Then in the 14th century the Infante Don Juan Manuel continues this literature in the *Libro del cavallero e del escudero*, a theory of the social skills of chivalry; the *Libro de los estados* (modeled on the *Barlaam*), and *El Conde Lucanor*, an exercise in dialogue between a count and his counselor, Petronio, who replies to the count's questions on themes of government with examples and fables[10]. The sapiential literature of Greek origin is contaminated here with that of Indian origin.

It is impossible to follow the long history of this doctrinal literature; let it suffice to recall the *Rimado de palacio* by the Chancellor Ayala, the *Manual del caballero cristiano* by Alonso Fernández de Madrid, the *Relox de Príncipes* by Fray Antonio de Guevara, the *Idea de un Príncipe Político Cristiano* by Saavedra Fajardo or the *Política de Dios y Gobierno de Cristo* by Quevedo. This theme took various different courses in the hands of Boscán, Machiavelli, Gracián and so many others, but the origin is in our now familiar sapiential works. In relation to this, I remind the reader of what we have said about the medieval collections of "sayings" of the sages, especially the Seven Wise Men, which reached the 16th century (Pedro Mexía, Hernán López de Yanguas).

And in these sapiential works we also find the origin of the flourishing of collections of maxims and adages. Among various titles we can mention in the 14th century, Don Sem Tob with his *Proverbios Morales*; in the 15th, the Marqués de Santillana with his *Proverbios*; in the 16th, Juan de Mal-Lara with his *Filosofía vulgar*, Juan de Timoneda with his *Sobremesa y alivio de caminantes*; Juan Rufo with his *Seiscientos apotegmas y sentencias*.

And then, too, there are the debates, for example the abovementioned *Disputa de un cristiano y un judío*; in the 15th century the *Proceso entre la soberbia e la mesura*. This is a genre that is interwoven with sapiential literature; confrontations of this kind are found in the *Lives*, in the fable and in "examples" of a Cynic and also Jewish type going back to Antiquity, and later in medieval Latin literature.

And we have the genres of the story and of the novel. I am not speaking here of so-called the Greek and Byzantine novel, but of the realistic novel linked to sapiential literature, as we have seen in the *Life of Aesop*, *The Golden Ass*, the *Satyricon*, etc. We have found echoes of this in the Greco-Christian works translated into Castilian. I have maintained elsewhere the thesis of

10 See J. Gimeno Casalduero, "El Conde Lucanor: composición y significado", *Nueva Revista de Filología Hispánica* 24, 1975, pp. 101–112.

the immense influence of this genre, and quite specifically of the *Life of Aesop*, on the Archpriest of Hita[11] and the *Lazarillo*[12].

As can be seen, here I do not go into the theme of the enormous influence of Greco-Latin literature in general on our literature; I simply give a few themes derived from sapiential literature and, within this, from the line represented by our four works. I believe that its influence is important and should not be forgotten; it deserves a thorough study. Naturally, at a certain moment, this influence intersects that of the greater literature and the new currents of thought.

The capacity of sapiential literature to last and be transformed without losing its essential identity is astonishing, no matter that it be anonymous, popular and without artistic pretensions. I have studied this as regards the fable in my *Historia de la Fábula Greco-Latina*; the case of these works, which are related, moreover, to the fable, is similar: my interest in the theme began with that study.

From the time of ancient Sumer and ancient Egypt, through multiple phases in Greek literature, sapiential literature, also cultivated by Muslims and Jews, reached our Castilian literature via unpredictable routes, where it was disseminated and flourished anew. This was not only a literary renewal but also an ideological one relating to moral themes, to novelistic themes and to the idea of the Christian monarchy. In the following centuries this ideology was widely projected throughout Europe. It is not the mission of this book to follow these new developments.

11 See my article "El Libro de Buen Amor y la Vida de Esopo", in *Serta Philologica F. Lázaro Carreter*, Madrid, Gredos, 1983, II, pp. 427–433. This is something that continues to be unknown, cf. for example F. Rico, "Sobre el origin de la autobiografía en el Libro de Buen Amor", *Anuario de Estudios Medievales* 4, 1967, pp. 301–325; it discusses only Ovid and the medieval Pseudo-Ovid, important sources without doubt, but less central in my opinion. For the crossing of the Greek and Indian sapiential lines, see my article "Aportaciones al estudio de las fuentes de las fábulas del Arcipreste", "Aportaciones al estudio de las fábulas del Arcipreste", in *Philologica Hispaniensia in honorem Manuel Alvar. III. Literatura*, Madrid, Gredos, 1986, pp. 459–473.

12 See my "La Vida de Esopo y la Vida de Lazarillo de Tormes", *Revista de Filología Española* 58, 1976, pp. 35–45. This work is, strangely, unknown: F. Rico in his edition (Madrid 1998) mentions Apuleius and Lucian, influences less direct than that of the *Life of Aesop*, which he does not cite. It was translated into Castilian earlier than the *Lazarillo*. Much altered, the plan of the journey and of the servant who, with jokes and truths instructs his master, is preserved in the *Quijote*. My paper and many others can be found now in my book *De Esopo al Lazarillo*, Huelva, Universidad, 2005.

These are popular and modest genres that, nevertheless, have made history and deserve to be studied in more detail. This book merely introduces the topic. Putting ancient Greek literature in contact with medieval and later Castilian literature is no small feat for sapiential literature. We have given some first results. It will be necessary to continue exploring the Castilian works and the antecedents preserved in Greek as well as sapiential works in Syriac and Arabic that did not pass into Castilian but are likewise of Greek origin.

And so, in summary, it was the Christianized Greek culture that by way of Arabic and Latin culture, much more creative this last, that contributed to the formation of our own. The enemies of the Greeks – Romans, Christians and Muslims, even Jews – brought the Greeks to us; they re-Hellenized Spain to a certain extent. And Spain was the key point for passage to Europe. The Castilians too were transmitters. It was only much later that the Greeks exerted a direct influence all over Europe.

Castile was a privileged point of passage to Europe for Greco-Roman-Christian culture. The Arabic route is one of the channels by which it arrived. In the end, the Greco-Christian ethic and the Greco-Christian political theory became European and assumed their place as part of the intimate nucleus of Europe.

Addenda to the 2001 edition of *"Modelos Griegos"*

I. Commentaries on various publications or extracts from publications

1. Commentary on a paper on Castilian prose, given at Zaragoza on 12 February 2002, which was sent to me by Professor José Fradejas.

As part of the bibliography Fradejas cites Marta Haro, *Los compendios de castigos del siglo XIII*, 1995; as well as Professor Valero's edition of *La doncella Teodor*. And he offers certain observations, also in relation to the treatment of the theme in *Modelos*.

To be sure, I do not care for his comments on this theme, in which he suggests that I am conditioned by my background as a Hellenist. My capacity as a Hellenist is not a conditioning, it is an excellent base, because I can contribute data that are generally unknown by those who confine their comments to speaking of the "oriental" character of this tradition, which is to say practically nothing.

Fradejas says that the Greek origin of this tradition is certain (p. 15), but the transmission via Byzantium, hypothetical. The adaptation and translation were probably Syrian-Arabic: this is true.

He accepts the sum of elements in our works: gnomologies from the 5th to the 8th centuries as earlier elements; (p. 16) the novelistic or biographical form, epistolary novels, the function of the "mirrors for princes."

Sapiential Greek literature, he says, passed into Pehlvi and from here into Arabic. But actually there are two lines: Greek > (Syriac) > Arabic (then Greek, Castilian, etc.); and (Sanskrit) > Pehlvi > Arabic (and from there to Greek, Castilian, etc.).

On p. 17 he affirms, in relation to all my works, that out of the Greek and Arabic versions, an original Castilian creation arose, which he calls Castilian gnomic prose. This refers to works such as the *Libro de los siete sabios, Flores de Filosofía, Libro de los Cien capítulos, Libro del Consejo y los Consejeros, Castigos de Sancho IV*, which I mention in my book. I have already said that these works have two sides: the original, that of all ancient and Arabic sapiential literature, and that of being the model for later Castilian literature.

Fradejas continues to waver regarding affirmations such as Ms. Valero's "a radical Arabic origin." He and the other scholars of the medieval tradition have never really accepted that the origin of this tradition is in the ancient Greek and pre-Greek sapiential tradition.

2. *Commentary on a review of* Modelos griegos de la sabiduría castellana y europea, *by H. O. Bizzarri in Emerita 71, 2003, pp. 155–157.*

Bizzarri essentially accepts the ideas in the book, which says that "in general terms, we must say that our four works were created on the base of Greek genres of which we have direct knowledge" (p. 157). He subscribes to this affirmation and to the insistence on arriving at the Greek base of these works, going against a tradition wide-spread among Arabists and medievalists. But really he shows his adherence to this latter tradition when he discusses the concept of the model, which he reduces to basically generic, denying any historical authority to the prologues that mention Greek originals. I have insisted that late Greek works, which in turn rest on a long series of older strata, have undergone Arabic and Christian remodelations that we cannot situate exactly: remodelations more extensive than anywhere else in *Donzella Teodor*, possible fusions of various elements (it is difficult to specify the period) in *Buenos Proverbios*, various additions in *Bocados de Oro*; there are different medieval versions of *Poridad de las Poridades*. Bizzarri follows the old tendency to think that only individual maxims come from the Greeks, with no organization whatsoever.

I believe that this is a prejudice derived from the lack of attention to this literature on the part of the Hellenists and Latinists and from the avidity of the medievalists, as I said, to channel the water into their own mills. The Greeks, according to them, would be the remote source of some individual items, the rest is "oriental" or "Arabic" or Christian.

But the fact that Greek books lie at the base of the translations can be deduced not only from the maxims, *khreîai* and anecdotes (many literally Greek), or from what the prologues say (which there is no reason to doubt), but also from the partial elements included (pseudo-epigraphic letters, debates, etc.) and from the type of organization of the realistic novels, in which short novelesque-biographical sketches are followed by debates, maxims, etc., all connected and unconnected, easily amplifiable or replaceable.

The content is Greek, the compositional schemes are Greek, the maxims and *khreîai* are Greek, and the themes are Greek, or Greco-Christian (and Cynic, Pythagorean, Hermetic, etc.).

Bizzarri praises my insistence on distancing myself from the tradition that I criticize; he says that one must think it over … but at bottom, he shares its views. The old traditions are hard to shed, even for competent specialists. They try to see the facts free of old interpretations, but it is difficult for them, which is only natural. Of course there are no Hellenists among them.

"Model", then, is not a generic term. It refers to specific works, perhaps later modified, amplified, reworked, but real works. I have written about the concept of "model"[1]: it refers to works read and assimilated, later translated, imitated, sources of inspiration. Not something that is followed slavishly, but, I repeat, specific works which can produce things that are new. In this case they are models followed quite faithfully: translated twice, basically, but reworked without doubt, as I have said.

But this ancient Greek cultural stratum has always prevailed (really various successive Greek strata, as I have explained, giving details). There is very little that is Islamic, more in *Donzella Teodor* as I have said, and little that is Christian. There are, nevertheless, things that could suit the old Christian mentality, including the Byzantine mentality, and at the same time concur with the Muslim and Castilian mentalities, especially in the religious and moral aspects: God, the king, the world, virtue, etc.

Finally, Bizzarri criticizes the fact that I speak of "Castilian and European wisdom". He says that the European tradition is independent. Often it is, as I say, for example in the case of the *Secretum Secretorum*; elsewhere I have spoken of the fable. This is why I say "and". But at other times this European wisdom reached Europe from Castile: there is testimony of this in many examples.

Therefore, the relation of these four books with the Greeks is not the same as *El Conde Lucanor*, for example, could have with them. Incidental additions apart, we are dealing with translations of Greek works. I believe I am correct when I speak of "models", a less explicit term. And of course they were the models for so many later works; I have given some examples.

1 "El modelo clásico como constante histórica", *Revista 1616* 2, 1979, pp. 47–57.

3. *An extract from a review by Elvira Gangutia of the author's book "De Esopo al Lazarillo", Huelva, Universidad, 2005 (in* Emerita *73, 2005, pp. 373–381).*

The book that concerns us does not refer only to the small-format work written by Rodríguez Adrados in parallel with the creation of the *Historia de la fábula greco-latina*; many of the works included (some of them unpublished to date or published earlier in foreign journals) go beyond the date of the work mentioned and permit us to observe the progress afforded by Rodríguez Adrados in the extremely complex field of the fable and in other related ones, providing the bases for works by the same author, such as *Antología del cuento erótico griego, latino e indio* (Madrid 1993) and *Modelos griegos de la sabiduría castellana* (Madrid 2001).

Our book comprises a brief prologue by the author and three parts, each divided into detailed chapters that include works organized thematically. The third part of the book is devoted to reviews on books about the genre of the fable, several of which are extensive works of great density, ... (see, for example, the review on M. J. Luzzato and A. La Penna *Babrii mythiambi aesopei* (Leipzig 1986) and the work "La fecha de la *Augustana* y la tradición fabulística antigua y bizantina", 1992).

It is impossible to describe in this review the innumerable points elucidated in which Rodríguez Adrados provides incontestable findings. The work reveals how many of the discoveries were forged as the scholar himself was studying a great and fragmentary literary mass that universally goes beyond individual cultures and languages, escaping as well the limits of its own "genre". Therefore, we will attempt to follow certain general lines (definition and formal expression of the "genre", its origins and evolution, its content and thought), which we will illustrate with references to the articles published in this book....

The "center" or "hard nucleus" of the genre can be defined by the preeminence of animals that speak, endowed from ancient times with fixed characteristics. But also, in a manner parallel to the myth, gods, certain forces of nature, like a torrent, and also plants with fixed and opposing characteristics (rigidity/flexibility), like the reed and the oak can be the protagonists of the fable.

In spite of its chameleonic capacity over the centuries, the fable has proved to be an extraordinarily constant genre. Compared with the great literary genres, more fixed and conservative, the fable would seem to belong to an "inferior" level. Nevertheless, its anonymous (throughout history the presence of great creators is almost irrelevant), traditional and formally flexible essence makes it particularly adaptable and resistant.

Formally, the fable is initially an "example" in a narrative, as in Mesopotamia, in India or in the Middle Ages (the "enxiemplos" in Spain). The archaic Greek fable is also like this, initially in verse, in which Rodríguez Adrados identifies metric formulas that are interchangeable, as in the oral fables. Around the 5th century B.C., fables are submitted to a process of conversion to prose, which affects other Greek genres. This can be observed in the Socratic dialogue, in Xenophon, in the Cynic Antisthenes, down to Demetrius of Phalerum, who creates the first collection of fables. With this the fable becomes part of the "anthological genres" and goes from being a relatively extensive unit to its well-known brevity and concision. ("Hechos generales y hechos griegos en el origen de la sátira y la crítica", 1978; "La fábula griega como género literario", 1982; "Nuevos fragmentos de poetas yámbicos arcaicos y clásicos. Estesícoro, Semónides (?), Auctor incertus", 1982: "Fábula y cuento popular de tradición antigua en los Balcanes", 1991; "Mito y fábula", 1993).

The flexibility and adaptability of the genre has complicated the activity of the philologist when it comes to making editions of the fables. A critical edition attempts to establish the original state of a text, and this can hardly be done here because that original state has never existed: these are texts of the "open tradition", somewhat like our romances, which the first printing transformed from being basically oral into the fixed situation, at times illusory, of "literature". And here I want to recall our late friend, M. Ferrer Chivite, who, after the discoveries of Barcarrota, informed us that the Lazarillo might be considered an "open work". Professor Rodríguez Adrados considers that progress has been made and that it is possible to produce better editions of the fables, but he believes that other philological techniques should be explored, like those tested for the glosses or in *Vetus Latina*, although given the even greater complexity of the genre, one would have to resort to a completely computerized edition with special programs. The metric elements are extremely important: they would not only permit us to point out the characteristics of the so-called "open tradition", but would also allow us to establish an ancient *"corpus"* from which the old collections and later ones come ("Sobre una redacción bizantina de las fábulas esópicas", 1958; "Desiderata en la investigación de la fábula antigua", 1978; "Problemas de crítica textual en la transmisión de la fábula greco-latina", 1986).

What can be said about the origins and evolution of this genre? The answer is, according to Rodríguez Adrados, the result of a long process of study. In Mesopotamia, in 2500 B.C. and in Egypt in the 14th century B.C. there were already figurative representations of animals (according to the author the artistic representation of fables is curious and little studied) that can correspond to themes of the fables; in the Neo-Sumerian period we find texts that will be copied in Old Babylonian, Accadian, Assyrian and Neo-Babylonian for more than two millennia. In India the written texts come later, which leads to the debated question of whether the Indian fable is earlier than the Greek one. Although after the conquest of Alexander there could have been a great diffusion of the fable in India, there are themes that are only found in India and in which the ancient influence of Mesopotamia can be felt.

In Greece the first fable considered as such *(The nightingale and the hawk)* is found in the epic poetry, in Hesiod's *Works and Days*; later remains of hexameters used in fables are also found in Paniasis. Professor Rodríguez Adrados considers that the archaic union of the fable with epic poetry fosters the appearance of burlesque animalistic epics such as the *Batracomiomaquia*. But it is in the Greek lyric that we have an important manifestation of the fable with evident traces of the oriental world: from Archilochus we have *The eagle and the vixen* which goes back to *The eagle and the serpent* from the Accadian epic *Etana*. There is the influence of the *Gilgamesh* in the fragment of Ibycus in which the drug against old age is mentioned ("El tema del águila, de la épica acadia a Esquilo", 1964; "Ibico 61 y el influjo del Gilgamés en Grecia", 1987; "Más temas fabulísticos mesopotámicos en Grecia y la India", 2003; *"El ratón y la comadreja",* una nueva epopeya paródica. *P.Med.* 70.1 re. and *P.Vindob.inv.G* 19813+29814", 2000). In Archilochus's fables about monkeys and in Semonides Rodríguez Adrados detects traces of Egypt ("Sobre el origen y evolución de la fábula del águila y el escarabajo", 1988/1989), The fable is also used by other lyric poets such as Semonides or Theognis (whose heroic/antiheroic lives, Professor Rodríguez Adrados recommends, should be reviewed in an Aesopian light). Nor does Pindar or the tragic and comic authors escape this current ("El poema del pulpo y los orígenes de la colección Teognídea", 1958; "El tema del león en el *Agamenón* de Esquilo", 1963).

Thus far we can speak of fables within long texts. But beginning in 300 B.C., as we have already said, the compilations in the form of collections appear, the oldest being that of Demetrius of Phalerum. After that we find the anonymous collections that are formed throughout the Byzantine period. The oldest, according to Professor Rodríguez Adrados, is probably the *Augustana* (IV/V A.D.) and then the *Vindobonense* (VI/VII A.D.) and the *Accursiana* (X A.D.) ("El papiro Rylands 493 y la tradición fabulística antigua", 1952; "Sobre una redacción bizantina de las fábulas esópicas", 1958; "Problemas de crítica textual en la transmisión de la fábula greco-latina", 1986; "La fecha de la *Augustana* y la tradición fabulística antigua y bizantina", 1992; "Nuevos testimonios papiráceos de fábulas esópicas", 1999).

In the same way as has been described for the oldest Greek fables, elsewhere, for example in India, the fable can be integrated into an epic poem (or other genre, there are even fables within other fables) and also, since the 2nd century B.C., they can be in the form of a collection. But there is another form of presentation, in which the fables can be included in the *Life* of the author of the fables, real or supposed, with a precedent in the Assyrian *Life of Ahikar*. Under the Cynic influence, a philosophical movement to which Professor Rodríguez Adrados accords a determining role in the evolution of the Greek fable and its successors, the *Life of Aesop* will become a real model for biographical literature. According to Professor Rodríguez Adrados, at a certain moment, following the conquests of Alexander, the Greek fable "reverts" to India, a phenomenon that occurs in Egypt as well. This is accentuated in the Byzantine epoch, when Greek fables pass into Syriac and from there to the Arabic fables, which in turn preserve traces of independent traditions, as can be seen in the Lokman collection. All this reverts again to Greek, with additions from the Indian tradition, as can be seen in the *Syntipas* ("El Pañchatantra, la fábula mesopotámica y la fábula griega", ined.; "Elementos cínicos en las 'vidas' de Esopo y Secundo en el *Diálogo de Alejandro y los Gimnosofistas*", *1978;* "La *Vida de Esopo* y los orígenes de la novela Antigua", 1979; "Siria, cruce de caminos de la narrativa bizantina y la oriental", 1983; "La fábula en Bizancio, entre Grecia, el Oriente y el Occidente", 1993; "Fábula y cuento popular de tradición antigua en los Balcanes", 1991; "La fábula en Grecia y Oriente", 2002; "Las fábulas de Lokman dentro de la tradición fabulística Griega", 2003).

The Greek fable is installed in the Roman world from a relatively early date. It can already be found in Lucilius, spreading via the Latin elegiac and epigrammatic genre. Afterward collections appear, which, now known by the names of the authors such as Phaedrus or Avianus, were given great importance in the Middle Ages ("El papiro Rylands 493 y la tradición fabulística antigua", 1952; "Fedro y sus fuentes", 1983; "Los más antiguos influjos de la fábula india en la Edad Media latina", 1984; "De la fábula griega a la fábula latina en dísticos elegíacos", 1991; "La fábula en Horacio y su poesía", 1994).

As has already been mentioned, Byzantium has a fundamental role in the codification of the fables. It is in this phase that there are created the great moveable *corpora* or anonymous collections such as the above-mentioned *Augustana, Vindobonensis* and *Accursiana* collections, formed by short units of fables, quite apt for diffusion, translation and instruction ("Sobre una redacción bizantina de las fábulas esópicas", 1958; "Fábula y cuento popular de tradición antigua en los Balcanes", 1991). We must mention here a television feature on Bhutan in which a schoolteacher can be seen teaching children English, a required language apart from the national language. When the camera focused on the rudimentary tablets, one could see that the text used to teach English to these children of a Himalayan country located between two giants like India and China was the fable of *The lion and the mouse.*

The process of transfer and retransfer, of "reversion", contamination, etc. was prolonged, according to Professor Rodríguez Adrados in some cases almost until our own times. One of the most important confluences of fables based on the traditions studied will occur in the Iberian Peninsula during the Middle Ages. In the *Disciplina clericalis* by Petrus Alphonsus there are traces of the Indian and Greek traditions, and Alfonso X's translations revert to Arabic models from the Bagdad of the 9th century A.D. ("La fábula de la golondrina de Grecia a la India y la Edad Media", 1980; "Más sobre la fábula de la golondrina", 1982; "Versiones medievales del tema de la serpiente desagradecida", 1991; "La zorra y el cuervo en la Edad Media latina", 1992). The Archpriest of Hita's *Libro de Buen Amor* will make use again of fables integrated in a biographical type of text, and in El Conde Lucanor, Indian compositional patterns are preserved ("Problemas de crítica textual en la transmisión de la fábula greco-latina", see on pp. 658–661 various *stemmata* on the evolution of the fable, 1986). The fusion of these traditions leads an enormous reinforcement in the Renaissance thanks to printing, with magnificent incunabula that present the fables preceded by the Life of Aesop and accompanied by extraordinary prints that renew and disseminate, in a way previously unimaginable, the artistic figurative tradition that lies in the origins of the fable from Mesopotamian and Egyptian times.

But before that the fable had diversified in contacts with genres like sapiential literature or the erotic tale, such as can be found in Bocaccio, Chaucer or Marguerite of Navarre. The Life of Aesop will make itself felt in the Lazarillo and even in the *Quijote* ("*La Vida de Esopo* y la *Vida de Lazarillo de Tormes*", 1976; "La fábula", 1981; "Documentación suplementaria de la fábula greco-latina", 1990; "El cuento erótico, de los cínicos al final de la Edad Media", 1992; "Literatura sapiencial antigua en la Haggadah y en Pedro Alfonso", 1993; "Un género literario greco-indio: el cuento erótico", 1994; ("El Pañchatantra, la fábula mesopotámica y la fábula griega", ined.; "El *Libro de Buen Amor* y la *Vida de Esopo*" [with *stemma* on p. 479], 1983; "Aportaciones al estudio de las fuentes de las fábulas del Arcipreste", 1983; "La fábula del lobo, el zorro y las gallinas en Mira de Amescua", 1985; "La fábula en la Edad Media y en el Renacimiento", ined.).

Does our persistent genre contain some equally constant message? As it appears in Greek iambic poetry (for example Archilochus), it has a popular and critical base; also, the lyric poet Stesichorus made use of the fable to dissuade the citizens from accepting tyranny, and even when it appears in poetry in hexameters, as in Hesiod, it is used to criticize unjust monarchs. But its adaptability allows it to serve different ideologies as a weapon: sometimes (Theognis, Herodotus, Sophocles), as in the fable of the torrent that sweeps everything away in a sudden flood, there is a comparison with the people, who at certain times can demolish everything ("El tema del torrente en la literatura griega arcaica clásica", 1965; "Nuevos fragmentos de poetas yámbicos arcaicos y clásicos. Estesícoro, Semónides (?), Auctor incertus", 1982; "Más fragmentos nuevos de poesía griega arcaica", 1984).

Nevertheless, the element of criticism of the strong and powerful prevails in general. There is an attempt to construct an equality and to demonstrate the possibility of the triumph of the intelligent but weaker person over the strong one, whose power is taken seriously into account in a way so realistic that at times, instead of criticism, the fable advises resignation. The Socratics and above all the Cynics, whose particular vision will endow the fable with characteristics that will spread universally, are the ones who will accentuate the element of social criticism latent in the genre: nature triumphs over wealth, arrogance and vanity ("Filosofía cínica en las fábulas esópicas", 1986; "Política cínica en las fábulas esópicas", 1987; "Géneros helenísticos en el Banquete de los siete sabios de Plutarco", 1996).

This characteristic, so evident in the Greek fable, is revealed in fables of other cultures: in India it serves to criticize the hypocritical ascetics, paralleling the criticism of the clergy in the Middle Ages ("Desiderata en la investigación de la fábula antigua", 1978; "Hechos generales y hechos griegos en el origen de la sátira y la crítica", 1978; "La fábula griega como género literario", 1982; "Las ranas pidiendo rey: origen y evolución de una fábula política", 1984).

4. *Extract from a review of the book by Oliver Overwien,* Die Sprüche des Kynikers Diogenes in der griechischen und arabischen Überlieferung. *Stuttgart, Franz Steiner, 2005. 500 pp. Reviewed by F. R. Adrados in* Emerita, *75, 2007, pp. 165–167.*

This is an important book for various reasons, the first being the study of the maxims, apophthegma and *khreîai* of Diogenes in the Greek and Arabic gnomological collections, the latter derived from the former, but with some differences. We are given a translation and commentary. The second reason: their origins and relations, studied and then explicated in various tables. This part takes from page 1 to page 209.

From here until the end the third theme is developed: the linguistic structure and that of the content of the maxims and the rest, their structure, there types, their relation with the Greek literary genres and with Cynic literature in general. The book ends with several very valuable indices. The whole book represents a huge effort of erudition.

Personally, without disdaining the other themes, the one that most interests me is the study of the Greek and Arabic gnomologies related to Diogenes. All of the works that have been published are adduced, thus producing a collection of the maxims of Diogenes more complete than Giannantoni's Greek collection (1990) or Gutas's Arabic one (1993), both used as a base. Nevertheless, I would like to have had a complete collection of the maxims in their diverse sources, with the variants of each; the different sources, I mean, be they Greek or Arabic.

The study of the gnomologies in the two languages is important. To begin with the Greek tradition, I believe that there has never been such a complete study of its various sectors, establishing the presence of each maxim or *khreía* in these diverse sectors, all of which is seen clearly in the corresponding tables, as is the general relation between the gnomologies shown by means of *stemmata.* For our author, the "*GV* Tradition" and the "*WA* Tradition" (centering respectively on the *Gnomologium Vaticanum* and the Vienese collection of apophthegma) are two great groups of gnomologies that form a body essentially different from another bloc, the maxims in Stobaeus. The *Corpus Parisinum* draws on *GVWS* and Stobaeus, while

Maximus and the related collections draw on the *Corpus Parisinum* and the two "traditiones". Diogenes Laertius stands apart.

All this is suggestive and, *grosso modo*, true, I believe. But the problem is: Do we have the right to draw general conclusions on the minimal part of the content of the gnomologies represented by the maxims of Diogenes? I doubt it; it would be necessary to extend the study to other sectors. I myself have attempted this in part as regards Alexander; see note below.

I would also like to point out the author's vast knowledge of the Arabic collections (of the published ones, that is) and the study of their internal relations with the Greek ones. But here I find a serious objection: besides Ibn Durayd and many others, he cites and studies the Arabic texts of Hunayn, *Adab al-falasifa* (pp. 94 ff.), and Mubassir, *Mukjtar al hikam* (pp. 243 ff.), but he hardly even cites the 13th century Castilian "translations" of these two works, namely the *Libro de los Buenos Proverbios* and *Bocados de Oro.*

Now, leaving aside this last, less important theme, my study of *Buenos Proverbios*, which the author is not familiar with[2], analyzes a work that only partially coincides with that presented by our author. Hunayn's work includes things that I find only in Mubassir (and *Bocados*), not in *Buenos Proverbios.* And on the other hand, Overwien's book lacks any reference to the central scheme of *Buenos Proverbios*, which centers on Alexander.

To be sure, the book I am reviewing and mine refer to themes that are partially complementary, in part different, but I feel that a study by Overwien of the Castilian works and my commentaries on them should have been unavoidable.

And he does not know the situation of the two Castilian works within the tradition of the Greek gnomology: they are translations of Greek originals found in Syria and Egypt by the Arabs; I believe I have established this without any doubt. They are works whose sources can substantially be established. The author of the book being reviewed, whose erudition is so great in other themes, is deficient in this one, as well as in the different influences of late Antiquity on these two works (not Persian, in my opinion).

All of this is followed, as I have said, by a long study on the form and content of the maxims and their relation to Cynic philosophy in general and to that of Diogenes in particular. Much can be learned from it, keeping in

2 In my *Modelos* ..., pp. 27 ff., 207 ff., etc. Neither is he familiar with my study of the treatment of Alexander in the gnomologies, which I have dealt with above.

mind that we are dealing with material that is uniform in general terms but with great variants (as in the case of Alexander).

It is important not to forget that the book studies a branch of the gnomological tradition that is very old and that is the forerunner of many things, for example, formal elements of maxims and *khreîai.* And it is within the Cynic tradition in general, from the time of Diogenes himself. The coincidences pointed out by our author with various Greek literary genres, such as the diatribe and the fable, are the result of their common Cynicizing character; I have written about this. To this Cynic point of view we must attribute formal elements and, also, the image of Socrates, the criticism of Plato, etc.

The book is long and dense, but in centering on Diogenes, it cannot give definitive solutions for the history of the gnomologies. To be sure, it advances in the knowledge of what there is in them that refers to Diogenes, to the relation, at least on this point, of the Greek gnomologies to each other (other elements of the Greek gnomologies are left somewhat aside) and to the relation of the Arabic gnomologies to the Greek ones (at least in part).

This is an immense field, in which the book achieves the advances I have mentioned and others as well. Many more things are still pending. And the omission of the Castilian sources, which go back to late Greek Antiquity (for Diogenes and many other matters), is lamentable.

5. *A note on the publication of the* Corpus Parisinum *by Denis M. Searby*[3].

This edition has finally come out, the absence of which we lamented in our book, p. 169, where we gave information about this manuscript (*Paris.Gr.* 1168) based on Gutas's references in his *Greek Wisdom Literature.*

This voluminous edition should be consulted to see if it contributes anything new to the sources in the Byzantine epoch of the maxims studied here. It definitely is made clear that it is here, and not later in Maximus, which is a derivative of the *Corpus* as I have said, that the maxims of the Ἱερά of Johannes Damascenus were fused with the previous tradition. For the history of the γνῶμαι during the Byzantine epoch knowledge of this collection is important.

3 This edition is: "The *Corpus Parisinum*: A Critical Edition of the Greek Text with Commentary and English Translation (A Medieval Anthology of Greek Texts from the Pre-Socratics to the Church Fathers, 600 B.C.–700 A.D.)". Two volumes, Mellen Press, 2007.

A thorough study of the topic should be made, but this is not the appropriate place. Nevertheless, the conclusions on the gnomologies of the Hellenistic and Roman periods do not change.

In any case, I give here an index of the Collection: 1. *Florilegium Christianum* (Bible, Church Fathers, Philo). 2. *Oracula theosophica*, a brief collection. 3. *Florilegium Profanum* (arranged by authors). 4. *Excerpta of Stobaeus.* 4b. *Series secunda e Stobaeo.* 5. *Democriti, Isocratis, Epicteti.* 6. *Gnomologium alphabeticum.* 7. *Menandri sententiae.*

II. New studies by the author on works of sapiential literature

1. *Resumé of the article "Alejandro, Plutarco y las gnomologías griegas", in* Plutarc a la sua època: paideia i societat. *Barcelona, Universidad, 2005, pp. 33–50.*

Here I would like to discuss the main conclusions of this work.

a. Exposition of the Question

Over a long series of studies on Plutarch's *Banquet of the seven wise men*[4], on the images of Alexander[5] and, especially, in the present book *Modelos* ..., on ancient gnomological and sapiential literature, I have been noticing dark points in the knowledge of the literature referring to Alexander, in Plutarch and elsewhere. And specifically in the case of sapiential or wisdom literature.

I say this especially insofar as it concerns the Plutarchian treatment of the theme of Alexander and this sapiential literature. Alexander was important for Plutarch and for all Greek thought under the Roman domination: it was a counterbalance for the honor and culture of Greece as opposed to the empire, especially after the defeat at Carrhae[6]. Alexander was the phi-

4 See Adrados, F. R., 1996: "Géneros helenísticos en el *Banquete de los siete Sabios* de Plutarco", in *Estudios sobre Putarco: Aspectos formales. Actas del IV Simposio sobre Plutarco*, Madrid, pp. 125–142.

5 See F. R. Adrados, "Las imágenes de Alejandro", in *Alejandro Magno, Hombre y Mito*, Madrid, 2000, pp. 15–31.

6 See Maria Rubina Cammarotta, "Il *De Alexandra Magni Fortuna aut Virtute*", in *Ricecbe plutarchee a cura di Italo Gallo*, Naples, 1992, pp. 105–124.

losopher in action, in whom a whole line of Greek heroes culminated. And he turned out to be a model imitated by Roman generals and emperors from Pompey to Augustus, Trajan and the Severi.

And he was a useful model for the new "Antoninian politics" that attempted to unite authority and freedom and was defended by writers such as Dion of Prusa, or Pliny the Younger and by Plutarch himself, although he insisted on the rational elements and on those derived from the ancient Greek city-state in its best times[7]; and, of course, on Platonic idealism, tempered by the realism of Aristotle and Theophrastus[8].

This is why Plutarch wrote about Alexander again and again: everyone recalls the *Vita Alexandri*; the two rhetorical treatises, thought to be works of his youth, known as *De Alexandri Fortuna aut Virtute* and the passage on the Macedonian king in the *Regum et imperatorum Apophthegmata*. Not to mention the lost work πῶς Ἀλέξανδρος ἤχθη, which would have shed light as much on Alexander as on Plutarch (the same as another lost work, *Alexander or on Colonization* and, without doubt the *De Regno*).

Now, in my "Las imágenes ..." I presented the panorama of the "image" that Alexander wanted to offer of himself and I spoke of how this image exploded, the victim of inevitable contradictions, and of how, in this way, the different images of Alexander arose: that of the hero, of the good virtuous king, of the *felix praedo*, and others as well. But I feel that I did not leave the place of Plutarch in this literature sufficiently clear.

In short, it would be necessary to make more precise the position of Plutarch in his writings relating to Alexander[9]. And we should also study Plutarch's relation to the "image" of Alexander disseminated by Alexander himself and his "cabinet", an image which inherits the tradition of the Greek heroes from Achilles to Pericles, plus the Platonic image of the governing philosopher, and which adds a certain monarchism typical of the 4th century, which I have already mentioned. And at the same time we should study his relation with the unfavorable image defended by the old moralism, including one sector of Cynicism, and also the favorable ones advo-

7 See Agostino Masaracchia, "Sul Plutarco Politico", *RCCM* 36, 1982, pp. 4–40, 1994. Also C. J. D. Aalders, *Plutarch's Political Thought*, Amsterdam, 1982.

8 From this would come the *Gerendae rei publicae praecepta* and the *An seni gerenda sit res publica* according to A. Masaracchia, 1994, art. cit., pp. 5–40.

9 On Plutarch and Alexander see, apart from my cited study, Mercedes Lopez Salvá, "Plutarco y Alejandro Magno", in *Plutarco y la Historia. Actas del V Congreso Español sobre Plutarco* (C. Schrader et alii eds.), Zaragoza, 1977, pp. 261–270.

cated by the other. And, more specifically, Plutarch's relation to the "popular" sapiential literature so widely disseminated beginning in the 4th century. This is my main theme here.

b. General panorama of Plutarch's works on Alexander

But first we must make certain general observations on the three Plutarchian works on Alexander: we must see his "image" of Alexander, to then go on to study what tradition he did not include and that, nevertheless, has reached us. Although we must not neglect a point that cannot not always be determined exactly: the date of the various elements within the gnomological tradition that I am alluding to. Of course, the Neo-Platonic, Neo-Pythagorean, Hermetic and Christian elements are later than Plutarch. But the Socratic, Platonic, Cynic, Stoic and some other elements inherited from a prior time are, in general terms, earlier than Plutarch. And to see to what extent he has or has not taken advantage of them is what we are attempting to do. First, however, we must summarize the general exposition of the various works of Plutarch on Alexander.

Really, and very concisely, the *Vita Alexandri (VA)* continues the line of encomium for Alexander as the maximum representative of valor, nobility, munificence and humanity, and as the illustrated philosophical man; a line replete with more or less historical anecdotes and also with fantastic elements: prodigious happenings, dreams, supernatural events, although within more modest limits than those of the Pseudo-Callisthenes; Plutarch denies some of those that appear in that work.

In Plutarch Alexander has a fervent love and need of philosophy (7), he abhors the senseless luxury of the powerful and the victorious (24, 40), he respects women (22.5), his meals are frugal (22.7, 23.10), he knows that he is human because he sleeps, because of his relation with women (22.6) and because he has blood and not *ichor* (28.3); he does not steal victory and he battles with loyalty (29, 59), he is very generous (39), he keeps his word and pardons the chief of the Gymnosophists (64) and others too. But he has a high opinion of himself as king: he would sign a treaty with the enemy if he were Parmenion, but he is Alexander (29).

He is, in short, the culmination of the traditional hero, valiant and loyal, an Achilles with characteristics from the teachings of the philosophers, acquired from Aristotle and from his reading (8), legendary characteristics, to be sure. Plutarch adds Alexander's attempts to assimilate himself to the

Persians and to make them assimilate as well (*VA* 47). All of this continuing the line of the Pseudo-Callisthenes, and, I should add, the line of the "image" of Alexander that he himself and his "cabinet" fostered.

I would like to point out several things. First, that some of these anecdotes and χρεῖαι are common to Plutarch *VA* (sometimes also to the rest of the Plutarchian works on Alexander) and to one or more of the gnomologies, and also to various authors. Secondly, some anecdotes and χρεῖαι from the gnomologies are missing in *VA* (and at times in the other works); he chooses from among them (in the sense that they do not contain later material). I will discuss all this below. But I would also like to point out that in Plutarch *VA*, there are materials that are, from what we can see, purely his: he takes from the gnomologies things that have reached us only through him.

In my study I give a list of the citations from *VA* that only appear here or, at most, in some other passage of Plutarch or some single author, but not in the known gnomologies.

In general we have well-known themes: disdain for incompetence and cowardliness, luxury, money; praise of valor and the kingly qualities, generosity, munificence, respect for women and sexual self-control. The vanity of considering himself a god is missing, he is human. It is clear that there was an ample repertory of anecdotes of this type, of a Socratic, at times even Cynic morality, and the old tradition of aristocratic and kingly valor. Plutarch chooses features that we do not find elsewhere, and we will also see the opposite, as I say. But the image, in general terms, is the traditional one fostered by the Macedonian king.

But there is in Plutarch something that is missing in the Pseudo-Callisthenes and in the gnomologies: the dark areas of Alexander's conduct, as when he kills the Indians in his retreat (59. 6–7) and the deaths of Clitus, Philotas, Parmenio and Callisthenes (49, 51, 53 ff., etc.), which the author does not conceal: he tries to pass over them rapidly, attributing them to drunkenness or circumstances of ingratitude. Neither does he use them to give an unfavorable view of Alexander, as happens in Cicero or in Seneca.

Plutarch is, then, a continuer of the encomiastic and legendary history, which presents the new, humane kind of philosophical king, derived from the new thought of the 4th century, although with the differentiating nuances that I have pointed out. I should add that, somewhat marginally, there appears both in the Pseudo-Callisthenes and in Plutarch the theme of the relation of the king with the Cynics, in which the king almost has the role of a Cynic or admires them.

The thesis is this: the triumphs of Alexander are owing to his virtue, not to his good fortune. What dominates is virtue more than valor (but this also). These different virtues are expounded successively, illustrated with examples from the life of the hero, who stands out for his love of knowledge: "It is typical of the philosophic soul to love wisdom and above all to admire the sages. This trait was characteristic of Alexander as of no other king" (1.331 C–D). These virtues are: φρόνησις, σωφροσύνη, ἀνδρεία, ὁσιότης, ἐλευθεριότης, etc., all of them of the traditional Socratic-Platonic type. It is a true fusion of the Socratic-Platonic philosophy and the traditional virtues. Alexander is the philosopher in action.

Apart from this, the number of anecdotes and χρεῖαι is much lower than in the *VA*. Some are common; I have already mentioned them. Others appear in the gnomologies as well; I will speak of them below. Also, there are some that are found only here (or here and in *AApoph.*).

Similarly to the way I have proceeded thus far, I would like to refer in the first place to the anecdotes that are common to *VA* and/or *AF (De Alexandri Fortuna)*; and secondly to those that are only in *AApoph. (Alexandre in Regum ... Apophthegmata)*. Later, in another chapter, we will study those that the gnomological tradition adds to some of these sources. But first I will consider those that are in *VA* and/or *AF* and in *AApoph.*

These are variations on the same themes. It is easy to see that the anecdotic material was copious but coherent; it is always a matter of praise of Alexander within the coordinates indicated. This will be completed when we add the gnomological and other materials. All of this was loosely organized in the following way:

At the beginning, the education of Alexander, at the end, his death; in the center, themes of valor, the royal man (including the theme of the gifts), the humane and clement man, his restraint at meals, his opposition to the *eros*, to luxury and wealth, and to hubris as well. The theme of death scarcely appears in the collection, unlike the Pseudo-Callisthenes and especially its medieval continuers.

In summary, the traditional agonistic morality is amalgamated with Socratic morality, sometimes with Cynic tints. The entrance of ethical themes, not always exactly linked to the life of Alexander, coincides with the definition of him as a philosopher in our works, but above all in later ones.

c. Alexander, Plutarch and the gnomologies

Everything said up to now shows that Plutarch knew various gnomologies, some without doubt relating to Alexander. And this in spite of the fact that he is really only minimally cited in the collections of γνῶμαι. In Giannantoni[10], Plutarch, with reference to *AApophth.* and *VA,* is cited only four times, with regard to dialogues between Thrasilus and Alexander and Harpalus and Crates, and the themes of Diogenes and Onesicritus, all of which I have alluded to above. And Giannantoni does not cite *AF.* No doubt he does not consider Plutarch a philosopher, only, perhaps, a transmitter (and this only to a slight degree). But the fact is that Alexander is not mentioned even once.

This is an error of the modern collectors of gnomologies. It can, perhaps, be accepted that Plutarch is not considered except as a source, but not that Alexander is not mentioned. For Alexander was, for the ancient gnomologists, a philosopher of the Socratic school, a disciple of Aristotle. This is true as much for the gnomologies preserved in Greek as for those preserved in Arabic translation. I have alluded to this in my *Modelos griegos de la sabiduría castellana y europea.*

Of course there are a few cases where maxims of Alexander are found both in Plutarch and in the gnomologies and various authors: this bears witness to the fact that he worked within an open tradition, of which he is one of the reflections. But there is a loose relation; there are examples, not very numerous, that I will present before offering other more frequent ones in which γνῶμαι about Alexander appear in various gnomologies and sources, but not in Plutarch.

I cite, among the gnomologies, *GV* (*Gnomologium Vaticanum*), *GB* (*Gnomica Basileensia*), *Flor. Barocc. = Florilegium Baroccianum*, *Flor. Monac. = Florilegium Monacense*, *Vind. = Excerpta Vindobonencia*, *OM* (Oxford Manuscript), *MC* (Maximus Confessor), *VG* (various Vatican codices), *AM* (Antonius Melissa), Arsenius, as well as derivatives in various authors. And I add *ID* (Ibn Durayd), in Arabic but very close to the Greeks. I give the complete data only for the first gnomology cited in each case. Here it must be remembered that we are dealing only with:

1. Γνῶμαι on Alexander in Plutarch and in gnomologies or other sources;

10 G. Giannantoni, *Socraticorum Reliquiae*, Rome, 1983.

2. Γνῶμαι on Alexander in various gnomologies and sources but not in Plutarch. Aside from the repetitions there are only two variants.

   A brief commentary. It is true that some of these maxims can be later than Plutarch, but given the frequent coincidence among the maxims in Plutarch and those of the gnomologies, we must postulate, I insist, the existence of a long series of gnomologies of similar orientation. Plutarch chose from a very broad array of maxims (which in turn can come from the Pseudo-Callisthenes and from lost literature of a similar orientation). He chose them in his three works or in one or two of them.

   His orientation is the one we are familiar with: the themes of the king granting gifts and benefits, not allowing suspicion, conscious of his valor and superiority. He is tempering, respectful of women, he disdains money and false beauty, he is a king and not an executioner or a master. His model is in Homer.

   Perhaps one must point out the Cynic cast that sometimes infiltrates the maxims. The connection with Diogenes and the Cynics in general (their image is reflected in the Indian Gymnosophists) comes from the Pseudo-Callisthenes and is in Plutarch: the old hostility of the Cynics toward the powerful is tempered by Alexander's admiration for them. So then, here new anecdotes are added that are unknown to Plutarch (*GV* 96, 97, 104, *ID* 8, 10). And in *GV* 102 there is a series of maxims of Cynic character.

   What is not present, here or in Plutarch, is hostility toward the Macedonian; his cruel deeds are not even alluded to. All of this is an apologetic literature.
3. Γνῶμαι on Alexander in the medieval gnomologies. But I believe that the anecdotes and maxims regarding Alexander do not end with the Pseudo-Callisthenes, Plutarch and the ancient gnomologies, some of which reached us in their Byzantine phase or in individual citations from various authors. In the gnomologies known through Castilian translations we find, on the one hand, the same maxims, and on the other hand, new ones. So the existence of the maxims known from far back makes it probable that some of the new ones may actually come from Antiquity; others can have been created based on them[11].

11 The two medieval works are unfamiliar with Plutarch, so that the coincidence with him (rare in any case) derives from the common gnomological tradition. On only one occasion is Plutarch cited (Polutocus, *BO*, p. 168) with a theme that is really Christian.

It must be made clear that I am not dealing here with the legend of Alexander in the Byzantine and Arabic periods, or in *BP*, *BO* and *Poridad*: I have spoken of this in *Modelos*. I am only concerned with the maxims and anecdotes, although, clearly, there is some relation. But is seems to me that this is, in general terms, an older tradition.

In my article I indicate whether the anecdotes and maxims are also in the ancient tradition that has reached us. I include those of:

a. *Buenos Proverbios*
b. *Bocados de Oro*

It can be deduced that *BP* and *BO* have common sources: many of the γνῶμαι are either identical or similar with slight variations. And these sources, on many occasions, are the same ones that the gnomologies we have mentioned so far drew on. But there are hardly any coincidences with Plutarch: it is clear that there were gnomologies used by Plutarch and others that were not, with common elements existing in both; and that our two texts are derived from the latter, the non-Plutarchian ones. Naturally, the Plutarchian ones were used to a different extent in the three works of the author from Queronea. (See Figure 1).

With respect to the content, there are no great differences among all the gnomologies: the theme is fundamentally the same, praise of Alexander from the point of view that we are familiar with – they unite the heroic, the kingly and the philosophic.

Now, elements of *BP* and *BO* that do not figure in the gnomologies derived from the "non-Plutarchian" ones can come from the sources of these texts: thus *BP* and *BO* fill the gaps left by the non-Plutarchian gnomologies.

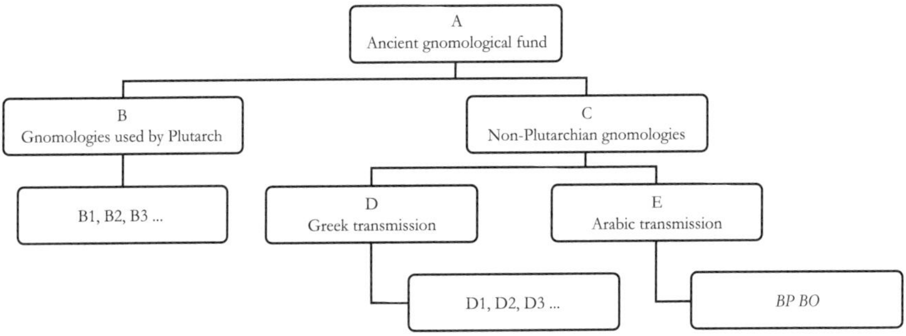

Figure 1.

In consequence, the γνῶμαι that we have considered as new, which do not appear elsewhere, can come from this fund of "non-Plutarchian gnomologies", as we have said. But they can also be derivations or creations of the common source of *BP* and *BO* when they are in both collections. When they are in only one of the two, they can be creations of these collections or of intermediate sources.

All this "new" material does not differ essentially from material we know from the other sources. But I believe that it offers certain nuances of its own, especially in *BO*. It joins emphasis on the themes of "instruction of princes" and moralist themes in general, sometimes with no connection any more to the theme of Alexander: the same thing occurs in another work we have mentioned: *Poridad de las Poridades*.

These γνῶμαι do not stray far from the themes that we have been considering. But, although epic or heroic themes are not lacking, there is great emphasis on ethical themes such as justice, truth, the intellect linked to the tongue and to writing, the king who governs free men, who thinks of his people day and night and benefits them by day, the theme of the family and woman (respect, modesty), the obedience of the people and, nevertheless, the keeping one's distance from the king who is in "muddied waters", etc. All this comes from Antiquity, but it has been reinforced, without doubt (unless it has been eliminated from the gnomologies that we know).

The same must be said of the Cynic themes, sometimes derived from others that we have seen in connection with Diogenes, but that here are more frequent: the theme of fine clothing joined to a lack of intelligence, of the bones of kings being undistinguishable from those of others, of misogyny (not letting oneself be defeated by women).

There is a reinforcement of the moral and Cynic themes, but on existing bases from the ancient gnomologies.

d. Conclusion

Plutarch's three works on Alexander belong to the encomiastic genre, derived, in the final analysis, from the Pseudo-Callisthenes and lost works of the same type. This is the same genre as that of the gnomologies that existed on Alexander and that brought together royal, chivalric and epic features with other moralistic ones. As for the three works, their differences are due, more than to anything else, to dictates of the literary genre. They all choose from the same fund of gnomologies.

All these elements appear both in Plutarch, in his three works, and in the gnomologies that we preserve directly in Greek, which at times in late Antiquity underwent amplifications that have reached us either via Byzantium or by the West. But it seems that Plutarch had only partial access to the ancient fund of gnomologies, since those that have reached us in Greek on occasion contain elements missing in Plutarch (in others we find the same ones). And the gnomologies of the 6th and 7th centuries that were translated from Greek into Arabic and from there into Castilian are familiar with this same fund, at least in part, but they also know elements that only they preserve.

Many of the elements of the gnomologies not accessible to Plutarch, without being radically different from those that were available to him, emphasize the ethical values, including those of the prince, and within these, the Cynic themes that, to be sure, are not absent from Plutarch (and are earlier than the Pseudo-Callisthenes), although not in any great measure.

2. Studies by the author on ancient sapiential literature and Cervantes. Summary.

In a series of three papers that go beyond some earlier ones already used in *Modelos* …, the author has proposed the existence of an extensive influence of the old realistic novel (apart from *The Golden Ass* and *The Banquet of Trimalchio*, which are well known) and a series of Cynic themes, first on the *Lazarillo* and the picaresque novel in general; then on *El Licenciado Vidriera*, certain others of the *Novelas Ejemplares* and, especially, the *Quijote*. This connection with the picaresque novel has been studied by various authors; the bibliography is given.

This line of the picaresque novel and Cervantes (that is to say, a part of Cervantes), which inaugurate the western novel, derives, then, from the Greek realistic novel of a Cynicizing type, although in other modern novels the root is, as we know, in the so-called Greek, later Byzantine novel.

I am going to give a summary of the three papers that I have devoted to this topic and that are later than *Modelos* … (where, furthermore, the theme is already touched on, see p.86).

a. *"De la Vida de Esopo al Lazarillo y Cervantes", in* Charisterion Francisco Martin Garcia oblatum. *Cuenca, Universidad Castilla-La Mancha, 2004, pp. 21–33.*

To be sure, Francisco Rico and others have mentioned the two novels cited above plus the *Baldo* and the *Crotalón* as inspiring the *Lazarillo*, but I add, among others, the *Life of Aesop* (in Latin since 1479, in Castilian since 1489, widely disseminated and much earlier than the well-known 1554 edition of the *Lazarillo*). I add other possible sources, namely, various medieval Latin ramifications derived from this type of literature. And I must emphasize the influence of all of them on Italian works like the *Bertoldo* or French ones like *Gargantua and Pantagruel.*

I propose that not only the *Lazarillo* but also earlier works like *El Libro de Buen Amor*, *El Conde Lucanor* and various collections of maxims and aphorisms are within this same environment. And this can be said, too, of well-known works by Chaucer and Boccaccio.

Our study also is concerned with the theme of the comic hero, about which Papademetriou has written. I indicate its ancient precedents going back to Archilochus and its presence in the Archpriest and the *Celestina.*

It is a jump, of course, to the *Lazarillo*, whose similarities with the *Life of Aesop* I study in detail. Some themes are also common to the *Guzmán de Alfarache*, which Cervantes was familiar with. I conclude that "the marked similarity of the fictional plot of the two texts and their ideological orientation, as well as the central characters, who share many important features, can serve as an indication of a formative influence of the ancient text with respect to the modern one."

I also allude to *La lozana andaluza*, whose Rampín shares many of the characteristics of the Aesop of the *Life* and also of the Lázaro; and to parallels in Cervantes as well, in *Rinconete* and the *Coloquio de los perros*. All of this was already known.

Finally, going on to the *Quijote*, I should point out that Elvira Gangutia and later Holzberg, Papademetriou and I have all suggested that the name of Sancho (*Sanctius* in Latin) comes from *Xanthos*, Aesop's master in the *Life*. Following that I study the possible relations between Sancho and this Aesop and I also speak of the *Coloquio de los perros* and *El Licenciado Vidriera*, which I compare with the *Quijote* in the themes of madness, of the master and of the servant (secondary in the *Quijote*, it was not in the *Entremés de los romances*, which appears to be the original model). Furthermore, this theme is present in ancient theatre and in Spanish theatre from as far back as the 15th century.

In short, I consider that the direct source of the *Quijote* is in the *Lazarillo*. Cervantes may have known the ancient sources and have used them at the same time as he used the *Lazarillo*, but this is only a hypothesis. In any case, Sancho has aspects in common with the Aesop of the *Life*, although there also are, without doubt, popular Spanish sources.

El Libro de Buen Amor, the *Lazarillo* and *El Licenciado Vidriera* are the works that are closest to the *Life of Aesop*, while the *Coloquio* is closer to *The Golden Ass*. As for the *Quijote*, it is close to the *Lazarillo* without any doubt, and perhaps also to some ancient popular and Cynicizing literature, including the *Life of Aesop* (and possibly other *Lives*). In the following works I explicate this point.

b. *"Cervantes and the ancients", in* La España y el Cervantes del primer Quijote. *Madrid, Real Academia de la Historia, 2005, pp. 45–70.*

The beginning of this article stresses the scant relation of Cervantes with the great ancient classics; the *Quijote* is a popular, realistic novel which connects with the corresponding genres of Antiquity. It is the common people who fill its pages, just as they do in its Castilian and ancient precedents. The author gives more examples of this literature in Antiquity: *Lives*, maxims, various satires, debates.

He considers unfortunate that the *Life of Aesop* is not given attention by the scholars of Spanish literature, in which he highlights episodes of a Cynic character. Aesop travels the world from adventure to adventure and imparts wisdom, in fables, anecdotes, satires and maxims, to his master, the philosopher Xantos and to his philosopher friends as well as to King Croesus and the Delphians. He is a kind of antihero, ugly but intelligent. He has notable forerunners in the Greco-Latin tradition.

The author studies the continuation of this line in the *Lazarillo* and the *Quijote*, in which, nevertheless, the erotic episodes are lacking: demands of the times.

For Cervantes and other authors, the ancient world is dominated by the Greek novel, the pastoral genre and the others that I have mentioned. In the Middle Ages all of them survived the downfall of the great Literature (which regained its influence in the Renaissance, with no loss of the earlier genres).

Another point of contact of the *Quijote* with the ancient and medieval works of popular wisdom is the theme of the discovery of a rare manuscript. The greater part of Cervantes' work, with its ancient and medieval precedents and the concomitant features that kept it alive among the people, can, in a broad sense, be placed within sapiential literature.

On the other hand, it does not seem right to situate Cervantes among the Erasmians: this was a matter of theologians and philosophers; there can be echoes of popular satire, but Cervantes remains in the discrete background in matters of religion. As in the literature that we are discussing, everything in the *Quijote* reflects pure humanity, everything can be transplanted to any country or period.

What would Cervantes have done, back in 1597, in the prison of Seville, on the eve of the death of Philip II, alone and with no books? No doubt build on his memories, imagine what would happen in his Spain to a knight like those of the idealizing books that he knew so well. Defeats when defending justice, common women instead of idealized heroines, flocks of sheep but no armies, echoes of the readings of the ancient popular Greco-Latin literature, perhaps in translation or heard read aloud, also Italian and Castilian works.

As we know, the beginning of the *Quijote* presents the knight alone in his first disastrous sally, whose model was surely the *Entremés de los romances*. Cervantes found he needed a squire in order to make dialogue possible, a sly, rustic companion, skeptical but secretly ambitious, a help to his master: Sancho. Here we can emphasize the features he shares with various ancient, medieval and contemporary antiheroes; Aesop is one of them.

At the end of the article there is a discussion in general terms of the coincidences of the novel and other Cynicizing genres and the *Quijote*: voyages, sayings, debates, anecdotes, satire (especially on women and physicians), stories, short novels, criticism of the powerful and of falsehood, the theme of the world reversed (Sancho as governor), counsels (including Don Quijote's "counsels for the prince" addressed to Sancho), etc. This was a genre that was pleasing to Cervantes, the hero ill-treated by fortune. The old Cynic antihero and the more recent "pícaro" were adapted to the circumstances of contemporary Spain.

Passages like those of the Golden Age and others that depend on the great classics do not require a direct knowledge of those works; they simply become one more piece of the multicolored mosaic.

A strange alchemy of Cervantes, that of placing all this alongside a parody of chivalry. The derivation of this alchemy from minor genres is the beginning of the great western novelistic tradition, a noteworthy case.

The article ends with a detailed description of the features of the old Cynicizing literature in *El Licenciado Vidriera*, even clearer here, and in other works by Cervantes.

In summary, one must recuperate the world of ancient wisdom that was palpable in the environment and was read in popular works, which were doubtless the most translated ones, and that was present in the origin of a large sector of the antecedents of the great modern novel in Castile, Italy and France. Of course, there is still the sector of the idealistic novel, which comes from a different ancient tradition. And so the great ancient literature began to make its influence felt decisively in the 15th century.

c. "El género literario del Quijote", BRAE *CCXCI–CCXCII, 2005, pp. 573–584.*

This work returns to the previous themes and carries them further. The ancient sapiential tradition in its Cynicizing adaptation invades the entire Middle Ages and goes beyond that. It should be emphasized that in Antiquity the "Counsels for the Prince" belonged to these genres, passing on to the Christian ones and to the Middle Ages, later even reaching Quevedo. Attention must be drawn to Lucian (known by Cervantes), Seneca, the maxims of various authors and of the gnomologies, Christian preaching, etc., among other routes of access.

This literature contained a certain erotic element (mitigated in Cervantes) whence came the tradition of Boccaccio and the others, and various other elements already described, as well as stories, debates, parodies, etc., as I have said. In the *Quijote* there is an amalgam of these various Greek, Latin and medieval genres. But Cervantes broke the pattern by introducing a main character foreign to this tradition, Don Quijote. The *Quijote* is both an old realistic novel linked to a conglomerate of sapiential elements and a new genre, the extensive modern novel, centering on Don Quijote. Later, this combination broke up into various different genres, which were really of an earlier origin

This multiplicity is strongly reminiscent of the vital experiences of Cervantes, which I am not going to recall here. I must only say that if they were painful, they also added to his experience of the world, to his humanity and wisdom. It all combined easily with the ancient and medieval literary universe that enveloped him, from the Cynic antihero to the "pícaro" and the rest. But the criticism of the *Quijote* is not crude, but humane, as Ayala and others have correctly remarked.

Curiously, Cervantes passed from literary criticism, characteristic of the Cynics, to social criticism (actually, the Cynics used both). He used the same elements for this, adding others, such as the pastoral novel.

Thus, it is right to define the *Quijote* as the beginning of the modern novel, but this does not seem enough. I have spoken of its sapiential and Cynic precedents, but Cervantes, in his use of them, has gone much further. The length of the *Quijote* , in any case, made it necessary to combine a multitude of elements, but always respecting the central line of the hero who idealistically wants to change the world and who naturally fails. And who is accompanied by the squire whose model can be found in the old antiheroes.

An interesting debate. Don Quijote coincides with ideas that were floating about: discontent with the world, asceticism, holiness, the need for change. He anticipates the rationalisms and idealisms of future centuries. But, strictly speaking, he should not be included with the Erasmians, as I have said.

Thus, the *Quijote* encompasses a long tradition (or traditions) and a modern world. From it comes the novel in its entirety, as we know. But the novel pruned away elements and strengthened the central or dramatic line at the expense of the marginal elements, discarding many that were of ancient origin. The *Quijote* is still at a halfway point. It is not simple.

It looks forward, but it depends on earlier roots. Cervantes, as the child of his times that he is, creates from his times. But he is strongly rooted in certain sectors of classical Antiquity, those that were most accessible to him, and which I have attempted to make clear. He combined these with his own ideas and experiences and incorporated them into a new central scheme centering on Don Quijote, who, furthermore, had his origin in the old parodic genres.

III. Selected supplemental bibliography of sapiential literature

Alonso Troncoso, Victor, "La *paideía* del príncipe en tiempos de los diádocos", *AHB* 14, 2000, pp. 22–34

Bizzarri, Hugo Oscar, "Non omnis moriar. Sobre la fama del sabio en la Edad Media castellana", *Thesaurus* 45, 1990, pp. 3–6

—,"Técnicas del sermón medieval en el *Libro de los gatos*", *Cultura Neolatina* 55, 1995, pp. 101–116

—,"Una disputa entre filósofos y teólogos: la concepción de la naturaleza en las colecciones sapienciales castellanas", *Medioevo* 22, 1996, pp. 303–334

—,"La estructura de *Castigos e documentos* del rey Don Sancho IV", *Incipit* 17, 1999, pp. 83–138

Díaz Martínez, Eva. Mª, "Tradición e innovación en los tratados de educación de los príncipes de los siglos XVI y XVII. Una revisión del fenómeno", *Analecta Malacitana* 23, 2000, pp. 493–519

Egido, Aurora, "A la tercera. Nuevos relieves de discreción quijotesca", in S. Redondo, ed., *Releyendo el Quijote, cuatrocientos años después*, Paris, Presses de la Sorbonne Nouvelle, 2005, pp. 87–113

Fernández Delgado, José Antonio, "*Auxesis* en el uso plutárqueo de la fábula", in A. Pérez Jiménez and F. Titchener, eds., *Valori literari delle Opere di Plutarco*, Málaga-Utah I.P.S., 2005, pp. 111–120

—,"La fábula en Plutarco: de la historieta ejemplarizante al ejercicio progimnasmático", in M. Jufresa et al, eds., *Plutarc a la seva època*, Barcelona, 2005, pp. 77–84

—,"Enseñar fabulando en Grecia y Roma: los testimonios papiráceos" *Minerva* 19, 2006, pp. 29–52

Fuentes González, P. P., "Thales reconsidered", *Mnemosyne* 51, 1998, pp. 1–19

—,"El atajo filosófico de los cínicos antiguos hacia la felicidad", *Cuadernos de Fil. Clás. Estudios griegos e indoeuropeos* 12, 2002, pp. 202–251

—,"¿Necesitaban de un amigo los cínicos antiguos?", *Bitarte* 31, 2002, pp. 51–72

Fuentes González, P. P., "Epictète", in R. Goulet (ed.), Dictionnaire des Philosophes Antiques, III, Paris, *CNRS*, pp. 106–151

—, "Eratosthène de Cyrène", in R. Goulet (ed.), Dictionnaire des Philosophes Antiques, III, Paris, *CNRS*, pp. 188–236

González Barrera, Julián, "La historia de la doncella Teodor: una invención greco-bizantina, un cuento de *Las mil y una noches* y, finalmente, un pliego de cordel", unpublished doctoral thesis, U. Sevilla

Haro Cortes, Marta, "Erotismo y arte amatoria en el discurso médico de la *Historia de la donzella Teodor*", *RLM* 5, 1993, pp. 113–125

—,"Una nueva coleccíon de sentencias: proverbios o sentencias breves espirituales o morales", *RLM* 13, 2001, pp. 9–43

—, "Narratividad y práctica literaria en la literatura de sentencias medieval" in Lacarra and Cacho Blecua, eds. *Tipología de las formas narrativas breves románicas medievales III,* Zaragoza, 2004, pp. 235–266

Ladero Quesada, M. A., "El emperador Trajano como modelo de príncipes en la Edad Media", *Anuario de Estudios Medievales* 1999, pp. 501–525

Laplana, J. E., "Aldonza en el convento y Cervantes resucitado", in *Colecciones aragonesas,* Zaragoza, 2005, pp. 17–32

Pérez Jiménez, Aurelio, "El ideal del buen rey según Plutarco", in *La imagen de la releza en la Antigüedad*, Madrid, Editorial Coloquio, 1988, pp. 89–113

Overwien, G., "Das Gnomologium Vaticanum und die Tradition", *Gottinger Forum für die Altertumswissenschaft* 4, 2001, pp. 99–131

—,"Zwei literarisch-philosophische Vorbilder für Lukian und seinen *Demonax*", *Gymnasium* 110, 2003, pp. 533–550

Searby, D. M., "The sources of the so-called *Gnomologium Parisinum*", *Revue d'histoire des textes* 29, 1999, pp. 295–300

—, *The Corpus Parisinum. A Critical Edition of the Greek Text with Commentary and English Translation (A Medieval Anthology of Greek Texts from the Pre-Socratics to the Church Fathers, 600 B.C.–700 A.D.)*, Lewinston - Queenston - Lampeter, The Edwin Mellen Press, 2007, 3 vols.

Tardieu, M., "Aristotle et la sagesse des nations", *Journal Asiatique* 294, 2006, pp. 67–79

Van Dijk, Gert-Jan, "Transmission and Reception of the Classical Fable Tradition", in *Favolisti Latini medievali e Umanistici XIII*, Genova, 1988, pp. 9–31

List of works cited

Acosta, E. and Angeli, E., *Filodemo. Testimonianze su Socrate*, Naples, Bibliopolis, 1992

Adrados, F. R., "La lengua de Sócrates y su filosofía", *Methexis* 1952, pp. 29–52

—, "Aristóteles en la Atenas de su tiempo", *Estudios Clásicos* 108, 1955, pp. 43–55

—, "La Vida de Esopo y la Vida de Lazarillo de Tormes", *Revista de Filología Española* 58, 1976, pp. 35–45

—, "Desiderata en la investigación de la fábula antigua", in *Actas del V Congreso Español de Estudios Clásicos*, Madrid, 1978, pp. 215–235

—, "Elementos cínicos en las Vidas de Esopo y Secundo y en el Dialogo de Alejandro y los gimnosofistas", *Homenaje a Eleuterio Elorduy*, Bilbao, Universidad de Deusto, 1978, pp. 309–329

—, "Hechos generales y hechos griegos en el origen de la crítica y la sátira", *Homenaje a Julio Caro Baroja*, Madrid, Centro de Investigaciones Sociológicas, 1978, pp. 43–63

—, "The Life of Aesop and the Origins of the Novel in Antiquity", *Quaderni Urbinati di Cultura Classica* N.S. 1, 1979, pp. 93–112

—, *Historia de la fábula greco-latina*, Madrid, Universidad Complutense, 1979–87, 3 vols. [English revised edition (by the author and Gert-Jan van Dijk), Leiden, Brill, 1997–2003]

—, "Siria, cruce de caminos de la narrativa bizantina y oriental", *Aula Orientalis* 3, 1981, pp. 17–29

—, "El Libro de Buen Amor y la Vida de Esopo", in *Serta Philologica F. Lázaro Carreter*, Madrid, Gredos, 1983, II, pp. 427–433

—, "Más fragmentos nuevos de poesía griega antigua", *Studi in onore di Adelmo Barigazzi, Sileno* 10, 1984, pp. 1–10

—, "The earliest influences of Greek Fable on Medieval Latin writing", *Classica et Mediaevalia* 35, 1984, pp. 243–263

—, "Aportaciones al estudio de las fábulas del Arcipreste", in *Philologica Hispaniensia in honorem Manuel Alvar. III. Literatura*, Madrid, Gredos, 1986, pp. 459–473

—, *Filosofía cínica en las fábulas esópicas*, Buenos Aires, Centro de Estudios Filosóficos, 1986

Adrados, F. R.,, "Las fuentes de Hesíodo y la composición de sus poemas", *Emerita* 54, 1986, pp. 1–36

—, "Política cínica en las fábulas esópicas", in *Filologia e forme letterarie. Studi offerti a Francesco della Corte,* Urbino, Università degli Studi di Urbino, 1987, I, pp. 413–426

—, "Problemas de crítica textual en la transmisión de la fábula greco-latina", in *La crítica textual y los textos clásicos. III Simposio de la Sección de Filología Clásica de la Universidad de Murcia (9 y 10 de abril de 1984)*, Murcia, Universidad, 1987, pp. 131–148

—, "Documentación suplementaria de la fábula greco-latina", *Euphrosyne* 18, 1990, pp. 213–226

—, "El cuento erótico, de los cínicos al final de la Edad Media", *Argos* 12, 1990–91 [1992], pp. 185–194

—, "La fecha de la Augustana y la tradición fabulística griega y bizantina", *Prometheus* 18, 1992, pp. 139–149

—, "La fábula en Bizancio, entre Grecia, Oriente y Occidente", *Studi Italiani di Filologia Classica* 11, 1993, pp. 195–204

—, "Literatura sapiencial antigua en la *Haggadah* y en Pedro Alfonso", *Illinois Classical Studies* 18, 1993, pp. 229–236

—, *El cuento erótico griego, latino e indio*, Madrid, Ediciones Clásicas, 1994

—, "Géneros helenísticos en el Banquete de los Siete Sabios de Plutarco", in *Estudios sobre Plutarco: Aspectos Formales*, Salamanca, Ediciones Clásicas - Universidad, 1996, pp. 125–142

—, "Orígenes del teatro español en Salamanca", in *Salamanca y la Literatura. Ciclo de conferencias pronunciadas en Fundación Ramón Areces (Febrero 1996)*, Madrid, Fundación Ramón Areces, 1996, pp. 13–38

—, "Nuevos textos sapienciales griegos en obras árabe-castellanas", *Emerita* 67, 1999, pp. 195–217

—, "Las imágenes de Alejandro", in J. Álvarez and S. M. Blázquez (eds.), *Alejandro Magno. Hombre y Mito*, Madrid, Editorial Actas, 2000, pp. 15–31

—, "Tradición sapiencial antigua y obras árabe-castellanas", in *Studia Graeca in memoriam Jesús Lens Tuero*, Granada, Athos-Pérgamo, 2000, pp. 1–17

—, "Las fábulas de Lokmann dentro de la tradición fabulística griega", in *Studi di Filologia e tradizione greca in memoria di Aristide Colonna*, Napoli, Edizioni Scientifiche Italiane, 2003, pp. 1–15

—, *De Esopo al Lazarillo*, Huelva, Universidad de Huelva, 2005

—, "Alejandro, Plutarco y las gnomologías griegas", in *Plutarc a la seva época: paideia i societat. Actas del VIII Simposio Internacional de la Sociedad Española de Plutarquistas*, Barcelona 2005, pp. 33–50

Alexiou, M., *The ritual lament in Greek Tradition*, Cambridge, Cambridge University Press, 1974

Alvarado, S., "Paralelismos entre la literatura etíope clásica y las antiguas literaturas eslavas", *Boletín de la Asociación Española de Orientalistas* 34, 1998, pp. 313–330

Bádenas, P., *Barlaam y Josafat: redacción bizantina anónima*, Madrid, Siruela, 1993

Bat Moshe, S., "Fuentes judías. Leyenda del Talmud y del Midrash", Jerusalem, World Zionist Organization, Department for Education and Culture in the Diaspora, 1980, pp. 132–151

Baumstark, A., *Aristoteles bei den Syrern vom 5. bis 8. Jahrhundert*, Leipzig, Teubner, 1900 [= Aalen, Scientia-Verlag, 1976 (reprint)]

—, *Syrisch-Arabische Biographien des Aristoteles*, Leipzig, Teubner, 1900

Beck, H.-G., *Kirche und Theologische Literatur im Byzantinischen Reich*, Munich, Beck, 1959

Bergson, L., *Carmina praecipue choliambica apud Pseudo-Callisthenem reperta*, Stockholm, Almquist, 1989

Beschorner, A., "Griechische Briefbücher berühmter Männer", in N. Holzberg (ed.), *Der griechische Briefroman*, Tübingen 1994, pp. 169–190

Bizarri, H., "Consideraciones en torno a la elaboración de *El libro de los doze sabios*", *La Corónica* 18, 1989, pp. 85–89

—, "La estructura de *Castigos e Documentos* del rey Don Sancho IV. Apuntes para la historia de la formación de la ciencia política en la Castilla del siglo XIII", *Incipit* 17, 1997, pp. 83–138

Borkowski, J.-F., *Socratis quae feruntur epistolae*, Stuttgart, Teubner, 1997

Bouffartige, J., "Du grec au latin. La traduction latine des Sentences de Sextus", in *Études de Littérature ancienne*, Paris, Presses de l'École Normale Supérieure, 1971, pp. 81–95

Brock, S., "The laments of the philosophers over Alexander in Syriac", *Journal of Semitic Studies* 15, 1970, pp. 205–218

—, "From antagonism to assimilation: Syriac attitudes to Greek Learning", in *East of Byzantium* (N. Garsoian et alii, eds.), Washington, 1982

—, "A Syriac collection of Prophecies of the Pagan Philosophers", *Orientalia Lovaniensia Periodica* 14, 1983, pp. 203–246

Brocker, M., *Aristoteles als Alexanders Lehrer in der Legende*, Bonn, 1966

Budge, E. A. W., *The Alexander Book in Ethiopia*, London, 1933
Calvo, J. L., *Textos de magia en papiros griegos*, Madrid, Gredos, 1987
Cañas, J., *Libro de Alexandre*, Madrid, 1988
Carlini, A., "Le Sentenze di Sesto nella versione di Rufino", *Studi forogiuliesi in onore di C. G. Mor*, Udine, Arti Grafiche Friulane, 1984
Cary, C., *The Medieval Alexander*, Cambridge, Cambridge University Press, 1956
Chadwick, H., *The Sentences of Sextus*, Cambridge, Cambridge University Press, 1959
—, *Florilegium*, in *Reallexikon für Antike und Christentum* 7, 1969, cols. 1131–1160
Chevalier, M., "Prólogo", in Mª.J., Lacarra, *Cuento y Novela corta en España. 1. Edad Media*, Barcelona, Crítica, 1999
Copenhaver, B. P., *Hermetica*, Cambridge, Cambridge University Press, 1994
Corpus dei Papiri Filosofici Greci e Latini (CPF), I 1***, Florence, 1999
Crombach, M., *Bocados de oro. Kritische Ausgabe des spanischen Textes*, Bonn, Romanisches Seminar der Universität Bonn, 1971
Daly, L. W., *Contributions to the History of Alphabetization in Antiquity and the Middle Ages*, Brussels, Latomus, 1967
Daly, L. W. and Suchier, W., *The Altercatio Hadriani Augusti et Epicteti philosophi and the question-and-answer dialogue*, Urbana, University of Illinois Press, 1939
Darbord, B., "La tradición del saber en la *Donzella Teodor*" in *Actas del V Congreso de la Asociación Hispánica de Literatura Medieval*, Granada, Universidad, 1995, pp. 13–30
Diels, H., *Doxographi Graeci*, Berlin, de Gruyter, 1929[2]
Dihle, A., "Zur antiken Biographie", in W. W. Ehlers (ed.), *La biographie antique*, *Entretiens sur l'Antiquité Classique* 44, Genève, Fondation Hardt, 1998, pp. 119–146
Elter, A., *De Gnomologiorum Graecorum historia atque origine commentatio*, Bonn, 1893–97
—, *Sententiae Pythagoreorum*, in *Gnomica Homoeomata* 5, Bonn, 1904
Endress G., (ed.), *The ancient tradition in Christian and Islamic Hellenism*, Leiden 1997
Fernández Delgado, J. A., "La poesía sapiencial griega en Grecia y los orígenes del hexámetro", *Emerita* 50, 1982, pp. 151–174
—, *Los oráculos de Hesíodo. Poesía oral mántica y gnómica griega*, Cáceres, Universidad de Extremadura, 1986

Franceschini, E., "Il Liber philosophorum moralium antiquorum", in *Acta della regale Accademia dei Lincei, Classe di Szienze morali, storiche e philologiche* 3, 1930, pp. 355–399

Gallé Cejudo, R. J., "La carta ficticia griega y el diálogo", *Excerpta Philologica* 4–5, 1994–95, pp. 41–51

Gallo, I., *Frammenti biografici da papiri*, II, Rome, Edizioni dell'Ateneo, 1980

García Gómez, E., *Un texto árabe occidental de la leyenda de Alejandro:* according to manuscript ar XXVII in the Library of the Junta para Ampliación de Estudios, Madrid, 1929

Gerhard, G. A., *Phoinix von Colophon*, Leipzig, Teubner, 1909

Gerresch, C., "Un récit des Mille et Une Nuits: Twadduh, Petite Encyclopédie de l'Islam médieval", *Bulletin de l'Institut Français de l'Afrique Noire* 25, serie B, 1, 1973, pp. 57–175

Giannantoni, G., *I presocratici. Testimonianze e frammenti*, Bari, Laterza,1969

—, *Socrate. Tutte le testimonianze*, Bari, Laterza, 1971

—, *Socraticorum reliquiae* II, Rome, Bibliopolis, 1983

Gimeno Casalduero, J., "El *Conde Lucanor*: composición y significado", *Nueva Revista de Filología Hispánica* 24, 1975, pp. 101–112

Gómez Redondo, F., *Historia de la prosa medieval castellana. I*, Madrid, Cátedra, 1998

Grignaschi, M., "Les *Rasā'il Aristātālisa ilā-l-Iskandar* de Sālim Abū-l-'Alā et l'activité culturelle à l'époque Omayyade", *Bulletin d'Études Orientales de Damas* 19, 1965–66, pp. 7–83

—, "Le roman épistolaire classique conservé dans la version arabe de Sālim Abū-l-'Alā", *Le Muséon* 80, 1967, pp. 211–264

—, "La figure d'Alexandre chez les arabes et sa genèse", *Arabic Sciences and Philosophy* 3, 1993, pp. 205–234

Gutas, D., *Greek wisdom literature in Arabic translation. A study of the Graeco-Arabic gnomologia*, New Haven, CT, American Oriental Society, 1975

—, *Greek thought, Arabic culture. The Graeco-Arabic translation movement and early 'Abbāsid society (2nd–4th/8th–10th centuries)*, London-New York, Routledge, 1998

Guy, J.-C., *Les apophthegmes des Pères*, 1, Paris, Éditions du Cerf, 1993

Hadot, P., "Fürstenspiegel", in *Reallexikon für Antike und Christentum*, vol. VIII, Stuttgart 1972, cols. 555–632

Hägg, T., "The oriental reception of Greek Novels", *Symbolae Osloenses* 61, 1986, pp. 99–131

Haro, M., "Erotismo y arte amatoria en el discurso médico de la *Historia de la Donzella Teodor*", *RLM* 5, 1993, pp. 113–125

Henry III, P., "A Mirror for Justinian: the *Ekthesis* of Agapetus Diaconus", *GRBS* 8, 1967, pp. 281–308

Hock, R. F. and O'Neil, E. N., *The chreia in ancient Rhetorik*, I, *The Progymnasmata*, Atlanta, Scholars Press, 1985

Holzberg, N., *Der griechische Briefroman*, Tübingen, 1994

Huit, C., "Les épistolographes grecs", *REG* 2, 1889, pp. 149–163

Jaekel, S., *Menander*, Leipzig, Teubner, 1974

Kasten, L. A., "Poridat de las Poridades. A Spanish Form of the Western Text of the Secretum Secretorum", *Romance Philology*, 5, 1951–1952, pp. 180–190

—, *Poridat de las poridades*, Madrid, 1957

Kaufhold, H., "Die Überlieferung der *Sententiae Syriacae* und ihr historischer und literarischer Kontext", *Akten des 26. deutschen Rechtshistorikertages*, Frankfurt am Main, Klostermann, 1987, pp. 505–518

Kindstrand, J. F., *Bion of Boristhenes. A collection of the fragments with introduction and commentary*, Upsala, Almquist, 1976

—, *Anacharsis. The legend and the apophthegmata*, Upsala, Almqvist & Wiksell, 1981

—, "Florilegium Baroccianum and codex Hierosolymitanus Sancti Sepulchri 255", *Byzantion* 54, 1984, pp. 536–550

—, "Florilegium e Basilio Magno ineditum", *Eranos* 83, 1985, pp. 113–124

—, "A collection of Apophthegmata in an Oxford Manuscript", in S.-T. Teodorsson (ed.), *Greek and Latin Studies in Memory of Cajus Fabricius*, *Studia Graeca et Latina Gothoburgensia* 54, Gothenburg, 1990, pp. 141–153

Klauser, P. and de Labriolle, E., *Apophthegma* in *Reallexicon für Antike und Christentum*, I, 1950, cols. 545–550

Knust, H., "Flores de Filosofía", in *Dos obras didácticas y dos leyendas*, Madrid, Sociedad de Bibliófilos Españoles, 1878

—, *Mitteilungen aus dem Eskurial*, Tübingen, 1879

Krämer, J., "Arabische Homerverse", *ZDMG* 106, 1956, pp. 486–506

Lacarra, Mª. J. and López Estrada, F., *Orígenes de la prosa*, Madrid, Júcar, 1993

Lambert, W. G., *Babylonian Wisdom Literature*, Oxford, Clarendon Press, 1960

Lamberz, E., *Porphyrii Sententiae ad intellegibilia ducentes*, Leipzig, Teubner, 1975

Leo, F., *Die griechisch-römische Biographie nach ihrer literarischen Form*, Leipzig, Teubner, 1901 (Hildesheim, Olms, 1965)

Lida, Mª. R., "La leyenda de Alejandro en la Literatura medieval", in *La tradición clásica en España*, Barcelona, Ariel, 1975

Lippert, J., *Studien auf dem Gebiete der griechisch-arabischen Übersetzungliteratur. I. Quellenforschung zu den arabischen Aristotelesbiographien*, Braunschweig, Richard Sattler, 1894

Manns, F., "Une source de l'Aggadah juive: la littérature grecque", *Liber Annuus* 29, 1979, pp. 111–144

Manzalaoui, M., "The pseudo-Aristotelian Kitāb Sirr al-āsrār", *Oriens*, 23–24, 1974, pp. 147–247

Marín, M., "Legends on Alexander the Great in Moslem Spain", *Graeco-Arabica* 4, 1991, pp. 71–89

Mariño, R. Mª. and García Romero, F., *Proverbios Griegos. Menandro: Sentencias*, Madrid, Gredos, 1999

Massignon, L., "Inventaire de la littérature hermétique arabe", appendix to J. P. Festugière, *La révelation d'Hermès Trismégiste*, vol. I: *L'astrologie et les sciences occultes*, Paris, Gabalda, 1944 (reed. 1981), pp. 384–400

Mazzaoui, M. M., "Alexander the Great and Arab Historians", *Graeco-Arabica* 4, 1991, pp. 33–44

Megaw, P., "A Syriac Collection of Prophecies of the pagan philosophers", *Orientalia Lovaniensia Periodica* 14, 1983, pp. 203–246

Menéndez Pelayo, M., "La *Donzella Teodor* (un cuento de *Las Mil y Una Noches*, un libro de cordel y una comedia de Lope de Vega)", in *Homenaje a D. Francisco Codera en su jubilación del profesorado,* Zaragoza, Mariano Escar, 1904, pp. 483–511

Menéndez Pidal, G., "Cómo trabajaban las escuelas alfonsíes", *Nueva Revista de Filología Hispánica* 5, 1951, pp. 363–380

Merkelbach, R., *Die Quellen des griechischen Alexandersromans*, Munich, Beck, 1954

Merkle, K., *Die Sittensprüche der Philosophen, Kitāb ādāb al falāsifa*, Leipzig, O. Harrassowitz, 1921

Mettman, W., *La historia de la donzella Teodor. Ein spanisches Volksbuch arabischen Ursprungs*, Mainz, Akademie der Wissenschaften und der Literatur, 1962

Miquel, A., "Twadduh la servante", *Sept contes des Mille et une Nuits*, Paris, Sindbad, 1980, pp. 13–49

Mitchell, J. F., "Consolatory Letters in Basil and Gregory Nazianzen", *Hermes* 96, 1968, pp. 299–318

Nock, A. D., "Diatribe Form in the Hermetica", in *Essays on Religion and the Ancient World*, Oxford, Clarendon Press, 1972, pp. 26–32
Nock, A. D. and Festugière, A.-J., *Corpus Hermeticum*, vols. I–IV, Paris, Les Belles Lettres, 1946–54
Odorico, P., "Il 'Corpus Parisinum' e la fase costitutiva dei florilegi sacro-profani", in *Studi Bizantini e Neogreci, Atti del IV Congresso Nazionale di Studi Bizantini*, Galatina, Congedo, 1983, pp. 417–429
Offenloch, E., *Caecilii Caleactini fragmenta*, 2nd ed., Stuttgart, Teubner, 1967
Oliver, P., *Los diálogos entre el rey y el sabio en época helenística*, unpublished doctoral thesis, Murcia 1988
Packmohr, A., *De Diogenis Sinopensis apophthegmatis quaestiones selectae*, Münster 1913
Papadimitriou, J. Th. A., *Aesop as an archetypal Hero*, Athens, 1997
Perry, B. E., *Aesopica*, Urbana, University of Illinois Press, 1952
—, *Secundus the silent philosopher*, Ithaca, New York, Cornell University Press, 1964
Peters, F. E., *Aristotle and the Arabs*, New York, New York University Press, 1968
Phillips, M. B., "Some Remarks on the Manuscript tradition of the Maximus Florilegium", *Illinois Classical Studies* 7, 1982, pp. 261–275
Plezia, M., *Aristotelis privatorum scriptorum fragmenta*, Leipzig, Teubner, 1977
Pohl, S., "Die Aristotelische Ethik im *Kitab al-Sa'ada wa-l-is'ad*", in G. Endress and R. Kruk (eds.) *The Ancient Tradition in Christian and Islamic Hellenism. Studies on the transmission of Greek philosophy and sciences dedicated to H. J. Drossaart Lulofs on his ninetieth birthday*, Leiden, 1997, pp. 201–235
Poirier, P., "À propos de la version copte des Sentences de Sextus", *Laval Théologique et Philosophique* 36, 1980, pp. 317–320
—, "Le texte de la version copte des sentences de Sextus", *Colloque International sur les textes de Nag Hammadi*, Québec-Louvain la Neuve, Presses de l'Université Laval, 1981, pp. 383–389
Pötscher, W., *Epistula ad Marcellam*, Leiden, Brill, 1969
Puche López, Mª. C., *Historia de Apolonio rey de Tiro*, Madrid, Akal, 1997
Reitzenstein, R., *Poimandres*, Stuttgart, Teubner, 1966 (1st ed. Leipzig, Teubner, 1904)
Renau Nebot, X., *Textos herméticos*, Madrid, Gredos, 1999
Richard, M., "Florilèges grecs", in *Dictionnaire de Spiritualité*, París, 1962, cols. 475–512

Rico, F., "Sobre el origen de la autobiografía en el Libro de Buen Amor", *Anuario de Estudios Medievales* 4, 1967, pp. 301–325

Rosenthal, F., *The Classical Heritage in Islam*, London, Routledge, 1975

—, "Sayings of the Ancients from Ibn Durayd's *Kitab al-Mujtana*", *Orientalia* 27, 1958, pp. 29–54.

Schenkl, H., *Epicteti dissertationes ab Arriano digestae*, Leipzig, Teubner, 1916

Schneider, J., "Brief", in *Reallexikon für Antike und Christentum*, Stuttgart 1954, p. 573

Sodano, A. R., *Le sentenze "pitagoriche" dello pseudo-Demofilo*, Rome, Accademia Nazionale dei Lincei, 1991 [205]

Stanzel, K. H., *Dicta Platonica. Die unter Platons Namen überlieferten Ansprüche*, Würzburg, 1987

Steiger, A., "Tradición y fuentes islámicas en la obra de Alfonso el Sabio", *RIEI* 3, 1955, pp. 93–109

Strohmaier, G., "Ethical sentences and anecdotes of Greek Philosophers in Arabic Tradition", *Actes du Ve Congrès International d'Arabisants et d'Islamisants*, *Correspondance d'Orient* 11, Brussels, 1970, pp. 463–471

—, "Die arabische Sokrateslegende und ihre Ursprünge", in P. Nagel (ed.), *Studia Coptica*, Berlin, Akademie Verlag, 1974, pp. 121–136

Sturm, H., *The Libro de los buenos proverbios. A critical edition.* Lexington, University of Kentucky Press, 1971

Suárez de la Torre, E., "La epistolografía griega", *Estudios Clásicos* 23, 1979, pp. 19–46

Suchier, W., *L'enfant sage*, Dresden 1910

Swift Riginos, A., *Platonica. The anecdotes concerning the Life and Writings of Plato*, Leiden 1976

Sykutris, J., "Epistolographie", in *RE*, Suppl. V, 1931, pp. 185–220

—, *Die Briefe des Sokrates und der Sokratiker*, Paderborn, Schöningh, 1933

Timpanaro, M., *Pitagorici. Testimonianze e frammenti*, Florence, La Nuova Italia, 1964

van Dijk, G.-J., *Ainoi, Logoi Mythoi*, Leiden, Brill, 1997

Vernet, J., *La cultura hispanoárabe en Oriente y Occidente*, Barcelona, Ariel, 1978

von Fritz, K., *Quellenuntersuchungen zu Leben und Philosophie des Diogenes von Sinope, Philologus*, Suppl. Bd. 18.2, Leipzig, Dietrich, 1926

von Grunebaum, G. E., "Greek Form Elements in the Arabian Nights", *JAOS* 62, 1942, pp. 277–292

—, *Medieval Islam*, Chicago, Chicago University Press, 1947

Walsh, J. K., "Versiones peninsulares del *Kitāb ādāb al-falāsifa* de Hunayn ibn Ishaq. Hacia una reconstrucción del 'Libro de los buenos proverbios'", *Al-Andalus* 41, 1976, pp. 355–384

Wesselski, A., "Die gelehrten Sklavinnen des Islams und ihre Byzantinischen Vorbilder", *Archiv Orientální* 9, 1937, pp. 353–378

Zeegers-Vander Vorst, N., "Une gnomologie d'auteurs grecs en traduction syriaque", in *Symposium Syriacum 1976*, *Orientalia christiana analecta*, 205, Rome, Pontificium Institutum Orientalium Studiorum, 1978, pp. 163–177

Ziakas, G., "On the Problem of the Origin of the pseudo-Aristotelian Arabic Works", *Graeco Arabica* 2, 1983, pp. 39–50

Index

Sapheneia: Contributions to Classical Philology

As indicated by its name, this series is devoted to the interpretation of ancient Greek and Latin texts. It accommodates not only studies of special subjects and individual authors, but also annotated editions as well as commentaries. In the tradition of critical scholarship the collection is uncompromisingly philological without however excluding new approaches and methods of exegesis. Each of the volumes represents independent and original research which contributes to the understanding of ancient texts whether in the form of critical exposition or the investigation of specific problems. It is in this sense that they genuinely further the discipline of classical philology. At the same time the series welcomes studies of the reception and influence of ancient texts including in particular the history of their transmission as well as the historical development of philology in its various aspects.

In order to reach as wide a readership as possible, publication is restricted to works written in those languages most commonly in use in classical scholarship. Special importance is attached to clear presentation and a choice of language that can be readily understood. Authors are moreover encouraged to provide translations wherever they would aid comprehension.

Ultimately *Sapheneia* should not only advance classical studies, but also deepen our understanding of the intellectual tradition of the western world.

The Editors:
Margarethe Billerbeck and Bruce Karl Braswell

Vol. 1: Poltera, Orlando. *Le langage de Simonide*. Etude sur la tradition poétique et son renouvellement. 686 pages, 1997.

Vol. 2: Grossardt, Peter. *Die Trugreden in der Odyssee und ihre Rezeption in der antiken Literatur.* 493 pages, 1998.

Vol. 3: Hummel, Pascale. *L'épithète pindarique*. Etude historique et philologique. 677 pages, 1999.

Vol. 4: Guex, Sophie. *Ps.-Claudien, Laus Herculis*. Introduction, texte, traduction et commentaire. 244 pages, 2000.

Vol. 5: Billerbeck, Margarethe / Zubler, Christian. *Das Lob der Fliege von Lukian bis L.B. Alberti*. Gattungsgeschichte, Texte, Übersetzungen und Kommentar. 272 pages, 2000.

Vol. 6: Amherdt, David. *Sidoine Apollinaire, Le quatrième livre de la correspondance*. Introduction et commentaire. 592 pages, 2001.

Vol. 7: Billerbeck, Margarethe/Guex, Sophie. *Sénèque, Hercule furieux.* Introduction, texte, traduction et commentaire. 617 pages, 2002.

Vol. 8: Hummel, Pascale. *Philologus auctor.* Le philologue et son œuvre. 438 pages, 2003.

Vol. 9: Amherdt, David. *Ausone et Paulin de Nole: correspondance.* Introduction, texte latin, traduction et notes. 255 pages, 2004.

Vol. 10: Guichard, Luis Arturo. *Asclepíades de Samos. Epigramas y fragmentos*. Estudio introductorio, revisión del texto, traducción y comentario. 583 pages. 2004.

Vol. 11: Neal, Tamara. *The Wounded Hero*. Non-Fatal Injury in Homer's *Iliad*. 352 pages. 2006.

Vol. 12: Laplace, Marcelle. *Le roman d'Achille Tatios*. «Discours panégyrique» et imaginaire romanesque. XV, 797 pages. 2007.

Vol. 13: Braswell, Bruce Karl / Billerbeck, Margarethe. *The Grammarian Epaphroditus*. Testimonia and Fragments edited and translated with Introduction, Notes, and Commentary. 454 pages. 2008.

Vol. 14 Rodríguez Adrados, Francisco. *Greek Wisdom Literature and the Middle Ages*. The Lost Greek Models and Their Arabic and Castilian Translations. 392 pages. 2009.